CHINESE CIVIL JUSTICE, PAST AND PRESENT

ASIA/PACIFIC/PERSPECTIVES
Series Editor: Mark Selden

Crime, Punishment, and Policing in China
edited by Børge Bakken
Woman, Man, Bangkok: Love, Sex, and Popular Culture in Thailand
by Scot Barmé
Making the Foreign Serve China: Managing Foreigners in the People's Republic
by Anne-Marie Brady
Marketing Dictatorship: Propaganda and Thought Work in China
by Anne-Marie Brady
The Mongols at China's Edge: History and the Politics of National Unity
by Uradyn E. Bulag
Transforming Asian Socialism: China and Vietnam Compared
edited by Anita Chan, Benedict J. Tria Kerkvliet, and Jonathan Unger
China's Great Proletarian Cultural Revolution: Master Narratives and Post-Mao Counternarratives
edited by Woei Lien Chong
North China at War: The Social Ecology of Revolution, 1937–1945
edited by Feng Chongyi and David S. G. Goodman
Little Friends: Children's Film and Media Culture in China
by Stephanie Hemelryk Donald
Social and Political Change in Revolutionary China: The Taihang Base Area in the War of Resistance to Japan, 1937–1945
by David S. G. Goodman
Gender in Motion: Divisions of Labor and Cultural Change in Late Imperial and Modern China
edited by Bryna Goodman and Wendy Larson
Islands of Discontent: Okinawan Responses to Japanese and American Power
edited by Laura Hein and Mark Selden
Women in Early Imperial China
by Bret Hinsch
Civil Justice in China: Past and Present
by Philip C. C. Huang
Local Democracy and Development: The Kerala People's Campaign for Decentralized Planning
by T. M. Thomas Isaac with Richard W. Franke
Hidden Treasures: Lives of First-Generation Korean Women in Japan
by Jackie J. Kim with Sonia Ryang
Postwar Vietnam: Dynamics of a Transforming Society
edited by Hy V. Luong
The Indonesian Presidency: The Shift from Personal towards Constitutional Rule
by Angus McIntyre
Nationalisms of Japan: Managing and Mystifying Identity
by Brian J. McVeigh
From Underground to Independent: Alternative Film Culture in Contemporary China
edited by Paul G. Pickowicz and Yingjin Zhang
Wife or Worker? Asian Women and Migration
edited by Nicola Piper and Mina Roces
Social Movements in India: Poverty, Power, and Politics
edited by Raka Ray and Mary Fainsod Katzenstein
Biology and Revolution in Twentieth-Century China
by Laurence Schneider
Contentious Kwangju: The May 18th Uprising in Korea's Past and Present
edited by Gi-Wook Shin and Kyong Moon Hwang
The Inside Story of China's High-Tech Industry: Making Silicon Valley in Beijing
by Yu Zhou

CHINESE CIVIL JUSTICE, PAST AND PRESENT

Philip C. C. Huang

ROWMAN & LITTLEFIELD PUBLISHERS, INC.
Lanham • Boulder • New York • Toronto • Plymouth, UK

Published by Rowman & Littlefield Publishers, Inc.
A wholly owned subsidiary of The Rowman & Littlefield Publishing Group, Inc.
4501 Forbes Boulevard, Suite 200, Lanham, Maryland 20706
http://www.rowmanlittlefield.com

Estover Road, Plymouth PL6 7PY, United Kingdom

British Library Cataloguing in Publication Information Available

Library of Congress Cataloging-in-Publication Data

Huang, Philip C., 1940–
Chinese civil justice, past and present / Philip C. C. Huang.
p. cm.
Includes bibliographical references and index.
ISBN 978-0-7425-6769-6 (cloth : alk. paper) — ISBN 978-0-7425-6771-9 (electronic)
1. Justice, Administration of—China—History. 2. Civil law—China—History. 3. Practice of law—China—History. I. Title.
KNQ1572.H84 2010
349.51—dc22

2009039999

™ The paper used in this publication meets the minimum requirements of American National Standard for Information Sciences—Permanence of Paper for Printed Library Materials, ANSI/NISO Z39.48-1992. Printed in the United States of America

Contents

Tables

Author's Note

THIS BOOK WAS BEGUN IN 1990, almost twenty years ago now, when I did the first of my field visits and began to gather materials for the book. The original intention was to write a single book on Chinese civil justice spanning the Qing down to the present. It soon became clear, however, that the topic was too broad for just one book. So I finished writing and published first my 1996 book *Civil Justice in China: Representation and Practice in the Qing*, and then my 2001 book *Code, Custom, and Legal Practice in China: The Qing and the Republic Compared.*

This third book got stalled for a few years. First of all, the subject of civil justice in contemporary China, especially of the Reform era, is far broader than that in the Qing, as well as in the Republic. The main reason has been rapid marketization and urbanization and the host of accompanying legislation. For several years, therefore, I thought that I might not write a third book and would just publish articles on selected topics, keeping to the original emphasis on those aspects of the legal system most important to the lives of common people, especially those of the countryside.

But then, to my own surprise, I found that my study of those and other selected dimensions of the story eventually added up to a single larger argument with implications for all of Chinese civil justice. As I taught in China and wrote for Chinese audiences these past five years, I was very much struck by the extent to which mainstream Chinese legal thinking has internalized Western modernism (or what some might call "Orientalism"). That modernism has become the principal foil for the arguments of this book and, ironically, has lent it the thematic coherence it had not had earlier. To the extent that we in Chinese legal history studies in the West have shared in those modernist assumptions that so dominate the Chinese legal profession today, the arguments should prove relevant to us as well.

It should be pointed out here that the specific topics covered in this book are very far indeed from making up a complete picture of the entire story of civil justice. The latter, of course, remains a rapidly expanding and changing story, as Chinese economy and society become ever more complex and multifaceted. This, then, is deliberately a partial story covering only selected aspects. For the book, the previously published articles have been revised, trimmed or expanded, and updated as needed to form a coherent whole with the rest of the study.

Numerous colleagues in the profession, as well as friends and students, read and commented on various parts of the book along the way, especially the individual articles that were published in these past three years. They include Donald Clarke, FAN Yu, Huaiyin LI, Hanchao LU, Yusheng PENG, Bradly Reed, William Rowe, Matthew Sommer, Preston Torbert, Elizabeth VanderVen, WANG Hui, Yang WANG, Margaret Woo, XIA Mingfang, Liu YANG and ZHANG Jiayan. I wish to thank especially Kathryn Bernhardt, who read and commented on every draft of every article and chapter. XU Anqi helped me greatly in obtaining from a northern and an eastern county the 336 case records spanning the 1950s down to the 1990s. WU Ruozhi was the source of the 45 most recent cases from a southern county. DONG Leiming's investigations of recent changes in community mediation, cited at some length in chapter 2, helped me update that part of the book. Finally, my most recent students, here and in China, have been helpful during the past year when the book took final shape. I thank especially Fangchun LI, YU Shengfeng and YOU Chenjun. This book was written mainly for their generation.

A word, finally, about the process of publication. I feel fortunate to have met up again with an editor, Susan McEachern, who somehow manages to have the time, and the intelligence and knowledge, to actually read a manuscript and form her own judgment. I am grateful to Mark Selden for pointing me in her direction, also to the constructively critical referee whom she had the perspicacity to select, and to her efficient editorial team. For someone who had published five books with a single publisher, the new realities of academic publishing came as quite a shock. Ever-expanding Internet access and ever-shrinking budgets, yet also ever-increasing numbers of submissions, have forced university presses to impose impossible workloads on their editors. Gone are the days when editors had the leisure to actually read manuscripts, acquire near-professional acquaintance with their fields, and provide cordial attention to authors. Add to that the fact that good referees are harder and harder to secure given the mounting numbers of manuscripts and the realities of a highly factionalized profession, one cannot help but feel for younger scholars who have to navigate their ways through such minefields, with tenure at stake. Perhaps Rowman & Littlefield's combination of exceptional leadership with commercialized efficiency is one truly viable way for the future.

Preface

Why Do We Need a Different Approach to the Study of Chinese Law?

I WISH TO BEGIN HERE BY ADDRESSING MAINSTREAM legal opinion and legal history study in China, to highlight the problems of the extreme legal modernism that is so widespread and predominant there today. American scholars, of course, work and study in a different context and are not burdened by their Chinese counterparts' sense of a recent history of profound national humiliation, nor by the much more highly ideologized academic environment. For American scholars, it may in fact require some empathy and imagination, rather than normal scholarly expectations, to grasp and relate to the problems of the discursive world of Chinese legal scholarship. I myself have only come to the thoughts below after my recent years of teaching in China and writing for a Chinese audience. For me personally, full realization of the extent of the predominance in China today of an extreme modernist outlook has been nothing short of startling. How could China, "Maoist" and "revolutionary" until so recently, have become so quickly the great stronghold in the world of what is very close to American-style neoconservatism, complete with its market fundamentalism, modernizationism, and self-righteous legal modernism?

While some of what follows may strike some U.S.-based scholars as irrelevant or tangential to our concerns, or as just rather obvious, I have nevertheless decided to begin with this preface, which had originally been written for a Chinese audience. In part, it is because I think some of the issues raised are very real for an American audience as well, if perhaps to a lesser degree and in more subtle forms. I wonder how many of us have not taken for granted the universal applicability of the modern Western discourse of rights? How many of us can truly say that we have been entirely free of the Orientalist assumptions that so afflict mainland Chinese scholars today? And how many have truly thought about how concretely traditional Chinese law might figure in present-day lawmaking? These issues are writ large in China and therefore are more starkly clear than they might be in the United States.

Lest some might further object that legal history scholarship in China can only be of secondary concern to scholars working in the United States, I should point out that the academic endeavor of Chinese legal history study can enjoy genuine vitality only if it does so within China itself. Even with its sharp decline in recent years, the number of scholars engaged in Chinese legal history research in China still number in the multiples of hundreds, if not thousands, to those in the United States. If that endeavor were truly to be dead-ended in China, it could not help but affect Chinese legal history study elsewhere. One need only imagine what things would be like if the study of American legal history were to be dead-ended in the United States itself, and the few dozen Chinese specialists of U.S. legal history were to write mainly for one another. The fate of U.S.-based study of Chinese legal history, in other words, is in fact unavoidably tied to the fate of legal history study within China itself.

To turn now to the Chinese context, China's legal tradition, first of all, suffered three devastating blows in the past century. The first time was during the final years of the Qing and in the Republic when, under pressures from foreign powers, traditional law was completely abandoned in favor of imported Western law for the sake of regaining national sovereignty. The second time was during the revolutionary period, from the Communist "liberated areas" to Mao Zedong's rule, when traditional law was once more rejected, along with the Guomindang's transplanted laws from the West. One was dubbed "feudal law," while the other was equated with "bourgeois law." The only part of tradition that met with approval was rural customary mediation. The third time was during the new Reform period, when traditional law was rejected yet again, along with Maoist law, in favor of the wholesale transplanting of Western law. Today, what is "modern" is equated entirely with the West, while China's own tradition is considered "premodern" or "unmodern" and, as such, unable to meet the current needs for modernization and the development of a market economy.

In the current world of legal discourse in China, traditional Chinese law has, in effect, been completely severed from the present. It may have historical value and may contain the wisdom of the Chinese people, but it has no contemporary relevance; it may be relevant for understanding past dynasties, but, under the current agenda of modernization and marketization, it can have no significance for actual lawmaking or the real lives of the people.

In this larger historical and discursive context, the study of China's legal history has declined steadily in importance during recent years. At the major law schools in China today, courses taught and research undertaken all have mainly to do with modern Western law. Whether in the "fields" of "jurisprudence" (*fali*) or different "sectoral laws" (*bumenfa*) (i.e., civil law, criminal law, and so on), the teaching materials and the research topics all concern mainly Anglo-American and European law. While contemporary (Western) legal studies are booming, the study of Chinese legal history is ever more marginalized, seen as ever less relevant. Faculty staffing declines year after year, and legal history courses matter less and less in the training of the younger generation of legal professionals.

A Legal History Field Severed from Reality

What have survived in Chinese legal history studies in China are mainly the fields of legal thought (*sixiangshi*) and legal institutions (*zhidushi*). Here we need to note at the outset that numerous Chinese scholars have made valuable contributions in these two spheres, sorting out with precision and rigor past legal thought, writings, codes, and institutional designs, setting thereby solid foundations for further study. Some have placed particular emphasis on major concepts, such as the importance of rites (*liyi*) and ethics in past Chinese law;[1] others have pointed to the reliance on *qingli* (human relations and moral principles) alongside law;[2] others have explained how Legalism was "Confucianized" with the ideals of benevolent government (*renzheng*) and harmony (*hexie*);[3] still others have pointed to the fine qualities of a system that emphasized mediation, and so on.[4] Needless to say, these are often accompanied by emotional assertions about the "greatness" of Chinese tradition, a reflection, of course, of the nationalistic ideology of the nation-state. In the Chinese context, differences between the approaches of those in "legal history"—*falüshi*, housed in law schools—and those in regular history, housed in history departments, loom quite large, but those will not be considered here; suffice it to say that both have the major characteristics just outlined.

1. See, for example, Ma Xiaohong (2004).
2. Many have argued this point of view, the most important being actually the work of the Japanese scholar Shiga Shūzō, whose point of view continues to enjoy immense influence in China. See especially the book edited by Wang Yaxin and Liang Zhiping (1998).
3. Ch'ü T'ung-tsu's (Qu Tongzu) (1961) classic work, widely respected and accepted in China today, remains the best example of this argument.
4. Nowhere more strongly put than in official claims made about mediation in the Mao Zedong period. See chapter 4.

But on the whole, these kinds of studies of Chinese legal history all lack practical relevance for present-day China, unable as they are to rise above the historical background of traditional law's having been rejected time and again by the nation's leaders and lawmakers during the past century. The blows suffered have been so devastating that even legal history specialists themselves have largely given up any right to a voice on current realities and lawmaking. Even those who have argued that China must maintain and continue its great legal tradition have done so only at such a high level of generality as to be devoid of any specific and concrete implication for current realities. Few have questioned the predominance of Western modernist assumptions in mainstream legal studies, accepting, in effect, the view that only Western laws can be of use to present-day China.

In this larger context, some Chinese legal historians have developed attitudes that might be likened to those of a museum curator. On the one hand, they emphasize the great value of China's legal history, implicitly with themselves as the designated custodians; on the other hand, they insist that traditional Chinese law is completely different from that of the West, thus setting up an either/or binary between China and the West in which traditional law can have absolutely no relevance to contemporary lawmaking, for it belongs entirely in the museum.[5] When faced with an outsider's attempt to go beyond such a binary, to try to move traditional Chinese law out of the museum into the realities of present-day life and society, they almost instinctively object, feeling those efforts to be threats to the value of their treasured museum pieces.

In my view, such an orientation tells above all about the pained historical background of this field of study in China. Ultimately, the tendencies originate from the repeated rejections of China's legal tradition by the nation's own top leaders and lawmakers. Precisely because almost all modern Chinese laws have come from the West, the new legal system embodies a nihilistic present without a history, while the old traditions are encased in a history without a present or a future. Those are two sides of the same coin. Of course, there have been some important voices that have argued for moving Chinese legal studies out of such a dead end, and even a few that have tried new directions of inquiry.[6] For the field of legal history as a whole,

5. Tian Chengyou (1996) offers an insightful insider's analysis of what may be termed the special angst of Chinese lawmaking and legal studies, with its exaggerated faith in Western law (and complete rejection of the Chinese legal tradition), even while faced with the insurmountable problem of a great disconnect between transplanted law and Chinese social realities, and between legal intent and actual implementation. Legal history studies, undertaken in that larger context, can only be either iconoclastic or of the museum-curator variety.

6. Liang Zhiping (1996) and [Zhu] Suli (1996, 2000) are among those who might be seen as examples of such. Younger scholars, like Jiang Shigong (forthcoming) and Zhao Xiaoli (1998) are additional examples.

however, there can be no mistaking the basic fact of its complete severance from present realities.

Divided Intellectual and Emotional Commitments in Legal Studies

Under these circumstances, legal studies in China today show divided intellectual and emotional commitments. On the first level, the mainstream of so-called modern legal studies equates "modern law" with Western law, while legal historians either do not concern themselves with or abdicate their right to a voice about present-day realities. Precisely for this reason, there is little or no dialogue or mutual influence between the two. In terms of approaches to research, both tend toward a one-sided emphasis on theory/thought and institutional structure, without concern for practice or actual operative realities. If we were to analogize society to a person, this amounts to someone who completely refuses to connect up his own past with his own present, dividing himself into two disconnected abstract constructs. This is the first level of division.

At another level, there is something of a fracture between emotion and intellect. Some researchers emotionally identify with China and the Chinese people out of patriotism; yet, intellectually, they identify completely with so-called modern law and legal studies and believe in (or at least do not object to) the assumption that the West's is the only kind of true law there is.[7] Given the decisions made by the nation's top leaders and lawmakers in the past century, one really could not expect otherwise of the great majority of researchers. In this way, emotional and intellectual commitments are deeply divided, forming a kind of split identity on a deeply psychological level. The tendency described above to insist on the complete opposition between Chinese and Western law, while guarding zealously the uniqueness and museum quality of Chinese law, is a manifestation of just such a fracture. The two tendencies stem from what may be seen as the same emotional "knot."

Toward a Different Perspective

It should be said first of all that all of this is entirely understandable, the consequence of a century of external pressures and domestic crises. At the same time, however, it must be acknowledged that this kind of perspective violates what would be our normal sense of history and of reality. From a historical

7. Joseph R. Levenson (1953), of course, wrote about such a division in Liang Qichao (and the "mind of modern China") fifty-five years ago. I believe the analysis is far more apposite for some May Fourth wholesale Westernizers and contemporary modernists than it is for Liang.

point of view, Chinese law today obviously comes from three major traditions: namely, the imperial past, the modern revolution, and transplants from the West. All three are part of an inseparable heritage that makes up China's present, the three together forming an amalgamated entity that is China today, that cannot be understood fully if any of the three is ignored. Mainstream legal study in China today, however, equates "tradition" only with the imperial past severed from the present, while excluding the Maoist period from both "traditional" and contemporary China. In other words, it completely rejects two of the three main traditions and stands for simple wholesale transplanting of Western law.

Such a view of the legal system as something without a past is neither realistic nor healthy. The views that are predominant today were in truth forced upon China by a combination of foreign aggression and domestic crises. A more confident China of tomorrow will likely sooner or later leave such views behind, along with the attendant emotional and intellectual traps. There will likely come a new view of the traditions of the pre-twentieth-century past and of the twentieth-century revolution, not only for the sake of a better understanding of the past, but also for a better grasp of the present and the future. We in the United States who have wittingly or unwittingly gone along with the dominant modernist thinking of our age, reinforced by the mainstream Chinese point of view, might wish to do the same.

At the same time, it should be acknowledged that the dead-ended bind described above is partly of the legal historians' own making. To move toward genuine understanding, there needs to be critical reflection not only upon the modernism that dominates the legal field in general but also upon the field of legal history study itself. To simply reject all of Chinese legal history and adopt an ahistorical view of law, as so many mainland Chinese scholars have done, is one deep-seated reason why a simple-minded modernism has come to predominate in China to the extent it does today. To ignore the actual practice of Chinese law in the past, and construct in its stead an abstracted, idealized system without the stuff of real life, as have most past Chinese legal historical studies, is to rule out any possibility of critical reflection about the extreme wholesale Westernization-ism and modernism of the present.

Going Beyond Orientalism

To accept the irrelevance of their own legal history as Chinese lawmakers have done in the past century, and as so many mainland Chinese legal scholars do today, is tantamount to a kind of indigenous "Orientalism." It is to believe that Chinese tradition represents only "the Other," suitable only for bringing out the universality of modern Western law.[8] To be content with just studying Chinese legal thought and institutions as a system unto itself, of the past only for the sake of the past, even if filled with nationalistic sentiment, is in the end to treat China's past only as a foil for modern Western law.

For Chinese legal studies in China to break out of this intellectual trap, this premise must be overturned and our understanding of China's past and present must be reconstructed. We can then establish the relevance of China's legal history for an understanding both of the past and of the present. We need first to leave behind a framework of study that does not consider practical application and operative realities. If we look only at theory/thought, Chinese legal history of the past hundred years indeed appears as a series of ruptures and flip-flops, from the adoption of the German model in the late Qing and the Republic to the antifeudal, anticapitalist legal system of the Maoist period to the readoption of wholesale Westernization in the Reform period. The legal history of the imperial era indeed seems to carry no legitimacy or meaning whatsoever, and in the Reform era, the same seems to apply to that of the Mao period. Seen purely from the point of view of theory and legal codes, Chinese legal history of the past century indeed appears to have undergone complete and nihilistic change, without any tradition or continuity to speak of.

However, if we see things from the point of view of actual legal practice, then the record of the past hundred years appears quite different. There were changes, to be sure, but there were also continuities and cumulative experience. Practice is different from theory, first because it comes with its own "subject-hood,"[9] for it does not allow simple wholesale transplantation, but rather asks that law be adapted in practice, and even in legal principle, to Chinese realities, including the will of the people. Practice is also more open and tolerant than theory. It permits the merging of China and the West, allows them to engage in tugs-of-war, to influence, accommodate, and compromise with one another. Legal theory, on the other hand, demands logical consistency. If our view of law is limited to theory/thought, then we can only see Chinese and Western law as mutually opposed, in an either/or framework, without the possibility of coexistence or interaction. But present-day Chinese realities do not permit such a simple choice, neither of a simple restoration of the past nor of a simple wholesale Westernization divorced from Chinese history. What present-day realities in China demand are precisely coexistence and interaction. Practice, finally, is what makes the past relevant for the pres-

8. I am of course employing here Edward Said's (1978) concept, but, as I have written elsewhere, I disagree very much with his nihilistic epistemological attitude, which maintains that all knowledge is in the end no more than a discourse or a construction (see Huang, 1998).
9. The Chinese term here is *zhutixing*, or autonomy and independence, emphasized by most Chinese intellectuals.

ent, and vice versa. Divorced from practice and limited only to theory, there can be no possibility for the present of selecting the strengths of one to make up for the shortcomings of the other, even less can there be any possibility of building a distinctive Chinese legal system appropriate for current realities.

At the same time, I would like to make clear that I am advocating here the history-of-practice approach only as a method and not as an end. To spotlight a history-of-practice approach is to correct for past tendencies in legal history scholarship in China to study only theory, representation, and institutional structure and to disregard practical application and circumstances. But it is not at all to say that history is only the history of practice, or to say that only practice is real. Obviously, practice can only be one part of any broad view of history and reality, and it cannot be severed from theory and representation. Practice might be sensible and positive, but it might also be unreasonable and negative. And, in itself, it carries no prospective (i.e., forward-looking) ideals, no logical unity, nor exact and systematic concepts. Obviously, practice needs the prospective view of ethical ideals and theory; otherwise, it can only be retrospective and empiricist. This is one reason for this book's emphasis on the persistent "practical moralism" mode of Chinese legal thinking, whose value is attested to not least by its tremendous longevity. My research has always stressed that Qing law's basic character consists neither simply in its representation nor in its practice, but rather in the paradoxical combination of the two, with built-in tensions and conflicts, as well as compromises and accommodations. That is the true secret to the longevity of China's legal tradition. What I want to advocate is in the end a broad view of history and reality that includes both material and ideational dimensions, both social-economic structures and individual agency, both institutions and processes, changes as well as continuities, broad historical forces as well as contingencies and individual choices. In the end, what we need is to understand the past and present of Chinese law from a broad historical perspective and a down–to-earth sense of reality.

If we return now to the field of academic legal studies, past studies of legal thought and institutions by Chinese legal scholars are important resources for us today. They need to be supplemented with considerations of practice and of historical circumstances to make up for what they lack, but this is not to say that they need to be discarded. In the end, what is needed is to combine the study of practice with that of thought, which is to say the new research with the old. Only then can the study of legal history in China come to have true vitality in this new age of ours.

1
Introduction
The History-of-Practice Approach to Studying Chinese Law

IN ORDER TO JOIN TOGETHER the past and the present in Chinese law, what this book emphasizes is a particular research method and several major themes. Since the themes were arrived at through the method being advocated, they can be read also as explanatory illustrations of the method.

The method I wish to advocate is the study of the "history of practice." The word "practice" here carries mainly three overlapping yet somewhat different meanings. First is practice in its conventional sense, namely, practice as opposed to theory, referring mainly to action. This meaning is close to and yet not quite the same as a second meaning of "practice," as used in the sense of my 1996 book *Civil Justice in China: Representation and Practice in the Qing*, where it is juxtaposed against "representation." Both of these meanings should be distinguished from a third meaning of "practice," as in Pierre Bourdieu's (1977) usage, where practice is juxtaposed mainly against institutions and structures.

In the tradition of the Chinese Revolution, "practice" was used in a sense close to yet narrower than conventional usage, and the term referred mainly to the problem of how to apply "universal" (Western) Marxist theory to the Chinese Revolution. But since that usage spotlights the issue of disjunction between theory and practice (and therefore required the intermediation of "Mao Zedong thought"), it is directly related to the central theme of this book. My own work has stressed that China's own representation may also be inconsistent with its practice. Bourdieu's concept of "logic of practice," on the other hand, calls for searching out the "logic" contained in the process of practice, rather than in institutional structures, in order to uncover the fundamental characteristics of a society and to transcend the long-standing problem in Western thought of binary oppositions between the subjective and the objective, and structure and agency.[1]

In addition to these three meanings of "practice," I wish to place particular emphasis on the historical dimension. Mao Zedong's idea of practice attended to time and space, and yet was also intended to be a universal transcending time and space. My "history of practice," by contrast, aims mainly to spotlight the historicity of the humanistic and social spheres of life. Bourdieu, of course, emphasized process, and distinguished it from institutions and structures, but his concept of process paid little attention to history, and was mainly the conceptual tool of an anthropologist focusing on contemporary society.[2] The difference between "history of practice" and simple "practice" is that the former incorporates not only the kinds of practices outlined above but also their interactions over time with theory, representation, and institutions, as manifested also in practice. Let me turn to illustrate these points with examples.

Practice as Opposed to Theory: Legal Formalism and the History of Practice of American Law

What will be explained here is first the difference between practice (meaning action) and theory. Chinese scholars often emphasize how Western theories are abstractions from Western experience and do not accord with Chinese reality. That point, of course, contains its grain of truth, but what I wish to emphasize here is that Western theory, especially theory that has been turned into ideology sponsored by the power of the state, also does not accord with the West's own history of practice.

America's so-called classical orthodoxy tradition of legal theory is a good example. Its origins are usually traced to Christopher Columbus Langdell, who became dean of Harvard School of Law in 1870. Because this tradition emphasized especially the universality and scientific nature of law and the use of deductive theory to arrive at absolute truths, scholars have also dubbed it "legal formalism." From the 1870s to the 1920s, it did in fact occupy a dominant position in the American world of legal studies. Yet at the same time,

1. Clearly, "practice" as used here overlaps with and yet is different from Aristotle's usage in his three-way distinction of *theoria*, *praxis*, and *poiesis* (production). It is broader than Marx's usage of "revolutionary praxis" to mean the merging of theory and practice. It is also broader than James Scott's recent usage (Greek *mêtis*) to mean mainly the perfecting of techniques through repeated use (Scott, 1998).
2. To be sure, Bourdieu's "habitus" seeks to deal with cumulative experience as an intermediary between structure and agency, but the concept of history used in this book is much broader than Bourdieu's.

it was challenged from the start by Langdell's colleague at Harvard, Oliver Wendell Holmes (later a Supreme Court justice). Holmes stressed especially the historical nature of law, rather than its universality beyond time and space; he also argued that law must be tested in actual use and evaluated on the basis of its practical consequences. Scholars generally consider Holmes the founder of the American tradition of legal pragmatism. This tradition was followed in the 1920s by the new legal realism.

At the level of legal practice, Supreme Court decisions have not come simply from the "classical orthodoxy" tradition of theory, but rather mainly from the long-term tug-of-war between orthodox formalists and their pragmatist-realist challengers. The former dominated the Court until the 1920s when, under the presidency of Franklin D. Roosevelt, the latter came to occupy a majority among the nine Supreme Court justices. Many important American labor and welfare decisions of the Court come from that period. The non-"orthodox" jurists would maintain their upper hand in the Court until, under the neoconservative administration of George W. Bush, jurists of the orthodox persuasion once more occupied the majority. Looking back at the history of practice of American law, it is clear that its real essence lay not in any single theoretical tradition, but rather in the long-term coexistence and competition among its different theoretical traditions.

Practice as Opposed to Representation: Qing Law

Because of the apparent disconnect between Western theories and Chinese realities, some Chinese scholars have advocated the use of China's own concepts to generalize Chinese experience, but what I want to point out here is that China's own representations can also be at odds with its history of practice. My first volume, about Qing justice, emphasized how Qing representations and practice diverged from one another and yet were combined to form a single system. That is to say, between representation and practice there were disjunctures and tensions, yet also mutual adaptation and joining together.

More concretely, Qing representations give us a three-point picture. First, there were few civil lawsuits. In the official ideology of the state, such lawsuits should not happen and, even if they did, they were only about "minor matters," which the central government would not be unduly concerned with and would leave largely to the local governments to deal with "on their own authority" (*zili*). Furthermore, most "good people" (*liangmin*) would not become involved in a lawsuit; if they did, then they usually did so only on the instigation of evil "litigation mongers" (*songgun*) and "litigation masters" (*songshi*). Finally, when magistrates dealt with such minor lawsuits, they usually acted in the manner of "father-mother officials" (*fumuguan*) handling disputes among children, employing mediatory methods, and edifying the "children people" (*zimin*) with moral principles, without resorting to adjudication by law. Needless to say, these representations were closely tied to the Confucian ideology of benevolent government (*renzheng*). They have profoundly influenced past scholarship.

However, archival records of actual cases demonstrate a very different picture. First, "civil" lawsuits accounted for about one-third of all cases at the county yamen level. This is my conclusion based on records from the three counties of Baxian in Sichuan, Danshui-Xinzhu in Taiwan, and Baodi in Shuntian prefecture. The so-called minor matters cases in Qing official representations in fact accounted for a significant and important proportion of cases handled by the local yamen.

Second, most litigants were common people who went to court out of necessity and for the sake of protecting their rightful claims. From a total of 628 cases, I identified the background of precisely 500 litigants, of whom 189 were common peasants, 20 rural hired workers, 51 common landlords, 82 common town residents, 25 degree-holders, and 33 merchants. The remainder were variously big landlords, big money lenders, corporate entities, and so on. These were not consistent with the images given in official representations of litigants.

Third, when the county courts dealt with such disputes, they either allowed the disputes to be settled by community or kin-group mediation or they made decisions on the cases at court in accordance with the law (without excluding, of course, appropriate considerations of *qingli*, or human compassion/relations and moral principles). The magistrates very rarely conducted mediation at court. Of the total of 628 cases examined, 221 went on to a formal court session (the others being resolved by community or kin mediation, or simply went unresolved). Of those, just 11 underwent a kind of arbitration, in which the magistrate ordered both sides to compromise. All others were decided in clear-cut judgments for or against. From the actual records of cases, at least, Qing magistrates very rarely indeed undertook mediation in the manner of official representations.

A moment's thought will make clear that a magistrate was unlikely to undertake, indeed could not have, the "Ma Xiwu style" of handling cases—referring to the manner in which Ma Xiwu, a superior court judge of the central Shaan-Gan-Ning base area (who was later to become vice president of the Supreme People's Court), conducted on-site investigations and discussions with neighbors and kin and others concerned in order to arrive at a resolution, often through mediation—that characterized Maoist courts of the pre-1949 "liberated areas" and the post-1949 period before the reforms. They had neither the intent nor the leisure. They generally simply "adjudged at court" (*zuoting pan'an*). Furthermore, even though in their writings they liked to represent themselves as morally superior gentlemen, in accordance with the habit of official discourse of the time, they were in reality the bottom rung of a complex bureaucracy, in which the safest behavior for the sake of their own advancement was to act according to law and to regulations. Moreover, litigants who persisted all the way to a formal court session were usually among the most truculent, or else entirely committed to their rightful claims in the belief that the other side had violated them. Such people could not easily be persuaded by mediation. Under those circumstances, the most realistic thing to do for the magistrate was to adjudicate outright.

On this point, the famous Qing jurist Wang Huizu was the clearest and most realistic. As he put it, "While adjudication is done by law, mediation is done by human compassion." The magistrate is someone who adjudicates by law (*duan'an*). It is the kin and the neighbors who mediate, not the magistrate. He explains further, "When it is a matter of law, then there has to be a clear-cut position for or against. But when it is a matter of human compassion, then right and wrong can be compromised some." What he means is that once the case is at court, the magistrate can only act according to the law, distinguish clearly between right and wrong. That way, the losing side is likely to harbor lasting animus, and the two sides are likely to remain hostile toward each other for a long time, unlike the cordial resolution that can be arrived at through mediation by friends and kin, and no lasting animosity results. Precisely because he believes that the magistrate must adjudicate according to the law, he admonishes them to regularly study the code, "Whenever one has time after a day's work, one should study carefully one or two statutes and substatutes. Within a few months, one will be familiar with the essentials" (cited from Huang, 1996: 205–6).

By the formalist logic of Western Continental law, the Confucian ideals and actual Qing legal practice would seem to be contradictory (and therefore cannot coexist); but for Chinese jurists, there was no problem here of logical inconsistency. Confucian moralizing has to do with the ideals of the legal system, while actual application can allow for practical principles and for adjudication, even if those seem opposed to the stated Confucian moral ideals. In Chinese legal reasoning, Confucian moralistic representations are about what ought to be, while the practical provisions and the adjudicatory actions of the judges are about adapting to real-life circumstances that cannot fully accord with moral ideals. Actual realities determine certain kinds of actions, just as Confucian teachings point to a picture of an ideal world. The main argument of my book *Civil Justice in China: Representation and Practice in the Qing* can be summarized this way: in the history of practice of Qing law, what was said was one thing; what was done was another; and when the two were joined together, that was yet another thing.

Practice as Opposed to Institutions: Male and Female Inheritance Rights and Their Actual Operation

"History of practice" includes also the meaning, à la Bourdieu, of distinguishing between institutional structure and actual operation. For example, the Guomindang's 1930 Civil Law adopted from German law the principle of gender equality in inheritance, but in actual operation, the new law was not applied in the countryside. This is a conclusion I reached on the basis of 247 cases from the four counties of Shunyi (Republican Hebei province), Wujiang (Jiangsu), Yibin (Sichuan), and Yueqing (Zhejiang). The reason was simple. At the time, most rural women "married out" into other villages, and parents in their old age had to be maintained by sons who remained in the natal villages. Their land therefore could not go to their daughters. For this reason, the courts of the Guomindang period in practice for the countryside generally only recognized the inheritance rights of the sons. But lawmakers did not revise the text of the code accordingly; instead they permitted the legal provisions (institutional structure) to coexist with incongruent practice, amounting, in effect, to closing one eye over rural customary practice.

This disjunction between codified legal provision and judicial practice was not dealt with formally in legislation until the 1985 Law of Succession of the People's Republic of China, when the right to inheritance was linked by law to the obligation for old-age maintenance. That way, rural sons were to inherit their parents' property because they fulfilled the obligation for their old-age maintenance, not because they were male; daughters, if they fulfilled the obligation for the parents' old-age maintenance, could likewise inherit their parents' property. Thus did legislators both uphold the principle of gender equality in inheritance rights and attend to rural realities, thereby resolving the inconsistency between institutional structure and legal practice. This was a resolution that was arrived at only after many years of actual practice. It was a principle that cannot be found in Western law.

At least on this matter, legislators of the People's Republic were not limited to the simple ideology of wholesale Westernization. Yet, in the Reform period, that ideology has once more become predominant. But the history just summarized above demonstrates for us legislative innovation and its possibility.

The History of Practice vs. Formalist Theory

The reason I have chosen to emphasize the history of practice as the approach to the study of law is because formalism and its mode of thought predominate in today's legal studies (as well as the various social sciences). Formalism is more concerned with theory than with reality, and it emphasizes especially deductive logic, aspiring to attain thereby universal truths that stand above the particularities of time and space. This kind of absolutist propensity lends itself readily to ideologizing by the state, as has happened time and again in Western history, beginning with the Reign of Terror after the French Revolution. Nineteenth-century imperialism and recent American neoconservatism are other particularly notable examples.

Max Weber can be seen as one of the best representatives of the Western modernist tradition, and also one of its best analysts. He made clear the deep-seated premise and belief of modern Western civilization, the key being its view of formal rationality. As Weber points out, the key difference between modern Western law and other legal traditions consists in its "formal rationality." In Weber's view, legal formalism in the modern Western Continental tradition demands logical consistency in codified law and also between codified law and its application to concrete fact situations (Weber, [1968] 1978: 657).

Qing law, by comparison, in Weber's view, was substantivist, or instrumentalist, concerned more with the ruler's wish to maintain social order than with the protection of individual rights, and therefore also more prone to arbitrariness (Weber, [1968] 1978: 844–48). For Weber, even Anglo-American common law is a kind of "empirical justice," and not the rational-formalist law he approves of, for it is based on precedents, not the universal principle of rights, and it relies on a jury comprised of common folk, not specialists employing legal logic (Weber, [1968] 1978: 976, 891).

Weber's views have profoundly influenced the study of Chinese law. In accordance with his views, scholars have regarded Qing law as containing only concrete and particular regulations, not universal abstract principles/norms. At the same time, they think that the Qing had little or no civil law to speak of. Even the fine study done by Derk Bodde and Clarence Morris (1967) was not able to rise above this kind of presupposition. And scholars have maintained that Qing judicial practice, because it did not employ the kind of reasoning used in formalist law, did not adjudicate in any true (namely, Weberian) sense of the word (see, for example, Shiga, 1981: 74–102). Scholars have also argued that revolutionary China had no civil law at all to speak of. True Chinese civil law has existed only since the Reform period, with the massive importation of Western laws (William C. Jones, 1987: 309–31). (Before that, only the Guomindang's laws might be considered genuine law.)

I will demonstrate at length that the true difference between Qing law and Continental formalist civil law consists not in Qing law's lack of provisions to guide legal judgments but rather in its insistence on embedding its conceptual system in concrete fact situations for the purpose of resolving actual problems. Qing law did not try to develop abstracted principles of universal applicability; rather, it seemingly postulates that only when joined to real legal practice can abstract principles be properly clarified and carry real meaning and applicability.

Practical Moralism

Let me illustrate with an analytical theme of mine developed from the history-of-practice approach. It should be said at the outset that what I mean by the "history-of-practice" method is not a purely "empiricist" method of research. In my opinion, mere accumulation of empirical information does not have a great deal of meaning. Experience must be linked up with theoretical concepts. What I wish to advocate in method is to develop from the history of practice theoretical concepts appropriate to Chinese realities. At the same time, by "history of practice" I also do not intend a purely retrospective approach, but one that is accompanied by prospective (i.e., forward-looking) moral visions. What the method emphasizes is to search out, through actual history, not mere theoretical speculations, but avenues for pursuing given moral ideals (e.g., harmonious human relations, social justice, people's rights).

This book will demonstrate in detail that a particularly important characteristic of Chinese law is that, with respect to the duality of experience and theory, it privileges experience, but not to the neglect of theory. What it seeks is the close interlinking of concept and empirical situation. In contrast to the European Continental tradition of formalist law represented by Weber, Chinese law has sought to embed abstract concepts in concrete fact examples, rather than to seek to elevate abstractions into universal principles independent of concrete fact situations. For example, on property rights, traditional Chinese law did not abstract the principle of private property rights in the manner of modern Western law, but rather, within the circumstances of the time, provided for legal punishments against "fraudulently selling [another's] land or house" (*daomai tianzhai*) (as for example by falsely representing others' property as one's own to sell or forcibly occupying another's property), against "stealing-eating the fruits of another's plot or garden" (*shanshi tianyuan guaguo*) and other such invasions of others' properties, and against "the young using [familial] wealth without [parental] authorization" (*beiyou sishan yongcai*), and so on. On marriage, as a further example, Qing law did not advance the abstract principle of marriage as a contract, but rather provided for punishments against various false representations and violations in a marital agreement, such as "promising again to marry another" (*zaixu taren*), or "to represent a crippled person as not" (*you canji zhe, wangzuo wu ji*), or "to forcibly marry before the agreed-upon time" (*qiyue weizhi er qiangqu*), or "to deliberately not marry when the agreed-upon time arrives" (*qiyue yizhi er gu weiqi*), and so on. The same approach was used with respect to debt and inheritance, the other two main spheres of civil law.

Some scholars (including Weber) have believed therefore that traditional Chinese law attended only to specific concrete situations and lacked abstract concepts and principles, but this belief is based on a misunderstanding. Qing law's difference from modern Western formalist law consists not in its inability to formulate abstract principles about nonconcrete problems, but rather in its different mode of thinking as to how to join experience and theory. Formalism demands that abstract universal principles be created through legal (deductive) logic, while Qing law asks that abstract principles be embedded in concrete examples. A very good illustration is Qing legislation on homicides. All the laws are organized around a very abstract issue—intent. Homicides were separated into six grades, depending on the degree of intent. The severity of punishment varied with the degree of deliberate intent. (Xue Yunsheng, [1905] 1970: 849–57). The distinctions employed, as we will see, were in fact finer than the mere two categories of intentional killing and negligent killing adopted by the Guomindang from German law. Precisely for that reason, Republican judges in actual practice often turned back to Qing law for its concepts and distinctions to adjudge cases (for detailed analyses and documentation, see Neighbors, 2004). Those Qing distinctions were not purely abstract concepts (intentional or unintentional), but rather came from closely joining together abstract concepts with concrete fact situations. These are points I make at some length in this book in chapters 6, "Civil Adjudication, Past and Present," and 8, "Whither Chinese Law?"

At the same time, Qing law was definitely not just a retrospective law, based only on what has happened in the past. (Some have criticized American legal pragmatism on precisely these grounds for its lack of a clear agenda for lawmaking, arguing that it is, in the end, mainly just a reaction against "classical orthodoxy.") Rather, Qing law was a legal system with a strong prospective vision. Its view of the future of society rested on its moral visions, as for example the ideal of a harmonious society (of course, Confucian discourse equated this kind of ideal with the ancient era of the sage kings), in which there would be no lawsuits among the people, in which disputes would be resolved entirely by moral principles, and in which even when lawsuits happen, they would be resolved by the "father-mother officials" through moral edification.

While harboring such moral ideals, Qing law in practice also very pragmatically established a judicial system for dealing with disputes over what it termed "minor matters" (roughly equivalent to the modern "civil" category), relying first on community and kin mediation, and then the "third realm," involving an interaction between community mediation and court intervention (more below), and, finally, if the dispute was still not resolved, then by the county courts "on their own authority." And magistrates, while they espoused Confucian moral discourse, in actual practice consistently employed the very practical method of outright judgments (*duan'an*), clearly distinguishing between right and wrong according to law. I call this combination "practical moralism." This is a theme that I developed in my first volume, *Civil Justice in China: Representation and Practice in the Qing*; the present volume develops the theme further in chapters 6 and 7.

The purpose of using "practical moralism" to conceptualize Qing law is first of all to highlight its merging of moral representations with practical action, the two being at once inconsistent and yet combined together. This is what I characterize as: what this system said was one thing, what it did was another, but these two combined was yet another thing. Another purpose is to spotlight its rather distinctive mode of thought, which contrasts sharply with Weberian formal rationality.

This mode of thought was evident even in the Maoist period. To be sure, Maoist rule built a totalistic state ideology, making even more absolutist claims than Western modernism. But at the same time, it carried a tradition akin to pragmatism, which we can term its practice-orientation. That was born mainly of the Chinese Communist Party's own experience in revolution, in reaction against the doctrinaire Marxism of the party's early period. After the failure of the Great Revolution (in 1927), the party turned to the countryside, with which most party members of the time were not well acquainted, thereby setting the stage for rethinking the relationship between theory and experience. Later, in the War of Resistance period, large numbers of intellectuals from the coastal areas who made the trek to the Yan'an area had little understanding of the local situation and were, in fact, not even able to communicate with the local peasant "masses," thus creating a critical problem for the party: how to unite the two groups. That was part of the historical background for Mao's essay "On Practice." He called for the intellectuals to go deep into the countryside, first to obtain "perceptual knowledge" and identify with the "class feeling" of the peasants, and then to raise the level of their understanding with the help of (Marxist) theory to arrive at a higher level of knowledge, which was in turn to be tested in actual practice. Based on that kind of revolutionary epistemological outlook, the entire party developed the demand to "investigate and do research" ("no investigation, no right to speak") (Mao, [1941a] 1971: 196), resulting in a particular style of operation for the entire party. Even today, many Chinese social science instructors take their students down to the countryside to do on-site investigations of concrete conditions, something hard to find among social science instructors in the United States. This is a point that I have made in two published essays in Chinese (Huang Zongzhi [Philip C. C. Huang], 2005a, 2005b).

Even under the wholesale transplanting of Western laws in the Reform period, we can still discern the continuation of the original mode of thought that privileged practice. Here we might briefly introduce the illustrative example of tort law discussed in this book. It was imported from German law; Qing law contained no provisions about torts. The crucial concept is "wrongful acts" (i.e., violations of others' rights). In the manner outlined by Weber, this principle starts from the doctrine of natural rights, deducing therefrom a host of provisions: wrongful acts stem from the fault of violating others' rights, and fault results in the obligation for compensation; if there is no fault of violating another's rights, then there can be no compensatory obligation to speak of. Chinese law, however, has lent all this a different interpretation. As I will show in detail (chapter 7), the 1986 "General Principles of Civil Law" lent this a distinctive reading based on the Chinese practical-moralism mode of thought. First, in light of the empirical reality that civil damages occur both in disputes that involve fault and those that do not, the law must deal with both kinds of situations. For this reason, the "General Principles" provides, on the one hand, for obligations for compensation in the event of fault in violating another's rights and, on the other hand, also provides that even in the absence of fault, the party involved might have to bear obligation for appropriate civil compensation.

From the point of view of the formalist mode of legal thought, these two are contradictory provisions that cannot coexist. But for Chinese lawmakers, the key point is the reality of the different fact situations, and law has merely provided appropriate provisions accordingly. Logical consistency is simply not an issue. In my view, this is another example of how China can create its own distinctive modern law.

Divorce Law Practices and the System of Court Mediation

The history of the practice of divorce law reveals the same mode of thinking, and furthermore shows the nature of the very distinctive court mediation system that has continued to this day. In the Mao Zedong period, in response to specific historical needs, the system of court mediation was developed to operate over and above community mediation. The origins lay in the need to deal with strong rural opposition to the party's early radical promise of freedom of divorce (to be granted upon either party's petition); in the face of that opposition, the decision was eventually made to deal with disputed divorces case by case through mediation, in order to minimize tensions between the party and the peasantry. After a sustained period of practice, the legal principle emerged of using the quality of the emotional relationship of the couple (*ganqing*)[3] as the standard to decide whether to grant divorce or not. The key question became whether the relationship of the couple "has truly ruptured." That way, it was thought, the party could both avoid divorces based on so-called bourgeois cavalier attitudes of "liking the new and tiring of the old" (*xixin yanjiu*, referring especially to revolutionary cadres who came to prefer women comrades to their village wives), while still carrying forward the revolution against "feudal marriage" practices (that ignored the feelings of the couple)—such as polygamy, slave girls, *tongyangxi*,[4] parentally imposed mates, and purchased wives. For this, a distinctive court mediation system was invented in the Mao period, developing in time an entire set of methods, procedures, and style of work. Judges were to go deep into rural village communities; "interview" (*fangwen*) the "masses" (kin, neighbors, and the local party organization); and investigate and do research, in order to arrive at an understanding of the marriage's background and present condition and analyze the roots of the couple's marital problems (*hunyin maodun*). They were then to intervene actively, using all kinds of methods, including political education, organizational pressure, material incentives, and so on, to try to save the marriage of the couple. The purpose was to arrive at "mediated reconciliations" of the great majority of the divorce disputes. On the basis of 336 cases from a North China county (A county) and a Jiangnan county (B county), this book documents in detail the above system. In the Reform period, this Maoist "Ma Xiwu style" of court actions, especially its more authoritarian parts, have fallen into relative disuse, but the other parts of the court mediation system that developed alongside divorce law practice, especially with disputes involving no-fault fact situations, continue today to form an important part of the Chinese legal system. Chapters 4 and 5 examine this historical process.

---

3. The Chinese term ganqing has no exact English equivalent. In the semiofficial Foreign Languages Press version, this stipulation is translated, "In cases of complete alienation of mutual affection," which is close. But *ganqing* allows for gradations—"very good" (*ganqing henhao*), "poor" (*buhao*), "ruptured" (*polie*), and so on—while "mutual affection" does not. Here and later in this book I will render *ganqing* as "emotional relationship," or simply "relationship," which seems to me to come closest to capturing the meaning of the Chinese term.

4. Neither of the two commonly used English terms for *tongyangxi*—"child bride" and "adopted daughter-in-law"—is quite accurate, as I have pointed out elsewhere (Huang, 2001: 160n). "Child bride" suggests that the girl was married very young, which was generally not the case. "Adopted daughter-in-law" is also misleading, for no formal process of adoption took place. I therefore use the original Chinese term throughout.

If we shift our perspective at this point from the "what was" of the "history of practice" to the "what ought to be" of China's search today for its own "modernity," the standard of "whether the emotional relationship of the couple has ruptured," formulated during the course of the practice of divorce law, may be seen as the "logic of the history of practice," or of "modernity," contained within Chinese marriage law. It is different from the "freedom of marriage" principle; it is a legal principle born of years of legal practice, and it was not formally incorporated into the codified law until the 1980 Marriage Law. In my view, there is every reason for this "tradition" born of China's modern revolution to be developed further today in conjunction with the from-reality-to-legal-principle-to-practice mode of thinking of Chinese law. At the same time, what is shown here is the practice-based spirit of lawmaking in the People's Republic: legal principles are incorporated into codified law only after an extended period of trial through practice.

Western legal formalism takes the abstracted principle of rights as its point of departure and asks that it be applied to all fact situations, resulting thereby in a strongly adversarial legal system. However, in the real world, there are both disputes with fault and disputes without fault (in the sphere of divorce, the West itself has since the 1980s turned to an approach that sets aside considerations of fault). In point of fact, Western legal systems today, faced with the high incidence of lawsuits stemming from the adversarial nature of its legal systems, are trying to find alternative ways to resolve disputes. China has accumulated much more experience in this regard than the West, and can develop further in this direction. Chapters 4, 5, 7, and 8 explore this question in detail.

At the same time, the tradition of mediation and of practical moralism no doubt carry with them a tendency to scramble up ("mixing up wet mud," *he xini*, in Chinese parlance) right and wrong and not distinguish clearly between disputes that involve violations of the law from those that do not, and between those with fault and those without. They can therefore lapse easily into treating one as if it were the other. Where the litigants involved are of unequal power, the system can easily slop over into abuse of power and connections. The importing of Western laws that are based on rights can be a corrective to such a tendency, and should be used in fact situations involving fault to clarify and protect rights, just as the Chinese mediation tradition can be employed in no-fault fact situations as a corrective for the excessively adversarial tendency of Western legal systems that insists on separating out right from wrong and winner from loser.

In my view, consistent with the start-from-concrete-reality mode of Chinese legal thought, what might be done today is to adopt the following guideline: in fact situations that do not involve fault, employ mediation, including court mediation, because it has proven to be most effective in such situations; where fault is involved, then adjudicate by law to protect rights and thereby incorporate the strengths of Western law.

At the same time, blind transplanting of Western systems should be avoided. One notable example is the recent changes adopted with respect to rules of evidence, which have completely discarded the accumulated experience of past practice under the People's Republic, doing away with the system of having judges bear the principal responsibility for investigation and evidence gathering (characterized in Chinese usage as "judge's authority-ism," *zhiquan zhuyi*), and adopting instead the West's system of leaving the burden of proof and evidence to the litigants (what is termed in Chinese "litigant-ism," *dangshiren zhuyi*). The intention for the changes was to protect the rights of litigants to present evidence themselves. That is well and good for criminal law where the state is an interested party, but it is not entirely apposite for civil law that deals with disputes among citizens. Furthermore, in the sphere of divorce law practice, because of the lack of necessary accompanying institutional practices, especially that of the use of witnesses, what has resulted is a system that is simply not working as intended, with strong tendencies toward utter disregard of substance in favor of formalistic procedures. Bureaucratic attention to form, without regard to substance, has been among the worst problems. This kind of practice may be considered the negative unanticipated consequences of the changes in evidence law. This fact is documented in chapter 5 on the basis of forty-five recent cases from R county in the south. The point is, practice and the history of practice can be positive, and a resource for searching out China's own kind of modernity, but they can also be negative, running counter to intended moral purposes.

What is being emphasized here is the difference between a practice-based historical outlook and a theory-based historical outlook. The latter can lapse easily into an utter disregard of reality, and if put to actual use, can result in a host of unintended negative consequences such as those just outlined. The former, however, tends to stay closer to reality. If combined with forward-looking moral values, the logic evinced in the history of practice can serve as a better guide for practical reforms. This too is part of what I mean by "practical moralism."

The Third Realm and Centralized Minimalism

This book presents another example of an analytical concept derived from history-of-practice methodology, to bring out another thread of tradition that has present-day implications. In chapter 5 of my *Civil Justice in China: Representation and Practice in the Qing* (1996), I highlighted "the third realm" in the Qing system for dealing with disputes. What community and kin did when faced with disputes was mediation, while what magistrates did in formal court sessions was adjudication; between the two there existed a vast third realm. Once a disputant filed a lawsuit, it would trigger an interactive process between the societal system and the official system. On one side were the renewed efforts at community and kin mediation, and on the other, magisterial comments on the plaints, counterplaints, and petitions of the litigants. Those comments were generally either publicly displayed or conveyed to the litigants, or the litigants saw them through other means and channels. These comments would often directly influence the ongoing societal mediation. If the litigants should reach agreement at that point, then they would petition the court to withdraw the case, and the court would almost without exception grant the request. In this way, the dispute would be resolved in this semiformal third sphere through the interaction of the societal and the official systems.

In another article from the same perspective, "'Public Sphere' / 'Civil Society' in China? The Third Realm between State and Society" (Huang, 1993a), I pointed out how state and society formed an either/or binary in Jurgen Habermas's very widely discussed concept of "public sphere," as well as in the later concept of "civil society." The history of practice in China was very different, for state and society overlapped and interacted across broad historical time spans. For that reason, I advanced the concept of the "third realm."

The present volume further illustrates that concept with the history of practice of Chinese basic-level governance. Modern Western theorizing about state/society relations, under the influence of the assertion of bourgeois rights against the state in the French Revolution, has developed a deep-seated analytical assumption about the either/or opposition between state and society. That presupposition is strikingly evident in theories ranging from Weber to Habermas, and in fact may be said to be present in virtually all of the theorizing in the field of historical sociology. The "state" refers mainly to the formal bureaucratic system, and "society" to informal endogenous organizations. Rarely is the sphere in between the two considered, resulting in a view of state and society as an either/or binary.

But in the history of practice of Chinese governance, what obtained much more often were interactive or joint state-society semiformal operations, outside the scope of direct control by the centralized state apparatus. This kind of semiformal governance was manifested first of all in the *xiangbao* system, positioned at the crucial nexus of state and society—in nineteenth-century Baodi county, each xiangbao generally oversaw about twenty villages. Different from formal bureaucrats, they were generally quasi-officials nominated by the community and then approved by the county yamen, who performed their duties without salary or paperwork. But different also from simple endogenous societal systems, they were formally approved and appointed by the state, and bore definite responsibilities to the state apparatus. That is why I refer to them as semiformal quasi-officials. Another similar example is the village-head (*cunzhang*) system initiated near the end of the Qing, which was similar to the xiangbao system. A further example is village education, also initiated in the last decade of the Qing, in which the villages themselves generally furnished the school buildings (often the village temple) and hired the teachers, the government providing only the blueprint for education without appropriating any funds (VanderVen, 2005). The origins of China's modern mass education system lay precisely in this kind of joint state-community effort. Yet another example is the Quanxuesuo (Education Promotion Offices) of the time, whose members were nominated by the localities and then confirmed by the county magistrate, also examples of semiformal governance. Like the xiangbao and the village heads, members of the Quanxuesuo were quasi-officials who performed their functions with little or no paperwork, were positioned outside the yamen's formal apparatus, and assisted the magistrate in overseeing basic-level education (VanderVen, 2005). Still another example is the merchants' associations that arose in the late Qing, which similarly were semiofficial, semipopular organizations, formed on the instigation of the state and participation of the local merchants.

The operating mode of these quasi-officials was very minimalist in terms of the method of administration, most of them having neither salaries nor paperwork, and with the formal state apparatus intervening only in the event of disputes or change of personnel. For example, the xiangbao generally acted as they liked; unless there were complaints against them from villagers or there was to be a personnel change, the county yamen would not intervene in their operation. For this reason, what we know about them comes mainly from county archival records of disputes involving them or their replacements. The same applies to the village heads and the Quanxuesuo personnel. (Of course, from the 1920s onward, we also have materials from anthropological field investigations.) Even the management of the county yamen itself went by these same methods. What we know about the actual operations of various offices (*fang*) of the yamen comes mainly from litigation records, such as disputes within a given office over the control of the office or among different offices over their respective powers and revenues (Reed, 2000). The magistrate intervened only then, in a manner similar to his intervention in village governance—using dispute resolution as the principal method.

I call these administrative methods "centralized minimalism," distinct both from the formal official bureaucratic system and from informal societal organizations, and possessing their own logic and method of governance. Chapter 3 focuses on this tradition of the history of practice. (See also Huang, 2008.)

Although my "third realm" conceptualized the space occupied by this sphere, it did not explain the manner and logic in which it actually operated. The subtitle of chapter 3, "Semiformal Governance by Quasi-Officials and Dispute Resolution," is intended to be a preliminary conceptualizing of its history of practice. This kind of administrative method came first from the minimalist governance ideal of Confucianism and was evident in the Qing state's promise to not raise taxes with the continued expansion of population (*shengshi ziding, yong bu jiafu*). Another aspect of this is the limit set by the Qing government on the numbers of clerks and runners a yamen could employ. Later, when faced with continuing increase of population and the real requirements of governance, it developed gradually this system of basic-level semiformal governance under the centralized system at the top. The system originated from long-term historical practice, not from any governing ideology, whether the Confucian ideology of minimalist governance or the more sophisticated formulation of "Confucianized Legalism" from Ch'ü T'ung-tsu (1961). It was born of the interaction between ideology and administrative requirement in the history of practice, and not simply of any ideology.

Here, if we turn once more from the "what was" of the historical practice to consider the "what ought to be" of systemic social or political reform, what "centralized minimalism" stands for is an approach that might possibly be relevant for the present. The needs of the welfare state of the new era, of course, would render obsolete a good deal of the content of the old minimalist tradition of governance, but the semiformal administrative method and the state-initiation-societal-participation model of minimalism might yet have a role to play—as for example in the provision of public services and in China's continued search for a distinctive political modernity.

Community Mediation under Minimalist Governance

Finally, a word about the community mediation system that is closely related to minimalist governance. On the one hand, there was the concept and method basic to Chinese governance that communities should deal with disputes over "minor matters" by themselves, that the state would intervene only when society itself was not able to resolve the problems. On the other hand, there was the development, endogenous to the tightly-knit communities based on a peasant economy, of a system for resolving disputes: respected individuals within the communities would come forth to listen to and consider the points of view of both sides, and then seek to work out, first separately with each and then together with both, compromise resolutions acceptable to both sides. In the process, both the laws of the state (*guofa*) and what people termed "reason/moral principles" (*daoli*) would be considered, but the main purpose was to work out compromises for the sake of maintaining good human relations (*renqing*). Then, on the basis of the voluntary agreement of both sides, a mediated resolution would be reached. It might employ "apologies" (*peili daoqian*), oral promises or written agreements, a shared meal, and so on, to lend the mediated resolution a ritualized kind of confirmation.

This set of concepts and methods was seen by the state as an integral part of its method of governance, and it was also a long-standing custom of crucial importance for the countryside. What is surprising is that despite the past century's repeated rejections of the Chinese legal tradition, the same concepts and methods have managed to continue, first in the Guomindang period, and then also in the collective era—even though mediators changed from the community's most respected people to its state-approved cadres, and even though the principle and method changed from the past "compromise/human relations first, law and reason/moral principle second," to "law-policy first, human relations and reason/moral principle second"—the basic principle and method, that the community would resolve its own disputes, remained. In the Reform period, even though the massive migration of peasant workers (*nongmin gong*) has impacted the entire system in unprecedented ways, still, community mediation has shown persistent and powerful vitality and has received the determined support and approval of the state. Today, despite the powerful ideological current of wholesale Westernization, it remains a critical component of the Chinese legal system, also its most distinctive aspect. This is the main topic of chapter 2, "Community Mediation, Past and Present."

This book will start with village community disputes and mediation to set the larger social context for civil justice. It will then move on to the political-economic context to analyze the two traditions of informal and semiformal governance in the history of practice and explore their present-day relevance. Next the book turns to the history of divorce law practice to bring out the origins, myths, and realities of court mediation, and then to consideration of recent changes in rules of evidence as they have impacted divorce law practice to explain the negative consequences of a blind copying of Western institutional arrangements. It will be shown that while the history-of-practice may be reasonable and positive, it can also be unreasonable and negative. From there the book turns to the consideration of how civil adjudication and court mediation, despite radical changes in their theoretical underpinnings, reveal in practice substantial continuities, as well as a host of innovations both conceptual and methodological. They reveal also the "practical moralism" mode of thinking and its present-day relevance. The final part is a prospective look at the (Chinese conception of the) problem of "modernity" to address the issue of choices and directions for Chinese law in the future. The conclusion provides a quick summary of the major empirical findings of the book.

The method of starting with the history of practice advocated here is obviously connected to the tradition in Chinese law of privileging experience and practical use. What that tradition reveals is a mode of thought different from modern Western formalism. This book suggests that it is a mode of thinking that can serve as the basis for constructing China's own modern epistemological method and theorizing. It can be used to transcend the either/or binary of experience/theory; it can be the key to joining closely theoretical concept with experience. Once joined to theory, one can rise above the simple descriptive, retrospective, and particularistic character of experience; at the same time, once joined to experience, one can recognize the historicity of theory, and avoid absolutizing and ideologizing tendencies that disregard time and space.[5]

My intention here is not to reject completely Weber's type of formalist theory and logic, because the building of new theoretical concepts needs to be done through a dialogue with formalized theory, and the systematizing of new concepts also needs the assistance of formal logic. What I object to is only their absolutizing and universalizing. My attitude toward positivist theory and research methods (and to postmodernist theories as well) is basically the same.

Practice obviously is not so clear or simple as formal theory; its strength is that it is closer to, more in accord with, reality. At the same time, the history of practice often embodies (though not necessarily so) coexistence and compromise, or mutual adaptation, between theory and action, and thus it will not be so unitary or one-sided as theory, but rather more tolerant of differences. In the examples given above, the history of practice, in its process of reconciling theory and reality, often embodies a certain kind of practical wisdom. It is the latter that can serve today as a possibly useful resource.

In epistemological terms, my point of view may be summed up this way: experience is one thing and theory another, but, joined together, they make up something more than either one or the other. The same applies to practice and theory: from the point of view of what is, practice is one thing; theory, representation, or institution another; but coexisting, interacting, combining, and differentiating in the course of the history of practice, they make up something more than either one or the other. From the point of view of the pursuit of what ought to be, the history of practice and the logic contained therein might be seen as a resource for more realistic and intelligent choices of what paths to follow in the pursuit of given moral ideals.

5. I have explored some of these issues also in Huang Zongzhi [Philip C. C. Huang] (2007b).

2

Community Mediation, Past and Present

RURAL CHINA AND THE CHINESE LEGAL system have both undergone repeated radical changes in the past century. First came the accelerated agricultural commercialization of the twentieth century and the adoption of the new Civil Code of the Republic of China in 1930. Then came the Communist-led Land Reform and collectivization, accompanied by complete penetration of grassroots society by the laws and policies of the new totalistic party-state. Then, in the Reform era, came first de-collectivization and rural industrialization, and the massive importation again of Western laws, followed from the 1990s on by the massive movement of rural labor into the cities for work,[1] impacting rural life in unprecedented ways.

However, the community mediation portion of the traditional legal system showed surprising resilience through it all, continuing through all of the momentous changes. A core concept and method of governance in the Qing legal system was to let lineages and communities handle disputes themselves by mediation. This was the deeper meaning of the term "minor matters" (*xishi*). Its surface meaning was that the state considered disputes having to do with "households, marriage, and land" (*hu hun tiantu*) relatively unimportant, as distinguished from "severe cases" (*zhong'an*); the term included also the meaning that such matters were to be dealt with using only relatively light

1. Though temporary, this was movement that "left both the land and the village" *litu lixiang* (to be distinguished from the earlier rural industrialization under which labor "left the land but did not leave the village," *litu bu lixiang*).

punishment. But its deeper meaning was that from the point of view of governance, these were matters that were preferably dealt with by society itself; the state would intervene only if the communities were not able to resolve matters themselves. That concept-method continued, albeit with modifications, through all the changes of the past century. Considering the scope and depth of those changes, the persistence of the concept-method itself attests to its fundamental importance to the traditional legal system.

Even today, it remains a major difference between the Chinese and Western legal systems. To take the United States as an example, despite the nearly half-century old movement for "alternative dispute resolution" (ADR), mediation still figures far less prominently than in China. When confronted with a dispute, most people still do not think of mediation as an option. In the face of serious threats to one's interests, most people will still see litigation as the only recourse. So-called arbitration is in large measure really a discounted trial that cuts costs by the use of retired judges and substitute "courtrooms"; its principle of operation remains basically the same as that of the court system, to arrive at a winner and a loser. (There is considerable misunderstanding in China of the American ADR system—something to be taken up in chapter 7.) By contrast, in China most people to this day will look first to mediation and some kind of peaceable resolution, and go to court only as the final resort. This remains a fundamental difference between the two legal cultures. It is also a good indication of the persistence in China of the traditional legal system in its broad sense.

This chapter starts with materials on the 1920s to the 1940s from on-site field investigations. After comparing them with records of court cases from the same period, and then with those from the same locality in the Qing period, it will seek to establish in broad strokes a baseline picture of community mediation in the prerevolutionary countryside to serve as our point of departure. Information is rather scarce for earlier periods, but we will look also briefly at some recent findings for the Huizhou area in the Ming and early Qing, to lend some measure of greater time depth to this discussion. We will then turn to look at changes and continuities through the Mao Zedong era, followed by the early Reform period (the 1980s to the mid-1990s). We will look finally at the changes in the "later" Reform period after the mid-1990s. The discussion of each period will progress in the following order: first the source materials, then the main content of the disputes, then the mediation personnel and the principle and method used.

As will be shown, there are two main types of community mediation in China today: those that are done by "informal" (i.e., strictly nonofficial) leaders that go unrecorded, and those that are done by "semiformal" community cadres (to be distinguished from "formal" state officials) that are recorded and counted. Both should be distinguished from court ("judicial") mediations and official or administrative mediations. As will be seen, the post-1949 period has seen first, in the collective era, "semiformalization," or "cadre-ization," in which community disputes came to be handled almost exclusively by community cadres, and then, in the later Reform period since the mid-1990s, partial informalization (or re-societalization), in which many community disputes have come to be handled once more by informal leaders of the communities.

Community Mediation from the 1920s to the 1940s

In the North China countryside of the 1920s to the 1940s, village disputes occurred mostly in the same categories as in the Qing, namely, over land, debt, inheritance and old-age support, and marriage. They were usually mediated by informal leaders of the communities. The main principle-method governing the mediations was compromise, based on considerations of human relations (*qing*), with law (*fa*) and moral right and wrong (*li*) as secondary concerns. It differed from the Maoist period, when mediations came to be handled by community cadres, and the main concern was with law-policies, and only secondarily with human relations and moral right and wrong. The content of the disputes also differed from the later period.

Source Materials

The Mantetsu (short for Minami Manshū Tetsudō Kabushiki Kaisha, or South Manchurian Railway Company) investigations of six North China villages undertaken in the late 1930s to early 1940s contain fairly detailed materials about rural mediation, covering the 1920s to the 1940s. This chapter uses the information from the three most thoroughly investigated villages—Shajing in Shunyi County, Houjiaying in Changli, and Sibeichai in Luancheng, all in Hebei Province—to try to construct a rough but usable prerevolutionary baseline. Unlike villages in Guangdong, Fujian, or Huizhou, where lineages were highly developed and held substantial properties,[2] these villages had little lineage property and their "lineages" might be better termed "common descent groups," generally with only common burial land and neither farmland nor ancestral halls. Because of the frequent natural disasters of the region, movement of people in and out of the villages tended to be quite common, and the communities consequently evinced a rather low degree of cohesion. However, relative to the more highly commercialized Jiangnan and other areas, the villages tended also to be more inward looking, with social

2. This was of course Maurice Freedman's (1966) original definition of the term *lineage*.

interactions largely limited to the community itself (in sharp contrast to Jiangnan's village of Huayangqiao that I studied in detail) (Huang, 1985: chap. 6). Overall, the villages were neither tightly knit nor highly integrated with the outside; they fall more into what might be considered the intermediate or common range, which was one of the reasons the Mantetsu researchers selected these villages.

The Content of Disputes

To be sure, no group of villages can represent all the different areas and all the villages of all of China. However, there can be no doubt that disputes in these villages show strong consistency with the Republican-period court records from Shunyi County (used in my earlier volumes). The content of the civil disputes of the time was basically the same, having to do mostly with land, debt, inheritance–old-age maintenance, and marriage. At the same time, the Republican-period court cases of Shunyi County were basically the same in content as those of the Qing period from nearby Baodi County. Land and debt disputes were basically the same; as for inheritance and marriage, even though the text of the legal code had changed quite markedly in the twentieth century, legal practice remained substantially the same. The family's land and house were still divided among the sons; rural daughters in practice still did not have those inheritance rights. The Guomindang's new civil code did indeed provide for gender equality in marriage and divorce, but in actual judicial practice in the countryside, divorce was still very rare, and those initiated by women rarer still.

As shown in table 2.1, land disputes, including disputes over boundaries, sales-purchases, and rental, made up one major category, accounting for 9 of the 41 cases (22 percent). Here we do not find the topsoil rights system of the Yangzi delta, and hence also not the kinds of disputes that stemmed from the new code's denial of those rights (Huang, 2001: chap. 6). But there was the more prevalent nationwide *dian* (i.e., conditional sale) system, which came from a long-standing rural custom recognized by law, permitting those forced by subsistence pressures to sell their land to retain advantageous terms of redemption (e.g., at the original dian price for a long period of time). It led many dian-makers to refuse even after decades to sell outright (*maiduan*) their dian land, or to seek repeatedly additional payments from the dian-holder for the difference between the original dian price and the current market value (a practice called *zhaotie*), thus causing many disputes.[3] In our three villages, dian was especially

3. For this reason, the Qing code added in 1753 the provision that redemption rights were thence not to exceed thirty years (Huang, 1996: 36–39; 2001: chap. 5).

TABLE 2.1
Disputes in Three North China Villages, 1920s to 1940s

	Shajing	*Sibeichai*	*Houjiaying*	***Total***
Land				
boundary	2		2	**4**
sale	1	2	1	**4**
rental		1		**1**
Debt	1		2	**3**
Marriage		2	1	**3**
Brothers & sisters-in-law	7	6		**13**
Inheritance		1		**1**
Old-age support		1		**1**
Administrative	2	1	3	**6**
Other	3		2	**5**
Total	**16**	**14**	**11**	**41**

Sources: Shajing, KC, 1–2; Sibeichai, KC, 3; Houjiaying, KC, 5.
Note: This table includes just those disputes elicited by the questions of the investigators. It should not be seen as comprehensive.

widespread in Sibeichai: of the 140 households, 70 had dianed their land at some time. But possibly because of the overwhelming power of the wealthiest landlord, Wang Zanzhou, there were no evident disputes over dian in the village (KC, 3, appended table; see also Huang, 1996: 39). However, in county-level lawsuits, disputes over dian rights occupied a substantial proportion of all cases (7 of 42 in Shunyi's land-related cases) (Huang, 1996: 38).

Debt disputes also accounted for a definite proportion of the village disputes (three, or 7 percent). There were both small "informal" loans (i.e., without a written document, middleman, guarantor, or security) among kin, neighbors, and friends, and larger "formal loans" (with a middleman, guarantor, or security, and usually with a written document). From county-level lawsuits we can see that the proportion of cases from informal loans was higher than that from formal loans. This was mainly because formal loans contained a built-in mechanism for dispute resolution, namely the middleman or guarantor. If problems arose at the time the loan came due, the middleman might arrange for an extension, turn to another source to pay the loan due, or even advance the money himself (KC, 4: 222; 2: 195–96, 215; Huang, 1996: 52–54). If the loan was secured by landed property, the middleman might take the next step and arrange for its change of hands. The middleman was in fact an important part of the mediation system for resolving disputes (KC, 2: 211; Huang, 1996: 51–54). Informal loans, by contrast, precisely because they were informal, left more room for nonpayment or misunderstandings. They were not less conflict prone simply because the principals involved were kin, neighbors, or friends. They in fact appeared more frequently in county-level lawsuits than formal loans.

Outside of land and debt, conflicts among brothers and their wives were quite common (thirteen of the forty-two, or 32 percent). The problem arose first from peasants' attempt to keep married brothers together in imitation of the elites and their Confucian ideal, as can be seen from the following provision of the Qing code: "If brothers, sons or grandsons should divide up family property during the lifetime of their parents or grandparents, they will be punished by 100 blows with the heavy bamboo stick" (Statute 87). Realistically, however, when adult married brothers lived together in the same house, friction from daily life was almost unavoidable, and household division became the main method for dealing with the problem. This was a reality that Qing law recognized by providing after the statute forbidding household division quoted above that "if the parents give their permission, then it may be allowed." (Substatute 87-1).

Chinese villages over time developed a set of methods to help avoid disputes over household division itself. The key was the middleman (*zhongjianren* or *zhongren*, in North China also called *shuoheren*, *zhongbaoren*, *zhongshuoren*, and so on), usually more than one, who may include kin, marital kin, neighbors, or community leaders. In Sibeichai, the process usually took no fewer than two days (KC, 3: 96). First, everyone involved including the brothers would participate in discussions to divide up the properties into equal portions, and then the brothers would draw lots to decide who gets which. The middlemen would draw up a household-division document (*fenjiadan*), listing in detail the properties being divided, to forestall future arguments (Huang, 1996: 26–27; KC, 1: 290–92, 319; 3: 93, 95–96, 102, 123, including the actual division documents).

Precisely because of the efficacy of this "procedure," there was not a single instance in our three villages of a dispute arising from the process of household division or from arguments after the fact over unevenness in the division. Those were also rare among county-level lawsuits: in the 72 cases involving landed property and inheritance from Shunyi between 1916 and 1934, there was not a single case related to household division. In 35 such cases of the nineteenth century from nearby Baodi County, there was just one, and in 142 such cases from Danshui-Xinzhu in Taiwan, just two.[4] The high frequency of brothers and sisters-in-law friction and disputes in the villages thus contrasted sharply with the rarity of household-division disputes in the county yamen's records, attesting thereby to the efficacy of the customary practices of household division as the way to resolve those disputes.

---

4. The Baodi case originated from the two sides seeking a remeasurement of the land years later; as for the two Danshui-Xinzhu cases, one had to do with an opium-addict brother who had been given a regular income rather than a share of the properties; he later sought a redivision. The other had to do with an uncle's swallowing up of the family property (Huang, 1996: 27–28).

Another kind of dispute was over old-age maintenance. In the three villages, there was just one instance, showing that as late as 1930, the old morality and legal provision for sons to maintain their parents in old age still functioned well. In addition, the "old-age-support land" (*yanglaodi*) system used widely in the villages—to set aside part of the land during household division for maintenance of the parents while they were alive and for funeral expenses when they died (what peasants called *shengyang sizang*)—was also quite effective (Huang, 2001: chap. 8). The only instance of an old-age-maintenance dispute in our three villages came when the elderly widow Xu, known in the village as something of a spendthrift, wanted to sell outright one *mu* (i.e., one-sixth of an acre) of the family's land that had already been dianed out. Her son, married and the head of the household, refused. To pressure her son, the elderly woman brought suit, charging that her son would not feed her. The court found her claim groundless (KC, 3: 153; Huang, 1996: 32, 62). The case obviously involved rather unusual circumstances. According to the testimony of one villager, if a family had just one son, there was usually no problem with old-age support. Only when the family had more than one son would there be disputes over who should do what. Even so, in the three villages, even families with multiple sons could usually reach agreement over the parents' old-age support. For example, the five Hao brothers of Sibeichai each provided an equal share of grain and spending money for the parents every year. In another family in Sibeichai, the mother ate at the three brothers' homes in turn, and each of them farmed one mu of old-age-support land for her (KC, 3: 79; Huang, 1996: 31). Of course, this does not mean there were no disputes. In Shunyi County, old-age maintenance disputes accounted for seven of the thirty (23 percent) lawsuits (related to inheritance–old-age support); in Qing Baodi, three of twelve (25 percent).

What needs to be discussed separately here are two spheres in which the new code made new provisions. First was marriage. The new 1930 code provided for gender equality in the letter of the law. But, in real life, its effect in the countryside lagged far behind the towns and cities. In our three villages, there was just one instance of a woman (in Houjiaying) petitioning for divorce, and that was because her husband had gone away to seek work more than ten years ago and had not been heard from since (KC, 5: 139–40). This was basically the same as the pattern shown in the nineteenth century Baodi case records: of thirty-two marriage-related cases, only one was initiated by the wife, because her husband had gone off to work thirteen years ago and had not been heard from since (Baodi xian dang'an, 162, 1839, 6.1; Huang, 1996: 29). Such "abandonment" was among the very few conditions for "divorce" recognized by the Qing code, which required that it must exceed a period of three years (Substatute 116-1). Of course, in the county-level lawsuits of

Shunyi, there were more divorces initiated by wives (eight of thirty-three marriage-related courses, in which twelve were divorce cases), but they all came from the towns. The new Guomindang legal provisions still had relatively little effect on the countryside.

The other sphere was inheritance, for which the code also provided gender equality as in marriage. Here again the new law did not have the effect intended. In villages, only sons inherited. In our three villages, there was just one case of someone (a widow) who tried to use the new law to claim a share of the property of the father (for her two daughters). In the end, the dispute was resolved through mediation by the village head and two other respected individuals of the community, who arranged for the daughters to receive, according to usual village practice, what they would have received as dowries for marriage (Huang, 1996: 63–64; see also KC, 3: 155, 338–39). As for the county court, cases claiming women's inheritance rights came mainly from the towns and not from the villages.

The forty-one disputes from the three villages included six lawsuits involving village governance. At the time, with the imposition of the new special levies (*tankuan*), such as the school levy (*cuntan xuekuan*) and the police levy (*cuntan jingkuan*), many original village leaders refused to continue to serve as village heads in order to avoid the high-pressure demands of the state's bureaucratic apparatus. The result was something of a power vacuum that allowed ne'er-do-wells (*wulai*) and local bullies (*eba*) to insinuate themselves into power, leading to corruption and abuse, which in turn prompted villagers to file complaints with the county government. Those lawsuits were intimately linked to the special historical circumstances of the time; given our long-term perspective and concern with community mediation here, we will not dwell on those.

Finally, it should be pointed out that the disputes in the three villages were born of social conflicts that were already openly manifested, and mainly between those in positions of roughly equivalent power and status, such as those involving land, debt, inheritance, and marriage. But records of such open disputes also conceal the tensions and frictions among people of unequal power, since those, suppressed by the fact of unequal power, were not likely to reveal themselves openly. The most obvious example is the relationship between mothers- and daughters-in-law. Houjiaying village provides us with one unforgettable example: a seventeen-year-old daughter-in-law was picked on almost daily by her demanding mother-in-law until the summer of 1942, when she had, as usual, worked for four days gathering wheat stalks for someone in the village. She had earned 3.20 yuan in pay and as usual was going to visit her natal family on her day off. Her father-in-law had accepted the pay in her stead and then, short of change, simply gave her 4 yuan. On that account, the mother-in-law threw a fit and ended up going to her in-laws' house to demand the 80 cents back. Angry things were said, and the young woman became extremely upset. That night, after she returned, she jumped in the well and killed herself (KC, 5: 49–50, 40; Huang, 1996: 70).

In another case, from Shunyi County in 1927, the seventeen-year-old son, Changjiangtou, of rich and powerful Liu Langui, raped Lu Lansheng's seven-year-old daughter. The girl died from the injuries. But Liu cajoled, paid, and pressured Lu to agree to withdraw his charge. He also bribed the county government into treating the matter as a civil dispute. And he got seventeen local individuals of high repute (including Zhou Shutang of Shajing village) to come forth, ostensibly to "mediate," employing the standard rhetoric, to the effect that "the two sides have met and followed the appropriate courtesies . . . and both now wish to end the lawsuit." He managed thus to obtain the county government's permission for the case to be withdrawn and closed (Shunyi 2: 485, 1927.6.6; Huang, 1996: 69).

Such case examples show us that the community mediation system worked best among people of roughly equivalent power. If the positions of the two sides were too unbalanced, then there was room for the kind of abuse shown above. Below we will see how, in the 1980s, the incidence of recorded disputes between mothers- and daughters-in-law would climb steeply, precisely because the growing power balance between them allowed what had been suppressed to come out into open disputes. But then, in the later Reform period, imbalance returned, now because of the decided advantage in earnings of the younger generation, and the frequency of open disputes declined again.

Mediation Personnel

To resolve their disputes, the North China villages relied mainly on the mediation mechanisms of the communities themselves. As has already been seen, at the most basic levels of human interactions, the villages relied widely on the middleman system. Household divisions and formal loans, marriage, land sales-purchases and rentals, hiring of agricultural workers, and so on generally used middlemen and the mediation mechanisms they brought with them. In case of friction, the middlemen would serve as mediators (Huang, 1996: 52–58). As for disputes within common-descent groups, they were usually settled by people from within the group. Household division was itself a good example of such (of course, as noted above, it may on occasion rely on those from outside the common-descent group). Here I will not dwell on these basic-level, relatively narrow-in-scope relationships, but will concentrate instead on community-level mediation mechanisms.

The Mantetsu-investigated villages each had a number of respected mediators whom everyone could name. The great majority were informal leaders of high community esteem. In Shajing, interviewees named seven such individuals, among whom were three of the ten so-called *shoushi*, or informal leaders of (public) affairs of the village, all of them rich peasant types: Li Ruyuan, age sixty-five, with 76 mu of land, head of the Li common-descent group and also the village doctor; Yang Yuan, forty-four, with 40 mu of land and also a jewelry store in town; and Zhang Rui, forty-two, the wealthiest man in the village with 130 mu and currently the deputy head of the village (*cunfu*). Then two well-to-do middle peasant types: former village head Zhou Shutang, elderly, with 33.5 mu of land, and Zhang Shaoting, fifty-six, with 16 mu of land and also renting 30 mu. Then there is Yang Yongcai, sixty, the eldest member of the Yang descent group, with 18 mu, who also looks after the village temple (for which he receives 100 yuan a year). Finally, Chong Wenqi, forty-nine, who had a cake shop and wide associations. Most, in other words, were substantial property owners and middle-aged or above (Huang, 1996: 58–60).

In the village of Sibeichai, the two individuals who did the most mediating were former village head Zhang Yueqing and current village head Hao Guoliang, showing thus the change that had come with the beginnings of penetration of the village by the state apparatus. Zhang and Hao were not just individuals of high repute in the village but also people recognized by the state apparatus for village governance. Their authority was therefore even higher than that of the typical village elite (Huang, 1996: 58–60).

Lengshuigou villagers mentioned especially the moral qualities expected of a mediator. According to them, a mediator needs to be someone who keeps his word and is trustworthy, or is "elderly and moral." Another interviewee said that he should be someone who is "just" and "knows how things work." In Houjiaying village, there was someone whose reputation reached beyond the community itself. Dubbed the "good man of the township" (*yixiang shanshi*), he reportedly could make "big problems turn into small problems, and small problems into nonproblems." After Hou Yongfu died, none of the other six or seven acknowledged mediators of the village enjoyed that kind of reputation (Huang, 1996: 58–60).

The above makes clear also that the endogenous "traditional" village "elite" and "leaders" were all men; multiple factors saw to it that women occupied only a limited place in the public space of the community.[5] But that was not always the case. In the 1930s and 1940s, in the single-surnamed hamlet Lujiada of the village of Huayangqiao in Songjiang County near Shanghai, the most respected person in the entire hamlet was a woman named Lu Danan. Villag-

5. Margery Wolf (1972: 38–41), on the basis of her research in Taiwan, singled out especially the "women's community" based on the socializing that took place during the women's clothes and vegetables washing.

ers said she was straight, able, and generous, and she kept her word. Because of that, the members of the descent group would all turn to her when they had problems or disputes. Her many deeds led people to respect her as someone who helped people in difficulty. Everyone referred to her as "big sister." In 1939, when she underwent household-division with her twenty-six-year-old brother, Guantong, she made sure that he received more land than she did.[6] (People say that Guantong was an acquisitive fellow who, because of his opposition to cooperativization in 1955, was classed a "rich peasant"—something not corrected until 1979.) For this reason, brother Guantong was always most respectful toward his big sister. Lu Danan's was obviously a rather unusual case (Huang, 1990: 150–51).

Principle and Method of Mediation

From the many examples of mediated resolutions of disputes in the Mantetsu interview records (Huang, 1996: 58–75), we can see that the main principle and method of mediation was human relations (qing) and compromise, with the mediators facilitating the working out of a solution that both sides could accept. And the main purpose of mediation was, in this "society of the well acquainted" (*shuren shehui*), to resolve problems, keep peace (*xishi ningren*), and avoid long-term enmity.

But this is not to say that laws (fa) and moral right/wrong (li) were not important. In *Civil Justice in China: Representation and Practice in the Qing*, I recounted at some length the dispute over easement "rights" between Li Zhuyuan and his nephew Li Guang'en of Shajing village in 1941 (KC, 1: 162–70; Huang, 1996: 65–68). For many years, Guang'en had relied on a path through Zhuyuan's courtyard to get to his own house. But now Zhuyuan sold his house-courtyard to a newcomer, Zhao Wenyou. Zhao wanted to build his house to extend over the easement path. That, of course, would cause Guang'en much inconvenience. For this reason, the two sides got into a protracted dispute.

The case involved multiple dimensions. According to the custom of the village, when land was sold, the neighbors on four sides had the first right of refusal. This was, of course, a custom that had evolved over time, precisely in order to avoid problems such as this one. But Zhuyuan, in order to obtain a higher sales price (100 yuan), deliberately went around the custom, used a middleperson from outside, and registered the sales transaction at the town

6. This was a village where a substantial proportion of the families took in "married-in" sons-in-law (*ruzhui*), and it was not uncommon for the daughter along with her married-in husband to receive a share of the family's land.

of Renhe, some distance away. Zhuyuan's behavior was, strictly speaking, legal, since the law had no requirement about the right of prior refusal of the neighbors. It was also the reason Zhuyuan was able to register the transaction without difficulty.

Faced with the disjunction between custom and law, the three mediators (Zhou Shutang, Zhao Shaoting, and Yang Yongcai, all from among the seven most respected mediators in the village) had to consider things not only from the point of view of moral/customary right and wrong, but also that of legality in the eyes of the law. The stance they took as mediators in the end was based neither simply on custom nor on law, but rather was mainly concerned with seeking a compromise between the two parties in order to solve the problem and keep peace. They suggested that Zhuyuan should return 20 to 30 yuan of the sales price to Zhao Wenyou in return for Zhao's agreement that he would allow Guang'en to continue to use the easement. But Zhao, who was a semi-stranger to the village, insisted on building his house over the easement, since it was perfectly legal, or else he would demand that Zhuyan concede the entire sales price of 100 yuan. Zhuyuan, of course, refused. The mediation therefore failed. It was clear that while Guang'en was clearly morally in the right, Zhuyuan and Zhao had the law on their side.

Confronted with the dilemma, the mediators asked Li Ruyuan, the most respected elder in the Li kin group, to come forth to try to resolve the problem. Li, for his part, also turned to compromise. He suggested that he would provide a path for Guang'en through his own courtyard for free, and hoped that Guang'en would accept that as the solution. But the path that Ruyuan offered was on the north side of Guang'en's house, not nearly as convenient as the original easement, which ran from the road to the south of the house. Guang'en therefore refused the offer. And things once more reached an impasse.

At this point, Zhao Wenyou began construction of his new house, leading to an argument with Guang'en, followed by a fight. Zhao went off to file suit at the county court that very day. Faced with this intensification of the conflict, the three mediators redoubled their efforts. This time, they raised the figure of "20 to 30 yuan" up to "30 to 40 yuan." The Mantesus researchers on the scene threw in another 10 yuan. In the end, Zhao Wenyou was paid a total of 50 yuan in return for agreeing not to extend his house over the easement.

Clearly, the principle-method of mediation was to consider mainly qing, or human relations, but not without considering also law (fa) and moral right/wrong (li). The overriding purpose was to resolve the dispute in order to keep peace, and the principal resort was to compromise, though in conjunction with considerations of law and of moral right/wrong. This "traditional" mediation principle-method would undergo sharp changes in the post-1949 period.

A Different Example from Huizhou of the Ming-Qing Period

What about the way things were before the 1920s? Can this picture of the "traditional" be extended back into the Ming and early Qing? Recent studies using Huizhou documents have made important advances, providing us with some basis for comparison and guesswork. They suggest substantial continuity in the content of disputes and also in some aspects of mediation. But the role played by semiofficial community leaders might have been very different from the later period.

First is the work of Xiong Yuanbao. Xiong relies mainly on the diary of a *shengyuan* (i.e., holder of the lowest examination degree) named Zhan Yuanxiang (the *Weizhai riji*) from Qingyuan village in Wuyuan County (Huizhou Prefecture), who recorded forty-seven disputes occurring in that village in the early Qing from 1699 to 1705, plus one each for 1696 and 1698.[7] On that basis, Xiong has reconstructed a fairly detailed picture of the content of the disputes there, even if not of the principle and method of mediation (Xiong Yuanbao, 2003: 153–57).

Qingyuan village was, of course, different from our North China picture, both in geographical location and historical period. Here social differentiation of the countryside was more pronounced. Qingyuan contained residents who were degree-holders (five from the late Ming to the early Qing, including two *jinshi* (i.e., the highest examination degree); and the nearby village of Duanxin actually counted twenty-four degree-holders, including five *jinshi*—Xiong Yuanbao, 2003: 169–70). The village also had large numbers of low-status "tenant-servants," *dianpu.* And it differed in the landholding system: here there was the so-called one-field-three-owners (*yitian sanzhu*) system, more complex than Jiangnan's one-field-two-owners (*yitian liangzhu*) system, and resembled the "big rent" and "little rent" system of Taiwan. There were numerous landlord-tenant servant disputes. At the same time, lineage organization was highly developed (related of course to the presence of degree-holders), with substantial lineage property that was rented out to tenant-servants. Qingyuan also experienced more friction with the outside than our North China villages. It was involved in a protracted dispute with neighboring Duanxin and it was renowned for its "litigiousness" (*jiansong*).

However, there were also important similarities with our North China villages. There was quite pervasive use of middlemen in basic transactions and also reliance on lineage members for dispute resolution. The village had many disputes that were similar to those of North China later, such as disputes related to land (like encroachment on others' land and land-rentals), debt,

7. Including one case each from 1696 and 1698.

marriage contracts, and so on. In addition, there were disputes over ancestral grave land, which, though relatively uncommon in North China, were widespread in Sichuan's Baxian in the Qing (Huang, 2001: 79–81)

On the other hand, to judge by two other studies using Huizhou materials from the Ming period, the official institutional framework was quite different. According to Nakajima Gakushô's (2002) research, based on seventy-five dispute cases between 1522 and 1645 drawn from both official (*guan wenshu*) and private documents (*si wenshu*), and Han Xiutao's (2004), based on thirty-eight cases drawn from (what Han calls) dispute-resolution contracts (*jiefenlei qiyue*) between 1427 and 1637, the quasi-official *lizhang* and *yuebao* (merging the terms *xiangyue* and *dibao*, much like the later Qing *xiangbao*) in the Ming performed their functions differently from the later Qing xiangbao.[8] Their role was more formalized. According to Nakajima's materials and analysis, disputants throughout the Ming commonly filed written complaints (*tousu*) with the lizhang or yuebao, accounting for some 45 percent of Nakajima's cases (Nakajima, 2002: 254). As for Han Xiutao's thirty-eight cases, there were fourteen (37 percent) that were resolved with the lizhang acting as the main mediator (Han Xiutao, 2004: 69).

By contrast, the Qing xiangbao were prohibited after 1765 from interfering in disputes by the following substatute: "The county officials must handle personally [the minor cases filed by the people] and not allow the xiangdi [xiangyue dibao] to deal with and resolve them." (Substatute 334-8; see also Huang ,1996: 113). To judge by the Baxian case records, this restriction seems to have been effective from the mid-eighteenth to the mid-nineteenth century, but then xiangbao interventions in disputes returned in the late nineteenth century. Even so, we do not see in that later period the officially condoned, formally submitted complaints to the lizhang and the yuebao like those in the Ming.

Beyond the differences and similarities noted above, however, existing materials regrettably do not permit us to analyze further the principle and method used in mediation at the time. What the available information allows us to see are some basic continuities in the content of disputes and the role played by middlemen, and community and lineage leaders, in helping to resolve disputes through mediation.

Community Mediation in the Collective Period

In the collective period, with the virtual end of private property, disputes over land, debt, inheritance, and household division largely ended. New frictions

8. On the xiangbao, see the more detailed discussion in chapter 3.

that arose had mainly to do with new institutional arrangements. As for the personnel, system, and principle-method of mediation, they became (what might be termed) cadre-ized or semiformalized, replacing the old endogenous village leadership with state-approved and appointed personnel. When disputes touched on state laws-policies, the principle-method of mediation also tended to become more coercive. However, the communities became even more tightly knit than before, and their disputes continued to be resolved mainly by the villages themselves.

Source Materials

The source materials used for this portion of the chapter come mainly from my three visits to Ganlu village (Huayangqiao Township, Songjiang County, of the municipality of Shanghai, which had been the site of my earlier books on rural economy and of repeated visits since the 1980s) in 1990, 1991, and 1993, mainly in interviews with village cadres and disputants. Interviews thirty years after the fact, of course, can only yield broad-stroke information. Nevertheless, by using the information in conjunction with the more detailed materials from the county court for that period, and with more detailed information from both the earlier and the later periods, we can still get a fairly reliable picture.

Content of Disputes

In the revolutionary era, first came disputes related to land distribution during the Land Reform, and then disputes related to the process of cooperativization and collectivization, mainly having to do with one relatively well-to-do peasant's resistance, and also problems connected to an outsider who had moved into the village. Then, under the collective system, land buying-selling and renting were basically eliminated and related disputes along with them. The same with debt disputes: the villagers related that everybody was too poor; there was no money to borrow. Of course, there were still the "private plots" and some land-boundary disputes. But on the whole, private property no longer figured much in people's lives, and disputes over inheritance also became very rare. The old household-division system no longer played much of a role—the villagers said that household divisions at the time became very simple (involving mainly the house, since there was no land to divide up), basically a matter of "what the father says goes." Compared to the pre-1949 period, these were dramatic changes.

The collective system also brought a host of other related changes in human relations. It brought some new types of disputes, for example, over the determination of workpoints by the production team and over work assignments. But generally speaking, under the control of totalistic authority, people's autonomy over their daily lives dropped sharply, and open conflicts in human relations also declined. There were simply fewer disputes than under the marketized small-peasant economy of old.

Divorce stands out as something of a special sphere. In the marriage law movement of the early 1950s against "feudal marriages," unprecedented numbers of women sought divorce unilaterally. By the early 1960s, a certain steady state returned, and the number of divorces would not rise again until the 1980s. Compared to other disputes, those over divorce were far more frequent and to a considerable degree made up the main content of Chinese civil litigation until the Reform period.

During the Land Reform, the villagers and the cadres say, the main disputes had to do with the distribution of land, because everyone wanted the plots closer to the village, or else those of the more well-to-do villagers, because those had generally been better fertilized than the rest. But given the passage of time, no one could say more concretely what the disputes were and how they were resolved.

One lasting memory that stands out was of an incident that came from the later cooperativization period. The slogan of the time was "lend a hand to the poor peasants," to let one's farm animals, implements, and such "means of production" be sold cheaply to the poor peasants. The prices were low and set by the village cadres. For example, an ox that had a market price of 20 *shi* would be valued at about 10 shi.[9] Everyone remembers how Lu Guantong refused to sell his ox at such a price. For this, he was "struggled" at a mass meeting, labeled a "counterrevolutionary" and "rich peasant," and imprisoned for five years. After his release from prison, he was placed under "supervised labor" (*jiandu laodong*, which meant that he had to be the first at work and the last to quit and received only nine workpoints a day; that he had to do twice the amount of voluntary labor, *yiwugong*, of everyone else; and that he could only leave the village with the cadres' permission). In the "big four cleans" movement in 1965, he was struggled yet again. He was finally "rehabilitated" as a "middle peasant" only in 1979 (INT93-3; cf. Huang, 1990: 276–77).

The other lasting memory from the time of collectivization was of what happened to Gao Yongnian from Henan, who had worked on the railroad and married into the Xilihangbang hamlet of the village. Though Gao was strong, he did not know how to transplant rice, and was called "white claws"

9. A shi is a volume measure of about 160 catties, at 1.1 pound per catty. Huayangqiao village had adopted in response to the inflation during the later period of the Civil War a barter system based on rice-weight that continued down to the cooperativization period.

for his lack of farm experience. Assigned to work transporting rice shoots to the fields, he proved to be unable to balance himself with the weighted carrying pole on the field banks. He had a bad temper and would swear at people and insult the women. In the "self-reporting and public-discussion" (*zibao gongyi*) process to determine workpoints, he was angry that "the masses" gave him only nine points and swore at everyone. For this, he was struggled in open meetings no fewer than ten times during the "big four cleans." (Still he refused to "confess," saying that "whether I laugh or cry, you beat me; the worst you can do is to open up a couple of holes in me, then I won't laugh any more." For this, everyone admitted that he was a "hard bone," *yinggutou*). Like Lu Guantong, he was placed under "supervised labor" (INT93-3; cf. Huang, 1990: 276–77). Chen Ximing, who served as commune civil affairs assistant (*wenshu*, changed to *minzheng zhuli* in 1978–1981) from 1958 to 1981, recalled that he dealt with several cases of complaints about workpoints. Of course, as the judicial "official" of the commune, the way he handled them was mainly by administrative *tiaochu*, rather than *tiaojie* through compromise (INT93-6).[10]

Then there were the boundary disputes, as people still had private plots of land. One villager recalled that in the 1960s, Gao Boren of Gaojiada hamlet had repeatedly encroached on the plot of his neighbor, Gao Buying, each time by a few centimeters. On account of this, the two got into a dispute that was later resolved by team head Lu Haitong (INT93-3). Another time, a peasant allowed his chickens and ducks repeatedly to wander into the other person's plot to feed until finally that person killed a few of them. That, too, required the mediation of the village cadres (INT93-3). According to the commune's civil affairs assistant, Chen Ximing, such disputes were among the ones he most commonly handled.

There were also the disputes over work assignment. Because requests sometimes came for villagers to work outside, and those generally paid more, there were usually many who wanted to go, and the production team leaders had to choose among them. Supposedly, they did what they could to be just and fair, but dissatisfaction was unavoidable (INT93-2).

The main disputes were those having to do with marriage. Our village had two divorce disputes in the 1950s, both from Xuejiada hamlet. One concerned a woman who had married into the village quite young, but then the husband grew up "short and ugly," the marriage was an unhappy one, and she went back to her natal family. In the early 1950s during the marriage law

10. In the old liberated areas, tiaochu and tiaojie were clearly distinguished, the former applying mainly to administrative handling, usually quite coercive, while the other emphasizing voluntariness more, aiming to obtain the disputant's voluntary acceptance of the resolution. After 1949, of course, the line between the two blurred. The rather coercive "mediated reconciliations" in divorce disputes were a good example—see chapter 7.

movement, she managed to obtain permission for divorce on the grounds of opposing a "feudal" marriage (INT93-1). In another similar case, a girl had been adopted into the family at an early age and later married to one of the sons, but they did not get along. Since the marriage fell under the category of *tongyangxi* (see chapter 4), she was able to obtain a divorce (INT93-9).

Compared to the villages of the 1920s to 1940s, these instances of women obtaining divorce on such grounds are striking. As we have seen, nineteenth-century Baodi County had just one instance of a wife seeking divorce, and that was by a woman who had been abandoned and had not heard from her husband for thirteen years. And our three Mantetsu-investigated villages also had just one instance, that from a woman of Houjiaying who had been similarly abandoned for ten years. The eight divorce cases from Shunyi County that were initiated by women all came from the towns. Compared to Songjiang County after 1949, the contrast is quite sharp. As shown in table 2.2, Songjiang had many more divorces; they would decline only after the early 1960s. The fact is that from 1950 until the early 1960s, under the rather liberal climate of the time toward divorce, many women seized the opportunity to demand divorce. But then, by the mid-1960s, those who had the gumption to use the new marriage law to seek divorce had already done so. At the same time, the courts became increasingly stringent, requiring that all disputed divorces first undergo high-pressure mediation by the administrative entity, the work unit, and the court, before divorce could be granted. In Huayangqiao, there was not a single instance of divorce in the 1960s and 1970s. Under the relatively more relaxed new 1980 Marriage Law, the incidence of divorce rose again and, with the still more relaxed "Fourteen Articles" (namely, "Some concrete opinions of the Supreme People's Court regarding how the people's courts in judging divorce cases are to determine whether the emotional relationship of the husband and wife has truly ruptured"—Zuigao renmin fayuan, [1990] 1994), more quickly still. Though "conservative" on divorce by comparison with Western countries, the People's Republic still provides a fairly sharp contrast with the "traditional" village.

Mediation Personnel, Principle and Method

Compared to prerevolutionary times, the big change in the collective era was the "cadre-ization" of the mediation personnel. In the past, mediators had been endogenous individuals of high social esteem in the community; now they were the cadres of the revolutionary party-state, though still members of the communities and, to judge by the example of Ganlu, also well-respected leaders. Most mediations of the time were handled by production team heads, party branch committee members (including the women's chair), the village security chair, the production brigade head, and the party-branch secretary.

This was quite different from how things were represented in the official documents of the state. According to the 1954 "Ad Hoc Principles for the Organization of People's Mediation Committees" (Renmin tiaojie weiyuan hui, 1954), the village mediation committees were "mass organizations" (though under the "direction" of the basic-level people's governments and courts). They were supposed to be elected by the "township people's congresses" and were to comprise one chair and one or two deputy chairs "to be elected by one another from among the members in the mediation committees." Even the 1989 "Regulations for the Organization of People's Mediation Committees" (Renmin tiaojie weiyuanhui, 1989) still provided that the committees were "mass organizations." But in actual operation, mediation was carried out mainly by the village leadership/cadres, whose top members were the party secretary and the brigade head. They handled the most serious disputes. It was not until the Reform period that mediators from "outside the system" (*tizhiwai*) would play a role again, to differing degrees according to the circumstances of the village.

Even so, the collective era's village mediation shared with the periods both before and after one basic fact—namely that disputes inside the village would basically all be handled by the village itself. To be sure, the semiformal village cadres of the collective period were much closer to the authority of the party-state, but they were still members of the community and part and parcel of its social networks. In dealing with problems, they could not but act at the same time as a member of the community (and even though a cadre appointed by the state apparatus, they still ate "collective grain," different from the "state cadres" on government salaries). Despite the violent social-economic changes, not only were village communities not dissolved but they became even more tightly knit because of collectivization. From the state's perspective, the original basic concept and method of governance—village society was to deal with its own internal disputes in order to minimize the burden on the state apparatus—still held.

But cadre-ization did bring changes in the way mediation worked. When matters of state policy (or politics) were involved, the mediations were in truth more administrative resolutions (tiaochu) employing coercive methods than simply mediated compromises (tiaojie). Lu Guantong's imprisonment was an extreme and highly politicized example. In his and Gao Yongnian's cases, state law and policy was obviously primary, in contrast to the primacy of human relations and compromise earlier. In the new context, when state law-policy was involved, compromise working mediation was considered unprincipled "mixing of wet mud" (*he xini*).

When state policy was not at issue, as for example in disputes over land boundaries and (the rare) household division, the old principle-method of

TABLE 2.2
Songjiang County Civil Cases by Category and Divorce Cases as a Proportion of All Cases, 1950–1990

Year	Land[a]	Debt	Divorce	Other marriage	Inheritance	Old-age support	Child support	House	Compensation	Other	Total	Divorce as % of total
1950	33	135	150	138	9	0	0	32	19	111	627	23.9
1951	6	64	145	101	5	0	0	12	6	35	374	38.8
1952	16	55	211	66	2	0	0	12	1	41	404	52.2
1953	30	94	287	121	21	0	0	21	0	51	625	45.9
1954	4	12	232	5	2	0	2	3	0	12	272	85.3
1955	0	3	113	12	0	0	0	1	0	5	134	84.3
1956	0	19	257	5	2	0	5	2	3	38	331	77.6
1957	2	21	169	23	1	0	0	19	5	22	262	64.5
1958	3	19	172	16	1	0	0	13	1	12	237	72.6
1959	0	7	203	0	0	0	0	1	0	11	222	91.4
1960	0	0	179	2	0	0	0	1	0	1	183	97.8
1961	0	0	251	5	1	0	0	5	0	0	262	95.8
1962	1	2	317	11	2	0	0	10	0	0	343	92.4
1963	1	2	267	35	1	0	0	15	0	3	324	82.4
1964	0	0	182	21	3	0	1	4	2	0	213	85.4
1965	0	2	191	4	1	0	1	5	0	0	204	93.6
1966	1	0	76	1	0	0	1	3	1	0	83	91.6
1967–1969 n.a.												
1970	0	0	20	0	0	0	0	0	0	0	20	100.0
1971	0	0	29	0	0	0	0	0	0	0	29	100.0
1972	0	0	22	0	0	0	0	0	0	0	22	100.0

TABLE 2.2 *(continued)*

Year	*Land*[a]	*Debt*	*Divorce*	*Other marriage*	*Inheritance*	*Old-age support*	*Child support*	*House*	*Compensation*	*Other*	*Total*	*Divorce as % of total*
1973	0	0	18	0	0	0	1	7	4	1	31	58.1
1974	0	0	36	0	1	0	4	16	17	38	112	32.1
1975	0	0	24	0	0	0	2	3	3	0	32	75.0
1976	0	0	41	0	1	0	2	0	0	0	44	93.2
1977	0	0	33	0	0	0	0	1	1	0	35	94.3
1978	0	0	61	0	0	1	0	6	1	0	69	88.4
1979	0	0	65	0	2	1	0	9	4	1	82	79.3
1980	0	1	103	0	13	3	1	17	6	6	150	68.7
1981	0	1	182	0	12	19	1	33	9	18	275	66.2
1982	0	3	199	0	12	29	8	29	25	20	325	61.2
1983	1	5	207	0	15	27	14	36	19	48	372	55.6
1984	0	8	246	0	13	43	13	39	30	20	412	59.7
1985	0	6	180	0	6	25	10	31	24	36	318	56.6
1986	2	18	230	14	28	8	9	45	40	8	402	57.2
1987	0	37	329	9	9	26	15	38	48	3	514	64.0
1988	1	66	453	14	9	33	35	25	67	12	715	63.4
1989	3	123	557	6	4	28	33	22	70	11	857	65.0
1990	0	112	623	19	1	38	34	32	76	9	944	66.0
合计	104	815	7,060	628	177	281	192	548	482	573	10,860	
%	1.0	7.5	65.0	5.8	1.6	2.6	1.8	5.0	4.4	5.3	100.0	

Source: Data supplied by the Songjiang County Court.

Note: Data are for cases received that year, not cases concluded.

[a] In the data for the 1980s, this is listed as "residential plots."

compromise, with its emphasis on peacemaking and on human relations and moral right/wrong, still played an important role. In Huayangqiao's only instance of a household-division dispute, in the early 1960s, Gao Sitang of Gaojiada hamlet had problems with his married daughter and the two wanted to divide up. The matter was handled by team head Lu Guantong. In the end, the resolution was for Gao Sitang to make concessions, reserving just one room of the house for his own use and turning over the rest to his daughter's family. Both sides then voluntarily accepted the arrangement (INT93-3). More concrete examples of such mediation can be seen in the same kinds of disputes of the later period.

Mediation in the Early Reform Period

In this period, the main change in Ganlu village in Huayangqiao was the vigorous rural industrialization and the new independence it gave the young. Generational tensions became more pronounced and openly manifested, leading to greatly increased incidence of disputes between mothers- and daughters-in-law, as well as over old-age maintenance. At the same time, with the rise in rural incomes and the building of new houses came new disputes over residential plots (*zhaijidi*). And with the liberalization of divorce that came with the 1980 Marriage Law, open disputes between husbands and wives increased. Finally, with the monetization of the economy and of human relations, there were many more (monetary) compensation cases. In the face of such disputes, what the villages relied on were still mainly the highly cadreized but nevertheless intracommunity mediation mechanisms of the Mao period.

Source Materials

The source materials for this portion of the chapter are relatively more abundant, coming mainly from my three on-site investigations and interviews of cadres and mediation personnel in 1990–1993; the statistical data on disputes provided by the local government on the villages of Ganlu and neighboring Xiangshan between 1984 and 1990, a total of 114 cases (table 2.3); the record book of the Ganlu mediation committee for the years 1989–1992, with details on a total of 32 mediated disputes of the village; and the record book of the township government's legal services office, with concrete details about 41 disputes (table 2.4). The statistical data in the following discussion come from tables 2.2 and 2.3, and the concrete case examples from those tabulated in table 2.4.

Content of Disputes

As table 2.3 shows, in this period, mother- and daughter-in-law disputes were the single most frequent type of dispute in the village. In this community of 500 to 600 people (523 in 1980), they accounted for sixteen of the forty-three disputes (37 percent). Along with old-age-maintenance disputes, such intergenerational conflict amounted to 44 percent of the village's total disputes.

As the villagers explained, the key factor here was the employment of the young in off-farm work in the new rural industries. The new township enterprises generally paid the salaries in cash directly to the workers themselves, and

TABLE 2.3
Ganlu and Xiangshan Villages and Huayangqiao Township Disputes, 1984–1990

	mother-daughter-in-law	*neighbor*	*husband wife*	*old-age support*	*residential plots*	*compen-sation*	*other*	*total*
Ganlu	16	6	7	3	4	2	5	43
%	37	14	16	7	9	5	12	100
Xiangshan[a]	18	16	4	12	13	5	3	71
%	25	23	6	17	18	7	4	100
Huayangqiao Township[b]	3	6	56	15	17	21	40	158
%	2	4	35	10	11	13	25	100

Sources: Supplied by township cadres.
[a] Data for 1985 to 1990.
[b] Data for 1988 to 1990.

TABLE 2.4
Disputes Handled by Ganlu Village Cadres, 1980–1992, and Disputes Handled by Huayangqiao Township Legal Services Office, 1990

	mother-daughter-in-law	*neighbor*	*husband wife*	*inher-itance*	*residential plots*	*compen-sation*	*other*	*total*
Ganlu, 1980–1992								
1980–1988	2	0	1	3	3	0	2	11
1989–1992	3	4	6	0	2	1	5	21
Total	5	4	7	3	5	1	7	32
%	15.6	12.5	21.9	9.4	15.6	3.1	21.9	100.0
Huayangqiao Township, 1990								
1990	3	2	20	5	3	5	5	43
%	7.0	4.7	46.5	11.6	7.0	11.6	11.6	100.0

Note: Ganlu village cases from 1980 to 1988 are from interviews with villagers; 1989–1992 cases are from the village "Mediation Record Book." Huayangqiao Township cases are from the record book of the township Legal Services Office.

not in workpoints (even though individually computed) to the head of the household. For this reason, the younger generation's independence was greatly enhanced. Their incomes were the main source for the financing of the wave of new housing construction of the 1980s, and they understandably developed strong feelings of ownership toward the new houses, in contrast to the past when everyone thought of the homes as belonging to the parents. Moreover, under the collective the elderly could earn some income from the community's vegetable garden or childcare center, but after the dissolution of the collective, the retired elderly no longer had any source of income. Many sons and daughters-in-law came to see the elderly as a burden. The daughters-in-law became less and less willing to be the first up in the morning, the last to go to bed, and the one responsible for the heaviest and dirtiest work (like emptying out the chamber pots). The mothers-in-law, on the other hand, still expected to be served by their daughters-in-law, as they themselves had once served their own mothers-in-law. Relations between the two were thus fraught with tension.

What triggered open conflict were generally small frictions from daily life. For example, in 1989, Xilihangbang hamlet's sixty-three-year-old Gao Yindi fought violently with her thirty-three-year-old daughter-in-law Yang Yafang. What brought things to a head was that Yang struck her child, and Gao thought she should not. A fierce argument ensued (Ganlu cun 1989–1992: 3). Another similar case involved the irascible fifty-seven-year-old Zhu Yindi. When she could not find her monosodium glutamate, she was certain that her daughter-in-law had taken it. In the argument, the older woman slapped the younger woman, who then fought back. Angry at both, and to show his impartiality, the son struck both of them. He accidentally injured his mother, who had to be taken to the hospital (Ganlu cun 1989–1992: 13). Such mother/daughter-in-law disputes were, however, relatively minor (unless of course they became a dispute over old-age maintenance or the cause of household division). Comparing the incidence of mother/daughter-in-law disputes in the village with mother/daughter-in-law disputes at the township level shown in table 2.3, we can see that the majority of these disputes were resolved within the village and few became complaints at the township level. At the county court level, as shown in table 2.2, mother/daughter-in-law disputes did not count as a separate category.

Old-age maintenance was a related intergenerational problem. In the early 1980s, neither of He Pinjuan's two sons wanted their parents to live with them. So the elderly couple lived in the back of the house of the younger son, in a room converted from the old pigpen. The number two daughter-in-law thought the arrangement unfair, since she was bearing a heavier burden than the older brother and his wife. She thought that the parents should take turns eating at the two brothers' homes. However, because the homes were about 500 meters apart, too far for the elderly couple to walk, they ended up eating only at the second son's home. Very upset about this, the second daughter-in-law frequently said to her husband in front of the parents: "Only pigs don't work," "a person must work," and the like. So He Pinjuan went to village party-branch secretary He Yonglong for help (INT93-4). In another dispute, the elderly parents lived together with their youngest child, a seventeen-year-old son. The first and second sons thought they should continue to work and support themselves and did not want to provide living expenses for them. The old couple also went to secretary He for help (INT93-4). A third example involved the three Xue brothers, who also did not want to be responsible for their parents' maintenance.[11] Compared to just an argument or fight between a mother- and daughter-in-law, such maintenance disputes were more serious, involving money and longer-term arrangements, and harder to deal with. They accounted for roughly the same proportion of cases at the township level as at the village, and also for a significant proportion of county-level court cases.

Intergenerational conflicts such as these led the local leadership to advocate the formalizing of old-age-maintenance arrangements with "contracts." Expanded familial properties were also a factor for turning to formal contracts. By the early 1990s, Ganlu village saw the reappearance of formalized household-division and old-age-maintenance agreements, in contrast to the earlier "what the father says goes." The brigade accountant Zhang Bingyu was among the first to adopt such an agreement in his household division with his three sons in 1988. The family house consisted of five large rooms and three small ones; there were also construction materials left over from the old house. The two elder brothers each got two large rooms and one small room. The youngest got just one large room and one small room, but, adding the building materials, he actually got more than his older brothers. Bingyu and his wife planned to live with the youngest son, and even had the division document spell out that the youngest son would be the one mainly responsible for their funerals. According to Bingyu, the eldest son had already worked for quite some time and had substantial savings, and the second son had graduated from a technical university. Neither objected to the youngest brother getting more. After everybody talked things over and reached agreement, Bingyu invited his brothers and sisters and their families to share in a meal to mark the

11. Under the new circumstances, a villager explained, the young people think an old woman is easier to maintain than an old man, mainly because the old woman can at least help with the housework, while the old man is usually accustomed to being served, and "knows only to sit and drink tea." From the point of view of the elderly, on the other hand, a daughter was considered better than a son because, at the time of old-age maintenance, the key variable was not the man but the woman. They would rather count on their own daughter to carry the burden. In Huayangqiao, married-in sons-in-law had always been quite common (INT93-2).

agreement, formalized with a written document, with one copy for each of the three sons (INT93-1).[12]

Then there were the disputes between neighbors. In addition to land boundary disputes such as those in the past, there were a substantial number of residential plot disputes that arose with the building of new houses in the village. (Old-fashioned pre-1949 disputes over land and debt were however rare.) The majority of the residential plots in the village had been allocated during Land Reform. In the collective era, when everyone just lived in their old homes, there were no residential plot disputes to speak of. With the wave of house building in the 1980s, such disputes became common. One example is Xuejiada hamlet's Xue Wenhua, whose old house was situated between Xue Delin and Zhang Degui's houses. Xue Wenhua wanted to build his new house farther out to the front (southward) than his neighbors', because that would give him a better view and because it would allow him to have his yard to the back of (northward) (and hence, also the smell of his farm animals downwind from) the house. But that way his house would affect his neighbors' "light and air." For this reason, they objected strongly. However, if Xue Wenhua were to build his house flush with Delin, his house would jut out 2.5 meters into Zhang Degui's yard. The three thus got into a dispute (INT93-5; Ganlu cun 1989–1992: 11, 15). Another example involved Xue Baobao and her neighbor, who also wanted to build his house farther out front than hers. He managed through connections to obtain approval from the village authorities for the building plan. The foundation had in fact been laid already. As in the other case, the house would impact Xue Baobao's "light and air" (housing regulations do not recognize considerations of the view). For this, Xue Baobao went to the township authorities to complain, threatening to sue if the problem were not rectified. As Baobao pointed out, "These days we've gotten gutsier. In the past, we didn't even dare go to the brigade office." Now, she had brought her case to the township office. In the end, the township government found her in the right and ordered the village authorities to cover the costs of having the foundation relaid (INT91-9). As table 2.3 shows, residential plot disputes were also relatively severe and hard to deal with. They occupied about the same proportion of total disputes at the township level as at the village. At their height in 1985–1986, these disputes accounted for more than 10 percent of all lawsuits at the (Songjiang) county court (dropping to 3.4 percent by 1990).[13]

12. Zhao Xudong's study of Li village in Hebei contains four such household-division documents from the same time period, and the record of a lawsuit over household division (Zhao Xudong, 2003: 65–75).

13. They were first grouped under "houses," which included house buying-selling and renting. The Supreme People's Court then instructed that a separate category "other immovable property" be established, and under that category a subcategory "residential plot use rights" be set up to take account of these lawsuits. My thanks to Professor Xu Anqi for clarifying this for me.

The liberalization of divorce that came with the 1980 Marriage Law (allowing, for example, a petition for divorce without first going through the relevant administrative entity and the work unit) brought an increase in open husband/wife disputes in the village. There were a total of seven serious husband/wife disputes in this period, four of which went on to court, and two of them ended in divorce. In the hamlet of Xubushanqiao of Ganlu, middle-aged Yang Chengzhang and his wife Yang Jinxiu always had trouble getting along. He was the barefoot doctor of the village but was lazy and liked to play mahjong and gamble, often staying out all night. She was parsimonious and did not want him to gamble. The two argued frequently. In the liberalized climate for divorce of the 1980s, Yang finally went to court to seek a divorce (Ganlu cun 1989–1992: 1; INT93-1). In Xuejiada, another hamlet of the village, Xue Yonglong and his wife, Chai Lingzhen, had financial difficulties. He did not take work seriously, often scolded her and beat her, and sometimes stayed in bed all day and just told her to get lost. She finally went back to her natal home and petitioned to the court for divorce (INT93-1).

Overall, marriage disputes were generally the most difficult to resolve. As shown in table 2.3, they accounted for just 16 percent of all disputes in Ganlu (and just 6 percent in neighboring Xiangshan), but 35 percent of those at the township level; they made up the great majority of all cases at the county court level (table 2.2). In the Cultural Revolution period, they amounted to nearly 100 percent of all lawsuits in Songjiang County. Low in terms of absolute numbers in the Cultural Revolution period, they rose in the 1980s back to the magnitude of the 1950s and 1960s and, by the late 1980s, had come to exceed by wide margins the numbers of the 1950s.

Finally, there were the "compensation for wrongful acts" cases that had not existed in the Qing and would greatly expand in the later Reform period. They were based originally on provisions imported from German civil law, formally adopted into the 1986 General Principles of Civil Law. Ganlu village had just one instance of such a case, and Huayangqiao Township five. As an example, the Xus thought that their neighbors' (the Zhangs) compost pit had encroached into their residential plot. So they filled in the pit and planted a tree at the spot. The two families got into an argument, and then a fight. Mr. Xu was only lightly injured, but Mrs. Zhang had to be taken to the hospital. The mediators thought that the Xus should bear the bulk of the responsibility, that they should pay 70 yuan of the 117-yuan medical bill. The Xus would not accept the arrangement and took matters up with the township government. It was re-mediated at that level (Huayangqiao, 1990: 26). Another case was when a woman worker injured her left hand at the village factory. The factory paid 2,000 yuan in damages, plus 800 yuan in medical fees. But this worker sought additional compensation to cover rehabilitative care. The factory refused. So she appealed to the township (Huayangqiao, 1990: 31). From the source materials at our disposal, compensation cases look to be relatively rare at the village level, rising markedly at the township and county levels. They were much more common in the towns and cities than in the villages. We can see from table 2.2 that there were few such cases in the Mao era, but mounting numbers in the 1980s.

Mediation Personnel, Principle and Method

The mediation personnel did not change much in this period. They were still mainly the semiformal village cadres, and still differed from the representation of them as "mass organizations" by the 1954 Ad Hoc Principles and the 1989 Regulations for organizing mediation committees. In Huayangqiao, there were nominally nine members on the supposedly strictly nonofficial mediation committee. The nominal chair was a young woman named Zhang Guofang, who served mainly as a secretary to the committee, keeping records of the disputes in the "Record Book of Mediations" (Ganlu cun 1989–1992). She handled only the most minor of the disputes, like mother/daughter-in-law spats. The more serious ones were usually handled by the key members of the community government. Those involving women were often handled by the "woman's chair" and party-branch committee member Li Peihua, who was well respected in the community, and the most serious by party-branch secretary He Yonglong (succeeded by Xue Delong, and then Jiang Shunlin), also highly respected. In other words, things remained much as they had been in the earlier cadre-ized system.

Compared with the Mao period, however, there was no longer the mass movement type of highly politicized approach to problems—as with Lu Guantong and Gao Yongnian. And compared to pre-1949, there was still a high degree of emphasis on state law and policy, differing substantially from the "traditional" system. In the triad of qing, li, and fa, its primary emphasis was on state law-policy (fa, or *guofa*) and only secondarily on human relations (qing, or *renqing*) and moral right and wrong (li, or *daoli*), unlike the traditional system, which made renqing primary, and guofa and daoli secondary. A simple example is the old-age maintenance case of He Pinjuan. Party-branch secretary He Yonglong believed from the start that the two young couples must bear responsibility for the maintenance of the parents, this in accordance with the law (of course, also with custom). For this reason, he explained to the young couples from the start their legal obligations. At the same time, he also paid some attention to human relations and urged the parents to try to take on more of the housework. But the ill feelings between the two sides ran deep and could not be solved so simply. In the end, He Yonglong turned to rather high-handed administrative methods. He simply took the parents' old-age support right off the top from the two young couples' workpoints and gave those directly to the parents. Apparently, the two brothers were quite happy with this arrangement, for they did not have to deal with further complaints from their wives (INT93-4). This kind of dispute resolution was, once again, more like tiaochu, in which law came first and high-handed administrative methods could be used, than the mediated compromise of tiaojie.

However, some of the disputes did not involve such clear-cut issues by law. In another case, woman's chair Li Peihua was involved in a dispute with her neighbor Lu Huojuan. Lu had built a wall that extended into Li's easement path. Angry, Li knocked the wall down. The mediation "chair," Zhang Guofang, mobilized Wu Renyu from the "house-building small group" and Jin Yongqing, the production team head, to help resolve the problem. The three mediators reached the conclusion that Lu was wrong to build a wall into the easement, for that was against building regulations. Also, her wall exceeded the regulation height of a maximum of 80 centimeters. On the other hand, Li should not have gone ahead and pushed the wall down; she should have asked the village government to deal with the problem. Thus, by moral "reason" (daoli), Li should compensate Lu 20 yuan for the cost of the section of the wall that did not jut out into the easement; as for Lu, she was not to build a wall extending to that point. A "mediation agreement" was thus drawn up with the consent and signatures of both sides (INT93-5; Ganlu cun 1989–1992: 14). This was a mediation that considered fa, plus qing and li. Li Peihua, it should be pointed out, as the woman's chair and party branch committee member, was the most powerful woman in the village. Seen in that light, the agreement seems fairer still.

The principle-method of "law-policy first and qingli second" can also be seen in divorce cases. There is, first of all, a case involving simple observance of law-policy. In the husband-wife dispute between Yang Chengzhang and Yang Jinxiu, mainly over Yang's gambling, the mediators thought simply that Yang was in the wrong, since his gambling violated the law. Therefore, the whole purpose of the "mediation" was to persuade and pressure him not to gamble (INT93-2; Ganlu cun 1989–1992: 1).

The dispute between Xue Yonglong and Chai Lingzhen was more complicated. As noted earlier, the two were under severe financial pressures, Xue regularly berated and beat his wife, and Chai had already gone back to her natal family, demanding divorce. This matter was dealt with by Li Peihua, assisted by the committee "chair," Zhang Guofang. They took as their starting point the law-policy to do everything possible to arrive at a "mediated reconciliation." For that, they persuaded Xue to go with them to the wife's natal family to apologize, but she would not even agree to see him. Then they went through the wife's two elder brothers to try to change her mind, but Chai still insisted on divorce. In the end, they worked with the township government's "legal services office" (falü shiwusuo) and arranged work for both husband and wife at the Dajiang company, with annual pay at 4,000 to 5,000 yuan (a much coveted figure for the mid-1980s). Apparently, the couple got along much better thereafter and, in 1993, at the time of my third visit, were planning to build a new house (INT93-1). This kind of mediated resolution was a legacy from the Mao period, something that might be considered part of the "modern revolutionary tradition," to be discussed in detail in chapter 4.

In the dispute between Xue Wenhua and his two neighbors over Xue's building of his new house, party-branch secretary Jiang Shunlin started from written regulations: the building of a new house must secure the agreement of the neighbors. But the way he talked to the disputants was not in terms of rules and regulations but rather of moral "reason," daoli. He persuaded Xue by saying, "If you build your house out in front of theirs, it would affect their light and air. How would you like it if someone were to do that to you?" As for Xue Wenhua's backup plan, to build his house flush with Xue Delin, Jiang pointed out: "If you do this, your house will encroach 2.5 meters into the yard of the other neighbor, Zhang Degui." Jiang then used a renqing argument: "That way, you will be in no end of conflict with your neighbor; how would you two get along in the future?" And, then also a daoli argument: "If someone were to do that to you, how would you react?" Xue Wenhua apparently had no response to this line of argument. What's more, Jiang explained that Xue Wenhua also knew that if Jiang refused to grant him permission, he would not be able to obtain a building permit from the village government and would not be able to build his house. The dispute was thus resolved, half coercively (INT93-5; Ganlu cun 1989–1992: 11, 15). Here we see once more the primacy of law, guofa, but also considerations of human relations, renqing, and moral right and wrong, daoli.

But many disputes did not touch on law-policy. In those situations, the mediators called mainly on human relations and moral right/wrong, in the manner of "traditional" mediation. To be sure, since mediators at this time and place were almost all cadres, they tended to use more high-handed methods. In the nearby village of Xiangshan, there was an instance of a young couple in a "de facto marriage" (they had a marital agreement, the "bridal gift" [*caili*] had been paid, the wedding banquets had been held, the two had started living together, but they had not yet formally registered their marriage). The wife had been pregnant twice but had miscarried both times. The couple drifted apart, and the man met another woman and asked for divorce. The wife was not opposed to divorce but wanted to be compensated, including expenditures for the bride's side of the wedding banquet, the work she missed on account of the miscarriages, "nutrition expenses," and "spiritual loss," totaling 2,000 yuan. The dispute was handled by party-branch secretary Jiang Shunlin. According to Jiang, he did not really consider law-policy at all, but was concerned mainly with finding a compromise resolution that both sides could accept. For this, he first emphasized to both that they were wrong to live together without first registering their marriage and that a court would reject a divorce petition under such conditions. He followed that tack, Jiang explained, because in his experience with such matters, the two would then be more prone to accept a compromise. In the end, Jiang persuaded both to accept the following resolution: the wedding banquets should not be considered, because both sides put them on willingly. But the woman should receive compensation for her missed work, totaling 60 days at 2.50 yuan a day, or 150 yuan. In addition, she should receive 200 yuan in "nutrition expense." That brought the total to 350 yuan. As for "spiritual loss," he said that couldn't really be computed. In the end, agreement was reached at 500 yuan. Thus, the husband was to compensate the wife a total of 850 yuan, and the matter was thereby resolved (INT93-5).

In short, compared with before the revolution, the mediation of this period still employed the triadic qing, li, and fa, with the difference that in the past, qing and compromise came first, law and moral right/wrong second, whereas now law-policy came first, qing and daoli second. At the same time, because the mediation personnel were mainly village cadres approved and appointed by the state, they commanded greater authority than the endogenous leaders of old, even if not necessarily greater social esteem. They tended more toward reliance on coercive pressures in mediating. All this would be impacted by changes of the later Reform period.

Mediation in the Later Reform Period

From the 1990s on there has been massive movement of the rural labor force into the cities to seek work, leading in turn to a host of changes in the mediation system.[14] The "society of the well acquainted" of many villages has become, to borrow He Xuefeng's expression, a "society of the half acquainted" (*banshuren shehui*) (He Xuefeng, 2000). At the same time, the scope of vil-

14. Wu Chongqing, on the basis of his investigation of Caixi township in Shanghang county in Fujian, points out that because the young and able-bodied have all left for work outside, there has resulted in the village a "society of the well acquainted without its principals," graphically shown in the fact that during the spring festival period, with their return to the village for the Chinese New Year's holidays, all of the accumulated conflicts of the year come to the fore, making that the peak period for dispute resolution (Wu Chongqing, 2002).

lage government functions has greatly contracted. With that has come the reappearance of the societal or informal mediation mechanisms of old, even while semiformal cadre mediation continues. At the same time, the role of the courts has greatly expanded, with law penetrating more deeply into the countryside and playing a larger role in people's lives, while the role of community mediation has contracted. Nevertheless, as we enter the twenty-first century, community mediation still shows considerable vitality, and the state continues to insist strongly on that original principle of governance—that communities resolve their disputes themselves as much as possible.

Source Materials

Songjiang County urbanized rapidly from the mid-1990s on. By 2004, Ganlu village had been formally incorporated into Shanghai City. Residents' lives now almost completely urbanized, it can no longer tell us about trends of rural disputes and mediation. The same applies to the village of Shajing in Shunyi County. For this reason, I turn here to the most detailed and reliable of recent research, a study by Dong Leiming of Song village (in Sanlidian Township in Runan County) in Hebei. Dong's materials consist mainly of the village's records of 109 dispute cases between 1992 and 2006 and his on-site interviews (Dong Leiming, 2008).

First a word about the difference between the villages of Ganlu and Song. Other than the fact that one village is in the Jiangnan region and the other in North China, Ganlu was the "seed brigade" (that raised the seeds) of its commune, much smaller than the typical brigade, with just one-sixth to one-fifth of Song's population of about 4,000. Ganlu had developed earlier, building new houses by the late 1980s, while Song did not do so until the mid-1990s. For that reason, the residential plot disputes of 1980s Ganlu did not appear in Song until a decade later. By then, control of the villages was even looser than earlier, and the incidence of residential plot disputes was even higher—twenty cases between 1992 and 2006, making up 18 percent of all disputes (some even involved encroachments on collective land, a problem that did not appear in Ganlu). Another difference was that Ganlu still maintained a machine-plowing brigade after de-collectivization, and Song did not. Because of that, many brothers in Song joined up to purchase small tractors, but in time that became a source of conflict (a total of five instances in 1992–1997). Finally, during Song's transition from the collective to the household responsibility system, there appeared a substantial number of land-boundary disputes between neighbors, partly because the land borders, generally marked by wood posts or lime, rotted or were moved, or faded with time, thereby leading to disputes, while Ganlu did not have that kind of problem. But those disappeared in Song too after 1996.

TABLE 2.5
Disputes in Song Village (Runan County, Hebei), 1992–2006

Year	*mother-daughter-in-law*	*neighbor*	*husband wife*	*old-age support*	*residential plots*	*debt*	*drunken disorder*	*production materials*	*daily life*	*other*	***Total***
1992	2	1			1		1	1	5	4	**15**
1993		3				1	1	2	1	1	**9**
1994		3	2		1		1		2		**9**
1995		4	2	1	4	1			5	2	**19**
1996	2	4							2	4	**12**
1997				1	2		2	2		1	**8**
1998	1				3		1			3	**8**
1999				1	2		1			2	**6**
2000				1	1		1				**3**
2001				1	1		2			1	**5**
2002	1				3		1				**5**
2003					1					2	**3**
2004			1						1		**2**
2005					1				1	1	**3**
2006				1			1				**2**
Total	**5**	**16**	**5**	**6**	**20**	**2**	**12**	**5**	**17**	**21**	**109**

Sources: Dong Leiming (2008, appendix).

On the other hand, Song village was like Ganlu in its intergenerational conflicts and maintenance disputes, stemming from similar reasons. Song had a total of six maintenance disputes during the fifteen years (more below).

Song village also shows the differences between the late Reform period and the earlier Reform period. One striking trend was the rapid decline from the late 1990s on in the incidence of recorded disputes. In the six years between 1992 and 1997, Song village had an average number of twelve recorded disputes a year, while between 2001 and 2006, it had just three a year (Dong Leiming, 2008: 71). Part of the reason, as Dong Leiming suggests, was the large numbers going outside to work, which resulted in much reduced personal interactions within the village, and the consequent decline in interpersonal conflicts.

Intergenerational disputes also went down. As Dong Leiming suggests, this is mainly because the younger generation now possessed an overwhelming advantage vis-à-vis the old because of their earnings. Also, given some measure of affluence, the old and the young both tend much more now to live separately. Dong calls the phenomenon "the nuclear-ization of the family" (Dong Leiming, 2008: 76, and chap. 2). In my view, another factor is that the old ideal of multiple generations living together, imitative of elite families, no longer commands much influence. The legal requirement that "if brothers, sons or grandsons should divide up family property during the lifetime of their parents or grandparents, they will be punished by 100 blows with the heavy bamboo stick" is very much something of the past; in its place are utilitarian considerations for "fewer hassles" and "greater convenience."

Another important reason, which Dong does not point out clearly, is that many disputes that used to be handled by village cadres are now being handled informally and are going unrecorded. One major example is the reappearance of informally mediated household divisions. According to the deputy head of the village, here most household divisions are done without the involvement of non-kin, relying just on the maternal or paternal uncle (30 percent), or the head of the common-descent group (here termed the *laozhangpanzi* inside the descent group, *menzili*) (20 percent). Only under unusual circumstances would village cadres be involved—the example given by the deputy secretary is the division between a remarried daughter-in-law and her father-in-law. These revived household-division procedures seem generally quite effective, like the household-division system of old; there were no recorded disputes related to household division in the village (Dong Leiming, 2008: 76). As has already been seen, this kind of development could already be seen in Ganlu village by the late 1980s, and in Li village of Hebei Province by the mid-1990s (as studied by Zhao Xudong, 2003: chap. 3).

Outside of the above were husband-wife disputes. Marriages of the past had been much concerned with continuation of the family line (of course, from the parents' point of view, old-age support was also a very practical concern), Dong Leiming observes, while the younger generation now think more about "love" and "how it feels." For that reason, marriages also split up more easily (Dong Leiming, 2008: 81). The 1990 Fourteen Articles that further liberalized divorce (those who applied to the court for divorce a second time were generally approved—see chapter 4) were also an important factor. Urban work, and consequent long separations between husband and wife, were a more important factor still. The rise in incidence of divorce after the mid-1990s is, however, not reflected in village records. In Song, there were just three divorce disputes recorded in the 109 disputes over the fifteen years from 1992 to 2006, and only one of those actually ended in divorce. What that fact tells is not that there were practically no divorces in the village, but rather that many divorces now simply circumvented the village mediation system and entered directly into the court system. In actual fact, there were five couples that divorced in Song between 1996 and 2006 (Dong Leiming, 2008: 80).

In addition, there were changes that came with the relaxation of control and order in the village. First were the disputes that accompanied daily life. One notable category was parents' disputes that stemmed from their children's fights. Another was "drunken disorder" disputes, a total of twelve in the period (though noticeably fewer after 2002—just one such in the most recent four years). Part of the reason was that people had much more leisure time than in the past (mainly on account of pervasive "hidden unemployment" in agriculture—Huang Zongzhi, 2006b). Such daily-life disputes accounted for a fairly large proportion of all disputes. Daily-life disputes became less frequent later with the great decline in personal interactions that came with people going outside to work, with the change from a "society of the well acquainted" to a "society of the half acquainted," or even "society of strangers," and the consequent reduction in numbers of disputes. Indeed, recorded village disputes of all categories declined quite dramatically from 2002 on.

Finally, we need to consider an unusual incident in Song village. In 2005 the county's "Bureau to Bring in Business" (zhaoshangju) arranged for an outside businessman to invest in a new private high school in the village and designated the Xuzhuang subvillage (*zu*, roughly equivalent to the old production team under the old production brigade, or administrative village) as the site, intending to requisition 130 of the zu's 200 mu of land for the purpose. The Bureau's initial plan was to compensate those peasants 900 yuan per mu a year, for twenty years. But the peasants thought that was too little. The offer was eventually raised to a onetime payment of 16,000 yuan. But many still refused. In the end, the authorities called on a gang of ne'er-do-wells, "*hunhun*," to make a show of force; one peasant was slashed with a knife. Only then were the authorities able to conduct the groundbreaking ceremony on 1 December as scheduled. But then villagers organized a group to go to Beijing to appeal (*shangfang*). As a result, the provincial government sent down an investigative team, the county was forced to make further concessions, and eventually paid 17,000 yuan per mu (Dong Leiming, 2008: 65–67).

Mediation Personnel, Principle and Method

The mediation personnel underwent a certain degree of what might be termed resocietalization or informalization in this period. We have seen how informally mediated household division reappeared, with involvement from just the kin group. Along with new-style agreements and contracts came the reappearance of middlemen, which can also be seen as a kind of return of the old societal mediation system. Then there were the husband-wife and intrafamilial disputes that, according to the village cadres, were now resolved mainly by kin and neighbors or the head of the descent group. Only more severe disputes went to the village authorities (Dong Leiming, 2008: 78). At present, when faced with a dispute, rural people no longer simply go to the cadres, as they had done in the Mao period, but are quite likely to turn to someone whom both sides respect for mediation. This was all the more true of disputes occurring inside the family or descent group.

Nevertheless, it is clear that the cadres still play a critical role. All the disputes recounted earlier were ones that the cadres had dealt with (and recorded in their disputes record book), and those varied from the smallest of frictions in daily life to larger property, land-boundary, residential-plot, old-age-maintenance, and marriage disputes.

On the basis of his field investigations of numerous villages throughout the country, Dong Leiming has advanced a six-type categorization of mediation systems according to the mediating personnel: first are the "no story" "no event" villages with few disputes (not unlike our Ganlu village of the collective era);[15] second are those in which mediation is done mainly by endogenous villagers of high social esteem (rather like our prerevolution villages); third are those in which disputes are mediated both by endogenous village elites and by cadres ("the state system's elites," *tizhi jingying*), the latter stepping in when the former are not able to deal with the problem; fourth are those in which mediation is done mainly by cadres (rather like Ganlu in the early Reform period); fifth are villages well on their way to industrialization (and urbanization, we might add), which rely more on the court system or the urban "societal mediation centers" (*shehui tiaojie zhongxin*) to resolve the more important disputes; sixth, finally, are villages that are near dissolution, in which illegal powers reign and brute force comes to dominate (Dong Leiming, 2008: 23–24).

Dong has not tried to quantify these types, but the third and the fourth, namely those relying on both societal elites and cadres, or simply cadres, are likely the more common types, followed perhaps by those relying mainly on endogenous societal elites. The highly industrialized-urbanized should be found mainly in villages of suburban areas. As for those under brute force and dominated by hunhun gangs, according to the research and analyses of Dong Leiming and of Chen Baifeng, they are on the rise, and are particularly common in the Hunan-Hubei region, especially along the lakefront areas where water-control systems have broken down. (The area studied by Chen Baifeng, [Hubei's] Chujiang County's Shaqiao and a number of other villages in the same county, seem to be of this description—Chen Baifeng, 2008.) As for the "no story" type, they are perhaps relatively rare. All in all, the most prevalent category might be where mediation is done both by societal elites and by the village cadres, as in Song recounted above.

Where law-policy is at issue, the cadres of Song village are clearly guided mainly by those. In one case example, a villager, Li, moved all of the land markers of the five plots adjacent to his responsibility land leftward each year,

---

15. My short two-day visit in May 2006 to (William Hinton's) "Longbow" village in Changzhi city in Shanxi suggests that village, too, might fit this category, resembling still in this respect villages of the collective era.

for several years in a row, and managed to enlarge his own plot by more than two meters that way. In the beginning, no one could figure out what was going on. But in the end, Li was found out, and the village committee came forth and measured the land, and Li admitted to what he had done (Dong Leiming, 2008: 89). Under those circumstances, the village cadres separated out legal (and also customary) right and wrong unequivocally.

In another dispute, one that did not involve law-policy, what the village authorities did was to adopt the compromise and peacekeeping approach, within the boundaries of the law. They also resorted to the use of administrative authority. Li Fendui and his neighbor Li Xingzhi argued over the boundaries between their plots and took their dispute to the village government again and again. In the end, the village cadres' solution was to carve out forty centimeters from each one's plot and make a paved path of it, thereby separating out their plots for good. No further disputes came from them again (Dong Leiming, 2008: 89).

Dong Leiming's investigations did not pay too much attention to mediation principles and methods, but we can see that the mediating cadres of Song pretty much operated by the principle of state law-policy first, peacekeeping second. Given the fact that laws and regulations are generally becoming ever better known with the massive propagation of the "rule of law" by the mass media, we might further suggest that law has come to figure more prominently in the later Reform period than in the early Reform period.

The Outlook for Societal Mediation

One influential current opinion among legal scholars is that, along with China's "modernization," marketization, and urbanization, Chinese villages can only become more and more like Western society and its rule of law. This kind of opinion has its basis in the decline in recent years of recorded community mediations and the rapid rise in numbers of civil lawsuits. Its deeper origins lie in what this book's preface spoke of as the distinctive background of China's legal history, of repeated severance of the past from the present by the nation's leaders and lawmakers, turning tradition into something with no relevance to current realities. What has come with that is a modernist ideology that sets up an either/or binary between Western and Chinese law.[16] From

16. The modernist ideological influence is so strong that some Chinese scholars believe that in China, because of its overly centralized state authority and consequent lack of pluralistic development of civil society, societal mediation could not develop until after the 1980s, when China began to imitate the West's modern alternative dispute-resolution system. What China needs today, they believe, is to model itself after that system (Peng Bo, 2007). Chapter 7 will take up the issue of differences and similarities between the Chinese and Western mediation systems.

that framework comes the opinion that China can only become more and more like the developed nations of the West. To be sure, some have argued that China's mediation system has distinctive strengths, but most think that the system is closely tied to the context of the "society of the well acquainted." When that gives way to the "society of the half acquainted" and the "society of strangers," the mediation system based on tightly knit communities will be completely replaced by the modern, urban Western legal system and culture. Thus will the old mediation system be left behind in the same way as traditional Chinese law.

As shown in the example of Song village, the mass movement of rural labor into the cities for work since the 1990s has indeed impacted the old community cadre mediation system in unprecedented ways. The weakening of village governments and partial dissolution of the old social bonds of the community have indeed led to a much diminished role for the old cadre mediation system. As shown in table 2.6, between 1985 and 2002, nationwide the number of recorded disputes handled by semiofficial community cadre mediation declined by more than half. If computed in terms of number per 100,000 population (thereby taking into account the growth in population), the decline still amounts to something on the order of 60 percent. At the same time, along with expansions in people's new social-economic activities and in the role played by the courts,[17] civil lawsuits have increased dramatically, amounting by 2005 to about eight times the number in 1980. Computed as numbers per 100,000 population, it was still a sixfold increase. The ratio of recorded extrajudicial mediations to court cases had been about eight to one in 1980; today it is just about one to one. Small wonder, then, that some people believe that mediation will be completely replaced by litigation.

However, such an opinion overlooks, first of all, the fact that official statistics record only the semiofficial mediations conducted by cadres, and not the purely societal mediations that do not involve cadres, such as household divisions and intra-common-descent-group disputes. The fact that official figures represent semiformal community cadre mediation as *minjian*, or societal mediation, makes the figures doubly misleading. Song village is in all likelihood representative of a larger pattern, showing considerable "resocietalization" of mediation, with nonofficial individuals of high esteem in the communities and kin groups taking on more and more mediations that go unrecorded. The decline in the number of mediations recorded is only of semiformal cadre mediation; it is accompanied by substantial expansions in the number of

17. Particularly in the rapid increase in so-called economic disputes—a category used by the State Statistical Bureau until 2002—which reached a height of 1.53 million by 1999 (*Zhongguo tongji nianjian*, 2004: 886).

TABLE 2.6
Numbers of Societal Mediations and Civil Lawsuits, 1980–2005

	Total population (10,000s)	*Societal mediations (10,000s)*	*No. Mediations per 100,000 people*	*Civil lawsuits (10,000s)*	*No. Lawsuits per 100,000 people*
1980	98,705			56.6	57
1985	105,851	633.3	598	84.6	80
1990	114,333	740.9	648	185.2	162
1995	121,121	602.8	498	271.9	224
2000	126,743	503.1	397	341.2	269
2002	128,453	314.1	245	442.0	344
2005	130,756	448.7	343	438.0	335

Sources: Zhongguo tongji nianjian (2006: tables 23-6, 23-191; 1991: 785; 1985: 801); Zhongguo falü nianjian (2007: 1080).

unrecorded informal societal mediations. The official statistics, in fact, greatly exaggerate the decline in total mediations.

According to a fairly systematic survey done in 2002, based on 2,970 completed questionnaires returned by peasants from thirty villages in six counties, of the three avenues of disputes resolution in the countryside—community mediation (tiaojie, which would include both semiofficial and nonofficial mediations), shangfang, and the courts—the proportion of disputants who say they were "satisfied with" the results was the highest among those who turned to mediation, 73 percent; less for shangfang, 63 percent; and lowest for the courts, 37 percent.[18] Of course, as the authors point out, people's degree of satisfaction or dissatisfaction depends very much on their expectations, which in turn depend greatly on their "costs" (expense and trouble). But there can be no doubt that in the minds of rural people, the mediation system as a whole, both semiofficial and nonofficial, continues to be seen as a system of low cost and high effectiveness, more effective than the court system.

The forecast of an end to mediation also overlooks the determination of China's leaders to maintain and develop mediation. There are, first of all, the two key decisions of 2002. The Supreme People's Court's "Some regulations for the people's courts in adjudicating civil cases involving people's mediation agreements" (implemented from 1 November 2002) provides explicitly that "mediation agreements shall have the same effect as civil contracts," which is to say that they will be upheld by the courts. At the same time, the Ministry of Justice's "Some regulations for people's mediation work" (implemented from 1 November 2002) required that funds be set up to compensate members of

18. Guo Xinghua and Wang Ping, 2004. See also a similar study of Beijing city, with similar results (Michelson, 2003).

people's mediation committees for their work and expenses (Renmin tiaojie gongzuo ruogan guiding, 2002: Article 42). This differed sharply from the earlier 1954 and 1989 regulations on the organization of mediation committees, which had not spoken of funding at all. In addition, the new regulations provide that, in addition to the old mediation committees of the different levels of the village, urban residents, town districts (*jiedao*), and enterprise units, there would be established new-style regional and trade/professional mediation committees (Article 10).

With this kind of support from the judicial sections of the government, the decline even of the semiofficial cadre mediation system has been reversed. As shown in table 2.6, the nadir was reached in 2002, with just 3.141 million disputes mediated nationwide that year. Thereafter, the number of cases mediated has steadily increased, up to 4.492 million in 2003, and steadying out in the 4.4 million-plus range in 2005. In 2006, there were a total of 4.628 million recorded cases handled by the cadre mediation system, compared to 4.382 million civil lawsuits handled by the courts. The mediated cases enjoyed a reported success rate of 92.1 percent (*Zhongguo falü nianjian*, 2007: 1065, 1080, 245).

Municipal and provincial governments are all pushing extrajudicial mediation. In recent years, many of these local governments have issued mediation provisions and regulations that echo and elaborate on the two 2002 central documents mentioned earlier. A preliminary search on the web turned up, for example: the "Suzhou City, People's Mediation Methods" (implemented from 1 February 2005), "Hangzhou City, People's Mediation Provisions" (implemented from 1 January 2006), "Shaanxi Province, People's Mediation Provisions" (implemented from 1 March 2007), "Chongqing City, People's Mediation Provisions" (implemented from 1 January 2008), "Anhui Province, People's Mediation Provisions" (implemented from 1 February 2008), and so on. These tell about the importance attached to mediation by those governments.

At the same time, new higher-level and broader committees have grown in the face of the new circumstances, accompanying the resocietalization of community mediation at the bottom. Shanghai City now has, under all its districts, new-style mediation "work offices" or "centers." As an example, Xiong Yihan has studied in some detail one such office, the "Yang Boshou people's mediation work office." Yang is someone who had had a lot of experience in government work (and even visited-studied at Cambridge briefly) and, since his retirement in 1994, has worked as a mediator. He was awarded the title "leading people's mediator" by Shanghai City in 2001, and was further recognized as "national model mediation committee member" in 2002. He works with three associates, all experienced mediators. Their office deals mainly with big disputes within their jiedao district (with jurisdiction over seventeen resident committees totaling 100,000 people). According to Xiong's analysis, Yang is able in his work to use flexible methods, to take account of human relations and moral right/wrong (qingli), and even circumvent law and the courts when needed to arrive at a resolution of the dispute (Xiong Yihan, 2006). A mediator like Yang is to some degree reminiscent of the "traditional" "good man of the township" and could perhaps be dubbed the "good man of the district." As Xiong points out, the "social capital" that Xiong relies on comes not simply from social esteem within the "society of the well acquainted," but rather from his accumulated reputation as a mediator, which can carry considerable import even in a society of strangers.

From the point of view of the disputants, as has been noted, community mediation as a whole, including both semiformal mediation and revitalized informal mediation, remains a low-cost and effective means to resolve disputes. In the present context of the monetization of everything, cadres mediation has indeed changed from the earlier purely service orientation to a kind of profession—the 2002 Ministry of Justice regulations, as has been seen, provided that mediation committee members be remunerated for their time and expenses. However, those same regulations still maintain what has been in effect since the 1954 regulations, namely that "the people's mediation committees will not charge fees for mediating disputes among the people." This is the main reason why even cadres mediation remains an inexpensive avenue relative to others, and why most people see mediation in general as the most likely to bring "satisfaction."

In short, community mediation, semiofficial and nonofficial, remains an integral aspect of the Chinese legal system. As for the future, will China's legal system really become just like that of the United States, such that the mediation system will fall almost completely into disuse, and the numbers of lawsuits per 100,000 people will rise another twentyfold?[19] I think perhaps not, and perhaps it should not.

19. In 1980, there were 6,356 civil lawsuits for every 100,000 people in the United States, more than 100 times the number in China. The majority were divorce, auto torts, and inheritance cases (Administrative Office of the U.S. Courts, 1981: 200; *State Court Caseload Statistics: Annual Report*, 1980: 14, 55; cf. Huang, 1996: 180).

3

Centralized Minimalism

Semiformal Governance by Quasi-Officials and Dispute Resolution

A VARIETY OF RECENTLY UNCOVERED archival evidence has shown us, surprisingly, that the basic principles and methods of the Qing civil justice system were also employed in many other spheres of Qing local governance. Enough evidence has now been accumulated to allow us to draw some preliminary conclusions about this aspect of Qing governance, which might in turn prompt us to rethink some of the main theoretical formulations about the nature of the imperial as well as the modern Chinese state.

To recapitulate briefly what we know about the civil justice system: the Qing approach to civil justice was encapsulated in the term "minor matters" (*xishi*), the Qing equivalent to the modern Western concept of "civil matters." Disputes over land, debt, inheritance, and marriage (and old-age support for one's parents) were deemed to be "minor": first, because in the state's eyes, offenses related to such questions were much less important than criminal acts (and warranted no punishment or only light punishment); and, less obviously, because the state thought that such matters were best handled by societal (i.e., community and kin group) mechanisms for dispute resolution, rather than by the courts. As has been seen in chapter 2, community or kin mediation did, in fact, resolve most disputes.

Nevertheless, many disputes concerning minor matters could not be resolved by such means and were taken to court. The state would then rely first on a semiformal process in which the court system would operate alongside the societal mediation that was usually reenergized upon the filing of a complaint. The liaison between the two systems was provided mainly by the *xiangbao*, an unsalaried quasi-official nominated by the local community and confirmed by the state. In that process, the magistrate generally commented briefly on complaints, countercomplaints, and petitions as they were received. Those comments were usually either posted or made accessible to the litigants, often through the xiangbao, and these preliminary expressions of magisterial opinion would play a major role as the mediation proceeded. One or the other side might become more willing to compromise, and a mediated resolution would follow. If such extrajudicial mediation succeeded, the magistrate would almost always prefer it to any possible court action.

The semiformal process involving quasi-official intermediaries and interactions between the court system and societal mediation was used so widely as to be routine, almost institutionalized. It resolved perhaps 40 percent of the total "minor matters" cases filed with the courts. The magistrate would hold a formal court session to adjudicate a dispute only after both the informal and semiformal processes had failed (Huang, 1993a; see also Huang, 1996: chap. 5).

That basic approach to governance—of acting only after complaints and of relying as much as possible on informal and semiformal processes—was applied, it turns out, not only in the civil justice system but also widely throughout Qing local administration. Unlike modern bureaucratic government and its emphasis on routinized supervision and paperwork, the Qing method of local governance by quasi-officials and by dispute resolution may be termed "minimalist," even though governmental power was highly "centralized" at the top. I begin this chapter by briefly summarizing the accumulated evidence, and then move on to some general observations about the implications of those findings for our understanding of Chinese governance, past and present.

The Evidence

Although county government records for late Qing and Republican China remain relatively scarce because of the devastations of war and revolution, a number of them did survive largely intact and have been studied in some detail in the past two decades. Each documents how the method of civil justice was used in other spheres of administration, including subcounty tax, educational, and judicial administration; village governance; and even administration of the county yamen itself. Together they give us a coherent picture of what may have been the main methods and distinctive characteristics of Qing local governance.

The Late Qing Baodi County Example

Archival materials from Baodi County in the late Qing (Baodi xian dang'an, preserved in the Qing archives for the capital prefecture of Shuntianfu, held at the First Historical Archives in Beijing) tell us about the actual operations of subcounty administration in that county, as opposed to the state's designs and intentions as manifest in its announced regulations and policies. They reveal the pivotal role of the xiangbao, each of whom oversaw tax collection and judicial affairs in an average of 20 villages (in this county of some 900 villages). These xiangbao—unsalaried quasi-officials who were nominated by and drawn from local society, and then confirmed by the state—served as the main liaison between the county magistrate's yamen and their community. They were Janus-faced, at once representatives of society and agents of the state. They might be the truly powerful leaders of local society or just buffers to protect the powerful from state demands; they might be advocates of societal interests or abusers of local society who exploited their state connections for personal gain. Some xiangbao did little more than deliver messages and information from and to the county yamen, while others wielded considerable influence, even settling disputes on their own authority. Much depended on the local situation and each xiangbao's personality (on tax collection, see Huang, 1985: 224–31; on judicial administration, see Huang, 1996: 127–31).

We know these things not from any paperwork on bureaucratic administrative routines but rather mainly from "cases" involving the appointments of xiangbao and complaints against them. The Baodi archives include ninety-nine cases regarding the appointment or reappointment of xiangbao that span the years 1830 to 1910,[1] sometimes revealing the jockeying among local individuals for the post and sometimes the opposite, as individuals did everything possible to avoid being named to it. Indeed, in numerous cases, nominated xiangbao or existing xiangbao ran away, and one man even repeatedly paid his would-be nominator extortionate fees to keep himself from being nominated (Huang, 1985: 228). Many instances involve complaints against xiangbao, generally for tax abuse or for exceeding their authority (e.g., Huang, 1985: 225, 228–30). The record is particularly full, for example, on one Tian Kui, who had been removed from office for abuse and then several years later, in 1814, again faced multiple complaints from local leaders when he attempted to get himself reinstated (Baodi xian dang'an, 87, 1814, 12.4; discussed in Huang, 1985: 229). Another xiangbao had been handpicked and installed again and again by a big landlord named Dong Weizeng, who owned 20,000 *mu* and had relied on this xiangbao to evade paying taxes on his land. The case came

1. Tallied by Wang Fuming, drawing on documents from five of the twenty *li* of the county (in Cong, 1995: 26–33).

to court in 1896 when other local elites joined together to bring a complaint against Dong and his xiangbao (Baodi xian dang'an, 94, 1896, 5; 1898, 2; 1898, 7.15; see also Huang, 1985: 230).

Such records enable us to form our picture of the xiangbao. Records of routine lawsuits of the county yamen, by contrast, give us only faceless xiangbao, ordered by the magistrate in boilerplate language to "look into the matter" or "investigate and report." From the cases and disputes involving the xiangbao themselves, we have learned about individual xiangbao—who they were, what they did, and the kinds of conflicts they were involved in.

But past scholarship, including my own, has not yet unearthed from such materials the distinctive method of governmental administration that is our focus here. In the absence of formal complaints, the xiangbao were left to operate on their own, free of official supervision and formal paperwork. They therefore figure little in the routine documentation of the county yamen. Substantial records were generated only when the magistrate was brought in because of a complaint against the xiangbao or because of a xiangbao's resignation or nomination. In those circumstances, the magistrate acted much as he did in civil cases. He preferred to allow the dispute to be settled by societal mechanisms; but should such mechanisms fail, he would render a clear-cut decision. Thus, in cases involving competing and unresolvable claims to the position of xiangbao, he would decide unequivocally for one of the candidates; and in persistent disputes involving xiangbao abuses, he would uphold the complaint—acting to discipline or remove the xiangbao—or reject it. The intent was to maintain the system with a minimum of bureaucratic effort.

As I have shown elsewhere with regard to "civil" lawsuits, the Qing magistrate had little inclination to engage in protracted mediation at court to work out voluntary compromises among those whom he saw as lowly people. It took much more time and effort to get the two sides to make voluntary concessions than it did to adjudicate or decide a case outright.[2] And, given the state's approach to "minor matters" as difficulties that it would prefer to see society resolve on its own, generally disputes persisted down to a formal court session with the magistrate only after both parties had dug in their heels and refused to make the kinds of compromises that societal mediators had urged on them. Such stubborn cases could rarely be resolved easily by magisterial moralizing, no matter how earnest or lofty. In practice, administrative expediency, if nothing else, dictated that the magistrate arrive at a clear-cut resolu-

2. The time-consuming difficulty of mediation is, of course, the reason why in the current Reform era, as caseloads mount, the courts have tended to replace it with simple adjudication (see chapters 5, 6, 7; Huang, 2006a, 2006b).

tion of the matter (Huang, 1996; 2006a)—an observation no less true of cases involving complaints against the xiangbao than of general civil disputes.

Yet such practicalities did not prevent magistrates from continuing to represent themselves in their writings or their published case samples in terms of the Confucian ideal, as someone who governed by moral example and moral suasion. And it is really because of those ideological representations that some scholars came to see the magistrate as a moralizing mediator at court.[3] In fact, most magistrates were careerist bureaucrats who, when confronted with otherwise irresolvable disputes, opted for speedy adjudications. Most, during their relatively brief tenure at a given locale, tried to interfere as little as possible and not rock the boat—in other words, they relied as much as they could on informal societal mechanisms and semiformal governance.

The Republican Shunyi Example

In the Republican period, the Chinese state unquestionably sought to expand its power in a manner commonly associated with "modern state making" or "bureaucratization" (discussed in more detail below). Thus, the Guomindang government sought to deepen its control over rural society by extending the state's formal bureaucratic apparatus below the county (*xian*) level, down to the newly established subcounty "wards" (*qu*), each with a salaried ward head (*quzhang*) backed by formal paperwork, police, and even military guards. This important bureaucratizing step came after the reforms that had begun in the New Policy period of the last decade of the Qing, when the state tried to tighten its grip on rural society by establishing the quasi-official position of village head (*cunzhang*) at the level of the natural village, rather than at the supra-village level as in the earlier xiangbao.

Nevertheless, alongside such twentieth-century bureaucratizing "state making," much remained still of the old minimalist approach to grassroots governance. Here, as with the Qing, our source of information is mainly paperwork that was generated only when the new village heads were appointed or dismissed, or were made the object of complaints. One notable batch of such materials comes from Shunyi County in Hebei, involving a total of eighty-eight petitions about village heads filed with the Shunyi County government in the years 1929 to 1931. Of those, seventy were from existing or nominated village heads who asked to be allowed to resign (Shunyi xian dang'an, 3:42 and 50, 1929.1-12; 3:170, 1930.9-1931.9). Six others were complaints against abuses by existing village heads, mainly in connection with their handling of

3. For more on this question of the magistrate as a moralizing mediator, the subject of my dispute with Shiga Shūzō, see Huang, 1996: 12–13.

taxes. The remainder consisted of five petitions submitted by other village leaders to nominate a new village head, five reporting deaths of village heads and the need for a new appointment, and two odd cases.[4]

These records tell us that the method of administration revealed in the Baodi records about the xiangbao was still commonly used in village governance. Like the xiangbao, each village head was nominated by local notables and confirmed by the county magistrate. Not a salaried official, he was more a representative of the village community than an official of the state. And he was pretty much left alone to perform his functions until and unless complaints arose or a new village head needed to be appointed (Huang, 1985: 241–44).

The spate of petitions to resign resulted from the new stresses on village government beginning in the late 1920s due to Guomindang attempts to tighten control and increase taxes, especially the miscellaneous levies—most importantly for police and military guard units and for schools—known collectively as the *tankuan*. The new state wanted to reach directly into natural villages through the village head, whereas the Qing state had attempted in Baodi County to exert its power via the xiangbao (overseeing, as noted above, about 20 villages each). The new state wished to hold the new village heads, not the xiangbao as in the Qing, responsible for tax collection. The new state sought to impose more taxes for modernizing reforms—to establish a modern police and school system—whereas the Qing state had for two centuries tried to leave things much as they were. Finally, during times of the Guomindang wars with warlords, armies passing through strategic locations would require villages to provide food, animals, lodging, manpower, and the like for logistical support (Huang, 1985: 278–80, 284–85, 288–89).

These new pressures were what many existing and prospective village heads sought to avoid. Some used the excuse of old age and infirmity or poor health; others pled illiteracy or inadequate ability or qualifications; and still others pointed to outside responsibilities and obligations. In several instances, a newly nominated village head turned right around to nominate someone else, who in turn submitted a petition insisting that the one nominated first was the better qualified for the honor. Many of the petitioners begging off from service as village heads referred to the increased burdens of the office in connection with the new taxes, and several mentioned the military requisitions.

4. One petition was a complaint by a village head against several villagers; another was submitted by three members of the newly (though far from consistently) established "supervisory committee" (*jiancha weiyuanhui*) against a village head for failure to properly post village accounts in accordance with new Guomindang instructions. In an earlier tally, I reported a total of "roughly 120" such petitions (Huang, 1996: 43–44). In that number are also 15 duplicate petitions, 10 having to do with issues other than village heads, and 6 that were just normal civil complaints lodged by individual villagers—a total of 119 petitions.

These materials confirm that village governance under the Guomindang in many respects changed little from that shown in the Qing Baodi archives. Just as the Qing state had done with the xiangbao, the new Guomindang state drew personnel from the locality itself, requiring that indigenous leaders nominate the village head from among the members of the community. Rather than appointing or assigning such village heads, the state limited its role to confirming nominations from the communities themselves. The new village heads, moreover, were to serve as unsalaried quasi-officials, just as the xiangbao had been. And also like the xiangbao, village heads so chosen were left to carry out their functions essentially on their own so long as tax expectations were met, until and unless they became targets of complaints, or until they tried to resign or asked to be replaced by new nominees. Thus complaints against them and petitions from them are our main source of information about them.

For the 1930s and early 1940s, the oral histories of Japanese Mantetsu (i.e., South Manchurian Railway Company) field researchers both substantiate and flesh out the archival records. Thus, the six North China villages surveyed by Mantetsu researchers in 1939–1942 illustrate in concrete detail three patterns resulting from this minimalist approach to village governance. From oral histories, and not from the county archives, we know that in Houxiazhai and Lengshuigou in northwest Shandong, earlier village heads, who had been nominated by community leaders, largely continued to serve through the 1930s and early 1940s. They generally represented village interests more than state concerns, and their communities dealt with the state as cohesive units. These were villages whose community bonds largely remained intact through twentieth-century changes, in whose affairs the county government did not have to intervene at all (Huang, 1985: 259–64).

In two other villages, in contrast, longtime village leaders resigned when faced with new stresses on the village economy and new demands from the state. The result was a power vacuum that allowed abusive bullies to exploit the post of village head for their own gain. However, community bonds were still strong enough that the villagers could complain to the county authorities about their mistreatment. In Shajing, near Beijing, this process occurred in 1939 under Japanese occupation; the village, with the neighboring village of Shimen, filed formal complaints with county authorities against the bully Fan Baoshan, who was removed and convicted (sentenced to two years in prison). In Sibeichai, in south-central Hebei, the process occurred early in the 1930s, when longtime village head Zhang Yueqing resigned and the bullying Li Yanlin took his place for two years; after the village complained to county authorities and obtained Li's removal, Zhang Yueqing returned to serve. Here our knowledge comes both from village oral history and from the county government records cited by the Mantetsu researchers (Huang, 1985: 264–70).

In the third pattern, exemplified in Wudian and Houjiaying villages in northeastern Hebei, old leaders of the community simply gave up on public service completely, allowing strongmen to monopolize the village government. At the time of the Japanese surveys of 1941–1942, both villages were under the rule of abusive village heads and neither had been able to unite and lodge effective formal complaints. As in the first pattern, the county was never involved and our knowledge of what happened comes entirely from village oral histories (Huang, 1985: 270–74).

These Mantetsu materials confirm that the Qing minimalist method of governance by semiformal personnel and by dispute resolution continued to be employed by the Guomindang government, and even the Japanese occupation government. They did not try to bureaucratize village government in the sense of putting in place salaried functionaries. Rather, they continued to use the minimalist approach, limiting themselves to approval and confirmation of leaders nominated from below. The government's bureaucratic apparatus entered the picture only on complaint of abuse or occasions of new appointments. (And that approach, we have seen, was very much open to abuse when new pressures and strains broke down old community bonds and allowed opportunists and bullies to insinuate themselves into positions of power.) In principle and method, such governance had much in common with the Qing's handling of "minor matters."

Tax Administration in Late Qing and Republican Huailu County

Huaiyin Li's study of the archives of Huailu in south-central Hebei (Zhili) province—another county distinctive for its well-preserved records, in this case running from the late Qing down to the 1930s—confirms the above observations. Here the key Qing subcounty official, comparable to the xiangbao of Baodi County, was the so-called *xiangdi*. Like the xiangbao, the xiangdi was unsalaried, nominated by the community (and usually serving on a rotating basis in accordance with long-standing "village regulations," or *cungui*), and confirmed by the county magistrate. Unlike the Baodi xiangbao, who typically oversaw twenty or so villages, the xiangdi were apparently generally tied to individual villages, one per village. As Li notes, this difference probably reflected the greater ecological stability and soil productivity of this area of Hebei, which made for more tightly knit village communities and a higher degree of community solidarity than in the less ecologically stable and less productive northeastern Hebei area of Baodi (H. Li, 2005: 9; see also H. Li, 2000: chap. 1). Greater community solidarity paradoxically enabled quasi-officials to reach more deeply into subcounty administration.

But the method of governmental administration was the same. Here again, the main source materials about the xiangdi are provided by disputes involving nomination and confirmation of the xiangdi, and by complaints against them for alleged abuse of their powers and functions. We see little in the formal archives of the government about the routine doings of the xiangdi, as one might expect of a bureaucratized organization. Instead, paperwork is largely limited to extraordinary "cases" or "lawsuits" that require intervention by a magistrate.

Taxes were handled in Huailu County mainly by the xiangdi paying the amount required, and then apportioning and collecting individual assessments from the members of his community. When all went well and the county government received the taxes due, each xiangdi was largely left to operate the process of tax collection on his own. It was only when the system ran into problems (as evidenced by disputes and complaints) or when personnel needed to be replaced that the magistrate entered the picture (H. Li, 2000: chaps. 5, 6; see also H. Li, 2005: chaps. 4, 5).

Under the late Qing New Policy reforms, followed by so-called modern state making in the Republican period, the xiangdi system persisted alongside the newly established village head system. But both operated according to the old principles of minimalist governance: unsalaried quasi-officials were left to work largely on their own until and unless disputes and complaints arose (H. Li, 2005: chap. 7).

Educational Administration and Village Schools in Haicheng County in the Northeast

Another important body of archival evidence comes from Haicheng County in northeastern China; this exceptionally well-preserved archive was the foundation of the dissertation work of Elizabeth VanderVen (2003). Here, beginning in the New Policy period, the central state called for the establishment of village community schools according to central guidelines. Such schools as existed in some natural villages had usually been the old private *sishu* schools, whose elementary curriculum centered on the "Three Characters Classic" (*Sanzijing*), the "Hundred Surnames" (*Baijiaxing*), and the "Thousand Characters Classic" (*Qianziwen*). (At the next level, the "Four Books" and "Five Classics" were taught.) The entire system was oriented toward the officially sponsored examination system by which officials were selected. Its replacement envisioned universal education for all village children and emphasized new-style subjects such as mathematics, geography, history, science, "Chinese," physical education, and music (VanderVen, 2003: chap. 3).

While the central state was quite specific in the blueprint it developed for these new village community schools, it allocated no official funding for them.

Villages, by and large, were to provide the necessary building, often from the village temple or village government revenues, and select and hire their own teachers. They were allowed to charge tuition to help offset expenses, but those fees generally remained low, for these were designed to be the community's "public" schools. Sometimes the new schools were reconfigured old sishu schools that combined the old and the new in their curriculum (VanderVen, 2003: chap. 3; 2005).

To administer local education, the late Qing (in 1906) set up the Quanxuesuo, or "Education Promotion Offices." These subcounty offices, partly formal and partly semiformal, were responsible for overseeing local and village education. They were not components of the county yamen or tied to any exact administrative division; in that respect, they were rather like the old xiangbao. Yet they were bureaucratized to the extent that the staff officers of the bureaus were salaried and were to regularly inspect the schools in their jurisdiction and to report their findings to the magistrate. The chief of the bureau was (at least in theory) to be nominated by the local community and then appointed by the magistrate, and that chief in turn (at least in theory) selected the other "board members" (*shendong*) and the staff of the bureau, subject to magisterial confirmation. Invariably drawn from the locality itself, the members of these educational offices were generally closely identified with local interests. Aside from submitting regular reports, these offices were left to operate essentially on their own, unless and until disputes or complaints arose (VanderVen, 2003: chap. 6).

Some of our information about the schools and the education offices comes from their bureaucratic periodic reports (complete with standardized forms) filed with the county government, covering everything ranging from quality of teaching, school management, and student performance to health, sanitation practices, and so on. But even more information, as was true of the xiangbao and the village heads, comes from "cases" involving village violations, special appeals, or disputes that then went to the magistrate for resolution. In such instances, the members of the education offices served as intermediaries between the village and the county yamen, much as the xiangbao had done. It was mainly in response to complaints and disputes that the magistrate intervened directly (VanderVen, 2003: chap. 6).

VanderVen's findings have been further confirmed by Huaiyin Li's more recent research on education in Huailu County in south-central Hebei. Li's materials, like VanderVen's, are drawn primarily from disputes and complaints involving the new village schools. They show the same partly bureaucratized and partly minimalist principles and methods as in Haicheng County (H. Li, 2005: chap. 8).

What is remarkable about the education story in these two counties is how very far-reaching and profound its consequences were. This approach, which combined state initiative with village community and local elite participation, marked the beginnings of nationwide village schools, and many that exist today date back to the founding efforts of this period. In particular, the village collective (brigade) schools established widely during the Cultural Revolution period show clear continuities with the early twentieth-century schools. Like their New Policy and Republican predecessors, these "modern" collective grammar schools were funded mainly by the villages (collectives) themselves, even while education followed centrally established guidelines and blueprints. They were in fact largely the products of active village participation in a minimalist initiative from the state.

Yamen Administration in Ba County, Sichuan, in the Qing

Finally, the Qing archives of the Ba County yamen in Sichuan Province, studied by Bradly Reed (2000), show us how the same principles and methods were applied even to the governance of the county government yamen itself. By governmental design, the magistrate himself was really the only centrally appointed and salaried official in the county yamen. Ch'ü T'ung-tsu's [Qu Tongzu] research long ago made clear the important roles filled by the magistrate's personal "private secretaries" (*muyou*), especially the judicial and tax secretaries he brought with him for his tour of duty, whom Ch'ü termed his "informal" staff. Those secretaries were paid by the magistrate himself, out of the "irregular" income (i.e., gifts and such) he earned in addition to his regular "salary" (Ch'ü, 1962). Reed's research has focused on the workings of the "regular" staff: the clerks and runners who managed the numerous offices (*fang*) that made up a yamen.

These personnel, too, were semiformal. The great majority of them were not supposed to exist at all, since Qing administrative statute explicitly limited such positions to just a few dozen—a fraction of the staff's actual numbers in the nineteenth century in most counties. Their pay was similarly capped by statute, again at a fraction of the real figure. These shadowy figures, who were extrastatutory, nevertheless performed regular administrative functions. They also exhibited a kind of quasi-bureaucratic ethic, likening themselves in qualifications and purpose to those who served in the formal bureaucracy (Reed, 2000).

The core of Reed's material is, once again, the records of "cases" having to do mainly with disputes. Some occurred within a given fang office, pertaining to appointments and reappointments or control over the office; others occurred between different offices disagreeing about the powers and revenues of the county yamen. The judicial office (xingfang) was particularly conflict prone, since, as Reed shows, it provided the bulk of the county yamen's revenue through fees charged for cases of local disputes. When such conflict erupted, one or the other side would file a complaint with the magistrate, whose intervention would be sought to resolve it (Reed, 2000: chap. 2).

It is mainly through these records that we learn of the operational realities of the different offices. Reed has emphasized what these cases tell us about how the yamen actually functioned on a day-to-day basis, about the self-contradictions that characterized the clerks and runners who made up the bulk of its regular staff—simultaneously illegitimate and regular "bureaucrats" ("illicit bureaucrats," in Reed's words) acting outside the statutes and yet performing the necessary functions of local government.

What I find particularly interesting in this material is the commonality in approach and method between such yamen administration on the one hand and subcounty judicial, tax, and educational administration on the other. Once again, we see the resort to semiformal personnel, sustained not by bureaucratic appropriation but by local society itself or, in the case of the yamen, by the fees the office charged for service. And the method was, once again, for the formal state apparatus to intervene as little as possible. Instead of employing the bureaucratic approach of routinized oversight and paperwork, the official bureaucracy, in the person of the magistrate, entered the picture principally to address complaints stemming from disputes. Otherwise, the system was left to run pretty much on its own.

The remarkable thing about this record is that the magistrate dealt with the different offices of runners and clerks under him almost as he did villages. Each office was allowed to nominate its head, subject to magisterial approval. Each office would support its own "representative" or quasi-official. Each office would rely first on its own internal mechanisms for dispute resolution. The magistrate entered the picture only when disputes could not otherwise be resolved or when abuse was charged. Then he would act to resolve the dispute or complaint, as he did in cases involving minor matters. This too was minimalist administration.

Centralized Minimalism

Max Weber drew important distinctions between his two governmental ideal-types, "patrimonialism" and "bureaucracy," the former characteristic of government under a ruler claiming the entire country as his personal domain, and the latter of modern states with specialized functions performed by an impersonal, salaried bureaucracy. It was part of Weber's genius that when faced with the historical reality of imperial China, he employed the concept of "patrimonial bureaucracy" rather than simply applying one of the ideal-types he advanced for clarifying theoretical connections. As I have noted elsewhere, Weber's suggestion may be viewed as a paradoxical formulation—a system that was at once "patrimonial" and "bureaucratic" (Weber, [1968] 1978: 1047–51; Huang, 1996: 229–34). While Philip Kuhn's study (1990) of the sorcery scare of 1768 emphasized the opposition between "monarchy" and "bureaucracy," I have stressed their interdependence within a single, paradoxical system.

Regardless, Weber's formulation has the power to clarify two important characteristics of imperial Chinese rule. First, despite the patrimonial claims of the emperor in theory, in practice he relied very much on a bureaucracy to ensure the stability of his rule and to counter the tendencies of patrimonial rule to fragment (into independent local patrimonial satrapies). And second, despite the predisposition of bureaucracy toward self-elaboration, and despite Weber's relative silence on the idea, it is clear that patrimonial rule dictated that the state apparatus remain minimalist to the greatest extent possible; otherwise, local officials would be separated from the person of the emperor by too many intervening layers, a separation that would threaten the bonds of personal loyalties that knit together the system, and decentralizing tendencies of local (patrimonial) rule might come to overwhelm the centralizing tendencies of bureaucracy (Weber, [1968] 1978: esp. 1047–51; cf. Huang, 1996: chap. 9). (Insofar as a patrimonial bureaucracy combines patrimonialism with bureaucracy, it also belies Weber's own rather unilinear scheme by which the premodern, prebureaucratic state changed to its modern, bureaucratic, and rational successor.)

But Weber's schema can have little place for the semiformal province of governance that has been the focus of this chapter. His characterization of the ideal-types and of the historical (as opposed to ideal-typical) Chinese state as a "patrimonial bureaucracy" was in the end limited to government's formal institutions and functions. It was predicated on a conception of state and society as an either/or dichotomous binary. Governance is by definition limited to the actions only of the formal state apparatus, in contradistinction to those of informal society.

Such a conceptualization can extend outside of formal governance to take account, as Weber did, of the strictly informal roles filled by the Chinese gentry elite and by Chinese lineages and clans, which have drawn so much attention in past China scholarship (for example, Chang, 1955, 1962; Ch'ü, 1962; Freedman, 1966), but it cannot encompass the semiformal xiangbao and xiangdi, village heads, and extralegal bureaucrats that have been the focus of the discussion above. It cannot, for that matter, encompass the "private secretaries" whom Ch'ü T'ung-tsu showed to be so crucial to local governance, or the gentry and merchant elites in the late Qing and Republic who, in conjunction with the state, came to take on an ever greater role in public services and local governance. The new "private" chambers of commerce illustrate this medial role particularly clearly: called for and regulated by the state (in 1904), they came to take on such governmental functions as the maintenance of new urban services, establishment of public security forces, and the mediation of disputes, even while simultaneously representing private merchant interests.[5]

Building on the work of Max Weber, Michael Mann has made the important distinction between the degree of centralization of governmental power (vis-à-vis other competing sources of power), which he calls "despotic power," and the degree of governmental reach into society, or what he terms "infrastructural power" (Mann, 1984; see also Mann, 1986). Thus, we might say that contemporary America is rather low in despotic power, given the separation of governmental powers into the executive, judicial, and legislative branches, their checks and balances on one another, and the power and prerogatives of civil society, yet very high in infrastructural power (whether one thinks of the Internal Revenue Service's powers or the reach of the police in a manhunt or the government's ability to prosecute a war). Imperial China, by contrast, was very high in despotic power, given the concentration of authority in the person of the emperor, but low in infrastructural power: the official bureaucratic apparatus reached only the level of the county magistrate, who, in the nineteenth century, oversaw a population of some 250,000 on average. High despotic power coupled with low infrastructural power is a useful way to sketch imperial Chinese government and to highlight its differences from contemporary American government.

Mann's insights are well supported by Wang Yeh-chien's research into imperial taxation. Despite the highly centralized nature of the Qing state, Wang shows, its taxes as a proportion of total agricultural output were relatively low: no more than 2 to 4 percent in the eighteenth and nineteenth centuries, compared to the 10 percent and more in Meiji Japan and European feudal states (not to speak of modern states) (Wang, 1973; see also Huang, 1985: 278–81). Taxation, of course, is a good indication of the scale of a state's infrastructural apparatus and reach. The small proportion of agricultural output taken by the late imperial state attests to the relatively low infrastructural power of that state. It obviously also highlights the constraints on the size of the bureaucracy imposed by limited funding.

Yet although it offers important insights, Mann's analysis, like Weber's, tells us little about governance outside of the formal apparatus of the state.

5. Rowe (1984, 1989) and Rankin (1986) first equated this trend toward the growing role played by gentry and merchant elites with a Habermasian "public sphere" juxtaposed against the state; they later came to view it more as something intermediate between state and society (Rowe, 1993; Rankin, 1993). My summary of these views is in Huang, 1993b: 220–21.

In juxtaposing the formal governmental structure to the informal powers of civil society, he has little to say about the semiformal governance that is our focus here. Mann's despotism-infrastructure distinction, in other words, cannot capture the method of governance outlined above, which occurred in the zone lying between formal government and informal society.

This is the context in which I advanced the notion of a "third realm" between state and society to spotlight the overlapping, collaborative sphere of governance between the two (Huang, 1993a, 1993b). In the civil justice system, that third realm lay between the formal court system and society's informal mediatory mechanisms. Rather than signaling the end of societal mediation, the filing of a formal complaint with the yamen generally galvanized more intensive efforts at such mediation. At the same time, preliminary expressions of magisterial opinion on the plaints, countercomplaints, and petitions often played a major role in renewed societal mediation to produce a compromise resolution, to which the formal system would almost always defer. The theory was that such mediated resolutions helped to minimize enmity between the parties and the likelihood of aggravation of the conflict or recurrence of the dispute (Huang, 1993a; see also Huang, 1996: chap. 5).

The xiangbao similarly represented something of a third realm in Qing governance, midway between the formal state apparatus of the county yamen and the informal mediatory mechanisms of society. He worked in the gray area between the two, answering at once to the magistrate and to those local people who had nominated him (Huang, 1993b; see also Huang, 1996: 127–31). We have seen above also how twentieth-century village heads, and even imperial yamen office heads, were alike in this respect. So too were the gentry and merchant elites of the twentieth century who came to fill new public service and governmental roles. Likewise, village education in the twentieth century belonged neither simply to society nor to the state, but was rather the product of the coworking of the two.

My purpose in advancing the concept of a third realm is not to deny the reality of the other two—the "state" (e.g., the formal bureaucratic apparatus) and "society" (e.g., the village)—but rather to go beyond the confines of a simple dichotomous binary: namely, that if it is not one, then it must be the other. Qing governance, we have seen, encompassed a vast sphere in between the two, in which they overlapped and worked in tandem.

But though my notion may help to identify that intermediate space and its quasi-officials, it does not quite capture the substance of the minimalist method of governance used in the third realm. The imperial bureaucracy could conceivably have opted for ever-expanding bureaucratization—a "maximalist" approach, specifying the functions of all offices and insisting that paper records be maintained for all activities of government. But it instead turned to something closer to a minimalist approach, insisting on quasi-officials rather than salaried bureaucrats, and preferring to do as little as possible until and unless disputes or complaints arose. Then and only then would the formal state apparatus intervene to ensure that this vast sphere of governance would continue to function smoothly.

To capture this approach to governance, as well as the government's overall organization, I propose here the term "centralized minimalism"—"centralized" because of the imperial claims to absolute (patrimonial) power in the person of the emperor. Administrative authority was not separated in relatively autonomous branches of government, or shared between the government and civil society, but concentrated and centralized. And this centralism, in turn, mandated a minimalist formal bureaucratic apparatus.

Though the imperial state had rather grandiose schemes for thoroughgoing control of society, especially the decimal organizations of households into the *baojia* and *lijia* systems (Hsiao, 1960), the logic of patrimonialism, as noted above, demanded that governmental machinery be kept to a minimum number of layers, lest the individual officials' personal loyalties to the emperor that bonded the system together break down and local patrimonial satrapies take over. Limited tax revenues from an involuted peasant economy served as an additional constraint. Thus, the Qing state had no formal officials lower than the county magistrate. This restriction was coincident with its wish to keep down the burdens that government placed on society. It thus passed legislation to minimize the number of sub-bureaucratic functionaries in the local magistrate's office to no more than a few dozen clerks and runners in each county (Ch'ü, 1962: 38, 58). It also promised not to raise taxes, despite the continual increase in population (*shengshi ziding, yong bu jiafu*).

Such a minimalist formal governmental apparatus, in turn, encouraged the use, instead, of quasi-officials and dispute resolution. Precisely because the formal apparatus ended at the county magistrate level, subcounty administration became the responsibility of quasi-officials. And because of the reliance on quasi-officials and societal mechanisms, the formal bureaucracy intervened only in the event of disputes or complaints.

This formulation of centralized minimalism, of course, is on one level reminiscent both of Weber's patrimonial bureaucracy and of Mann's high despotic power but low infrastructural power. But it differs from both in being intended to capture not just the nature of the formal organization of government but also the practice of actual governmental administration. It points up not just how formal government was organized but also how semiformal governance was practiced in the gray zone between the formal state and informal society.

Confucianized Legalism

Such semiformal governance is captured only in part by the official ideology of imperial government, which was a combination of Confucian with Legalist precepts, or what might be called "Confucianized Legalism."[6] The harshly Legalist ideology of government by laws, punishments, and bureaucracy was tempered by the Confucian ideals of benevolent government (*renzheng*).[7] At the level of local governance, the combination gave rise to the ideal of the magistrate as the "father-mother official" (*fumuguan*), who in effect brought together the stern Legalist father of punishments, discipline, and depersonalized administration and the kindly Confucian mother of humaneness, harmony, and government by moral example. Centralized authority was taken for granted by both elements in the mix, conveyed not least by the metaphor that cast government as a parent and subjects (*zimin*) as the children.

Confucianism embraced in addition an ideal of minimal interference in societal affairs. The Confucian political ideal was a moral society that would more or less govern itself. The state's role would be limited mainly to setting an example through its morally upright officials. Therein lay the origin of the legal ideal that society would settle its disputes without government interference, that the state apparatus would defer to societal mechanisms for dispute resolution. The state would intervene only when it had to, when such mechanisms had failed. Lawsuits were aberrations, and court adjudication was born of the necessity of coping with those aberrations. This was the ideological underpinning of the concept of civil justice as encompassing "minor matters." And such benevolent government was to burden the populace as lightly as possible—hence the roots also of the early eighteenth-century policies of minimizing the numbers of government officials and the scale of state taxes.

Here the reader may be reminded of the much-studied eleventh-century debates between Sima Guang and Wang Anshi. Sima Guang may be seen as advocating the aspects of Confucian minimalism under discussion: to keep the bureaucratic apparatus to a minimum and let society govern itself, insofar as it can. Whereas Wang would rely on salaried clerks, Sima would leave most of subcounty governance to the elite gentry (Bol, 1993: 169, 173–76, 177–81; cf. Hsiao, 1982: 515–17, 487–93). Sima's views were to become the mainstream and predominant Confucian political outlook that persisted through Ming and Qing China.

---

6. On the "Confucianization" of Legalist laws, see Ch'ü, 1961; cf. Bodde and Morris, 1967.
7. The Legalist ideology was also wedded to the Confucian vision of social hierarchy, as Ch'ü (1961) showed.

But such Confucian minimalism cannot in itself fully encompass the ideology of imperial rule—or the political outlook of Sima Guang, for that matter. The operative ideology of the imperial state, as we have seen, was born of a combination of Confucianism with Legalism, a combination whose historical roots long predate the eleventh-century Wang-Sima debate. Even Sima Guang himself took for granted well-developed legislation and regulations for ensuring the proper functioning of the imperial bureaucracy. Indeed, his political outlook might be characterized better as "Confucianized Legalism" than as simply "Confucian minimalism."

Even "Confucianized Legalism," as interpreted here, cannot fully encompass the dimensions of centralized minimalism outlined above. The resort to quasi-officials and dispute resolution as methods of governance was born of administrative practice, not ideological principle. That the quasi-official xiangbao would be used as liaison between the state bureaucracy and societal mediation to create a third realm of governance between the two, with the magistrate taking direct action in that intermediate sphere only in the face of otherwise irresolvable disputes, was not foreseen in either Confucian minimalism or Legalist governance. It was the consequence of a government that grew with an expanding population while its ideals of Confucian minimalism remained unchanged. Given the state's commitment to a number of somewhat contradictory aims—to maintain the ruler's patrimonial powers and at the same time to minimize the threat of fragmentation intrinsic to patrimonial rule, as well as to minimize the tax burden and hence to minimize the elaboration of the governmental apparatus—minimalist governance by dispute resolution was arguably the least burdensome and costly means of preserving the system.

At the same time, semiformal governance of course also came with its share of problems. It could lead, for example, to xiangbao abuse of their powers, without attendant checks that fuller bureaucratization might impose. That was surely part of the background for new legislation in 1765 forbidding magistrates to allow the xiangbao to deal with local disputes on their own authority. That new legislation checked informal and semiformal abuse by xiangbao for a time, until they returned again in the late nineteenth century (Substatute 334-8; Huang, 1996: 113; see also chap. 7, appended note).

Such pros and cons of semiformal governance might be seen as parts of the implicit logic of its practice, at best captured and expressed only partially by the phrase "Confucianized Legalism." Much less can Confucianized Legalism capture the dimensions of centralized minimalism discussed above that were born of modernizing imperatives of the twentieth century. The quasi-official village heads and partly bureaucratized, partly semiformal Education Promotion Offices established by the late Qing are ready examples, as are the new public service functions performed by local elites and the new chambers of commerce. Most important, perhaps, is the model of state initiative plus popular participation for the new village schools. Confucian minimalism took for granted the crucial role of the local gentry elite, so central to Sima Guang's political views, but twentieth-century villages had long since been largely devoid of such gentry elites. More often than not, popular participation in the new schools came from peasants and peasant leaders—in roles that lay outside the social vision of Confucianism. At bottom, Confucianized Legalism was the governing ideology of an agrarian state and its hierarchical order; it cannot encompass the practices of centralized minimalism in the twentieth century.

Bureaucratization and Minimalism in Contemporary China

Since Max Weber first schematized the steady expansion (and "rationalization") of the machinery of the governmental apparatus in modern Western nation-states, "bureaucratization" has come to be seen as *the* major governmental change from the premodern to the modern era. The Republican state and contemporary Chinese Communist party-state, if seen from that perspective, clearly evince much in the way of bureaucratization. They have pushed the state apparatus down to far lower levels of society than ever before, beginning with the establishment of the bureaucratized subcounty "ward" (*qu*) under the Guomindang, and the subsequent further elaboration of the subcounty bureaucratic apparatus in the "commune" or township (*xiang*) administration in the People's Republic. The numbers of officials paid by the state have expanded geometrically, from the 25,000-odd of the late Qing to the millions of cadres on state salaries in the post-1949 party-state—5 million in "governmental and public organizations" (*jiguan tuanti*) by 1979, and 10 million by 1989 (11 million in 1999 and slightly fewer in 2002, the latest year for which official statistics are available; see *Zhongguo tongji nianjian*, 1990: 114; 2005: 125). Elaborate bureaucratic rules, regulations, procedures, and paperwork have accompanied that unmistakable process of bureaucratization.

Given this obvious process of bureaucratization, it is easy to overlook the simultaneous persistence of aspects of the minimalist tradition of the imperial and Republican periods. Village "government," called "collective" government before the Reform era, in fact displayed many characteristics of the earlier minimalist method. The lowest level of state-paid cadres was the commune (township) level; the village cadres (i.e., production brigade and production team cadres) were not funded by the central state, but rather were conceived as self-funded—they "ate collective grain" instead of "state grain." They were, moreover, representatives of villages at the same time that they were agents or "officials" of the party-state. To be sure, the new party-state used the party apparatus to control such village leaders, with a reach well past where the formal state apparatus stopped. The party branch committee of the village was thus the Communist equivalent of the old village head, and it was subject to an unprecedented degree of centralized control. Nevertheless, much remained of the old practices, for members of the party branch were almost invariably members of the village community itself, deeply engaged with the village's interests, and inevitably identified not just with the party-state but also with their home village.

Rural governance in contemporary China in fact needs to be understood as an interaction between bureaucratization and the older minimalism, not just as characterized by one mode or the other. Village ("brigade") elementary schools provide one illustration of the complex history of the two. From the start of the rural education movement of the twentieth century, as we have seen, villages participated actively in the development of village schooling. Most village schools were started and funded principally by the villages themselves. The state set the guidelines, reviewed the schools, and sought to develop some measure of standardization, but within that context, the schools were mainly sustained and run by their communities. Much remained of that tradition after 1949, though a much higher degree of state control was imposed. In the Cultural Revolution period (1966–1976), especially, the formula of *minban gongzhu*, or "people-operated (i.e., by the brigades and the communes) and state-assisted," became paradigmatic, driving an unprecedented rise in universal education in the countryside (Pepper, 1996: 414ff.). Villages by and large administered and maintained their own schools, under state-set guidelines. Most even hired their own teachers, providing at least part of their pay in collective workpoints. Through this system, nearly universal primary school education was provided at close to no cost to almost all rural people, even if rural minban schools tended to be of a much lower academic standard than elite urban schools.

In the Reform era, however, new stresses from marketization and from declines in village and township government revenues (relative to their tasks) have brought semiformal rural education to a state of crisis. Free universal education was replaced by a money-driven system of high tuition fees and miscellaneous charges. Schooling became a heavy financial burden that many rural people could not afford. Budget shortfalls in townships and villages led to delayed payment or nonpayment of teachers' salaries, failure to meet assigned quotas of teachers, extensive reliance on cheaper substitute instructors, and so on, with the result that the quality of education declined sharply. The entire system, in fact, teetered on the verge of collapse (Li Liang and Xu Tonghui, 2005).

The central government has therefore recently proclaimed its intent to provide nine years of mandatory primary and junior middle schooling free, and the Ministry of Education has called for incorporating all of the nation's 3.8 million village school teachers into its regular budget to guarantee them a certain standard of pay ("Jiaoyubu," 2005). Such changes will likely be accompanied by greater national standardization and control of village schools, with a corresponding drop in semiformal participation by the local community.

Today, rural education seems poised before choosing a path through, or perhaps entering the whirlwind of, these different methods. One approach is the free minban education system provided by the brigades and communes of the earlier Mao period, with minimal state interference; another is the prohibitively expensive and malfunctioning system that succeeded it, after it was corrupted by the Reform era's marketization; and a third is the new twenty-first-century model of a bureaucratized welfare state, which would provide all with nine years of mandatory education, fully funded by the state. Just how this mix of the past and the present will work out remains to be seen, but it is possible that the older semiformal approach—state initiative plus community participation (based on local, self-interested commitments to public service, as opposed to a desire simply to make money)—may yet play a role. A similar logic may also apply to health care, currently also priced out of the reach of most rural people (Song, Xiong, and Zhang, 2003).[8]

These observations may also be expanded to cover general rural governance. The collective brigades and communes of the Mao era successfully provided virtually free education and health service, and impressive public security, but at the cost of lower standards and excessive "totalistic" control of village populations and economies by the party-state.[9] It was a paradoxical combination of a highly bureaucratized totalistic party-state with the semiformal minimalist approach of old. Indeed, rural governance under Mao may be seen as containing a strong strain of antibureaucratism, linked to the slogan of "simplify administration" (*jianzheng*) dating to the Yan'an period. The governmental apparatus of the Cultural Revolution might well have been more totalistic than the bureaucratized Communist party-state in its efforts to control culture and mentality, but it was surely more minimalist in terms of its degree of reliance on the formal state apparatus. Pointing out these commonalities by no means ignores the obvious differences between Maoist-movement politics and old-style minimalist governance.

8. Yang (2006) makes stimulating suggestions regarding a new "third way" model for public health.

9. "Totalism" (*quanneng zhuyi*) is preferred by Tsou Tang over the old term "totalitarianism" (*jiquan zhuyi*) (Tsou, 1994: 222ff.).

Reforms of the 1980s at first drew successfully on the combination of good village leadership and new market stimuli to drive "rural industrialization" and an impressive rise in the incomes and standards of living of rural people, but under marketization local governance gave way to the dictates of profit and careerism. First, as the party's importance shrank and calls for village self-governance grew louder, village and township cadres came to exercise much greater latitude than in the pre-Reform era. Indeed, beyond basic tasks like tax collection and birth control, to a considerable extent local governance often no longer focused on doing what the party asked but only on avoiding what the centralized party-state explicitly forbade. But as the morality of public service broke down, local cadres became ever more careerist and self-serving. Widespread abuses arose in local government (especially at the provincial and county levels) in the requisitioning of land (*zhengdi*) for enterprises and for real estate development, as the governments or individual officials sought to enrich their coffers, enhance their supposed administrative accomplishments (*zhengji*), or both; in the sales of state-owned enterprises to private owners for local government or personal benefit; and in the uses of arbitrary power to back such endeavors and suppress protest and opposition. These abuses occurred with relative impunity, as increasingly the bureaucratic apparatus of the party-state intervened only when state-set targets were not met or when disputes arose. The *shangfang* system—"appealing to superior authorities" by letter or in person—became overloaded with villagers' complaints against individual cadres or various levels of local governments.[10] The most severe of the abuses may be seen as combining the worst features of Communist totalism and traditional minimalism to create a kind of new-age local bureaucratized patrimonialism.

In the new century, a new model of local governance seems to be on the rise with the call for replacing the old controlling-extractive state with a public-service welfare state. The agricultural tax has been abolished, and the central government has declared its intent to overhaul rural education and health services. But the transition to the new model will not be easy and will likely bring many unintended consequences. Village cadres are increasingly becoming no more than salaried personnel, supported by appropriation from above rather than by taxes on the local communities—a change that might be considered suggestive of Weberian "bureaucratization" or "rationalization." But it is occurring as community resources and tax revenues fall markedly and the roles and functions of the village and township cadres sharply decline. (As they no

10. Since the promulgation in 1990 of the new Administrative Litigation Law, the courts have offered some remedy against abuses by agents of the party-state (Pei, 1997). To date, however, the more informal *shangfang* system remains the principal recourse of common citizens who suffer such abuses.

longer collect taxes, they lack the resources and authority to provide public services; if policies should relax, they may also do less in birth control.)[11] The danger is that the bureaucratization of village governance may be merely formal and not substantive, with its elaborate paperwork not matched by real work, as one recent investigation has reported (Dong, 2006: part 3). Whether the upper levels of the bureaucracy will be able to completely absorb and take over the provisions of public services remains to be seen.

In the highly industrialized and globalized China of today, of course, much of the imperative for a "Confucianized Legalism," which had been intended to meet the demands of an agrarian state, no longer obtains. The size of the bureaucracy is no longer constrained by the limited tax revenue generated by a predominantly agricultural economy. And modern needs, for education and health care as well as for transportation, marketing, and communication infrastructures, will force the new state to differ greatly from the old. Centralized minimalism can be relevant only if it can play a role in the current transition from a controlling-extractive state to a public service state. Nevertheless, the early twentieth-century precedent in self-governance and locally generated public services might yet prove instructive—and despite its totalistic excesses, so might the Mao period's use of central initiatives plus local participation, based partly on the minimalist governance tradition of old. Popular participation in, and control over, projects of local interest could also serve to strengthen community bonds that have been so dramatically weakened by the pervasive marketized atomization of recent decades. Given the long-term persistence of a peasant economy and of villages, simple reliance on the Western-style model of a bureaucratized welfare state may not be the complete answer.

It might be well here to recall the topic of community mediation that was the subject of the last chapter. As has been seen, despite all the sea changes of the past century, the pre-1949 informal mediation system as well as the post-1949 semiformalized cadre mediation system have both shown great resilience in present-day China and continue to make up an integral part of the total legal and governmental system.

For our purposes here, the important point is that changes in governance within the People's Republic cannot be understood simply in terms of our modern Western-derived categories of "bureaucratization," "rationalization,"

11. After the collective units were dismantled, education and health services for a time were supported by special local levies imposed under the township (*xiang* and *zhen*) governments. But those were eliminated in 2003 (for the express purpose of lightening the burden, *jianfu*, on the peasants). For a couple of years, the shortfall was made up by an expansion (a near doubling) of the agricultural tax; but the formal elimination of that tax in 2005 in effect completely "hollowed out" the township governments in terms of tax revenues and finances (Zhou, 2006).

and "modernization," or their opposites (e.g., de-bureaucratization). We need to also think in terms of the legacy of centralized minimalism and the method of administration by semiofficials and by dispute resolution that were so much a part of imperial and twentieth-century governance in practice.

There are obvious overlaps among the concepts discussed above: Weber's patrimonial bureaucracy, Michael Mann's high despotic and low infrastructural power, and "Confucianized Legalism." We might associate high despotic or centralized power mainly with Legalism, and minimalist governance mainly with Confucianism. We might also associate bureaucratic rule mainly with Legalism, and patrimonial rule (with its imperative for minimalism) mainly with Confucianism.

But these models tell more about the institutional structure and intent of government than about its actual operation or practice, and it is the latter that arguably lends real substance to the former. We must distinguish between the formal structures of government and the operational realities of governance, between governmental institutions and administrative practice. The imperial Chinese state apparatus, I have suggested, indeed needs to be seen in terms of the apparently paradoxical combinations of bureaucracy with patrimonialism, high despotic power with low infrastructural power, and Legalism with Confucianism. Yet it is the minimalist method of governance—that is, relying on semiformal personnel and doing no more than resolving disputes if and when necessary—that truly captures the operative realities of the imperial Chinese state at the crucial locus where it met rural society, which I have called "centralized minimalism." As has been seen, much remained and still remains of that tradition in Guomindang, Communist, and Reform-era governance. While new-age imperatives for a welfare state may render much of the old minimalism irrelevant, its tradition of semiformal governance and of state initiative plus local participation may yet play a role in China's ongoing search for its own distinctive political modernity.

4

Divorce Law Practices

The Origins, Myths, and Realities of Judicial "Mediation"

DISCUSSIONS OF CHINESE LAW CAN lapse easily into an either/or binary between Western modernism and Chinese tradition.[1] Neither point of view leaves much room for what might be termed "modern traditions"—that is, "traditions" forged in nearly two centuries of China's coping with its protracted contact with the West. In these times of the collapsing of Communist states and of "post-Communist" "transitions," there is even less room for considering revolutionary traditions. Yet there can be no question that Maoist tradition continues to powerfully shape Chinese justice today.

This chapter argues that divorce law practices made up the core of what might be termed "Maoist justice," which is the most distinctive part of contemporary Chinese civil law and indeed of the civil justice system as a whole.[2] They tell us about the origins, myths, and realities of judicial mediation in China. Divorce court mediations in China are very different from what we

1. The recourse to binarism is perhaps best exemplified by the debate in China between those calling for wholesale Westernization and those preferring to look to "indigenous resources." For an example of the modernist position, see Zhang, 2001. The "postmodernist-nativist" position is best represented by Liang (1996) and Zhu Suli (1996). For a discussion of what might be termed the "angst" of China's legal history studies and lawmaking, see Tian (1996).

2. Contemporary Chinese law sometimes separates out "family law" from "civil law"; this narrow conception of civil law is shown, for example, in the 1986 General Principles of Civil Law. On the other hand, civil courts in practice routinely handle marriage, divorce, and other family law cases, and it is this sense of civil law—employed also in Republican Guomindang law, based on the 1900 German Civil Code—that I use here. "Civil justice," in my usage, covers both codified law and legal practice, as well as the justice system generally, both formal (courts) and informal (community mediation)—that is, both judicial and extrajudicial.

commonly associate with the English word "mediation," as well as from traditional Chinese mediation. They also differ markedly from how they are officially represented. In the end, they can only be understood as practices that evolved out of the special circumstances of the Chinese Revolution.

The chapter is based on a total of 336 civil cases that I have collected, of which 216 concern marriage and divorce. They come from two counties, which I call A (near Shanghai City) and B (in northeastern Hebei Province). In gathering the cases, I attempted to draw a more or less random sample at regular intervals: for county A, 40 cases for each of the years 1953, 1965, 1977, 1988, and 1989; and for county B, 20 for each of those years, plus an additional 40 cases from 1995 to gain a glimpse at what happened in the 1990s, a decade in which divorce requirements relaxed. (Changes after the 1990s are taken up in the next chapter.) Two hundred of the 336 cases were gathered by photocopying the complete case files, including both the "main file" (*zhengjuan*), open to litigants, of written records of interviews with the litigants, their relatives, and neighbors and of court hearings and court-conducted meetings, and the closed "supplementary file" (*fujuan*), containing confidential materials such as records of interviews with the leaders of the litigants' work units and the internal "closing report of the case" (*jie'an baogao*) written by the head judge after reviewing all available materials. The remaining 136 cases were abstracted and outlined by hand at the archives. The chapter also draws on interviews with judges and lawmakers to supplement the information in the case records.

The first important departure of this study from past English-language scholarship is its use of a substantial number of archival records of actual cases, which the normal restrictions on relatively recent materials make difficult to access. The approach adopted here emphasizes actual legal practices rather than declared intentions of the law or representations of the legal system, whether official or popular. In addition, instead of just narrating what was done, I attend also to "the logic of practice," including those principles evinced in practice, even if not explicitly stated in the laws.[3] Marriage and divorce law in contemporary China, it will be seen, has come to operate by its own distinctive logic.

My approach and perspective are above all historical: I study contemporary justice not just synchronically but also diachronically, focusing on the process by which the civil justice system is formed and changed. Thus my approach emphasizes both practice and the history of practice as an open-ended process

3. Bourdieu meant these concepts to provide a way beyond the old binaries of objectivism and subjectivism, structuralism and voluntarism, but he failed to apply his own ideas to his study of the Kabylia peasants of Algeria (Bourdieu, 1977: 114–58), which is mainly structural and synchronic, and did not consider practice as process over time. My own preference, no doubt partly due to my bias as a historian, is for the study of practice as historical process.

that cannot be reduced to any simple construct such as tradition, modernity, or revolution.

This chapter, finally, brings together two areas of inquiry that have largely been treated separately in the past literature. We have, on the one hand, a substantial body of scholarship dealing with the nature of the post-1949 Chinese civil justice system, especially its great emphasis on mediation (Cohen, 1967; Lubman, 1967, 1999; Palmer, 1987, 1989; Clarke, 1991), and, on the other hand, works detailing marriage laws and their consequences (Meijer, 1971; Johnson, 1983; Palmer, 1996; Diamant, 2000). But little attention has been paid to the fundamental interconnections between the two. I propose to show how the former has been decisively shaped by the latter.

Maoist Justice

Past scholarship is right to point to mediation as the central characteristic of contemporary Chinese justice. But the term "mediation" can give a very misleading impression of the real nature of Chinese courts.[4] I begin by outlining official representations and giving a quick chronological overview, then provide a detailed illustration of the workings of a Maoist court on divorce, and finally characterize and analyze the practices of Chinese court mediation.

The Centrality of Mediation

The primary official claim about judicial mediation in China is that it is the cornerstone of the formal civil justice system. It is pointed out that as late as 1989, on the eve of the major changes in the legal system that occurred in the 1990s, 80 percent of all civil cases in the nation handled by the courts were mediated, and just 20 percent adjudicated (*Zhongguo falü nianjian*, 1990: 993). Even in 2000, more than two decades after the shift away from Maoist-style civil justice had begun, official figures still show mediated cases roughly equal in number to adjudicated cases (*Zhongguo falü nianjian*, 2001: 1257; see also Lubman, 1999: 270–71). As Wang Hanbin, chair of the Law Committee of the National People's Congress, put it: "Using mediation to settle disputes among the people and civil lawsuits is a fine tradition in the judicial work of our country" (Shanghai shi lüshi xiehui, 1991: 56). It is touted as the distinguishing characteristic of Chinese civil justice, past and present.

The emphasis on mediation is readily evident in divorce cases involving unilateral (contested, or ex parte) petitions. For one thing, the Marriage Law

4. Clarke (1991) and Lubman (1999: chaps. 8, 9) point out the complexities of "mediation."

of 1950 stipulated that mediation be attempted before a contested divorce petition could even be considered by the courts. According to Article 17, "Divorce shall be granted when husband and wife both desire it. In the event of either the husband or the wife insisting upon divorce, it may be granted only when mediation by the sub-district (*qu*) people's government and the sub-district judicial organ has failed to bring about a reconciliation." And this attempt usually followed an effort by the village or work unit at a more informal mediation process. Furthermore, "In dealing with a divorce case, the district or city people's court must, in the first instance, try to bring about a reconciliation between the parties. In case such mediation fails, the court shall render a verdict without delay" (Hubei caijing xueyuan, 1983: 17–18; Marriage Law, 1959).[5] In other words, even after extrajudicial mediation, the courts themselves must first try mediation before they can consider approving a contested divorce petition.

In cases in which there was "mutual consent," mediation to save the marriage did not come into play. The law, as we have seen, provided simply: "Divorce shall be granted when husband and wife both desire it." Though in some of the cases studied, permission was denied even when both parties jointly petitioned for divorce,[6] in most cases it was granted. When such mutual consent was present, the court's role was limited mainly to working out the specific terms of the settlement. If the parties agreed on the specifics worked out by the court, the case would be categorized as "mediated divorce" (*tiaojie lihun*); if they could not be brought to agreement, and the court had to resolve the dispute, the case would be categorized as "adjudicated divorce" (*panjue lihun*). That kind of mediation, which I will consider separately, was very different from the "mediated reconciliations" (*tiaojie hehao*) that are the focus here.

Chronological Overview

The court mediation required in ex parte divorce cases could be imposed either loosely or very strictly. Its application was rather loose in the early 1950s during the movement to put an end to old-style "feudal" marriages: namely, bigamy or polygamy (*chonghun*), female slaves (*binü*), *tongyangxi* (i.e., the practice of bringing a young girl into the home to be raised as a

5. The texts of the marriage laws are of course widely published. I rely here on the convenient compilation of source materials done by the Hubei caijing xueyuan, using the translation produced by the semiofficial Foreign Languages Press in Beijing. Alterations to these translations are made when necessary, and are so noted.

6. For example, in a case from county A in 1977 involving a party member (A, 1977–20), the "organization" (*zuzhi*; i.e., the party) took the position that the couple should set a good example for others and not divorce; that ended the matter.

prospective daughter-in-law),[7] marriages in which brides were purchased (*maimai hunyin*), and parentally imposed marriages (*baoban hunyin*). A petitioner could circumvent court-imposed mediation if he or she could convince the court that his or her marriage fell into one of those officially proscribed categories. By the close of the 1950s, however, since these specific forms of marriage were thought to have been largely done away with, divorce petitioners could no longer pursue that avenue (INT95-JP-1). In the 1960s and 1970s, the mediation requirement was so strictly applied that contested petitions were routinely denied in favor of vigorous efforts at "mediated reconciliations."

The requirement was relaxed somewhat under the 1980 Marriage Law, which guaranteed petitioners the right to choose to proceed immediately to the courts, without first going through mediation by the local government or the "sub-district" judicial agency: "When one party insists on divorce, the organizations concerned may try to effect a reconciliation, or the party may appeal directly to the people's court for divorce." But the court was still instructed to undertake mediation before granting divorce: "In dealing with a divorce case, the people's court should try to bring about a reconciliation between the parties. If the emotional relationship of the couple has truly ruptured (*ganqing que yi polie*), and when mediation has failed, then divorce should be granted" (Article 25) (Hubei caijing xueyuan, 1983: 41; Marriage Law, [1980] 1987).[8]

In the 1990s, the restrictions on divorce were further relaxed as a result of the "Fourteen Articles" issued by the Supreme People's Court on 21 November 1989; among other changes, they instructed the courts to grant divorce when a petitioner files for a second time, even if he or she had been the offending party in an extramarital affair (Article 8) (Zuigao renmin fayuan, 1994: 1086). Thus did the Supreme Court order an end to the long-standing practice of always denying the suit of an adulterous party against a spouse's opposition. As two judges of county A explained, that practice had been thought of as a way of punishing the offending party (INT93-9). But the easing of divorce restrictions in the 1990s was followed by new amendments, passed by the Standing

7. Neither of the two commonly used English terms for *tongyangxi*—"child bride" and "adopted daughter-in-law"—is quite accurate, as I have pointed out elsewhere (Huang, 2001: 160n). "Child bride" suggests that the girl was married very young, which was generally not the case. "Adopted daughter-in-law" is also misleading, for no formal process of adoption took place. I therefore use the original Chinese term throughout.

8. The Chinese term *ganqing* has no exact English equivalent. In the semiofficial Foreign Languages Press version, this stipulation is translated as "In cases of complete alienation of mutual affection," which is close. But *ganqing* allows for gradations—"very good" (*ganqing henhao*), "poor" (*buhao*), "ruptured" (*polie*), and so on—while "mutual affection" does not. Here and later in the chapter I will render *ganqing* as "emotional relationship," or simply "relationship," which seems to me to come closest to capturing the meaning of the Chinese term.

Committee of the National People's Congress on 28 April 2001, that again made requirements for ex parte divorce petitions more stringent.[9]

Reviewing the half century of divorce legislation and practices under the People's Republic of China (PRC), we might see the more stringent period, the 1960s and 1970s (and even the 1980s), as exemplifying what we can call in shorthand "Maoist justice," and the move away from those stringent requirements as characteristic of the more permissive or "liberal" Reform period.[10] That indeed is how practicing judges in China conceptualize the differences (INT93-9). Our first task here, then, is to clarify the Maoist baseline of PRC divorce law practices.

Procedures and Methods Illustrated

The Maoist court, as has been seen, was expected to favor active mediation rather than outright adjudication in divorce cases. Yet this "mediation" was not, as the English term would suggest, a process in which two adversarial parties, free of coercion, voluntarily worked with a disinterested third party to try to arrive at an agreement. Instead, Maoist mediation employed distinctive methods and a variety of subtle and not-so-subtle pressures, as well as material inducements, in ways that would be astonishing in an American courtroom.

The Maoist procedures were pushed across the nation and standardized in the years after 1952, when a vigorous campaign was launched to put an end to Guomindang court practices, dubbed "handling a case in isolation [from society]" (*guli ban'an*) and "handling a case by sitting in the courtroom" (*zuotang ban'an*) (INT93-8, 9). In Maoist court practices the judges, after talking with the petitioner and the defendant individually, were expected to "investigate" (*diaocha*) the facts of the case themselves, not just to render decisions in the courtroom. Doing so usually entailed going to the residence and workplace of the petitioner and defendant and talking to their "leaders" (*lingdao*). For rural petitioners, these might include the party branch secretary and brigade head; for urban petitioners, the factory head, school principal, party secretary, and

9. The amendments on divorce focused on the question of how to determine whether a couple's relationship had truly reached a point of rupture (*ganqing que yi polie*). They are quite conservative; for example, one situation that warrants the judgment that such rupture has occurred is "separation for two years" ("Guanyu xiugai 'Zhonghua renmin gongheguo hunyinfa' de jueding," passed by the Standing Committee of the Ninth National People's Congress, 28 April 2001; Chinese text available on the Web at www.people.com.cn, accessed August 2004). The new regulations governing (marriage and) divorce registration ("Hunyin dengji tiaoli"), enacted by the State Council on 1 October 2003, took the liberalizing step of removing the requirement for certification from the village or work unit, but only for uncontested divorces of mutually consenting parties.

10. Of course, these terms do not apply to the height of the Cultural Revolution—in county A, the years 1968 to 1974 (INT93-9)—when the courts largely ceased to function.

the like at the relevant work units. The judges would also talk to "the masses" (*qunzhong*), such as relatives, neighbors, and coworkers. They would seek to ascertain the facts and background of the situation, focusing especially on the nature of the marital relationship and its main problems ("contradictions," *maodun*). Usually, they would also inquire into the character and general work and political "performance" (*biaoxian*) of the parties in question, factors taken into account in the court's posture toward the case. Then the court would call in the parties concerned, usually first individually, to seek common ground and concessions required for agreement. This process would include not just the couple but also the parents, other important relatives, and the local leaders. Finally, if and when the terms of a "reconciliation" (*hehao*)[11] had been more or less worked out, the judges would convene a formal "reconciliation meeting" (*hehao hui*), often involving the local leaders and relatives as well. As part of the "mediated reconciliation," both parties would either sign or endorse the verbatim record of the meeting or execute a more formal "mediation agreement" (*tiaojie xieyi*).

A detailed look at one example will illustrate how things were done. In county B, on 5 September 1977, a twenty-five-year-old peasant woman of poor peasant family background, who had married four years earlier, filed a formal petition with the county court for divorce (B, 1977-16). She had written the petition herself, in grammar-school-level language and calligraphy.[12] As she tells it, she had married another peasant, who lived with his widowed father. The father-in-law had been nice to her at first. Then, about half a year after she had married into the household, and while she was sick, he feigned taking care of her, claimed to know enough to be "half a doctor," touched and felt her (*mo*) in various places, and promised to buy her things if she would just accommodate him. When she rejected his advances, he became nasty and ill tempered toward her, found fault with her in everything, and once even beat her. As for her husband, she said, he sided with the father and became angry with her and beat her when she said anything against his father.

There had been numerous arguments and fights between her and her husband for the past three years. Their marital problems had been mediated in the village by the brigade and team cadres along with their relatives. On that occasion, when everyone was gathered, she had told them what her father-in-law had done. According to her complaint, he denied it at first, but after two days and evenings of discussions guided by the mediators he eventually admitted his actions. Still, the mediators urged her to give him another

11. Two different characters are routinely used in the expression: he meaning "harmonize, reconcile," and *he* meaning "unite, put together," plus *hao* (good).

12. The cases collected also contain examples of complaints written by a court scribe or judge rather than by the complainant (e.g., B, 1965-2).

chance, and one of them even went to see her mother to persuade her to help the young couple to reconcile. But things only got worse after that, and her father-in-law continued to find fault with her. Her husband was afraid of his father, and on one occasion when his father beat him in a dispute over some missing meat soup, he even took poison to kill himself and was hospitalized for two months. She had gone back to her natal family in April, and had lived there for the past three months. She was now seeking a divorce.

In accordance with the usual procedures, she came to court in person two and a half weeks later, on 23 September, and reiterated these complaints orally in a meeting with one of the judges. The interview was recorded verbatim in a "written record of reception" (*jiedai bilu*), to which her thumbprint was affixed.

Two days later, on 25 September, the defendant husband too came to court for an interview to give his side of the story (also in accordance with the usual procedures). He confirmed some of the facts told by his wife—primarily, that his father had behaved inappropriately toward her. The father was in the wrong there, he said. He also confirmed that he was very much afraid of the old man and had indeed tried to commit suicide when his father beat him over the meat soup. But he pointed out that his wife had a weakness for nice clothes and was unhappy when his father refused to allow her to spend money on such luxuries. In addition, after he injured his lower back in the recent earthquake (the Tangshan quake) and became unable to work, their financial situation had deteriorated, increasing the tensions in their relationship. According to him, she complained that he was useless and refused to get up in the morning to cook breakfast. He was opposed to divorce, however, and hoped that he and she could build a house for themselves entirely separate from his father's house. Then most of their problems would disappear, he said. All this, too, was recorded in a "written record of conversation" (*tanhua bilu*).

At this point, the judges entered the picture to begin their work toward reconciling the couple. On 15 October, just three weeks after the wife's in-person visit to the court, the chief judge (*shenpanyuan*) and a "people's assessor" (*renmin peishenyuan*) of the court "went down" to the couple's village to investigate the case.[13] They first interviewed the brigade party branch secretary, who was rather critical of the wife. According to him, she was known by neighbors to be somewhat lazy; she also sometimes would secretly cook "a small pot" on the side for herself (rather than "a big pot" for the entire family, as was proper). She had complained crudely that her husband's "penis is not hard,"

13. Except for the simplest civil cases handled by a single judge, the "collegiate court" (heyiting) for a civil case comprised three members; they might include one or two lay judges or *renmin peishenyuan* (people's assessors), along with one or two professional judges (*shenpanyuan*).

and once even beat him with the help of her sister, but then later claimed that he was the one who had beaten them. As for the father-in-law, the secretary noted, he was rather stingy and talked dirty; it seemed quite possible that he might have behaved inappropriately toward his daughter-in-law. He, along with his own father, had indeed beaten the husband over something as trivial as meat soup that somehow went missing, and thereby caused him to take poison. But the root of the problem, the secretary said, was that the couple was in difficult financial straits and they didn't really know how to maintain a household. Otherwise, they had no great insurmountable "contradictions" in their relationship. This interview was recorded verbatim, in a "written record of interview" (*fangwen bilu*).

Next the judge and the assessor talked, on the same morning, with the local "chair of security and defense" (*zhi[an]bao[wei] zhuren*) and the deputy team leader of the husband's production team (who, as the lowest-level cadre, was closer to the family than the brigade secretary). They had been involved, they said, several times before in mediating between this couple. And, surprisingly, they reported that there was division of opinion within their own brigade party branch. Their view of the situation was different from the party secretary's: they were more critical of the father-in-law and less critical of the woman. Even though her father-in-law denied having made improper sexual advances toward her, they knew that he had a history of such behavior: when he was working as a tailor, he would improperly touch the women who had gone to him to have clothes made, until in the end no one went to him any more. The wife's problem was that she was a bit lazy and didn't like to go to work; that was known among her coworkers. But on balance, they said, the relationship of the couple was actually not bad (*ganqing buhuai*).

The judge and the assessor, as was standard, also talked with "the masses"—in this case, a twenty-nine-year-old uncle of the husband who was living in the same compound. This uncle had been party to the division of the household between the father-in-law and the young couple. At that time, the wife had asked for the sewing machine, and it was agreed that though the father-in-law would be allowed to use it, the machine itself would be given to her. Outside of that, the uncle confirmed much of what the others had said about the father-in-law, as well as about the wife. Asked by the judge to analyze the root of the contradictions, the uncle replied that it was their financial situation. Even though they had divided up the household (*fenjia*) and separated from the old man, they were not really able to support themselves.

After interviewing the village's above-mentioned leaders and masses about the couple, the judge and the assessor met with the forty-nine-year-old father-in-law of the petitioner. The judge, it is clear from the "written record of conversation," at this point already had drawn fairly firm conclusions about the father-in-law from the other investigative interviews. At the meeting, the father-in-law began by denying that he had molested the young woman. But the judge directly contradicted him, saying unequivocally that he and the juror had investigated and learned, not just from his daughter-in-law but also from "society" itself (*shehui*, an even broader and more elevated category than "the masses"), that his behavior toward his daughter-in-law "is improper" (*bu zhengpai*). Still, the father-in-law tried to deny he had done anything wrong, saying that he liked to joke around but had no sexual designs on his daughter-in-law. The judge, however, pronounced with finality that on this issue the father-in-law must henceforth pay close attention and do away with "bourgeois political thought." He added, somewhat threateningly, that such corrections would "work to your benefit in the future" (*jin hou dui ni you haochu*).

The judge then went on to lecture the father-in-law about his "rather severe problem of feudal thought and attitudes (*sixiang*)" when it comes to familial relations, declaring,

> There has been no place for Mao Zedong thought. . . . Your son dares not go against your wishes, and has no freedom at all. . . . Everything [you do] is completely of the old feudal ways, and is opposed to the new society's law. . . . You have direct responsibility in your daughter-in-law's clamoring for divorce (*nao lihun*). If this problem is not handled well, divorce might well be the result, and the one who suffers in the future will be you.

After this stern moral-ideological lecture, the judge continued: "You have now admitted in principle that you are responsible, but you have not yet arrived at a clear summation in concrete actions. You should consider things carefully, and talk about them this afternoon."

In the afternoon meeting, the father-in-law pointed out that when he had divided up the household with the young couple in the previous year, he had let them have more than 300 catties of grain, retaining just 40 for himself, and that he had paid for his son's hospital expenses (after having driven the young man to take poison). When the judge pressed him on what he was willing to contribute toward a new house for the young couple, he said that the maternal uncle was giving them a bench, and he himself had a tree ready to use and other "things," not specified. The judge concluded: "We will call all of you together. Would you be willing to acknowledge your mistakes and discuss things with them?"

On this same day, 15 October, another judge, the junior member of the team, went to the wife's village to investigate. He asked about the woman as a worker and a person, inquiring into her "political performance." The informant, whose identity is not noted in the very brief written record of interview (obviously, this judge was less thorough than the other), said that it was not bad and that all her family members were well liked, had no conflicts with others, and were good workers. Next the judge talked to the woman's father, in a conversation preserved in another written record of conversation. He repeated the same complaints as his daughter and said he was therefore in favor of the young couple's divorcing. Upon this testimony, this junior judge asked, "If we can reeducate your in-laws, would you tell your daughter to go back?" And before the man had a chance to answer, the judge instructed him: "Urge her (*quanquan ta*) to do so." After the father replied, "I am just afraid they [the husband and his father] will not change," the judge responded, again rather officiously: "From your attitude and the way you think [*sixiang*, that all-encompassing Maoist term], it is evident you have no faith. Do you not want your daughter to have a happy life?" The father said, "What if they beat my daughter again after a few days?" The judge answered, "If they do not change after we educate them, then we'll resolve the divorce problem." He ended the interview with an order: "Work on her."

Four days later, on 19 October, the senior judge and the assessor went to the wife's village to talk with her. She continued to insist on a divorce, reiterating her complaints. After letting her have her say, the judge focused on the division of grain when the household was divided: as already noted, the young couple had been given most of it, and the father just 40 catties. He asked: "Do you think he behaved properly on this?" She agreed yes, on that matter. Then the judge went on: "You don't want to live with your father-in-law, he too does not want to live with you. What then is the problem?" She replied, "Well, after the division, we still ate together for several months." After this exchange, the judge took her to task for what he considered her failings: "The way you tell it, even when your father-in-law behaves well, he's still no good. We think you lack correct thinking, blaming others for everything, and do not have an objective, true-to-the-facts attitude (*shishi qiushi de sixiang*), and do not respect the old and love the young. This is a bad case of bourgeois thought." When she countered with her complaints, the judge kept on attempting to make her more conciliatory and applying moral-ideological pressure: "We have investigated. When your husband was in the hospital, your father-in-law paid for the expenses. Of course, after the household division, your father-in-law did not give you much financial help, but you should see that things are difficult for him too."

The judge summed up for the wife their view of the situation and their plan of action:

> According to our investigation, your fights [with your husband] are not serious. Your financial difficulty is the main problem. As far as the "government" (*zhengfu*) [the term by which judges referred to themselves before litigants] is

concerned, we have worked with the commune and the brigade, and intend to make appropriate arrangements. At the same time, we have done education work with your father-in-law. Now your father-in-law intends to provide some bricks and wood, and your maternal uncle some more wood, and the brigade the land, to enable you to build a house. We want from all different directions to get you two to reconcile. Henceforth you two should build up your spirit of supporting yourselves independently (*zili gengsheng*) and lead a happy life (*haohao guo rizi*). Go and think about this.

Thus, the judge combined moral-ideological suasion with official pressure and material inducements (clearly arranged on the side with the brigade and commune leaders, even though these informal actions are not otherwise recorded in the official case record).

On the same day, this senior judge also met with the wife's father, in the presence of the village's deputy chair of security. As usual, he first allowed the other to speak. When the father grumbled in general terms, to the effect that his in-laws could not be trusted, that they said one thing and did another, the judge asked him to be concrete and specific. After he had aired a number of specific complaints and repeated his daughter's "request to the government to break up the marriage" (*yaoqiu zhengfu gei wo duankai*), the judge said, "Let us now go over the findings from our investigation. . . . The foundation of their marriage is quite good. The beginning of [your daughter's] demand for divorce was when the father-in-law misbehaved." He continued, "Through our criticism of the father-in-law, he has arrived at new understanding, agrees to give them bricks and wood for building their new home, and do all he can to help them financially. At the same time, the brigade has considered the problem of their livelihood, and will make appropriate arrangements."

Then, three days later, on 22 October, the senior and the junior judges and the assessor met at the wife's natal home with her and her mother, along with the local chair of security. This time the judges began by saying that they had criticized the father-in-law, and the husband had begun building a new house. They then asked: "What do you say?" The wife, whose position had clearly been softened by the two-pronged attack of both material inducements and moral-ideological pressure, exerted not just by the two judges in the formally recorded sessions but also by the village leadership and her relatives, said, "If the 'government' [again, *zhengfu*] succeeds in reeducating them, then we are most grateful." The judges continued to push her: "They have indicated that they are repentant and will change their ways (*huigai*). . . . We are here to urge you to go back. . . . If they do not change, then you can divorce later." They also asked, "Have you any other requests?" When the wife replied, "I can go back, but I want the sewing machine," the judges told her that the machine would go to her but the father-in-law should be allowed to use it. They explained:

because of his lame leg, he needed the machine to enable him to earn an income, thereby reducing the young couple's burdens. The wife said she would like a guarantee in writing that the machine would go to her, and the judges agreed to her condition.

On 27 October, the main judge returned to the couple's village and met once more with the father-in-law, and then the husband, in the presence of the village's chair of security. The father-in-law confirmed that he would not try to control the young couple from then on. And, he said, his son had borrowed 40 yuan to build the new house, which he had paid off, in the interest of "unity" (*tuanjie*). The husband told the judge that the new house was already completed,[14] and his father had supported the construction. The husband himself had gone twice to his wife's natal home; she agreed to come back, and his mother-in-law did not say anything to the contrary. "What else?" the judge asked. His wife was worried that he might not get transferred to work on the brigade's seed farm (*zhongzichang*), a better and less onerous job, but he thought that once they were living apart from the same compound as his father, there would be fewer causes of fights.

The stage was set for the final resolution, which took place a week and a half later on 6 November at the couple's new house—just two months after the wife had filed the initial petition. Present were the two judges and the assessor, the husband and wife, the father-in-law, the brigade's party branch secretary, the brigade head, and the chair of security. The judges opened the meeting by saying that the whole family was gathered that day for this "family reconciliation meeting" (*jiating hehao hui*). They announced that through work they had done in the two brigades, they had effected the reconciliation of husband and wife. First, turning to the father-in-law, they said, "You need to overcome your feudal thought, get rid of the old set of ideas, and let the two of them live their lives, not try to control everything. You should try to create good family relations." Then the party branch secretary and the brigade head in turn exhorted the three members of the family to do self-criticism (*ziwo piping*) and to make things right from then on. The father-in-law said what was expected of him: that he was grateful for "the concern shown by the leadership," that all the problems were the result of his old thoughts and of attitudes from the past, that he was determined to change, and that he would not make the same mistakes again. The wife-petitioner, for her part, said: "From here on, whoever is right should be the one listened to. I am talking straight. Please don't mind me in the future. We have borrowed a lot of money in building the house. The sewing machine must be given to me." And the father-in-law said, "I will

14. Houses in North China villages at this time were still relatively simple; they were typically built, with the help of other villagers, in just a few days (Huang, 1985: 220).

take responsibility for the debts incurred in building the house, but I must be allowed to use the machine." The husband said simply: "I will listen to what the leadership says. In the future I will correct my weaknesses, and make the relations good." The judges then concluded the meeting: "Today you have all exchanged opinions. We think it is very good. We hope that from now on you will all unite (*tuanjie*) and [using the dominant political slogan of the time] 'grasp revolution and promote production' (*zhua geming, cu shengchan*)." The husband, wife, and father-in-law all signed and affixed their thumbprints to the transcript of the mediation meeting (*tiaojie bilu*); this took the place of the formal mediation agreement used in many of the other cases.[15]

To Americans accustomed to thinking in terms of very high court fees and hourly charges by attorneys, this procedure must seem incredible. First of all, the two Maoist judges did not sit at the courthouse but rather brought the court to the site of the dispute. In the course of their work on the case, they made a total of four separate and joint trips to the couple's village of domicile and two to the wife's natal village. Separately or jointly, they conducted five formally recorded investigative interviews to ascertain for themselves the roots of the couple's marital discord and the possibilities for reconciliation, before they felt ready for the final meeting of resolution. And this accounting leaves out their numerous informal discussions with the brigade and team leaders to work out the specific material inducements.

The mediation also involved a mixture of coercion from the court and voluntary compliance from the couple. The judges used moral-ideological suasion as

15. Not all efforts at mediation ended by so completely satisfying the Maoist court's wishes. Sometimes the petitioner insisted on divorce despite the court's uses of ideological and moral suasion, official pressures, and material inducements. In that event, judges would sometimes resort to still more high-handed methods. Consider the following example, drawn from county A in 1989 (A, 1989-14). A local schoolteacher filed for divorce on the grounds that his wife frequently criticized and berated (*ma*) him as well as his parents, that she was no longer interested in having sex with him, and that their relationship (*ganqing*) had completely ruptured (*polie*). She, however, made clear that she was opposed to divorce. The judges investigated at both their work units. They determined that the couple's relationship had been quite good, and that their main problem had to do with their sex life. Her lack of interest stemmed from the pains she had suffered following a difficult Caesarean section—a problem that they thought could be overcome. The judges therefore used moral suasion, lecturing the petitioner that as a teacher, he should set a good example for others. They also tried to apply political pressure through the party organization, to which the man had applied for membership. And they offered the couple a material inducement: the principal of the school would arrange a position for her there, so the two of them would have more time with one another. But the husband remained adamant. The judges then informed him, "You do not have sufficient reason to seek divorce. If you insist, the court will adjudicate against divorce. We hope you will consider things carefully." Faced with that declaration, the petitioner gave in at the second mediation meeting convened by the court, presumably because he knew that nothing he did would make any difference in the court's decision. He withdrew his divorce petition (*chesu*). Judges interviewed in county A, however, say such a tactic is something of a last resort. The judges generally preferred to couch their statements in terms of what the law said, leaving no doubt as to how the court would adjudicate but stopping just short of the kind of bald threat used in this case (INT93-B-4).

TABLE 4.1
Outcomes of Divorce Cases

No Divorce *(buli)*		Divorce *(lihun)*	
by mediation *tiaojie hehao* *(tiaojie buli[hun])*	by adjudication *panjue buli(hun)*	by mediation *tiaojie lihun*	by adjudication *panjue lihun*

well as material inducements, exerting their own pressure and calling on that of the community and family to produce the results they sought from the couple and their relatives. They drew freely on the special ideological authority of the party-state and the powers of the local village leadership to effect a reconciliation.

Other Categories of Outcomes

Before a closer analysis of the characteristics and methods of the Maoist divorce court is undertaken, it would be useful to briefly place "mediated reconciliations" into the broader context of all divorce cases (schematized in table 4.1). After this type of case, reported also as "mediated no divorce" (*tiaojie bu lihun*), the other main outcome on the side of no divorce was "adjudicated no divorce" (*panjue bu lihun*); on the side of divorce, the outcomes were "mediated divorce" (*tiaojie lihun*) and "adjudicated divorce" (*panjue lihun*). These are the main categories according to which statistics on divorce lawsuits are kept.[16]

Adjudicated No Divorce

Sometimes petitioners remained insistent despite strong pressures from the court, and the court would end up adjudicating outright against divorce. National statistics (discussed further below) suggest that such occurrences were relatively rare in comparison with mediated reconciliations. Simple adjudication for no divorce most commonly involved third-party affairs. In one case from county B in 1965 (B, 1965-11), for example, the petitioner was a thirty-year-old man who had been born a peasant and had become a factory worker in nearby Tangshan. He was also a member of the party. He had married ten years earlier, in 1956—by the order of his parents, he said. The marital relationship had never been good; his wife had not been nice to his parents. She caused his mother so much aggravation, he claimed, that his mother's frustra-

16. Cases sometimes moved from one category to another during the process of litigation. Strong initial opposition to divorce could give way to agreement to divorce. In parallel to this shift, earnest efforts by the court to mediate could give way to acknowledgment that reconciliation was not feasible. In a 1977 case from county B, for example, both of these processes were evident (B, 1977-11).

tion and anger was partly responsible for her death. More recently, his wife had driven his father to leave the house. He therefore sought a divorce from this backward and ill-tempered woman. His letter of complaint was literate and had the tone of one good party comrade writing to another. The wife, however, took a strong position against divorce. In her testimony, she said that their relationship after marriage had actually been very good (*ganqing henhao*), that she had been good to his parents, and that she suspected he was having an affair with someone in Tangshan.

The court set out to investigate, talking with the leaders at the man's factory and the woman's village, as well as with selected members of the masses (especially his relatives and neighbors), in accordance with the usual procedures. In the course of their investigations, they learned that she, not he, was telling the truth: in fact the couple had married of their own free will, and their relationship had been very good. Only recently, since 1964, had the husband begun to treat the wife badly, a change entirely due to his involvement in an extramarital affair with a widow. That affair was the true reason for his insistence on divorcing his wife. The court's conclusion: the husband was guilty of a severe case of "liking the new and tiring of the old" (*xixin yanjiu*). They therefore adjudicated outright against divorce.

As two county A judges explained to me, judges commonly believed that the offending party involved in an affair with a "third party" (*disanzhe*) should never be "rewarded" with permission to divorce. Though the petitioner was often insistent on divorce, seeking to leave one spouse to gain another, the adulterer was seen as the offender, the other spouse as victim. This was the standard posture of the courts of the time, not questioned and criticized until the Supreme Court issued its Fourteen Articles in 1989 (INT93-9). In the example above, the court adjudicated against divorce (*panjue buzhun lihun*) on the grounds that it was acting "to protect the interests of the woman and the children" (*wei baohu funü yu zinü liyi*).

Mediated Divorce

The great majority of those cases that resulted in a divorce involved mutual consent. Generally the other party readily agreed to the divorce, or at least did not object strongly. In such situations, usually the court simply helped to work out the terms of a mutually agreeable settlement. The case would then be categorized and counted as "mediated divorce" (*tiaojie lihun*). To give a simple example from county A in 1965 (A, 1965-14): The husband was a soldier who had been away from home for some years, and the wife had an affair. He sued for divorce, and initially she claimed to be opposed. Upon learning that her husband was adamant, she said that she was not really opposed but did not want to go back to her natal home; instead, she wanted to stay at her in-laws until she found a new husband, and she wanted custody of their eight-year-old child. The court then mediated between the two sides, and got them to agree to the following terms: (1) the wife would be allowed to stay in her present home (a room at her in-laws' house) for another year; (2) she would have custody of the child, who would be supported by the father, during that time; and (3) the items in their room would be used by her until she left. Both parties agreed to the terms, and a formal "civil mediation agreement" (*minshi tiaojie shu*) was drawn up. The case was therefore recorded as a mediated divorce (see also B, 1988-12).

Adjudicated Divorce

In the other type of case ending in divorce, much rarer than mediated divorces, the court adjudicated for divorce. This usually happened when one party did not genuinely oppose the divorce but rather objected for what the court considered unacceptable reasons—usually to extract concessions or simply to spite the other, and not out of any genuine wish to reconcile. In one case from county B in 1965 (B, 1965-5), for example, the divorce petition had been filed at the end of 1964. The wife had gone back to her natal home the previous February and had not returned since. Her complaint was that her husband lied, was ill tempered, and was dull-witted. By making inquiries among the leaders of the brigade and her neighbors and relatives, the court learned that she was a good worker and was well regarded in the village; it also learned that the main problem was her feeling that her husband was dull-witted. The brigade and commune leaders had tried to mediate several times, but to no avail. The husband said he opposed the divorce, but not in the hope of effecting reconciliation; his desire instead was to have the 250 yuan given to her family before the marriage paid back and to be given all of their community properties.

The court's meetings with them to try to work out the specifics of a settlement to which both could agree were fruitless. Since the court considered the demand for full repayment of the betrothal-gift amount and for possession of all community properties unreasonable, it proposed that the man settle for 30 yuan. He refused. The court therefore adjudicated for divorce, stipulating what it considered reasonable terms of settlement. The judgment was formally rendered, and the case was classified as an "adjudicated divorce" (*panjue lihun*).

The National Picture

In many ways, 1989 was the final year when Maoist principles and methods predominated in divorce law practices. As already noted, in November of that year the Supreme People's Court issued what have come to be known as the Fourteen Articles, which made the conditions for divorce less stringent. The full implementation of those articles in 1990 and after would alter the divorce system substantially. But in 1989, the courts brought about no fewer than 125,000 mediated reconciliations and adjudicated outright against divorce in just 34,000 instances. Those numbers include almost all first-time ex parte divorce petitions. We should not be misled by the apparently high number of divorces that year: 377,000 mediated divorce cases and 88,000 adjudicated divorce cases (*Zhongguo falü nianjian*, 1990: 993).[17] As the sample cases suggest, the great majority of divorces were effected by mutual consent; the courts mainly helped to work out the specifics of each settlement. Adjudication came into play when a couple wishing to divorce could not agree on a settlement acceptable to both. In addition, the courts granted a certain number of second-time divorce petitions, anticipating the changes to come in the 1990s. But they rejected almost all seriously contested divorce petitions, either by bringing about a mediated reconciliation or by simply adjudicating against divorce.

By contrast, in 2000, at the close of what might be considered the "liberal" decade in divorce (and before the move to amend the marriage law in ways that tightened divorce requirements), the courts resorted less frequently to mediated reconciliations (just 89,000) despite the greater total number of petitions—1,300,000, compared to 747,000 in 1989. But the number of adjudications against divorce more than tripled, to 108,000 (*Zhongguo falü nianjian*, 2001: 1257).[18] Maoist practices, in other words, were no longer predominant.

The reason for the increase in adjudicated denials of divorce was explained by two judges interviewed in county A. The Maoist model, as we have seen, called for the judges to go down to the village to investigate and then marshal community and familial as well as official pressure to effect reconciliation, in a very time-consuming process. In the first case described in detail above, the judges made six trips to the couple's two villages to investigate and mediate; such expenditures of time became increasingly unrealistic as caseloads mounted in the 1990s with the return of litigation over other civil matters such as property, debt, inheritance, and old-age support. In response, litigants in the 1990s were allowed to present the evidence at court, and the judges sitting in court adjudged the case on that basis. This method, dubbed "investi-

17. In most of the remaining cases (about 122,000), the petitioner withdrew his or her petition (*chesu*) or the case was discontinued (*zhongzhi*) for another reason—for example, successful extrajudicial mediation. All numbers in this discussion have been rounded to the nearest thousand.

18. The 2000 figures do not separate out divorce petitions from "other marriage and family" cases, as did the 1989 statistics. The number of total divorce petitions here is arrived at by assuming the ratio of divorce to nondivorce marriage cases was the same in 2000 as it had been in 1989: roughly 6 to 1.

gate by adjudging at court" (*tingshen diaocha*), had been equated in the 1950s campaigns with the Guomindang courts (INT93-9).

The changes that came in the 1990s should not be exaggerated, however. As is well known, the party's gigantic propaganda apparatus often leads officials in the People's Republic of China to exaggerate the magnitude of change involved in each twist and turn of policy. My informant judges thus tended to frame as dramatic the shift from the Maoist style of justice requiring on-site investigations to the new practice of investigating by adjudging at court. Though such descriptions may give the impression that the treatment of divorce had changed completely and abruptly, from unilateral divorces being almost unheard-of to easily obtained, the national statistics tell a very different story. Much of the old resistance to unilateral divorce persisted, even in the "liberal" 1990s; and mediated reconciliations, though certainly reduced, still accounted for a large number of cases, with almost as many adjudicated denials in 2000 (89,000) as in 1989 (108,000). Furthermore, even these changes, that to divorce-prone Americans suggest rather modest movement in the direction of relaxing the laws limiting divorce, provoked a counterreaction and a demand for more stringent regulation. In the twenty-first century, as chapter 5 will show in detail, the Maoist coercive "mediated reconciliations" will largely fall into disuse, but the other kinds of court mediations that grew up alongside it will remain an important feature of the Chinese legal system.

The Characteristics of Maoist Divorce Law Practices

Ideologically and conceptually, the Maoist practice of mediated reconciliation is distinguished by its presumption that the party-state should intervene in the "(emotional) relationship" (*ganqing*) of couples. Superficially, this presumption calls to mind old notions of "totalitarianism"—the control by the party-state of matters that in Western societies these days are normally considered to be in the "private sphere," outside of public or government purview, though historically very much the concern of religious authorities (notably the Roman Catholic Church). It resonates with familiar Maoist formulations, most especially the idea of "nonantagonistic contradictions among the people"—the notion that once the "antagonistic contradictions" of class enemies are removed or set aside, the resulting society will live in socialist harmony (Mao, [1957] 1971; Han, 1982; see also Yang and Fang, 1987). The party was to take an active role in promoting such harmonious relations, including those between couples.

Some of the distinctively Maoist ways in which the party-state has intervened in marital relationships may not be so apparent. We have seen in the cases discussed above the subtle and not-so-subtle uses of party power. Coercion and high-handed pressure were ever-present but never used alone. There was a great deal of emphasis on moral-ideological "criticism" and "education." Part of the key to this kind of control was to "elevate" (*tigao*) small details of daily life into larger political principles, especially during the years surrounding the Cultural Revolution: hence relatives and neighbors were labeled "the masses" or even "society"; patriarchal attitudes and behavior, "feudal"; laziness and a desire for nice-looking clothes, "bourgeois"; work and lifestyle, "performance" subject to political evaluation by the party; and so on. In addition, moral suasion and ideological education were accompanied by genuine material inducements, such as the new house for the troubled couple discussed above (as well as a new job for the husband).

Less obvious still, perhaps, are the subtle ways in which the representatives of this system exercised their power. The judges routinely presented themselves, or at least allowed themselves to be perceived as, "the government," acting not just as officials of the court but rather in unison with the entire apparatus of the party-state's authority; hence local cadres were always made a part of any effort at mediation. And the emphasis on involving relatives and neighbors in the process also broadened the sources of the pressures brought to bear on each couple to the larger community and society.

Moreover, the use of political power was carefully cloaked so as to not appear arbitrary. Thus, the questioning of selected members of the masses was called "visits" or "interviews" (*fangwen*); "conversations" (*tanhua*) were held with the principals involved in a case. The senior judge in the case discussed above, unlike the junior member of the team, always encouraged the litigants to air their grievances and issues first, before stating his own position. And that view was presented as not merely an opinion but the objective truth, gleaned from a thoroughgoing investigation. The latter was itself a distinctive hallmark of Maoist governance and exercise of power, as exemplified by Mao himself—for example, his classic "Report on an Investigation of the Peasant Movement in Hunan" and his investigation of Xingguo County and Caixi and Changgang townships, "Preface to Rural Surveys" (Mao, [1927] 1971, [1941a] 1971). "Investigation and research" (*diaocha yanjiu*), far from being undertakings limited to academics, became integral to the language in which judges (and cadres) used and exercised power, and indeed to the Maoist "mass line" style of leadership and governance (discussed below). Mao's saying "If you have not investigated, you have no right to speak" (*meiyou diaocha jiu meiyou fayan quan*) (Mao, [1941b] 1971: 206) became one of the dicta most often repeated by judges, cadres, and officials throughout the Maoist era. Conversely, once such investigation and research had been done according to the accepted methods (interviewing trusted party leaders and the masses), the investigator's opinion carried much more weight. Thus a judge can refer to his findings as having the authority of society and the government.

The entire language associated with marriage and divorce itself conveys the posture taken by the party and the pressures exerted on those seeking divorce. The word for "reconciliation" is *he* (either "to harmonize" or "to unite") plus *hao* (good). And reconciliation is lent political significance by its (political) equation with "uniting (with others)" (*tuanjie*), as we saw above. There can be no mistaking the positive value associated with it. Divorce, in contrast, is the consequence of the "rupture" or "breakdown" (*polie*) of a relationship. And "third parties" who "disrupt" a marriage (*fanghai hunyin*) are offenders, as is the adulterous party; the other is the victim, even if not explicitly so labeled in the Marriage Law. Most of all, mediation is represented as highly desirable, a special attribute of China and Chinese tradition and something that local courts were to strive to maximize.

There was also a distinctive set of rituals associated with the process. As part of the "mass line" of Maoist governance, the judges would invariably "go down" to the village themselves to investigate, never just sit in court and summon witnesses—a style of behavior specifically targeted for criticism under Maoist justice. And the appropriate style for interviews and conversations, we have seen, was not to talk down to the litigants, or their relatives and neighbors, but to elicit their voluntary participation and an honest airing of their views. Perhaps most effective and important, the mediation effort would conclude not just with signed and fingerprinted mediation agreements but also with a mediation meeting, in which each concerned party was expected to announce, before a community public gathering of both the leaders and the masses, his or her plans for how to improve things in the future. Such practices gave concrete meaning to the subtle uses of official and social pressures on the couple to reconcile.

In its intent, method, language, and style, Maoist mediation clearly must not be simply equated with "traditional" mediation. I have shown elsewhere that court mediation in imperial China was mostly nonexistent; magistrates had neither the time nor the inclination to operate in the manner of Maoist judges (Huang, 1996). To be sure, extrajudicial mediation, such as might be undertaken by community or kin leaders in the village, had echoes in Maoist justice: for example, the use of moralistic language, the ceremony involving the public (i.e., other community members), and so on. But old-style community or kin mediation was predicated above all on voluntary compromise, brought about by a third-party intermediary—someone well respected in the community, to be sure, but usually lacking any official connections (see chapter 2 this volume; Huang, 1996: chap. 3). There was no resort to official coercion, nor anything like the imposition of party policy.

The Maoist Communist Party itself distinguished its mediation practices from the work of old-style mediators, whom it termed mere "peacemakers" (*heshilao*), interested only in working out compromises and lacking a clear-cut position (determined by ideology or policy) as to what was right and wrong. That kind of approach it dubbed unprincipled "mixing of watery mud" (*he xini*) (Han and Chang, 1981–1984: 3.426–27, 669). The Maoist court's attitude toward divorce was unequivocal disapproval, at least until mediation had proved impossible. Nor was the process voluntary in the same way that traditional village mediation had been. The petitioner for divorce might withdraw or give up, but he or she was not at liberty to seek the services of another individual or agency. The petitioner could obtain the desired divorce only by overcoming the local court's posture against divorce, by going through its required procedures of investigation and mediation, and by being subjected to its exercises of power in the distinctively Maoist manner of the Chinese Communist Party. To equate Maoist justice with traditional village mediation, in short, would obfuscate both.

Nor should Maoist mediated reconciliations be confused with conventional American notions of mediation. The so-called mediated reconciliation might in fact be described more accurately as coercive marriage counseling undertaken by the party-state through its court system, with no equivalent either in Chinese tradition or in the modern West. The Maoist Chinese state was unique in its attempts to intervene within a troubled couple's relationship, particularly in actively seeking to improve their emotional connection. This unprecedented enterprise can be best understood by looking at the historical circumstances that led to its rise.

Historical Origins

The Maoist system was shaped above all by two historical processes. The first was the evolution of legal practices from the party's attempt to steer a middle course between its early radical promise on divorce and the realities of strong peasant opposition. The second was the evolution of styles of work in the countryside, where the modern judicial apparatus that had developed in the Republican period under the Guomindang government was absent.

Radical Promise and Rural Realities

The radical promise on divorce dates back to the 1931 Jiangxi Soviet's Marriage Regulations of the Chinese Soviet Republic (Zhonghua suwei'ai gongheguo hunyin tiaoli). It was a period of considerable change in attitudes toward marriage.

Even the ruling Guomindang Party had promised gender equality in its 1930 Civil Code and had instituted relatively liberal standards for divorce (Huang, 2001: chap. 10). The principle of gender equality, at least in the abstract, was not open to question in the progressive climate of the time (and the Guomindang was not behind the Communist Party in laying claim to the mantle of progressivism). Perhaps more immediate and relevant was Article 18 of the 1926 USSR Code of Laws on Marriage and Divorce, the Family and Guardianship, which stipulated that a "marriage may be dissolved either by the mutual consent of both parties to it or upon the *ex parte* application of either of them" (*Soviet Law on Marriage*, 1932: 13; see also Meijer, 1971: 51).

The Chinese Soviet Republic in Jiangxi followed suit in its regulations; Article 9 declared, "Freedom of divorce is established. Whenever both the man and the woman agree to divorce, the divorce shall have immediate effect. When one party, either the man or the woman, is determined to claim a divorce, it shall have immediate effect" (quoted in Meijer, 1971: 281; for the Chinese text, see Hubei caijing xueyuan, 1983: 1–4). That was a far more radical posture than could then be found in any Western countries, where no-fault divorce would begin to take hold only from the 1960s on (Phillips, 1988: 561–72). On its face, this radical provision would allow millions of unhappily married Chinese women and men to obtain divorce on demand, regardless of the wishes of their spouse.

The first retreat from this position came almost immediately and for a very practical reason: the party wished to protect the claims of the Red Army's peasant soldiers to their wives. Thus, the formal (8 April) 1934 Marriage Law of the Chinese Soviet Republic, though repeating the radical provision of the early regulations (now in Article 10), added in the article immediately following: "Wives of soldiers of the Red Army when claiming a divorce must obtain the consent of their husbands" (Meijer, 1971: 283). The need for such an amendment had in fact already been fully spelled out in a 1931 document titled "Plan of Work among the Women," drawn up by the Special Committee for Northern Jiangxi of the Central Committee of the CCP: "We must refrain from imposing limitations on the freedom of marriage, since this would be contrary to Bolshevist principles, but we must also resolutely oppose the idea of absolute freedom of marriage, because it creates chaotic conditions in society and *antagonizes the peasants and the Red Army*" (quoted in Meijer, 1971: 39, emphasis mine). To threaten the interests of the peasant soldiers would be to endanger the very basis of the party's power, as Kay Johnson has pointed out (Johnson, 1983: 59–60).

For the peasants, the considerations at work here are obvious. Marriage in the countryside was a very costly event—affordable only once in a lifetime, given the expectations of customary expenditure and the income levels of most peasants. Allowing a dissatisfied woman to divorce her husband at will would strike not only the enlisted men but also their families as ruinous. To get a sense of the economic implications from the parents' point of view, imagine an American couple divorcing because of a marital spat—after the parents had purchased a home for the newlyweds. Such economic concerns were far more important than the injured feelings of the husband.

Moreover, some women joined the men in opposing unilateral divorce. Within the revolutionary movement itself, it was not uncommon for male Communist Party members to seek divorces from their (peasant) wives, disdained for their ostensible political "backwardness," in order to marry other (urban) women comrades—something that Ding Ling alluded to in her famous 1942 essay criticizing male chauvinism within the party on the occasion of International Women's Day (8 March) (Ding, 1942). That issue would remain contentious even into the 1980s (as discussed below).

Small wonder, then, that backpedaling from support for unilateral divorce was soon rampant. Nowhere were these concessions to popular displeasure more apparent than in the Communist base areas during the subsequent Sino-Japanese War. All dropped the Jiangxi Soviet's formulation, adopting instead provisions similar to those in the Guomindang Civil Code that laid out the conditions under which divorce could be granted, including bigamy, adultery, cruelty or ill treatment, desertion, impotence, and incurable disease. (At the same time, the border regions began to formulate laws based on a couple's emotional relationship, a new conceptual approach to marriage and divorce that would in the postrevolutionary years become dominant.) None repeated the Jiangxi Soviet stipulation that divorce be granted at the demand of either party.[19]

Specific provisions and elaborations to protect the interests of soldiers flourished in base areas as well as in post-1949 PRC legislation on divorce. Both the 1943 Jin-Cha-Ji and 1942 Jin-Ji-Lu-Yu Regulations provided that a petition for divorce from a soldier in the War of Resistance might be brought only when the soldier's whereabouts had been unknown for more than four years (Han and Chang, 1981–1984: 4.828, 840). The central Shaan-Gan-Ning base area did not treat the question of divorce from soldiers in its 1939 Regulations, but its 1944 Revised Regulations required the passage of "at least five years" of "no information from the husband" (Han and Chang, 1981–1984:

---

19. See the 1939 Marriage Regulations of the Shaanxi-Gansu-Ningxia (Shaan-Gan-Ning) Border Area, the 1943 Regulations of the Shanxi, Chahaer, and Hebei (Jin-Cha-Ji) Border Area, and the 1942 Regulations of the Shanxi, Hebei, Shandong, and Henan (Jin-Ji-Lu-Yü) Border Area, in Meijer (1971: 285–87, 288–94 [appendices 3, 4, 6]); for the original Chinese texts, see Han and Chang (1981–84: 4.804–7, 826–29, 838–41); compare the Guomindang provisions, which I discuss elsewhere (Huang, 2001: chap. 10).

4.810). The early 1950s, as we will see below, saw even stronger protections for soldiers.

But in retreating from divorce on demand, the party did not go back completely on its avowed goal of eliminating what it termed "feudal" marriages. In the early 1950s, the party especially targeted bigamy or polygamy, slave girls, tongyangxi, and marriage by purchase and by parental imposition. Many divorces were in fact granted, or marriages nullified, on the grounds that the unions fell into one of those categories, as the sample cases from 1953 clearly illustrate. Thus, in a county B case involving a tongyangxi, the court found: "The feudal marriage system is both irrational and immoral. . . . For this kind of marital relationship to continue would only add to the emotional suffering of both parties." The court therefore adjudicated for divorce (B, 1953-19). Another case involved a couple who had married at a very early age by parental imposition; the court ruled, "Both parties were still young. . . . They could never form a mutually affectionate, respectful, and harmonious family" (B, 1953-7). In a similar case, the court granted divorce because "the marriage had been imposed by the parents while the couple were still young, resulting therefore in the rupture of the relationship (*ganqing polie*) after marriage" (B, 1953-15). Data from Songjiang and Fengxian counties (discussed in the final section) show relatively large numbers of divorce cases each year through the early 1960s; indeed, these levels would not be reached again until the 1980s.

It is clear that obtaining a divorce was easier in the early years of the People's Republic than it later became. The mediation requirement of the Marriage Law, eventually imposed so strictly, was at first not stringently enforced. The movement against feudal marriages in fact created a generally liberal climate for divorce; even petitioners whose marriages did not clearly fall into the targeted categories could sometimes divorce. This liberal trend would end only after the old feudal marriages were thought to have been largely stamped out. Thus, in one case studied, a party cadre petitioned for and obtained a divorce on the grounds that his relationship with his wife had ruptured because she is filled with "backward feudal thought" (*fengjian luohou sixiang*) (B, 1953-1; see also B, 1953-5). Another cadre won a divorce because his wife was "just a housewife, is illiterate, and cannot work." The court granted the petition because "the two parties have different social occupations, and their *ganqing* has gradually ruptured (*zhujian polie*)" (B, 1953-7). And a woman cadre successfully petitioned for a divorce on the same grounds: her husband's thoughts and attitudes were backward, and he even objected to her going to meetings (B, 1953-20). Another woman managed to obtain permission to divorce despite the objection of her soldier husband, after she had gone through several failed attempts at mediation. The court explained its judgment as intended "to spare the two parties emotional suffering in the future, to promote production and avoid tragic consequences" (B, 1953-4).

But her case was an exception. Explanations and directives issued by the Supreme Court during these years show it repeatedly taking the position that when it came to soldiers, divorce was to be denied even if the wives had been tongyangxi (less consideration still was given to wives who had been purchased or married against their will by their parents). It invariably cited Article 19: "The consent of a member of the revolutionary army on active service who maintains correspondence with his or her family must first be obtained before his or her spouse can apply for divorce," a requirement that applied even to those seeking to break off engagements, otherwise not considered binding (Zuigao renmin fayuan, 1994: 1099). As the Court explained in response to a query from its northwest branch, the need for the soldier's consent, even in tongyangxi arrangements, was based on the principle of "the greatest benefit for the greatest majority of the people" (Zuigao renmin fayuan, 1994: 1090), as foundational a notion as the idea of allowing freedom of marriage and divorce.[20]

Yet this process of retreat must be viewed in conjunction with the parallel process of the party's campaign against feudal marriages. There can be no question that the marriage law campaigns of 1950–1953 attacked such marriages vigorously and that divorce practices were greatly liberalized during those years. The best evidence can be found in the scale and intensity of conflicts stemming from rural resistance to the campaigns. According to the Chinese Ministry of Justice itself, as Kay Johnson has pointed out, in each of those years some 70,000 to 80,000 Chinese women and men (mostly women) "committed suicide or were killed because of the lack of freedom in marriage" (Johnson, 1983: 132; *Guanche hunyinfa yundong de zhongyao wenjian*, 1953: 23–24).

To view the 1950 Marriage Law only in terms of its retreat from the radical promise of divorce on demand would be to overlook its important consequences. Indeed, as we have seen, those consequences were quite revolutionary in the context of Chinese rural society. The law's impact could be expected to be greater in the countryside, where the targeted old-style marriages were more prevalent than in the modernized cities. But at the same time, to convey an accurate picture of what actually happened, proper emphasis must be put

20. The actions of the legal system at that time had already been foreshadowed in the border regions. As we have seen, the original 1939 Shaan-Gan-Ning Regulations had not addressed divorce from soldiers, and it had also specifically banned tongyangxi, purchase of wives, and parentally imposed marriages; the 1944 Revised Regulations, however, added the stipulation about soldiers' consent and deleted the ban on tongyangxi, marriages by purchase, and parentally imposed marriages, retaining only the ban on bigamy (Han and Chang, 1981–84: 4.804–7, 808–11). It is thus clear that soldiers were already exempted from divorce on those grounds in the previous decade.

on the party's backpedaling from the Jiangxi provisions to protect the interests of soldiers and peasants. The two processes—a party-led campaign against the most objectionable varieties of old-style marriages and a retreat from the promise of divorce on demand—need to be seen together.[21]

By requiring mediation before contested divorces, the party steered its difficult course between the two competing principles. Divorces by mutual consent, it is clear, raised no concerns, since neither of the parties objected. Obviously, neither denying nor approving all contested divorces was an option: the first meant going back on the party's commitments to freedom of marriage and divorce, and the second was certain to be strongly opposed by rural society. In this context, mediation was an effective compromise. It could be loosely applied when the party wished to emphasize its attack on old-style marriages, as in the 1950s, and strictly applied when the party wished to take a more conservative stance on divorce, as in the 1960s and after. Most importantly, the procedure helped to minimize conflict by providing an institutional avenue through which the opposing voice could be heard and through which the party could try its best to work out, case by case, resolutions on which the two sides could at least nominally agree. In this way, the party tried to remain true to its goal of ending feudal marriages while at the same time minimizing peasant opposition. That, it seems to me, is the true origin and meaning of mediation in legislation about and the practice of divorce.

Rural Traditions Merged with Communist Practices

Though the analysis above explains the widespread resort to mediation in divorce, it does not address the specific methods, style, and form that those practices took. To understand the latter, we must turn to peasant traditions of mediation, and how those were and were not changed by the Maoist Communist Party. The practices need to be understood, in other words, neither as merely traditional nor as merely Communist, but rather as the product of a complex interaction.

The initial historical context is of the rural base areas. Driven underground and out of the cities by the White Terror after 12 April 1927, the party had to rebuild from the ground up after the collapse of the "First United Front." One consequence was its almost complete severance from the modern court sys-

21. In other words, Neil Diamant (2000) is right to emphasize the impact of the 1950 Marriage Law, especially on the countryside, while Kay Ann Johnson (1983) also tells an important story in emphasizing the party's retreat from its Jiangxi Soviet position. But Diamant's argument that the Marriage Law had a greater impact on the countryside than the cities, contrary to what he believes modernization theory might predict, is overly elaborate. He somehow overlooks the commonsense explanation that the old-style marriages targeted by the new law were much more common in the countryside than in the cities.

tem instituted by 1926 in perhaps one-quarter of all of China's county seats by the Republican government. Over the following six years, the new Guomindang national government would extend the modern system to nearly half of China's counties (Huang, 2001: 2, 40–47). The Communist-controlled hinterland fell largely outside these modern and semimodern cities; thus the Communist governments of the Jiangxi Soviet, and later of the border regions, had few models for modern courts and judicial personnel. The Communists were in any case as strongly opposed in principle to the Guomindang system as to the old Qing system. Those base areas, therefore, had to construct their legal apparatus almost completely from scratch.

Over time, a system evolved that drew on both traditional village and new Communist practices. From the former came the emphasis on mediation, predicated on compromise, with its distinctive methods of calling on respected local individuals to persuade disputants to resolve their differences in mutually acceptable ways. Such methods included talking with both sides to listen sympathetically to their grievances, using moral suasion to try to make each see the point of view of the other, bringing in neighbors and relatives when possible to aid in making compromises, and holding public ceremonies such as a meal or gathering to announce and give weight to a settlement.

All these were incorporated into the practices of the Communist Party. In fact, even today cadre mediators often fall back on the Confucian "golden rule" as they attempt to persuade disputing parties: "How would you feel if this were done to you?" (i.e., "What you would not have done to yourself, do not unto others") (INT93-12; chapter 2, this volume; Huang, 1996: chap. 3). Though the traditional meal to mark success was replaced by the mediation meeting, there was still an emphasis on each side publicly stating its concessions (albeit now in the form of Maoist "self-criticisms").

At the same time, distinctively Communist practices shaped the process. Hence the ultimate guide to right and wrong was party principles and policies, not Confucian or traditional popular morality (as discussed further below). Also influencing the procedure were the distinctive Maoist mass line instructions on how urban intellectuals were to behave toward villagers: to listen to them and talk to them as equals; to resort to persuasion, not arbitrary dictates; and to learn to live with and like the peasants, in the "three sames"—living the same, eating the same, and working the same (*tongzhu, tongchi, tonglao*) (Mao, [1943] 1971).

Those instructions were actually an outgrowth of a new theory of knowledge: it entailed learning first from practice, then proceeding to abstract theoretical knowledge, and finally returning once more to practice in order to test the validity of that knowledge (Mao, [1937a] 1971, [1937b] 1971). It was also linked to a method of study, which relied on systematic investigation through interviews with "the masses" (Mao, [1941a] 1971, [1941b] 1971). Together these elements formed what is arguably a distinctive revolutionary, and modern, epistemology (Huang, 2005).[22]

That epistemological posture in turn gave rise to a set of dos and don'ts for party members. Excessive reliance on theory to the neglect of concrete circumstances was criticized with a host of terms, such as "dogmatism" (*jiaotiao zhuyi*), "subjectivism" (*zhuguan zhuyi*), "party eight-leggedism" (*dang bagu*), "command-ism" (*mingling zhuyi*), "giving orders blindly" (*xia zhihui*), and even "mountaintop-ism" (*shantou zhuyi*). Single-minded preoccupation with facts to the neglect of theory, by contrast, is subject mainly to one criticism: "empiricism" (*jingyan zhuyi*). The Maoist prioritizing of practice over theory is of course best expressed by its mass line, which included emphasizing to cadres the need to obtain voluntary compliance and agreement from the populace (see also Mao, [1942] 1971). The new epistemology was thus accompanied by a theory of governance.

This blending of village traditions of mediation with Maoist party practices resulted in the unique mediated reconciliation of Maoist justice. Its distinctive methods and styles evolved from the interaction of the party and the village in the base areas. In other words, the truth about divorce law practices, especially those involved in mediated reconciliations, is told in those processes of change, and not in any simple dichotomous binary such as tradition/modernity, the village/the party, the peasant/the modern state.

From this interaction emerged what was called the "Ma Xiwu model." Ma Xiwu (1898–1962) was a superior court judge of the Shaan-Gan-Ning base area whose style of work Mao singled out for praise in 1943. In time, the "Ma Xiwu way of adjudging cases" (Ma Xiwu *shenpan fangshi*) came to be a kind of shorthand reference to all that Maoist justice stood for, not just in marital but in all civil disputes. Judges were to go down to the actual site of the dispute (*xianchang*) and investigate (*diaocha*) the real facts of the case. In so doing, they were to rely especially on the masses, who were thought to have "the clearest eyes" ([*qunzhong*] *yanjing zuiliang*). Once in command of the facts of the situation, the judges would work to dispel the "contradiction." And mediation accepted by both parties was thought to be the best way to resolve conflict and prevent its recurrence. The entire process was summed up in a three-clause formula: "rely on the masses" (*yikao qunzhong*), "investigate and do research" (*diaocha yanjiu*), and "mainly use mediation" (*tiaojie weizhu*)—the procedures, style, and rituals illustrated in the detailed case

22. Li Fangchun (2005) makes stimulating suggestions about a distinctive "revolutionary modernity." Under that rubric could be included this new epistemology, which is distinctive from both Confucian epistemology and Western Enlightenment epistemology. It also includes a new view of history from the ground up.

examined above. The Ma Xiwu style of justice, as we have seen, was aggressively propagated nationwide by the party in 1952 and after to replace what it considered unacceptable Guomindang practices. In 1954 Ma himself became the vice president of the Supreme People's Court (INT93-B-3; INT93-8, 9; see also Yang and Fang, 1987: 131–45).

Conceptual Basis

The Maoist divorce law practices outlined above were closely tied to the notion that the couple's ganqing, or emotional relationship, was *the* crucial basis for marriage and divorce. When divorce was denied, the grounds were that the ganqing was still good enough to repair; when it was granted, the grounds were that no such repair was possible. Even though that formulation did not appear in law until 1980, it was widely employed in practice from the 1940s onward. It served to provide at once the justification and conceptual spaces for those practices. Indeed, Maoist practices of mediated reconciliation can be understood only in light of the conceptual underpinnings that evolved with them.

Ganqing had not been a part of the original 1931 Jiangxi Soviet Marriage Regulations. Those, as noted above, were basically a copy of the Soviet Union's 1926 code, granting either partner in a marriage the right to ex parte divorce. That provision is rooted in the notion of marriage as a union entered into freely by two equal parties, which the will of either should be sufficient to dissolve. By the War of Resistance period, as we have seen, the border regions had already abandoned that original formulation in favor of something closely resembling the Guomindang's Civil Code of 1929–1930, which in turn was modeled on the German Civil Code of 1900. That code framed marriage as a civil contract, and divorce as a response to breaches of that contract in what might be termed "matrimonial offenses": adultery, willful desertion, ill treatment, and the like. Its treatment of marriage was itself based in the Western tradition of secular marriage law, which had moved away from the Roman Catholic Church's doctrine of marriage's sanctity and indissolubility (Phillips, 1988). The Chinese Communist Party, perhaps unwittingly, thus became to some extent heir to that tradition.

But even as the party of the base areas echoed the Guomindang approach, it was at the same time developing a formulation based on ganqing, which was not in Guomindang law. Because, on this understanding, the couple's emotional relationship was the most basic element of marriage, divorce should occur only if that foundation had never existed or had been undermined, resulting in a "fundamental incompatibility in the relationship" (*ganqing genben buhe*) of the couple. Similarly, in contemporary Soviet law, divorce was viewed as justified if the marital relationship was such as to make continuance of the marriage impossible, and hence divorce necessary (Sverdlov, 1956: 37ff.). This approach to divorce also had some affinity with the no-fault doctrine that was to become dominant in the West in the 1960s and 1970s, whereby "marriage breakdown" (a breakdown blamed on neither party) was made a sufficient criterion for divorce, replacing the "matrimonial offenses" found in earlier legislation (Phillips, 1988: 561–72).

At the same time, the notion of ganqing was distinctive. It emerged from the wish to replace both the Qing and the Guomindang conceptions of marriage. In the former, marriage was the acquisition of a wife by the husband's family: the husband alone was granted the right to divorce. More accurately, he had the right to "terminate" (*xiu*) his wife's marital relationship to him because of her failures, enumerated by the law as seven conditions: barrenness, wanton conduct, neglect of the husband's parents, loquacity, theft, jealousy, and chronic illness (Statute 116; cf. Huang, 2001: 164). (In practice, of course, there were social-cultural constraints against divorcing one's wife, legal theory notwithstanding.) Fundamental to the Communist Revolution's vision of a new social order was a new conception of marriage, based on love and the partners' free choice rather than parental will. Such a notion led naturally to the emphasis on ganqing as the sine qua non of a marriage.

At the same time, the party rejected (after a brief flirtation with it) the Guomindang's "capitalist" or "bourgeois" formulation of marriage as a kind of civil contract, a private matter outside the purview of the state, to be dissolved when that contract is breached. As the authoritative *Comprehensive Explanations* of China's laws puts it: "In our country, marriage is not a kind of civil contract, but rather a husband-wife relationship that is affirmed by law, including both property relations and human relations" (*Zhonghua renmin gongheguo falü shiyi daquan*, 1992: 510). It also rejected recent Western formulations of no-fault divorce, whose justifications for ending a marriage—the breakdown of the marital relationship because of "irreconcilable differences," or because the parties no longer "love" one another—became in the party's view mere rationalizations for cavalier bourgeois attitudes toward marriage and divorce. For the Communist party-state, the ganqing formulation was to emphasize freedom of marriage and divorce as well as long-term commitment to marriage.

To be sure, the 1950 Marriage Law of the People's Republic made no reference to ganqing, although the concept had been present in embryonic form in almost all of the wartime marriage legislation in the border regions. It also omitted any list of the kinds of offenses that would warrant divorce, as had been included in earlier laws. Instead, the 1950 Marriage Law focused almost entirely on procedures, an emphasis consistent with the Soviet Code of Laws on Marriage, the Family, and Guardianship (promulgated 1926; amended

1936, 1944, and 1945) (Sverdlov, 1956). It was also consistent with the party's wish then to stress practical considerations over principles.

Nevertheless, much contemporary evidence makes clear that almost all jurists and judges of the time had ganqing in mind as they applied and interpreted marriage law. Thus, the Ministry of Justice of the North China People's Government in 1949, as it in effect summed up the experiences of the base area governments, explicitly called a "fundamental incompatibility" in the couple's "(emotional) relationship" (*ganqing genben buhe*) the crucial criterion for deciding whether to grant divorce (Han and Chang, 1981–1984: 4.875). And the Supreme People's Court, in multiple explanations and directives issued in the early 1950s, referred repeatedly to the principle as determinative in interpreting and applying divorce law (see, e.g., Zuigao renmin fayuan, 1994: 1056, 1064). Perhaps most conclusively, the sample of divorce cases from 1953 shows that divorce petitions, as well as court decisions, were already routinely couched in those terms. The belief that ganqing was the proper foundation of marriage justified divorce when marriages involved bigamy, slave girls, tongyangxi, purchased wives, and parental imposition, as seen above.

It was only after the movement against feudal marriages was concluded that requirements for divorce tightened, and the mediation requirement came to be applied very strictly. In time, a fairly standard set of procedures and categories developed in connection with the ganqing formulation, already illustrated in the sample cases summarized earlier. The judges involved would always seek to ascertain first the foundation and the history of the couple's relationship, grading it "very good" (*henhao*), "good" (*hao*), "not bad" (*bucuo*), "average" (*yiban*), or "poor" (*buhao*). Thus, a couple who had been forced into marriage by their parents, against their own will, would be viewed as having a poor foundation. And if during the course of their married life they had fought frequently, their history would be seen as poor. These assessments would help the court to decide whether the relationship had truly ruptured (*ganqing polie*)—that is, whether divorce would be justified. On the other hand, a finding that the relationship's foundation and history were good would justify the court's insistence on a mediated reconciliation or its outright denial of divorce.

It remained for the 1980 Marriage Law to formally incorporate the idea of ganqing as something distinctively Chinese and deeply rooted in practical experience. As Wu Xinyu—deputy chair of the Legal System Committee of the Standing Committee of the National People's Congress, the formal body for writing laws in the People's Republic—explained at the time: "In our draft of the new law, we have added [to the 1950 Marriage Law] the expression 'if the (emotional) relationship has truly ruptured' to [the original sentence that reads] 'and mediation has failed, then divorce should be granted.'" Given the climate of reform, the revision was intended in part to be liberalizing. Wu cautioned, "While we oppose the kind of bourgeois thought that adopts a cavalier attitude toward marital relations and 'liking the new and tiring of the old,' we must not use law to forcibly maintain relationships that have already ruptured. That would only cause those involved to suffer, even for the contradictions to sharpen, and result possibly in homicides." He himself believed that "in the past, our courts in dealing with divorce cases had tended to be too strict" (Hubei caijing xueyuan, 1983: 46).

Wu's position finds ready justification in the plentitude of examples of hopeless Chinese marriages dragging on and on because of a court system overly intent on effecting mediated reconciliations, a state of affairs made familiar to English-language readers by Ha Jin's prize-winning novel *Waiting* (1999), whose main protagonist, the physician Lin Kong, despite his longtime love for his coworker Wu Manna, has little choice but to remain married to his peasant wife even though he tried again and again for divorce—"waiting" for no less than eighteen years before he finally is able to marry Manna. Indeed, improving the emotional relationships of couples is often beyond the power of any court, no matter how intrusive, whether it be congenial or overbearing, well-intentioned or rigidly following policy.

Yet Wu was expressing here just one side of the story. The Women's Federation chose to emphasize the other:

> In recent years, there has been an increase in "liking the new and tiring of the old" behavior, in perfunctory marriages and hasty divorces. Some people, once they have been promoted as cadres, or have moved to the city, or have gained admission to university, discard their old spouses . . . , using "rupture in the relationship" as their excuse. . . . They view proper morality as feudal dregs and worship the capitalist class's "freedom of marriage." We must undertake criticism and education of these people. . . . In real life, divorce often brings hardship to the women and the children. Under the new law we must seriously implement its stipulations about protecting the interests of women and children. (Hubei caijing xueyuan, 1983: 65–66)

That concern echoes the note sounded by Ding Ling some forty years earlier.

In any event, reliance on the idea of ganqing allowed the courts both to loosen divorce requirements for those couples whose relationship offered no hope for reconciliation and to tighten them for spouses who sought divorce out of momentary anger or a wish to replace an old mate with a new. Since any judgment of the quality of a couple's emotional relationship is inexact, the courts could make ad hoc determinations that best suited the circumstances of specific cases and the policy emphases of the moment. In other words, the formulation allowed practical concerns to take precedence over theoretical dictates. As Wu Xinyu put it: "This stipulation at once maintains the principle of freedom of marriage and also gives the courts considerable latitude, and is well suited to the real conditions of our country" (Hubei caijing xueyuan, 1983: 46).

The result is a conceptual framework that was, on the one hand, revolutionary in its origins, in some ways even anticipating today's no-fault divorce practices in the West, but that, on the other hand, grew out of and was enmeshed in practices dictated by the exigencies of the time. It served to justify, first, both the drive to put an end to targeted feudal forms of marriage and the efforts to minimize opposition among peasants and, in the later reform context, both the tendency to liberalize divorce requirements and the wish to conserve marriages. That twin-edged concept and its flexible application, perhaps, is the true "logic of practice" of the court's distinctively Maoist mediated reconciliations. It might also be seen as a major feature of what we can call the "revolutionary modernity" that went into the making of contemporary China.

As a diagnosis born of different and sometimes conflicting purposes and needs, "rupture of relationship" is of necessity elusive and vague. It thus is predictable that the question of exactly what qualifies as a ruptured relationship would become the center of all debates over marriage and divorce legislation in the decades after 1980. Future changes in marriage and divorce law will continue to revolve around that question, a focus that also seems to me part of the distinctive logic of the history of divorce law practices in the People's Republic.

Divorce Law Practices and Civil Justice as a Whole

We are left with a final question: What can this analysis of divorce law practices tell us about contemporary Chinese civil justice as a whole? For an answer, we need to look first at the general profile of civil litigation in the People's Republic.

It perhaps comes as no surprise that divorce cases generally accounted for the overwhelming majority of all civil cases in China, until the later Reform period, when "economic" cases came to outnumber divorce cases. Table 2.2, with data from the Songjiang County Court for the years 1950 to 1990, shows that divorce cases, which constituted about two-fifths of all civil cases in the early 1950s, soon overwhelmed those in all other categories once collectivization and "socialist construction" had largely eliminated land- and debt-related disputes. At the height of the Maoist period, divorce cases made up 90 to 100 percent of all cases. Only in the early Reform period of the 1980s did the numbers of civil actions in other categories rise again to create a profile resembling that of the early 1950s. Even so, divorces accounted for two-thirds of all cases as late as 1990 (when, nationwide, their proportion in all civil cases had declined to about two-fifths; see *Zhongguo falü nianjian*, 1990: 993).

Much the same picture appears in neighboring Fengxian County, another county court for which we have detailed data. (Even though divorce cases are not distinguished from other marriage cases, the data are very roughly comparable with those from Songjiang, since divorce accounted for the preponderance of all marriage cases from the mid-1950s on.) As shown in table 4.2, marriage cases made up about three-quarters of all cases in the early 1950s, but only about two-fifths of all cases in the reformist 1980s. Otherwise, the pattern very much resembles that in Songjiang, with marriage cases far exceeding all others at the height of the Maoist period. In fact, it would not be an exaggeration to say that Maoist civil justice was mainly its divorce law.

As we have seen, a central claim of Maoist justice is that mediation makes up the cornerstone of the entire system. In Songjiang County, for the same years as the cases sampled (1953, 1965, 1977, 1988, 1989), only 16 percent of all civil cases were reported as adjudicated; most of the rest were mediated (69 percent).[23] In Fengxian County, from 1977 to 1985, a total of 2,109 civil cases were reported as mediated and 215 adjudicated, for a ratio of nearly 10 to 1 (*Fengxian xian fayuan zhi*, 1986: 97). In other words, if Maoist justice was, above all, divorce justice, then divorce justice was, above all, mediation justice.

This is not to say that all mediation can be equated with the mediated reconciliations of divorce law practice. A substantial proportion of mediated divorce cases, as noted above, ended in divorce, not reconciliation; but they involved a different kind of "mediation." Again, these by and large were divorces by mutual consent, and the court's role was only to help work out the terms of a settlement—getting each side to make whatever concessions were needed. In that respect, it was quite similar to traditional mediation.[24] Mediated reconciliations, in contrast, required aggressive intervention: the court resorted not just to moral suasion but material inducements and pressures from the family, the community, and the larger society as well as from the judiciary.

In fact, judicial mediation in contemporary Chinese civil justice spans a range of court actions, from the merely pro forma to the aggressively adjudicative and interventionist, all placed into the same broad (and misleading)

---

23. Another 16 percent of the civil cases were withdrawn (*chesu*), discontinued (*zhongzhi*), or otherwise terminated (data provided by the Songjiang County Court).

24. Even in mediated divorces, the court could intervene quite forcefully to bring about a settlement considered fair by legal standards. In one case cited above, the court thought unreasonable the husband's demand for what amounted to a full refund of marriage expenses and for all community properties. When it could not get him to agree, it adjudicated. The difference between the PRC court and a contemporary American divorce court, which is guided by a set of general principles and rules of thumb in deciding the terms of a divorce settlement, is the premium placed by the former system on bringing both parties to (at least ostensibly) voluntarily accept the court's decision.

TABLE 4.2
Civil Cases in Fengxian County by Category, and Marriage Cases as a Percentage of All Civil Cases, 1950–1985

Year	Land[a]	Debt	Marriage	Inheritance	Old-age support	Child support	House	Compensation	Other	Total	Marriage as % of Total
1950	11	49	439	0	7	10	4	1	15	536	81.9
1951	7	34	298	6	0	0	3	1	16	365	81.6
1952	10	43	846	23	4	7	2	0	16	951	89.0
1953	56	83	532	11	0	0	11	0	37	730	72.9
1954	48	51	458	17	0	6	11	0	56	647	70.8
1955	2	15	371	1	0	5	4	0	51	449	82.6
1956	0	8	358	0	0	3	1	0	0	370	96.8
1957	0	6	381	2	3	6	1	2	0	401	95.0
1958	0	12	326	4	0	4	0	8	84	438	74.4
1959	0	3	472	0	0	3	3	2	2	485	97.3
1960	0	0	385	1	1	1	2	0	0	390	98.7
1961	0	0	558	2	0	2	3	1	0	566	98.6
1962	0	1	385	1	0	3	19	2	1	412	93.4
1963	0	3	296	7	0	8	30	5	10	359	82.5
1964	0	9	241	13	4	9	30	1	2	309	78.0
1965	0	5	194	4	5	7	0	2	5	222	87.4
1966–1976 not available											
1977	0	0	51	2	4	2	14	5	15	93	54.8
1978	0	0	56	0	6	2	30	6	22	122	45.9
1979	0	0	96	3	8	0	47	22	38	214	44.9
1980	0	0	72	3	7	0	36	28	22	168	42.9
1981	0	0	137	16	17	7	73	37	30	317	43.2
1982	0	0	179	8	38	14	62	92	64	457	39.2
1983	9	19	181	8	43	10	54	82	64	470	38.5
1984	8	5	227	12	39	11	26	50	42	420	54.0
1985	7	8	173	9	49	16	14	61	75	412	42.0
Total	**158**	**354**	**7,712**	**153**	**235**	**136**	**480**	**408**	**667**	**10,303**	
%	1.5	3.4	74.9	1.5	2.3	1.3	4.7	4.0	6.5	100.0	

Source: Fengxian xian fayuan zhi (1986: 94–95).
Notes: The data for a given year reflect cases concluded by the court, not cases received.
[a] Cases in the 1980s concern use of "residential plots" (*zhaijidi*).

category. At one end, "mediation" really means no more than the lack of active opposition from either litigant to the outcome of a case. Such cases differ little from those in imperial times when litigants were formally required to file a "willing acceptance" (*ju ganjie*) of the court's judgment. The contemporary twist is to represent the outcome as "mediated." At the other end, the court actively inserts itself not just into divorces but also into nondivorce civil cases (see chapter 7). This latter type of court mediation is strictly a product of the Chinese revolutionary process.

As we try to grasp the real nature of judicial mediation in contemporary China, and to sort out myths from realities, the Maoist mediated reconciliations in divorce law practices may be the most distinctive and revealing. They cannot be understood merely in terms of traditional mediation, which was centered mainly in the community and was compromise based. (Judicial mediation, we should recall, was very rare.) Nor can they be understood in terms of Western mediation, clearly separated as it is from the court's adjudication and coercion. The Maoist mediation deployed in the mediated reconciliations of couples, by contrast, was born of a distinctive history of divorce law practices that merged elements of both the traditional and the modern, the peasant and the Communist. It involved a cluster of practices and concepts that included the use of moral suasion, material inducements, and coercive pressures by the party-state and its courts against ex parte divorce in order to minimize active opposition; an organizing concept that held a couple's emotional relationship, ganqing, to be the crucial basis for marriage and divorce; and its logic in practice of terminating old-style unacceptable marriages without good ganqing, while striving to the utmost to conserve new-style marriages based on good ganqing. Those make up the core of Maoist divorce law practices, and hence also of Maoist civil justice as a whole. The next chapter will show that, in the new century, although the original coercive "mediated reconciliation" system has largely fallen into disuse, replaced by a newly formalized system of evidence procedures, other kinds of court mediations that grew up alongside it, especially those involving compromises in no-fault fact situations, remain a distinctive part of the Chinese justice system.

5

"Reform" in Evidence Procedure

Reasonable and Unreasonable Practices of Divorce Law

THE RECENT "REFORM" IN evidence procedure, from the evidence gathering mainly by judges of the Mao period to evidence gathering mainly by litigants today, has greatly impacted all of judicial practice. Even the mediation system of the Mao period has come to operate differently as a result of the reform. Using a sample of forty-five recent (1999–2004) divorce cases from county R in South China, this chapter focuses on the impact of evidence law changes on the practice of divorce law.[1] In this limited sphere, we can see that evidence law reform has not been a simple matter of a "transition"[2] from an old system vesting authority in the judges to a modern system guaranteeing litigants' rights, as was intended in theory, nor a simple matter of persistence of the old system, but rather something with a host of "unintended consequences."[3] The reforms reflect recent social-economic changes and make good sense; they are "reasonable" in the practical meaning of the word. Yet they have also brought negative consequences, the worst being the absorption

1. The cases were filmed by Wu Ruozhi from county R in the southeast coastal region, at regular intervals of one out of every twenty divorce cases. They are cited by the year and registration number of the case (not the archived number) (e.g., 2002: no. 270).
2. The term "transition," *zhuanxing*, generally used intentionally or unintentionally with the assumption that capitalism and legal formalism are the only possible directions of change in China, needs to be problematized. In my view, the future shape of China's "modernization" is still an open question, but it will certainly include aspects of both the "imperial" and the "revolutionary" traditions.
3. From Robert K. Merton to Anthony Giddens, the concept of "unanticipated consequences" or "unintended consequences" has been widely used and comes with much baggage. Here I use the term only in its most basic meaning as conveyed by the surface meaning of the term.

of the new procedures into the bureaucratic system's characteristic disregard of substance for the sake of formalistic appearances.

Recent survey research has shown how the legal system lacks credibility among the populace. In spite of the vigorous efforts by the government to propagate "rule of law" and promote education about law, the majority of the Chinese people remain rather skeptical about the legal system. Judges today actually enjoy less social esteem than those of the Mao period.[4] This chapter may be seen as an inquiry into some of the possible reasons.[5]

From On-Site to At-Court Investigation

The system today is very different from the Maoist system under which judges went to the site of the dispute and investigated through interviews with the local cadres and "masses" (i.e., neighbors, kin, and friends); it relies mainly on investigations at court, with the litigants bearing the principal responsibility for evidence. The 1982 Civil Procedure Law (for trial implementation) still affirmed that the main responsibility for evidence rested with the judges and not the litigants: "The people's courts should, in accordance with the prescribed procedure, collect and examine evidence comprehensively and objectively" (Article 56). But the 1991 Civil Procedure Law changed the provision from "collect and examine" to "examine and verify," and provided that the courts would investigate and collect evidence only "if, for objective reasons, a party and his agent ad litem are unable to collect the evidence by themselves or if the people's court considers the evidence necessary for the trial of the case" (Article 64). The main responsibility for evidence was thus shifted to the litigants. In 2002, the Supreme People's Court issued further rules for civil evidence ("Zuigao renmin fayuan guanyu minshi susong zhengju de ruogan guiding," 2002), now stating explicitly that the litigants are to bear the respon-

4. The reference here is to the study, cited in chapter 2, based on 2,970 questionnaires returned from thirty villages in six counties. It asked informants to evaluate the three different modes for dispute resolution in the countryside—community mediation; upper-level appeal, or *shangfang*; and court litigation—in terms of whether or not satisfaction was obtained. Seventy-three percent rated community mediation results as satisfactory (*manyi*), 63 percent rated shangfang results as satisfactory, and only 37 percent rated court litigation results as satisfactory (Guo Xinghua and Wang Ping, 2004). See also a similar study of Beijing City, with similar findings about the court system (Michelson, 2003). As for the Mao period, we do not have similar surveys but, on the basis of a variety of qualitative evidence, judges clearly enjoyed considerable social esteem, many of them actually attempting to work by the Maoist value of "to serve the people." See chapter 4; see also Wu Ruozhi's report of her interviews with elderly judges (Wu Ruozhi, 2007: 186–89).

5. Because the empirical evidence here is limited to divorce cases, this chapter cannot provide an analysis of the civil legal system as a whole, nor can it include a systematic look at the problem of possible judicial corruption that concerns many people.

sibility for evidence and that they are to suffer the consequences for failure to do so (Article 2).

From the perspective of mainstream legal theory of the modernization model, such a change represents obvious progress, because the new evidence law establishes the rights (and obligations) of the litigants to provide evidence and weakens the authoritarian powers of the judges, consistent with the general ideals of the "rule of law." Such thinking is, of course, valid with respect to criminal justice, in which the government and its agents (including judges, prosecutors, and public security organs) make up one side of a case and the accused the other. If the prerogatives for evidence as well as for judgment rest only with the government side, and the accused has no rights to present evidence, arbitrary use of authority would go unchecked that much more easily, the more so with political crimes. There is thus good reason, from the point of view of protecting the rights of the innocent, to guarantee the right of the accused to present evidence. There is all the more reason to do so in administrative cases where the government is itself the accused.

But civil cases are different. The government is basically a bystander seeking to resolve a dispute between two citizens. It is not party to the dispute and is therefore not in a position of "conflict of interest." Its objectivity in handling the case is not necessarily suspect. The present indiscriminate and unrestricted application of criminal law's logic of rights to civil evidence, to replace the government's collection of evidence with the litigants', has obvious flaws and limitations. It does not necessarily accord with the original intentions of the lawmakers, especially in the sphere of divorce law.

Moreover, there are different requirements for evidence between adjudication and mediation. In theory, while fairness in adjudication must be based on objective facts, mediation could disregard facts and seek only to reconcile the subjective wishes of the disputants. This is another difference between criminal cases (which use mainly adjudication) and civil cases (which use mediation more). That, too, argues against the simple equation of criminal and civil rules of evidence.[6] Of course, truly effective interventions in divorce disputes require command of the real facts. Moreover, in the Chinese court mediation system, the gathering of evidence for mediation and for adjudication is one and the same court process. If mediation fails, the court will simply proceed on to adjudication. Operationally speaking, therefore, although there are different evidence requirements for mediation and for adjudication, we cannot make the kind of clear-cut distinction between the two that can be made in theory.

The wide application of "litigant-ism" (*dangshiren zhuyi*) (i.e., for the litigants to carry the main responsibility for providing evidence) in the civil legal

6. My thanks to Professor Fan Yu for pointing this out.

system today is partly due to the influence of the formalist mode of thinking. It starts from the premise of natural rights. By that logic, the purpose of law is to protect rights, which leads naturally to an adversarial framework of right versus wrong, of either protection or violation of rights. In chapter 7, I shall show that the strength of such a system consists in its unambiguous posture about rights; its weakness, however, lies in its tendency to push into an adversarial frame even those cases in which the fact situations do not involve fault. The adversarial framework also leads easily to the idea of letting the two opposing sides bear separate responsibility for its version of truth,[7] and further to the notion of "courtroom truth," distinguishing between the truth that can be demonstrated under courtroom procedures from substantive truth. In that view, courts must content themselves with operating by the former, and not try for the latter, much less truth in some absolute sense—which can only be known to God. Such a train of thought, of course, leads to that much greater emphasis on procedures.[8]

This is obviously very different from the evidence system of the Mao period. The latter was predicated on the ideal of substantive truth, without distinguishing it from a courtroom truth, what can be demonstrated under legal procedures. What it demanded was for the judges to go to the site of the dispute to investigate and find out the truth and to deal with disputes accordingly, either by mediation and compromise or by adjudication as to right and wrong. Its point of departure was not the protection of the rights of the litigant, but rather to settle a dispute. It does not necessarily have to arrive at a distinction between right and wrong, but rather copes with the dispute according to the actual fact situation. It does not come with an adversarial framework or construction. Its strength is its ability, when no fault is involved, to arrive at a mediated resolution based on compromise and peacemaking; its weakness is that it can easily become wishy-washy about rights violations. Of course, during political movements, like the Land Reform and the Cultural Revolution, political and policy considerations were applied in addition to established norms, which itself became a reason for the turn to litigant-ism today.

The new system has two crucial components in civil actions: (1) the requirement that litigants provide evidence and exchange evidence (in a procedure resembling the American "discovery" system) before the trial, and (2) the requirement that in the course of the trial, after the plaintiff and the defendant each presents his/her evidence, the court asks the other side to respond (followed then by the mediation or adjudication phase of the trial)

7. Though it can also lead, as in Continental law, to the "judges' authority-ism" (*faguan zhiquan zhuyi*) (i.e., for the judges to bear the principal responsibility for gathering evidence).
8. This difference is pointed out clearly by Shiga Shūzō (1974–1975: esp. 33; 121–23). See also Max Weber on this point ([1968] 1978: esp. 809–15), cf. Huang (1996: 16).

(see, for example 2002: no. 36). Through the entire procedure, what the court relies on is mainly two methods: one is written documentation, and the other the "confrontation" (*duizhi*) of the accuser by the accused. In the latter, a procedure with deep historical roots, the operative principle is that something acknowledged to be true by both sides can be relied upon by the court. Otherwise, it must be proven. There is also procedure for use of witnesses, but in today's system they are of little consequence, something to be discussed more fully below.

The Changing Historical Context

These institutional changes have their roots partly in the altered historical context. One big factor is the increase in numbers of cases. The courts no longer deal with only a small number and can no longer undertake their own investigation as in the past. As the two Songjiang judges I interviewed in the early 1990s pointed out, the old system took up a great deal of time and is simply not practicable today (see chapter 4). Another factor is the massive importation of Western formalist laws, equating the old system with judges' authoritarianism and the new system with litigants' rights.

There are larger social-economic reasons. One is the movement of population. Since the 1980s, a total of 200 million peasants have entered into off-farm employment, about one-half in township enterprises and the other half in the cities. That has been accompanied by rapid urbanization, rising from 19.4 percent of the population in 1980 to 42.8 percent in 2004 (Huang Zongzhi and Peng Yusheng, 2007). Such a scale of movement has completely changed the kinds of control that obtained under the *hukou* system (with its rigid separation of the rural and urban populations) of the Mao period. To illustrate with a case example (2001: no. 270), the plaintiff husband asks for divorce from his wife. But the court, it turns out, was not able to find and notify the wife of the complaint. The archival record contains just a message from the street (*jiedao*) committee office of the county: "XXX was originally a resident of this residents' committee, but her hukou was moved out after her marriage, and her present whereabouts are unknown." The court could therefore only post a "public notice," asking the defendant to come to court in response, stipulating a deadline after which the court would rule on the case by default. What is reflected in this case is the new social reality: the government's control over the people is simply no longer as all-encompassing as in the past. In another case (2003: no. 168), the husband had gone off to work outside with a woman who is married. They apparently began living together. The plaintiff wife had not known about it until two years afterward (in 1993), when the other woman's husband came to her house to look for his wife. That time, the husband signed a "repentance document," *huigaishu*, promising not to do it again. Later, he went off to work again. By the time of the lawsuit, the couple had lived separately for three years. In response to the complaint, the husband said that he had started a business with XXX because the unit where he originally worked had collapsed. That was the reason he had been away a long time. These are the kinds of details that tell about the great social economic changes of the time.

Under the new realities, economic interactions have become far more complex and multifaceted, often beyond what the government can control. In one case (2003: no. 270), the couple wants to divorce, but their financial relationship turns out to be very complicated, with each side insisting on its version of the story. Both have been in business, and they have both community and separate properties, and community and separate debt obligations and claims. There is a car registered to the husband, worth 10,500 yuan, and a boat that the wife had bought together with some other people for 24,000 yuan (for her seafood business). The two show multiple debts and debt claims, some under individual names, others under both names. There are three debts, totaling 145,989 yuan; two bank account books, totaling 5,831 yuan; and three debt claims, totaling 95,358 yuan. Each side and his/her lawyer insist that the car and boat in the other's sole name is actually community property, and the debt in his/her sole name is actually a community debt that should be borne together, and the debt claims in joint names actually belong to himself/herself. In the end, the court ruled that the "house" (*fangzi*, which of course is an apartment or condominium, not a house in the conventional American sense) that the couple bought (though under the husband's name and transferred by him to the name of a relative, but obviously community property), worth 128,000 yuan, belongs half to each, and the husband (who will live in the house) is to compensate the wife for her half. As for the debts and claims, the court dealt only with those that were unequivocally documented and ignored the others, leaving them for the couple themselves to sort out. These kinds of financial relationships are products of the marketized era, quite unimaginable in the Mao period.

They suggest that in the larger marketized environment, it is often no longer practicable for the judges to go down to the village, town neighborhood, or work unit to interview the cadres and kin and neighbors on site in order to arrive at the truth of the situation, as they had done in the Mao period. It is often no longer feasible for them to bear the main responsibility for gathering evidence. Given the new social economic circumstances, the change from on-site investigations by judges to at-court presentations of evidence by litigants is an understandable one appropriate to the new circumstances.

In addition, given the decline in the party-state's control of the population and the expansion in the private sphere of people's lives, marital relations have to a considerable extent become a kind of private matter/secret (*yinsi*). In the new context, some of the private relations between husband and wife have become particularly difficult for the courts to verify. The cases contain many examples of wives accusing the husbands of abuse. In the Mao period, in an environment of tight control and close social networks, the judges could find out the truth through on-site investigations, since relatives and neighbors usually knew about such things. But now, under the new system, if each side insists on his/her version, and there is no written evidence, the courts can only exclude it from consideration as a non-ascertainable fact (more below).

As has been shown, the People's Republic has tended to privilege practical considerations in legislation. Before incorporating a provision into formal law, it has generally first tested the provision in practice in the forms of Supreme Court directives or explanations, in what I have characterized as a process of reality to trial legal provision to practice to formal law, with emphasis on a kind of "practical rationality" (see chapters 4 and 6). But practice is not necessarily "reasonable." My writings thus far have emphasized mainly the reasonable aspects of practice, to show that "practice" is generally closer to historical reality than theory and carries with it a practical logic that will not depart from reality and be carried to the extremes that formalist theory can. But the history of practice obviously can also come with multiple unreasonable elements—the most obvious being that a new system can easily fall in with the existing "political system" (*tizhi*), such that the best-intentioned designs end up utterly ineffective or bring results very different from, or even counter to, those intended. I use the expression "unintended consequences" here for such phenomena. This chapter therefore considers both reasonable (positive) and unreasonable (negative) consequences. The institutional changes described above appear reasonable in theory and in form, but we need to ask here: How did they actually operate?

The Evidence System in the Practice of Divorce Law

With reform has come a high degree of formalization of evidence procedure. In the Mao era, the contents of case records had mainly to do with substantive materials, mainly the interviews of the judges, and the result of the ideals of the "Ma Xiwu system," which relied on tight-knit organization and social networks and arrived at truths through the deep reach of the party organization and the "snow-clear eyes" of the "masses." In today's society, however, especially the highly fluid society of the cites and towns, with their very complex economic transactions, there is no longer such a high degree of cohesion;

even rural society, given its large numbers working outside, has loosened up greatly, changing from a "society of the well acquainted" to the "society of the half acquainted."[9] One source of change is that the party-state no longer commands the depth or scope of control as before; another is that complexities of market transactions have made truths much harder to ascertain. Under the new principles of at-trial investigation and litigant-ism, the courts can only rely for their judgments on the litigants' adversarial representations and on the courtroom truth that can be established under existing procedures.

All this is reflected in the case records. Today's records are dominated by written documents and the accompanying procedure of formal exchange of evidence. The court demands first of all the litigants' identity cards, marriage certificate, proof of power-of-attorney appointments, debt contracts, witnesses' testimonies, and so on. It expends much energy on such formalized evidence, whether they have substantive relevance or not. With the promulgation in 2002 of the Supreme People's Court's provisions about civil evidence, the courts have further required a formalized exchange of evidence before trial. They must notify both sides to come to court for such an exchange, which now occupies a good deal of the content of a case file. Then, at the trial, there are the formalized procedures of identity verification, the complaint and the response or countercomplaint, and arguments about evidence, all of which take up a good deal of space in the stenographic record. (Needless to say, also a good deal of time and personnel, the more so if the case is before a collegiate bench comprising three judges.)

As for the witness system, it plays only a very limited role today, contrary to the intent of the lawmakers. In form, what China has adopted is a mix of the Continental and Anglo-American systems: witnesses are examined mainly by the judges (although the litigants may also, with the permission of the judges, ask questions) as a part of the procedure of court investigation (in this respect resembling more the Continental system), but they serve at the request of the litigants (in this respect more like the American system). One result is that judges assume, much like under the American Common Law system, that a witness is necessarily a biased advocate for one side or the other. And, since there is no "cross examination" by opposing counsel as in the American "discovery" system,[10] the credibility of a witness is all the more suspect. In ad-

9. A 2003 study found that among rural workers, 31 percent do off-farm work. The sampling done by the study found that 58 percent only farmed, 16 percent worked off-farm, 15 percent did both, and 10 percent were unemployed (Lu Xueyi, 2004: 308–9). A 2005 survey of 1,773 villages (one or two villagers in each) found that 83 percent of peasant households contain at least one person working off-farm (Ye Jianping et al., 2006), although, as the authors themselves point out, their findings might be exaggerated on account of the fact that the villages studied were all within 10 kilometers of a city/town.
10. In part because of the relative shortage of lawyers and also the infrequent use of lawyers.

dition, there is no legal requirement for witnesses to appear; they are basically free to ignore a subpoena. There are no provisions to cover expenses for appearance at court, which also makes the system that much more impractical. In the end, because witnesses lack credibility and because most people refuse to appear, the courts have come to rely more and more on documentary evidence alone. The entire witness system has in fact become quite meaningless in actual practice (Xu Xin, 2006). It amounts to neither a Continental system (in which witnesses are called and examined mainly by the judges) nor an American Common Law system. It is basically just a hollow frame.

Yet by law, divorce courts need to consider facts that cannot be ascertained on the basis of documentary evidence alone. For example, are the foundation and current state of the emotional relationship of the couple good, bad, or average? Does the husband really abuse the wife? Is the husband really living with a "third party"? Does the husband really gamble all the time, as the wife charges? Such questions usually cannot be answered by written evidence. In the past, the facts were ascertained through neighbors and kin and the local party organization. Today, they need the help of witnesses.

To give a simple case example (2002: no. 245): The plaintiff wife says that her husband regularly beats and abuses her; she therefore seeks divorce. But the defendant husband claims that what the wife says is false; only one time, when she hit his elderly father, did he hit her arm twice in anger. (In addition, each claims that their debt of 35,000 yuan is the other's debt for which she/he bears no responsibility.) There is no documentary evidence for the beating(s), and neither side supplied evidence through a witness, whether in person or in written testimony. The court therefore basically disregarded the claim of abuse, concluding only that "the relationship between the couple is just average and, because of incompatibility in personality (*xingge buhe*), conflicts have arisen between them." The case ended in a judgment for divorce, and the court's posture amounted in effect to a no-fault approach.[11] In a similar case (2002: no. 339), the plaintiff says her husband frequently abuses her verbally and physically, but the husband completely denies it. The two sides also did not present witness testimony. In the end, the court again took no position as to fault and wrote simply in its judgment-report that "the relationship of the two after marriage was average and, because of financial difficulties, they frequently argued and fought."[12] This case ended in a mediated divorce, also without consideration of fault.

---

11. The court's judgment concentrated mainly on the question of the couple's debt. Since neither could furnish convincing proof, the court ruled that it was a shared debt for which both were to bear responsibility.
12. The final judgment of the court concentrated on the question of the debt obligation of the couple, concluding that because of insufficient evidence presented by the two sides, the debt was to be treated as a joint obligation for which both bore equal responsibility.

In the two cases above we can see that the operative reality in divorce law practice today, because of evidence problems, is a strong tendency toward a kind of no-fault approach—by default. This too is an unanticipated consequence. Although the law affirms the principle of fault (such as abuse, living together with a third party, gambling), in actual legal practice the courts are not considering fault. Since the court cannot verify whether a husband is abusing a wife, it can only disregard the issue. As the judges interviewed by Wu Ruozhi emphasized, domestic violence (or living with a third party) is very difficult to prove (Wu Ruozhi, 2007: 193), barring, of course, instances involving severe injury documented by hospital records (as, for example, in 2002: no. 25).

Although there is nothing intrinsically wrong with a no-fault approach to divorce—the West has basically adopted a no-fault approach since the 1960s and 1970s—it needs to be accompanied by legal provisions for the weak, and a public security and hospital system that will protect the victim and admonish and punish the offender. The present system lacks such protections. As Wu Ruozhi points out, although the 2001 Marriage Law upheld the principle of compensation for damages (Article 46) in divorce, it has not been implemented in practice, because of the present evidence procedure. The lawmakers' intent had been to establish gender equality and to give the weak a measure of protection through a legal weapon that can be used against the abuser. But in actual operation, the courts have in effect excluded domestic violence and living with a third party from consideration because of difficulties of proof, thus weakening the law's protection of the weak.[13]

The reality is that many facts that used to be known to neighbors and community cadres are turning into "private matters/secrets" of the couple. At the same time, given the problems with the new evidence procedure, the courts really have no way of verifying contested facts. The result is that facts that had been considered crucial to divorce cases in the past are being pushed outside of the scope of court consideration.

13. Wu Ruozhi uses the following case illustration: The defendant has beaten his wife publicly and has housed a lover for a long time, and also gambles regularly—things known to everyone in the community. But the plaintiff wife, except for evidence provided by the hospital of light injury sustained after a beating, did not even mention the other aspects of the husband's behavior, either because she was not able to provide any written evidence or because she thought they would do no good. Wu Ruozhi only learned of the facts through an interview with the woman after the trial. As for the hospital receipt submitted by the plaintiff, the defendant countered that it could only prove that she had been injured slightly, but not specifically that he had beaten her. Since no other evidence was presented, the court in the end did not find that the wife had actually been abused by the husband (Wu Ruozhi, 2007: 182–84; 277–87; cf. 2002: no. 309; 2000: no. 37; 1999: no. 2). In addition, as Wu Ruozhi points out, almost everyone present at the court trial was a relative of the defendant. The plaintiff, by contrast, had only her sister there for support. Under those circumstances, the plaintiff was unlikely to obtain justice (she sought 5,000 yuan in compensation but was given only 600 yuan).

Another problem for the courts is the debts of the couple. Most of those are informal loans from relatives and friends that do not have a documented contract and are concluded and maintained only through personal connections. Once a dispute arises and goes to court, such loans are very difficult to prove. For example, in a case involving a dispute over a house (2001: no. 46), the woman says she had handed her mother-in-law 62,800 yuan in cash to buy the home, but there is no written documentation. As for the husband, he claims that the house was purchased with money from his younger sister, who wired 50,000 yuan into his mother's account (but that too is not documented), and then later handed him an additional 40,000 yuan in person. Each side insisted on its version. The only proof the husband could provide was an affidavit from the original owner of the house, stating that he had sold the house to the husband's brother-in-law. In the end, the court was unable to reach any position with regard to the house.[14]

Under such circumstances, what the court normally does is simply consider only those facts that can be unequivocally ascertained, usually because both sides agree or because of written documentation. Other fact-claims are simply not considered. This is another aspect of the difference between the current system and the Mao period's. In the earlier period, there were few debts; today, they are many and complex. If the two sides should each insist on a different fact claim, the courts have no way of establishing what is true, and will simply set them aside. (There are numerous other examples, such as 1999: nos. 7, 9, 109, 209; 2000: nos. 19, 37; more below.)

From these multiple factors and tendencies have come a pervasive tendency to emphasize formalities more than substance, with emphasis on written documentation and procedures, often with a complete disregard for reality and truth. What follows below is a rather extreme example to dramatize this problem.

The Strictly Formalized Evidence Process in Operation

In the sample of cases from county R, especially the most recent ones, there are several that evince purely formalistic legal practices. There are couples that have reached agreement on divorce, including the terms of settlement with regard to disposition of the children and property, and want only to formally register their divorce and agreement. They come to the county court only because the county's Bureau of Civil Affairs, the entity that had handled the recording of mutual-consent divorces in the past, refuses to handle theirs.

14. And found that the couple's relationship had not yet ruptured and therefore denied permission for divorce.

What they find themselves confronted with is a highly bureaucratized and formalistic court system that demands of them pointless observance of procedures and expensive fees.

In the sample of forty-five cases, there are nine mutual-consent divorces (2001: nos. 7, 175, 374; 2002: nos. 36, 274; 2003: no. 199; 2004: nos. 292, 349, 355). To start with a rather extreme example (2003: no. 199): The plaintiff and the defendant had decided to divorce and had reached agreement on the terms, complete with a written text. They came to court only for the purpose of formalizing the divorce. But the court, in accordance with its fixed procedures, required them to pay first the "case acceptance fee" (*shoulifei*) of 50 yuan, and then also a 400-yuan charge (because the case involves property) "for other expenses" (*qita feiyong*). Then the court, by standard procedure, first met with the defendant for "inquiries" (*xunwen*). The defendant (according to the stenographic record) indicated that he agreed completely with the terms set forth by the plaintiff in her "complaint" (namely, that the two agree to divorce, that the mother would have custody of the two children, that the defendant would pay 500 yuan each month in child support "until the children are grown up"; that the plaintiff would live in the couple's old home—which belonged to the defendant's father—until she marries again; and that the couple's joint debt—borrowed from the defendant's father—would be the responsibility of the defendant). The plaintiff had in fact submitted from the start their formal written agreement and also a document from the district committee of their town, stating that in its opinion the couple's relationship had indeed ruptured and that they should divorce, and asking for the court's cooperation in the matter. However, even though there was no disagreement whatsoever between the two sides, the local court still went ahead and convened a "collegiate court" of three judges, plus a secretary, and went through all the motions of a formal trial. The stenographic record shows that the court stuck to its fixed procedure: first the rules of the court were read, then the identities of the plaintiff and defendant verified, then the two were asked whether there was reason for any one to be recused, then the presentation of the petition and demands and of evidence, then arguments, before the court entered finally into the mediation stage, during which it went over once more every item of agreement already reached, then drew up a draft agreement, which is typed up as the court's official "civil mediation document." This kind of court trial was really nothing but a high-priced show, imposing on the litigants a host of unnecessary hassles and expenses.[15]

---

15. In another case, the two sides had similarly reached agreement and came to court only to have their divorce formally recorded. In the process, the court had actually served the minor function of helping to spell out, on top of the already agreed-upon 150 yuan of child support per month to be paid by the plaintiff, the condition that the payments were to be made twice a year before the start of

Such formalistic practices may be traced to a state bureaucratic system that, through "marketization," has come to be preoccupied with profits for the individual sections of the system. What the litigants in the above case faced was, first, the Civil Affairs Bureau, which, out of considerations of income versus expenditure (of personnel and time and such), decided to refuse to take on the recording of no-dispute divorces. According to Wu Ruozhi's investigation, the charge for registering a divorce with the bureau had always been very low (just eight yuan), but if the couple should get into an argument during the process of recording the divorce, as sometimes happened, the officer doing the recording could get drawn in. Under the old ideology of service, the bureau bore such complications willingly, and handled large numbers of such recordings, along with occasional mediations. It continued to do so even in the early years of the reform, down to 1987. But then the bureau took the rather extreme position of refusing to handle any more such mutual-consent divorce recordings, thereby pushing everyone into the court system. Its main concern had been to do away with what it saw as a low-income but high-expenditure activity (Wu Ruozhi, 2007: 112–15; 135–36).

The result was that, in county R at least, these "cases" now all came before the court, which imposes on them the new evidence procedures. The local judges complain bitterly about the whole thing. This phenomenon of formalistic handling of mutual-consent divorces as if they were contested lawsuits is another unintended consequence of the evidence law reform. The judges complain that the civil affairs offices of the county and towns are shirking their own responsibilities and passing the burden onto the courts, causing much unreasonable waste of resources earmarked for litigation. According to the "responsible person" of the civil affairs bureau, some people have actually appealed this matter (shangfang) to the provincial civil affairs department, but to no avail. Under the current tendencies of the bureaucratic system toward formalization and profit seeking, this appears to be an as yet irresolvable matter.[16]

---

the school semester, and also that the court costs would be shared equally by the two. Still the court charged only a 50-yuan fee (2004: no. 349). In another case (2004, no. 292), the court charged the same amount and appropriately employed the simplified trial procedure (*jianyi chengxu*) of just one judge. There is also one rather exceptional case in which, during the course of the formalized procedure, a surprising substantive problem surfaced. The plaintiff and the defendant had reached prior agreement, complete with a signed written agreement, but at the trial the plaintiff suddenly claimed that she had been high-pressured into the agreement, that she in fact did not agree to the terms, and that she wanted the defendant to bear part of the tuition costs of the children (2002: no. 339).

16. Of course, the court system of the Mao period also had its share of concerns for formality, as for example in its exaggerated claims for the mediation system. In the ideology of the time, mediation was considered the main and proper way to resolve disputes, and there was therefore the demand to raise the reported incidence of mediations as high as possible, leading to preposterous claims that 80 percent to 90 percent of all cases were mediated. The courts typically reported mutual-consent divorces as mediated divorces (see chapter 4). The difference between today, after several decades of reform, and the earlier period is one of degree, and also of institutionalized complexities and fees.

The Continuation of Substantive Mediation

Even with massive marketization and the new evidence law, part of the court mediation system of the Mao period continues to operate and remains useful. This is an aspect that should not be overlooked. Even as the court system as a whole becomes ever more formalized procedurally, and adopts more and more the adversarial framework of the West, the mediation system born of ideals of substantive justice is still being applied to a substantial proportion of the cases (more below). Even as falsely represented and purely formalistic mediations increase, substantive mediations remain important.[17]

As in the Mao period, the most effective mediations are still those involving fact situations where the court need not concern itself with the question of legal right and wrong, and need only facilitate the working out of a settlement. One common situation is where both sides wish to divorce but are not able to agree on the specific terms. Under those conditions, the courts still play a crucial role today in helping the two sides to arrive at peacekeeping compromises that both can accept (see chapter 4). In one case (2002: no. 339), for example, the plaintiff wife says that her husband beats and mistreats her; she seeks divorce and the custody of the five-year-old daughter, the three-year-old son to go to the husband. The husband counters that he has actually been very good to her and is opposed to divorce. At the "trial," the court finds that the couple's relationship had been average, but then "because of financial difficulties, they often argued and fought." The plaintiff had by 1998 already left home for a year. Later, she went back on the urgings of others but left again a few months later to seek work outside. Apparently, the husband saw during the course of the proceedings that his wife was determined to divorce and, in the end, came to the position that if she insisted, he would go along. The court then helped the two sides come to terms on the specifics: the husband was to compensate the wife 2,000 yuan, the washing machine and other big items of the dowry were to go to her, the daughter to her, the son to him, and the court fees of 450 yuan were to be borne by her. On those terms, the two sides reached agreement voluntarily.

In another case (2000: no. 10; see also 1999: nos. 2, 10, 22), the plaintiff wife seeks divorce from her married-in husband. Her parents had wanted her to marry him mainly so they would have a grandchild. But he evidently turned out to be unable to have children. He denied the fact at first but, during the course of the trial, the court found that the hospital test record submitted by his wife as proof was legitimate. That was the key fact for the court; the two parties differed on a number of other questions, but those did not matter to

17. See chapters 4 and 7 for a fuller discussion.

the court. Its posture was that the plaintiff had a legitimate reason for divorce. All that was left then were just the specifics of a settlement. The defendant wished for 8,000 yuan in compensation, but the plaintiff was willing to pay only 3,000 yuan. The court then "worked on both" (talking first separately with each, and then with both at the same time) to arrive at a 5,000 yuan compromise figure. The two sides then agreed.

In the cases cited above, the court as a bystander of authority clearly performed a critical function. I will show in chapter 7 ("Court Mediation: Past and Past") that court mediations were generally most effective when no question of fault was involved, whereas matters involving legal right and wrong often led to coercive (but ultimately ineffective) interventions by the court, most conspicuously in the forced "mediated reconciliations" of couples seeking divorce. Under the Chinese legal system, if the litigants reject the court's mediatory efforts, they are faced next with outright adjudication by the same court in the same trial process. For that reason, they are under considerable pressure to accept the interventions of the court. They cannot simply opt out of mediation at will. Partly for that reason, court mediations enjoy a relatively high rate of success, far more than in European and American mediations that are entirely separated from the court system. They resemble more the "mediation-arbitration" (or med-arb for short) system that has gained some currency in the West in recent years (see chapter 7). The court mediation system is a legacy from China's modern revolution, and a system that is worthy of recognition and further development. The Supreme People's Court, in the face of the problems with the new evidence rules, has in fact already urged a reemphasis on the mediation system.[18]

The New Formalism and the Combining of Formal and Substantive Justice

The mediation cases just discussed may be seen as the continuation of the original (Maoist) substantive justice system, but I am of course not suggesting here that the new system has no merits and the old system is completely reasonable. The new system is in fact quite well suited to new social-economic realities, and has consequences that are undeniably positive.

In one case example from 2000, the plaintiff wife seeks divorce mainly because her husband gambles frequently. But the husband is not willing. The two had together operated a store, with fairly complex financial arrangements. The plaintiff presented evidence that her father had put up 200,000 yuan toward

18. On the rethinking of the system, see Huang Songyou, 2000; on the reemphasis on court mediation, see the text of the speech of Chief Justice Xiao Yang (2006) of the Supreme People's Court.

payment for the 320,000-yuan store. She wants the debt to be treated as a shared obligation. The defendant for his part presents proof that he had paid 120,000 yuan. There are three other debts, all in the name of his father, separately for 29,000 yuan, 79,000 yuan, and 15,000 yuan. He wants those treated as community obligations. Each side insists on its claims, and the court failed in its attempt to mediate. In addition, the couple confirms that they further borrowed 120,000 yuan with the store as security. The court, by examining the documentary evidence and hearing arguments from both sides, determined that the loan against the store was indeed a shared debt, for which both sides should be responsible. As for the three debts borrowed by the husband in his father's name, the court finds that they should not concern the plaintiff. As its judgment, the court finds, in accordance with the 1989 "Fourteen Articles" of the Supreme People's Court, that "if one side is lazy and does not like to work, and has bad habits like gambling,"[19] divorce would be allowed, and further, in accordance with the law, that "if the plaintiff has no stable employment or income, and is without fault, (s)he may be appropriately given special consideration." Thus, the court rules that half of the 200,000 yuan net worth of the store should go to the plaintiff, plus another 5,000 yuan in compensation, amounting to a total of 105,000 yuan. As for the two children (five-year-old son and three-year-old daughter), in accord with usual court practice, the parents should each receive custody of one. Of the 3,250 yuan in court fees, the plaintiff is to be responsible for 1,250 yuan and the defendant 2,000 yuan. Clearly, at least in this case, the court could not do as the courts of the Maoist period did, go on-site to determine the truth about the debts of each party, and could only adjudicate according to what could be proven with written documentation. But even so, its judgment seems substantial and well founded (2000: no. 170).

The same applied in another case. The plaintiff (wife) seeks divorce because her husband frequently stays out all night. A relative had tried to mediate, but to no avail. The couple has long since stopped sleeping together, and the plaintiff has already moved out and is living by herself. But the defendant refuses to divorce. The court failed in its attempt to mediate. The two sides have new-style and rather complicated financial relations. The defendant had set up a travel company, and husband and wife had each invested separately, with shares under their separate names. In addition, the plaintiff presents proof that the defendant had borrowed 49,000 yuan from her. In addition, the company owes two debts, one for 167,000 yuan and another for 130,000 yuan. These are all documented, and the court acknowledges them. Since

19. Zuigao renmin fayuan "Guanyu renmin fayuan shenli lihun anjian ruhe rending fuqi ganqing que yi polie de ruogan juti yijian," Article 10 (in "Zuigao renmin fayuan," 1994: 1086–87). In the 2001 Marriage Law, the passage about "lazy and not like to work" was deleted.

there is no question of fault at issue, the court basically gave each one-half of the property, dividing the company in accordance with what is in the name of each; the defendant was to pay back the 49,000 yuan he borrowed from his wife; as for the company's two debts, the one for 130,000 yuan was to be borne by the plaintiff, and the one for 167,000 yuan by the defendant. Here the new evidence system performed its role largely as intended (2001: no. 336).

There are also examples of the two systems working in tandem. We have seen, in the case already discussed above, how the court found on the basis of the hospital document (under the old system, the judge would have gone to the hospital to investigate) that the defendant husband indeed could not have children. Though he disputed the claim, he could offer no counterproof. The court therefore found that the plaintiff wife had a legitimate reason for seeking divorce. That adjudicatory posture was arrived at through the new evidence procedure. At the same time, through separate discussions with each party, the court "worked on their thought" and facilitated a voluntary compromise, compensating the defendant 5,000 yuan (he had wanted 8,000 yuan and she was only willing to pay 3,000 yuan). An example like this may be seen as a reasonable coworking of the new evidence system with the old mediation system (2000: no. 10).

The Abuse of Judicial Authority in Neither-Nor Actions

But we can also see tensions between the two models of justice. How are they to be reconciled? We have seen above a rather extreme example of how formalistic procedures joined up with the profit-seeking orientations of a "marketized" bureaucratic system. Given the tensions between the two models of justice, the greatest danger may be where legal practice works neither as one system nor the other, and ends in the abuse of judicial authority. In one example (2006: no. 302), after the plaintiff wife and her husband got into a physical fight, she came to court to charge that her husband was living with a third party (a thirty-something divorced woman). He countered that this was not true, and he did not want to divorce. The court, without investigating, concluded that this was a matter of a jealous woman with groundless suspicions. It reached its judgment just on the basis of the court "trial"—without, needless to say, the Maoist type of on-site interviews, or any effort to persuade the plaintiff that her suspicions were not true. It simply denied permission for divorce on the grounds that "the plaintiff has not sufficient reason to seek divorce" and that "the two sides can be reconciled."

The case shows, first of all, the formalistic tendencies of the new evidence law. The case record contains the registration cards of the two, detailed listings of their properties and the like, making up a rather bulky file of "evidence submitted by the litigants," plus the record of the procedural verification of the evidence during the "trial." There is no evidence, however, on the key question of whether the defendant indeed lives with a third party, nor any testimony from witnesses. The record evinces also the Maoist principle of aggressive court intervention into a couple's relationship, but without the accompanying investigations or the "thought work" on the litigants. The court simply concluded rather preemptively that the plaintiff's charge was groundless and therefore denied permission for divorce. The result was that three days after the trial, the couple got into another big fight and came back once more to court.

The court's behavior in this case shows the influence of both the Maoist attempt to minimize divorce and the new era's formalist logic, and yet it is really neither one nor the other, with neither the substantive investigation and persuasion of one, nor the documentary proof of the other. The result was a perfunctory judgment.

To give one more example, in a case discussed earlier (2003: no. 168), the plaintiff husband had lost his job (*xiagang*) ten years earlier, and went off to start a business with a woman, and then lived with her. Later he supposedly regretted what he had done (complete with a "repentance document"), and then went off again to work. By the time of the lawsuit, the couple had already lived apart for three years. Since he had been away for a long time, he was not close to the two children. They, a seventeen-year-old girl and a fifteen-year-old boy, had stated in their pretrial interviews at court that they wanted to live with their mother because "our father doesn't care about us, doesn't love us," and that "no matter how poor, we want to be with Mom."

But the judge basically disregarded the fact that the husband had lived with a third party (a fault by law), and did not consider the wishes of the two children. He simply informed the plaintiff in no uncertain terms that the court believes the couple should each get custody of just one child. To force agreement from the plaintiff, the judge began the trial with sharp interrogation of her as to what happened at the time of her marriage twenty years earlier: First, he asked her whether she was already pregnant when she got married. She said yes, that she was two months pregnant at the time. He then sprang on her the fact that their marriage certificate showed the date of marriage to be 5 December 1985, but the birth certificate of their daughter showed that she was not born until 25 September 1986. She thus could not have been pregnant at the time of marriage (and therefore had to some extent deceived the defendant). The plaintiff was taken completely by surprise by this "ambush," and could only fumble around to say that perhaps her memory was mistaken. With this tactic of proving first that the plaintiff had lied, the judge then high-pressured her into accepting an arrangement whereby each parent would get custody of one child, completely disregarding the children's plea that their father had not "fulfilled fatherly love" and that they wanted to live with their mother regardless of how hard their lives might be. We can only imagine the feelings of these two children upon hearing the judgment of the court. That judge also pressured the plaintiff to accept just one-half of the 10,000 yuan she had sought in compensation. With the supposed voluntary agreement of the plaintiff, he was able to report that the case had been "concluded by mediation."

What we see here is that the court, while pursuing the Maoist era's goal of resolving disputes by mediation, completely dispensed with the work of investigation and persuasion, and undertook "mediation" only in form and without substance. Such court behavior amounts to a neither-nor act more characteristic of a formalistic bureaucracy than a court. It is an abuse of judicial power (perhaps even of corruption?)—the kind that helps explain the low opinion that many people have of the court system.

The present evidence system, then, has multiple weaknesses. Part of the problem is that the new system is not yet fully set up—some parts are just hollow frames, most notably the witness system, which is not working at all. That greatly limits the scope of what can be verified at court. To be sure, the new system is in an experimental stage, feeling its way along and changing still. Other approaches are being experimented with, including a new "order to investigate" (*diaochaling*) system that might turn out to be useful.[20]

Part of the problem may also consist in the rather lopsided choice of institutional arrangement made by the lawmakers. Lawmaking today obviously privileges legal formalism, and has applied litigant-ism without modification to the (civil) divorce sphere. Such excessive reliance on formalized procedure has meant, at least in county R, that the system has taken on the weaknesses of a profit-seeking bureaucracy, with utter disregard for the needs of the litigants, ending in formalistic exercises for the benefit of bureaucratic sectoral interests. The poor coordination of the old and new systems has also resulted in the unintended consequence of neither-nor acts of judicial abuse.

But the new procedure has shown an ability to blend with what is left from the Maoist mediation system to meet the needs of new social-economic realities. In 2006, there were still 1.426 million court cases that were concluded by mediation, using new evidence procedures, compared to 1.744 million by adjudication (*Zhongguo falü nianjian*, 2007: 1066). What needs to be done, perhaps, is that along with the massive importation and systematic establish-

---

20. The Changning district of Shanghai began experimenting with this in 1998, to allow litigants to petition the court for an official investigation (with coercive power), in order to overcome problems intrinsic to investigation and proof by the litigant. The method is apparently being tried more widely in other areas as well. This may turn out to be one way to improve the current system (Jin Hua, 2005: chap. 4).

ment of foreign laws today, there should also be deliberate acknowledgment and development of the strong points of the old system. As Wu Ruozhi's interviews of eleven judges at county R shows, all are of the opinion that the strictly formalistic evidence procedure needs to be changed, that litigant-ism needs to be merged with the old judges' authority-ism (Wu Ruozhi, 2007: 192–94). Chief Justice Xiao Yang of the Supreme People's Court has already proposed the idea of steering a middle course and combining the two (Yang Zhongxu, 2007).

The key here may be to employ more the mode of thinking that starts from real problems rather than abstract theories. Imported formalist rights doctrines and evidence law accord with Chinese realities in some respects but not others; what is needed is to search through actual practice for legal models that fit Chinese realities, to bring together the old mediation system with the new rights system, and the old judges' authority-ism with the new litigant-ism. There should not be blind copying of the theoretical models of Western legal formalism. That is the reason for this chapter's simultaneous attention to positive and negative aspects in the actual workings of the present evidence system.

6

Civil Adjudication, Past and Present

THE PRACTICE AND LOGIC of civil adjudication in China, past and present, have been obscured by Confucian and Chinese Communist Party representations as well as some modernist presuppositions. According to the moral ideals of Confucianism, "civil" disputes among the people should be resolved through societal mediation, not court action. Similarly, according to the mediation ideology of the Chinese Communist Party, Chinese courts should engage mainly in mediation—touted as superior to the adversarial system of the West. Finally, by the standards of the formalist tradition of Continental modern Western law, Chinese courts do not judge cases consistently according to universal principles about rights, and hence from this viewpoint as well there is no real court adjudication in civil matters. This chapter will demonstrate that in the history of practice of Chinese civil law, adjudication was in fact always an important component of the system, not just in the Reform and Guomindang periods, but also in the Qing and Mao Zedong periods. The court adjudication system widely used today, in fact, has unmistakable historical antecedents.

The usage here of the words "mediation" and "adjudication" should be explained at the outset. "Mediation" (*tiaojie*), in both its English and pre-Maoist Chinese usage, means mainly voluntary conciliation through third-party facilitation or intervention.[1] Under Maoist justice, however, it came to

1. In nineteenth-century case records, *tiaojie* was used interchangeably with words such as *tiaochu* and *shuohe* to refer to mediation by relatives and friends, as in *jing qinyou tiaochu* / *tiaojie* / *shuohe*. Older terms for mediation included *tiaoting*, *shuohe*, and *hejie* (Morohashi, 1955–1960: 10.504, 485; 8.971).

incorporate also the sense *tiaochu*, which in some of the liberated areas earlier had been carefully distinguished from *tiaojie* and had been applied mainly to administrative organs.[2] Tiaochu was more high-handed than tiaojie and included the possibility of going against the will of the disputant. But the distinction between the two was lost after 1949.

"Adjudication" (in traditional Chinese, *duan*, *duan'an*, *duanding*, and also *pan*, *pan'an*, *panjue*; in modern Chinese, mainly *panjue*—see Morohashi, 1955–1960: 5.648, 2.233) may of course be defined differently by different individuals. My usage here distinguishes specifically between mediatory compromises and adjudicatory judgments according to law. In the former, there is no simple legal right and wrong, or "winner" and "loser"; in the latter, there is.

Post-1949 Chinese court practices, it will be seen, include both mediatory and adjudicatory actions, as well as a range of actions that fall in between. This and the next chapter on mediation therefore employ two additional categories: "mediatory adjudication," covering cases that are at bottom adjudicatory, though they contain mediatory features, and "adjudicative mediation," cases that are basically mediatory but incorporate some adjudication. These usages will become clearer as specific cases are discussed. Obviously, the shades of gray in real cases often make such labels difficult to apply. But conceptually, the acid test that distinguishes adjudicatory from mediatory cases is whether the resolution of the dispute is imposed against the will of one of the litigants. The focus of this chapter is on the adjudicatory sphere of Chinese civil justice; I will deal with the mediatory sphere in the next chapter.

Mediation has drawn more attention from past scholarship than adjudication, and my next chapter on mediation draws on and discusses those works (e.g., Cohen, 1967; Lubman, 1967, 1999: chap. 3; Hsiao, 1979; Palmer, 1989; Clarke 1991). Here, however, I approach the problem from the other end, by attempting to delineate those parts of the Chinese civil justice system that are better understood as adjudicatory. Past research on adjudication is taken up below, where relevant. As for the new book by Linxia Liang (2007), it is discussed in detail in the appended bibliographic note to this chapter (page 186).

Chinese court records, this chapter suggests, show us court practices that differ markedly from Confucian and Communist representations, as well as from formalist expectations. For the Qing period, I will refer to my collection of 628 court cases from three counties for which records have been

2. Thus, a 1944 Jin-Cha-Ji Border Region directive distinguished sharply between "village mediation" (*cun tiaojie*) and "ward government mediation" (*qu tiaochu*), making precisely the distinction drawn here (Han and Chang, 1981–1984: 3.640–43). In the central Shaan-Gan-Ning Border Region, by contrast, the terms "administrative mediation" (*xingzheng tiaojie*) and "judicial mediation" (*sifa tiaojie*) were used in addition to "popular mediation" (*minjian tiaojie*), foreshadowing the expanded usage of *tiaojie* to come (Han and Chang, 1981–1984: 3.630–33).

preserved—Baxian County in Sichuan, Danshui-Xinzhu in Taiwan, and Baodi County in the capital prefecture of Shuntian. For the post-1949 period, I employ the same sample of 336 cases from county A in the north and county B in the south, supplemented by interviews with judges in Songjiang County and with litigants and cadres in that county's Huayangqiao village (known as Ganlu village since the late 1980s), where I did extensive fieldwork for my 1990 book on the Yangzi delta (see chapter 4 for a more detailed discussion).

This chapter first reviews the adjudicatory "practices" of the courts, seen against formalist, Confucian, and Communist Party expectations and representations. One purpose is to delineate in broad outlines the adjudicatory sphere of the Chinese civil justice system, past and present, including the codified legal provisions that are intended to guide court actions (distinguished from those that set forth moral ideals). In addition, the chapter seeks to define some of the unspoken logics evidenced in court practices in the major areas of civil justice. A problem requiring special attention is the persistent combination, in both Qing and contemporary Chinese law, of official representations that emphasize mediation with court actions that employ adjudication. The tolerance for this evident inconsistency, I suggest, reveals a characteristic in Chinese legal reasoning that has persisted through all the transformations from the Qing to the Maoist and then the Reform period. It receives special emphasis here because it has tended to be overlooked amid the obvious changes.

Continental Formalism vs. Qing Justice

As Max Weber made clear, the basis of the rational-formalist, Continental legal tradition of the modern West is the derivation of law from abstract, universal principles about rights (Weber, [1968] 1978: 657, 844–48). As the German Civil Code of 1900 clearly exemplifies, civil law takes as its point of departure the rights of the individual person—rights (and obligations) with respect to debt and to property, to marriage and divorce, and to inheritance (*German Civil Code*, 1907). The German code would become the model for the Guomindang Civil Code of 1929–1930 and thus to some extent for contemporary Chinese law as well.

Weber went on to spell out the relationship in rational-formalist law between such universal principles and particular legal judgments. "Every concrete legal decision" was supposed to be "the application of an abstract legal proposition to a concrete 'fact situation.'" Moreover, "it must be possible in every concrete case to derive the decision from abstract legal propositions by means of legal logic" (Weber, [1968] 1978: 657).

For Weber, rational-formalist court judgments are what distinguish modern, rational law most crucially from other kinds of law—especially instrumentalist law that merely serves the purposes and whims of the (patrimonial) ruler, or substantive law in which facts are "evaluated upon an ethical, emotional, or political basis rather than by general norms." Indeed, not even the "empirical justice" of Anglo-American common law can compare to the rational judgments of Continental formalist law. According to Weber, in the former tradition judgments are rendered "not by subsumption under rational concepts, but by drawing on 'analogies' and by depending upon interpreting concrete 'precedents'" (Weber, [1968] 1978: 844–48, 656, 976). Such an approach to legal decisions (along with reliance on a jury system) gives common law strongly nonformalist, irrational characteristics (Weber, [1968] 1978: 891).

Weber's characterization of rational-formalist Continental law, while certainly idealized, does help to bring out the conceptual underpinnings of that legal tradition. It is thus useful as a foil for clarifying the very different conceptual approach of past and present Chinese law with which this chapter is concerned. At the same time, the modernist and Eurocentric biases of Weber's comparative typologies are problematic. One might easily conclude from them that Qing law contained only the concrete and the particular, not the abstract and the universals of formalist law. From there, it would be a short step to mistakenly suggest, as do Derk Bodde and Clarence Morris (1967) despite the very high quality of their work, that there was little civil law in the Qing. It would also be easy to take Confucian representations at face value and argue, as Shiga Shūzō (1981) has maintained, that Qing courts did not adjudicate in the sense of applying legal provisions consistently in rendering decisions. Along the same lines, William Jones (1987) holds that there was no civil law in China at all after 1949, only administration, until market and capitalistic reforms, and the adoption of Western laws, in the 1980s.

Yet though Qing law did not begin with abstract universals about rights in the manner of formalist Continental Western law, it did contain a substantial body of laws that guided court adjudication—and that were based on an epistemological outlook very different from that of modern legal formalism. Legal stipulations did not begin with abstract principles separated from and elevated above fact situations but rather with the situations themselves. Abstracted principles were meant to be embodied in, and were almost never expressed separately from, those illustrative situations. Instead of being explicitly stated, they were usually illustrated with specific situations, usually involving violations of the implicit principle. Additional fact situations related to the same principle were added on over time as elaborative substatutes, often originating (almost in the manner of Anglo-American common law) from memorials about real cases ("precedents") from officials on the scene.

What distinguishes Qing law from formalist Continental civil law is not the absence of legal provisions to guide adjudication but rather the insistence on grounding concepts in practice-based fact situations. The intention was never to abstract principles that would be universally valid. Instead, it was assumed that abstract principles could be formulated, and take on true meaning and applicability, only in conjunction with actual practice.

Thus, the Qing code never advanced the principle of the inviolability of property rights in the abstract, in the manner of the German Civil Code of 1900 or of the Guomindang's 1929–1930 Civil Code modeled after it. (The Guomindang code stipulated in Article 765, "The owner of a thing has the right, within the limits of the law or ordinances, to use it, to receive its benefits, and to dispose of it freely, and to exclude others from interfering with it.") Rather, it used concrete situations to illustrate the principle of property "rights," almost always in terms of punishments for their violation. Thus, fraudulently selling another's land or house as one's own (Statute 93—*daomai tianzhai*, "Fraudulently Selling Land/House") was an offense punishable by fifty lashes with light bamboo, to increase by one grade for every five *mu* of land or three *jian* (i.e., front "rooms") of the house, up to a maximum penalty of eighty blows with heavy bamboo and two years' penal servitude. Fraudulently occupying another's land/house was also punishable, as was falsifying its value. A number of substatutes then extended the same implicit principle to other fact situations: for example, monks selling (community) temple land as their own (Substatute 93-1), descendants fraudulently selling lineage land as their own (Substatute 93-4), slaves selling their masters' land as their own (Substatute 93-5), and so on.

Statute 87, on inheritance, began by specifying punishments for sons who divided up the family's property while their parents were still alive. The law, it would seem, insisted on the moral ideal of the extended (parents and sons living together) and joint (married brothers living together) family. But the law went on to stipulate in a substatute (87-1), "If the parents allow the division [of the family property], then it may be done." This practical provision accommodated the widespread social practice (stemming, among other things, from the reality of frictions among married brothers and their wives) of dividing up a household even while parents were alive. Yet it was not allowed to override the original moralistic vision, which was placed at the front of the main statute and indeed repeated in the first part of the substatute containing the practical concession.

The next statute dealt with the rights of sons to inherit their father's land. It began by stipulating punishments for those sons who arbitrarily used the family property against parental wishes, and then declared that the head of a household who did not divide up the family's property equally as he should was to be punished (Statute 88). Similarly, the obligation of sons to provide old-age support for their parents was conveyed by specifying the punishment for the failure to provide such support (Statute 338). No abstract claims were made about the right of sons to inherit or about their obligation to provide old-age support for their parents.

The same was true of the Qing code's approach to debt obligations, which fell under regulations governing usury (Statute 149, *weijin quli*, "Charging Interest at Forbidden Rates"). The statute first specified punishments against those who charged more interest for loans than the state-regulated maximum of 3 percent per month; the requirement of repaying a legitimate loan was a secondary concern. It stipulated that those who owed more than five taels and were three months late in repayment were to be punished by ten lashes with light bamboo, to increase by one grade for each month of delinquency, up to a maximum of forty lashes, and by one grade for every fifty taels owed, up to a maximum of sixty blows with heavy bamboo. The principle that legitimate debts must be paid remained implicit: only the concrete violations and their punishments appeared in the code.

Similarly, with respect to marriage, the implicit principle that marriage should be based on good-faith contracts between two families was not stated in the abstract but rather conveyed by specifying punishments for fraudulently betrothing an already-betrothed woman to another or for fraudulently representing a disabled woman or man as healthy (Statute 101). And the implicit principle that a marriage contract must be honored was conveyed by specifying punishments for those breaching the agreed-on time of marriage, whether the husband's family forced an early wedding or the woman's family deliberately delayed it.

Outside the realm of civil law as well, legal principles were expressed through illustrative fact situations (and punishments for violations). Qing homicide law, as Jennifer Neighbors (2004) has demonstrated, finely discriminated between six categories of killings (*liusha*), graded according to degree of intent, that most abstract of legal categories, and all expressed in illustrative situations. These ranged from premeditated murder (*mousha*), as with poison, to intentional killing (*gusha*), as in the heat of the moment, to killing in an affray (*dou'ousha*), differentiated by the nature of the weapon used, to killing while at play (*xisha*), further distinguished by whether dangerous games (such as fencing or boxing) were involved, to mistaken killing (*wusha*), including killing from negligence (as in playing with fire or with a bow and arrow), down to accidental killing (*guoshisha*), as by a runaway horse or cart (Xue, 1905: 4.849–57). Despite the absence of any abstract statement about intent, the prescribed punishments increased in severity with the degree of deliberate intent.

Republican law, by contrast, modeled on modern Western Continental formalist law, defined just two abstract categories, intentional killing and negligent killing, with no complex gradations for intent.[3] When confronted with real homicides, Neighbors further shows, Republican jurists often found the governing principles in their newly adopted code too abstract to serve as an adequate guide to adjudication. They therefore often turned back to the concrete markers employed in the Qing to help them to conceptualize and differentiate degrees of intent (Neighbors, 2004).

Moreover, Qing law relied on the principle of analogy to cover fact situations that were not specified in the code. The late-Qing code compiled in 1905 by Xue Yunsheng listed thirty statutes by analogy. Thus, an adoptive son who verbally abused his adoptive parents was likened to a natural son verbally abusing his parents or grandparents (Analogy Statute 27; analogized to Statute 329). By analogy, someone who fraudulently mixed water into meat, or sand or salt into rice, was to be punished as if he were a private merchant who added sand and soil to the government salt he was selling (forbidden in Statute 141, "Salt Laws," section 10—Analogy Statute 3). This mechanism enabled the extension of the principles implicit in the concrete illustrations. The key throughout was not the absence of principles or legal provisions but rather the insistence that abstract principles not stand alone, separated entirely from any illustration. Put another way, the code displayed an epistemological insistence on the inseparability of abstractions from practice, even while acknowledging that the latter's unlimited variability prevented exhaustive enumeration in the code—hence the recourse to the principle of analogy, a principle that was itself illustrated with some thirty concrete applications. Such fact-based stipulations made up a sizable body of laws to guide court adjudication.

This epistemological outlook of Qing law, it should be pointed out, is different not only from that of modern formalism but also of postmodernism, such as that of Clifford Geertz's "local knowledge," which has gained in recent years a good deal of currency among Chinese legal scholars. Qing legal reasoning did not deny the independent existence of facts; it actually took that independent reality as its point of departure. Geertz's point, however, is that "facts" are of necessity constructed, that fact and law are inseparable in that sense. According to Geertz, the way adversarial counsels construct facts in the modern courtroom shows that they cannot be dissociated from the spins put on them. For Geertz, the fault with modernist epistemology is

3. Contemporary Western homicide law, of course, distinguishes between (premeditated) murder and (voluntary and involuntary) manslaughter (in the United States, commonly labeled first-, second-, and third-degree murder, respectively).

that, among other things, it assumes the independent reality of facts, when premodern traditions did not (Geertz, 1983). But Qing legal reasoning, far from assuming that "true facts" cannot be known, saw the judge's task as to uncover the true facts. What Qing law would object to in modernist law is instead its elevation of abstract principles to universal applicability regardless of facts.

This is not to say that imperial Chinese lawmaking was purely fact- or practice-based and thus merely retrospective (looking back at past experience). It should be obvious that imperial Chinese law contained a strongly prospective dimension as well, most especially in its Confucian moralizing, which spoke more to what society ought to be like than what it was. The imperial law's conception of "civil" cases (i.e., *xishi,* literally "minor matters"), for example, first stressed that they ideally would not occur at all, because morally superior men would not stoop to such disputes or lawsuits. And when they did occur, they should be handled by societal mediation conducted by morally superior men of the community or kin group. Practically speaking, if such disputes came to court, they would be handled by county-level local courts on their own authority, without troubling the upper levels of the government (Huang, 1996: chap. 8). We might even say that the role played by Confucian moral ideals in imperial Chinese law in some ways resembles that of formalist principles about rights in precedent-based Anglo-American common law. Each system to some degree combines the ideal with the practical. The difference, of course, was that in Chinese law this combination, which I have termed "practical moralism" (Huang, 1996: chap. 8), did not demand that all court judgments be subsumed by legal logic under its moral ideals as required by Weberian legal formalism.

Confucian Representations vs. Qing Legal Practice

At the core of Confucian constructions of the law was the ideal of the Confucian moral gentleman who would cope with disputes through *rang,* "conciliation," and *ren,* "forbearance." By that logic, as noted above, being involved in a dispute or lawsuit at all was a sign of moral failing; thus civil disputes among the people were officially "minor matters" (*xishi*). In an ideal society of morally superior men, they would not exist at all. Should formal court procedures be initiated as a last resort, the court would always defer to community or kin-group mediation if that could at any point resolve the dispute. Finally, even if a dispute persisted, the court would ideally still engage in moral education and persuasion so that litigants would willingly accept its decision. The emphasis on voluntary acceptance found expression in the standardized court procedure of always requiring disputants to file pledges of "willingness to end the lawsuit" (*ganjie*) (Huang, 1996).

These Confucian representations underlie Shiga Shūzō's influential scholarly view that the traditional Chinese court undertook only "didactic conciliation," not adjudication. In Shiga's analysis, Chinese laws were conceptually founded on the triadic principle of *qing*, *li*, and *fa*: compassion based on Confucian humaneness (ren), moral principles governing both nature and society (*tianli*), and the laws of the state. He sees the three as operating together to make up the true source of laws (*hôgen*, to use Shiga's term), which themselves were relatively insignificant (Shiga likens laws to an iceberg in the ocean). Instead, the court's main guides were Confucian compassion and the moral principles of society. Mediation, or didactic conciliation, was the concrete manifestation of this view of law and governance (Shiga, 1981).

Though Shiga's analysis illuminates the logic underlying the official ideology, his focus on Confucian moralistic representations leads him to overlook the other crucial dimension of the Chinese justice system: its practical codified stipulations and the court decisions in accordance with them. Confucian moralizing notwithstanding, Chinese law readily acknowledged that disputes and lawsuits over "minor matters" did in fact exist: a substantial body of statutes guided court adjudications in such matters, as local courts rendered judgments about legal right and wrong.

Further, a number of other practical considerations are evident in the Qing courts' actions. The magistrates' caseloads were heavy enough to make unfeasible the time-consuming persuasion and moral education work (such as the later Maoist courts undertook) that "didactic conciliation" would have required. Moreover, litigants who persisted in a dispute through to a formal court session were usually among the most truculent; they had withstood the moral-ideological pressures against litigation built into the justice system and rejected the societal mediation that the filing of a lawsuit almost invariably galvanized. Such insistent litigants more often than not felt genuinely aggrieved or were convinced that the other party had violated the law, contrary to the Confucian assumption that usually both disputants were at least partially at fault. Consequently, in these circumstances magistrates generally adjudicated outright according to codified law. The litigants' filing of pledges of willing acceptance of the court's judgments was simply a formality.

My 1996 book used a collection of 628 Qing court cases from three counties to show that the courts almost never mediated in the manner described by Shiga. In the great majority of the 221 cases that made it to a formal hearing (most of the others being settled through societal mediation after a lawsuit was filed),[4] the courts ruled according to the law: in 170 (77 percent) of the cases, they found outright for one or the other party; in 22 other cases (10 percent), they adjudged that there was no clear-cut violation of the law by either party; and in another 10 cases (5 percent) they ordered further investigation. In just 11 of the 221 cases did the courts arbitrate, ordering the litigants to accept compromises fashioned by the court. In no case did the court engage in persuasion through moral education to obtain "voluntary" acceptance of its judgments, as Shiga's "didactic conciliation" analysis and the ritualistic requirement that litigants file pledges of such acceptance might lead us to expect (Huang, 1996: 241, table 3; see also p. 78). In a later volume, I examined in greater detail the specific legal provisions involved by comparing the Qing with the Republic (Huang, 2001).

What the case records show, in short, is that when minor matters reached court, magistrates generally adjudicated the disputes outright according to the law. Indeed, the well-known Qing jurist Wang Huizu specifically characterized mediation as what community and kin leaders did, while the courts made clear-cut judgments as to legal right and wrong (and for that reason were more likely to cause lasting enmity and, therefore, were less desirable than societal mediation) (Wang, [1793] 1939: 16; see also Huang, 1996: 204ff.). Others, including Liu Heng, Chen Qingmen, and Fang Dashi, similarly emphasized the importance of making unequivocal judgments to deter would-be litigation mongers and to ensure the upholding of the law (Huang, 1996: 205–6).

By the logic of Continental formalism, Confucian ideals and actual court actions seem inconsistent or contradictory; to Chinese jurists, however, there was no issue of logical consistency here. Confucian moralizing set forth the ideals of the system, which in application allowed room for practical stipulations and civil adjudication, even if those seemed to run counter to the Confucian ideals. In Chinese legal reasoning, it seemed obvious that Confucian ideals represented a vision of what the world ought to be like while the practical provisions of the code and the adjudicatory actions of the judges were responses to real-life situations that fell short of those ideals. Practical realities dictated certain actions even as Confucian moralizing continued to point to the vision of an ideal world. Indeed, a Weberian formalist might liken Qing court actions

4. Of the remaining 407 cases, 31 percent (126 cases) were closed because the litigants petitioned to withdraw the lawsuit after the dispute had been successfully resolved either by community/kin mediation (114 of 126 cases) or by the litigants themselves (12 of 126) (Huang, 1996: 241, table 3). For an additional 65 percent (264 cases of 407), cases stalled without any conclusion because litigants neither petitioned to close the case nor sought a formal court session, in many instances because societal mediation or the litigants themselves had successfully resolved the matter and no one bothered to return to court (Huang, 1996: 118–21).

to aspects of the "empirical justice" of Anglo-American common law, with its stronger empiricist or pragmatist emphases than Continental law.

Continental Formalism and Chinese Principles and Practices in Republican Civil Law

The imperial justice system and its epistemological posture were challenged by Western imperialism and the legal systems that accompanied it, most especially that of Continental formalist law. Modern Western law appeared to be an integral part of a modernity that, like industrialization, could not be rejected or even questioned. From the 1898 reforms on, the notion that Chinese laws, not just Chinese military power, lagged behind those of the West took hold widely among Chinese statesmen and intellectuals. They believed that the power of modern Western nation-states sprang above all from their legal systems, and that Meiji Japan's adoption of Western laws and institutions explained the superior power that had dealt China its shocking defeat in the war of 1894–1895.

Furthermore, imperialism itself had a dramatic effect. Chinese sovereignty had been severely compromised by the age of imperialism and the "carving up of the [Chinese] melon." Part of the rationale for imperialist "extraterritoriality" was the presumed backwardness of the Chinese justice system. To regain full international sovereignty, China had to demonstrate its determination to modernize by adopting Western laws. Those motivations were fully evident in Republican lawmaking.

Presented with the modern West's common law and Continental models, the Republican Chinese lawmakers opted for the latter. The reasons were perhaps most succinctly expressed by the chief Guomindang lawmaker, Hu Hanmin, who argued that in Continental law, the code reigns supreme over custom; common law, in contrast, is based on the formalization of custom, which could even take precedence over codified law. Given the backwardness of China and its customs, felt so painfully by the lawmakers in the face of imperialism, there could be no question as to the preferred approach: Hu, and indeed most other Republican Chinese jurists, unequivocally chose Continental law. For Hu, German law was the latest and the best that the West had to offer (Hu, 1978: 847–48; see also Huang, 2001: 65–68).

Republican Chinese civil law therefore came to look very similar to Continental civil law. The Guomindang Civil Code of 1929–1930, like its primary model, the 1900 German Civil Code—given an authoritative English translation by Wang Chonghui, the main legal specialist among the group overseeing the drafting of the code—began by stipulating rights in the abstract, holding them to be universals. The Guomindang code in fact closely followed the approach, structure, and language of the German code (Huang, 2001: chap. 4).

In hindsight, we can see that the ease with which Republican China (and indeed the Qing, in the legal reforms of its last decade) adopted the Western formalist, and adjudicatory, model of civil justice must be attributed in part to its own practical tradition in the Qing of court adjudication in civil matters. At the same time, however, much remained of the old system. The Guomindang Civil Code of 1929–1930 reintroduced, for example, the imperial legal (as well as popular and customary) category of *dian*, or conditional sales of land subject to rights of redemption. Though the draft had initially adopted from German formalist law the principles of unitary and exclusive property rights, which could be sold and purchased, rural realities led to the reintroduction of the principle that allowed the dian maker to redeem the land at favorable terms for a considerable period of time (first indefinitely and then, after 1753, for thirty years; see Huang, 2001: 73–74). This custom, made into an imperial law, was predicated on the moral principle of taking care of the weak and the poor, who in this case might find themselves forced to sell their land in order to survive. It also presupposed that land had a low degree of marketization and little price fluctuation. In the end, the dian formulation was incorporated into the Guomindang Civil Code, even though it ran counter to the overarching principles of property rights law and theory adopted from German law (Huang, 2001: chap. 5). Thus were traditional legal stipulations and imported formalist principles both accommodated in the code.

A similar holdover of old customs in Guomindang civil court practices was found in inheritance rights: despite the adoption of the formalist principle of equality between the sexes, rural sons, not daughters, were the ones entitled to inherit the family farm and obligated to maintain their parents in old age. In the Qing, punishment was stipulated for sons who did not support their parents in old age. Under Guomindang law, "lineal relatives by blood" had a "mutual obligation" "to maintain one another," without regard to gender (Articles 1114–16). In practice, however, the Guomindang continued with the old traditions in the countryside, because most peasant girls married out of their village and moved to the home village of their husbands. The sons were the ones who stayed on the family farm and therefore also bore the responsibility for maintaining their parents in old age. It was a responsibility born of the fact of a peasant economy in which the family farm was the principal source of livelihood, leading to what Fei Xiaotong terms a "feedback model"—the parents supporting their young children, who reciprocate by eventually supporting their parents in their old age; in contrast, the "relay model" of the modern West has no such requirement (Fei, 1983; cf. Huang, 2001: 136). The new principle of gender equality in inheritance was applied only in the towns and cities, where the peasant economy no longer obtained (Huang, 2001: chap. 8).

The Chinese Communist Party, it will be seen, would continue with the same approach, also despite adopting the principle of gender equality in inheritance. In the end, Chinese Communist law would make explicit the practical reality-based linking of inheritance to (old-age) maintenance, legitimating in the legal code the long-standing practice of inheritance rights for rural sons who stay in the village, and not for rural daughters who marry out.

Legal Formalism and Contemporary Chinese Court Practice

The coexistence of imported principles of rights with long-standing Chinese legal principles and practices becomes even more apparent in the legal system of the People's Republic. On the most obvious level, while the 1986 General Principles of the Civil Law of the People's Republic of China follows a format much like that of the Guomindang code (and hence of China's adopted German formalist model), stipulating rights (and obligations) in the abstract, official representations at the same time espouse the ideology of mediation, thereby claiming distinctiveness (and superiority) for the Chinese justice system.

Maoist language had couched this reliance on mediation over adjudication in terms of the "non-antagonistic contradictions among the people" in a socialist society, rather than relying on the Confucian morality of conciliation and forbearance (Mao, [1957] 1971). Nevertheless, the touting of mediation as the dominant characteristic of the Chinese justice system is the same. As late as 1990, some 80 percent of all cases were claimed to be mediated (*Zhongguo falü nianjian*, 1990: 993); even as the new century began, more than two decades into the Reform era, one-half of all cases were said to be mediated (*Zhongguo falü nianjian*, 2001: 1257).

While without question adjudication and mediation shade into each other on a continuum, we must somehow distinguish them conceptually, especially since Chinese courts themselves employ these categories. One useful way, as suggested earlier, is to consider the parties involved: if the final agreement is imposed regardless of the will of one (that is, if one "wins" and the other "loses"), then it does not appear to be a case of genuine mediation.

On this account, court adjudications make up a considerably larger proportion of court actions than official representations might have us believe. In addition to those officially classified as adjudicatory, many court cases are reported as "mediated" so long as the litigants nominally accept the court's judgment, almost in the manner of the traditional ritualistic *ganjie*. Many clear-cut court judgments as to legal right and wrong are represented as mediated because the litigant did not insist on, or saw no purpose in, objecting to the judgment. Concrete examples of such purely pro forma mediation, which might be termed "fictive mediation," will be provided in the discussion below of individual cases.

Another major category of cases is what I call mediatory adjudications, which can be termed "mediations" only in a rather distorted sense of the word. The best example is the denials of contested divorce petitions through court-imposed "mediated reconciliations," considered in detail in chapter 4 on divorce law practices. They begin with the adjudicatory denial of permission to divorce and employ high-handed measures to ensure a reconciliation, often against the will of the petitioner. These, too, appear in the sample of cases discussed below.

Many of the cases are adjudicative mediations, still within the scope of mediation though with adjudicative features. The court, for example, may help the litigants work out compromises with some measure of adjudicatory intervention. For instance, as discussed below, the court may see one party in a divorce as being the one at fault (e.g., the adulterous party) and therefore favor the other in helping to work out a settlement that both parties would accept.

To be sure, some cases approximate the original core sense of mediation. Those are discussed in more detail in the next chapter, which will attempt to define the logics underlying such mediation and also to distinguish between more and less successful cases of mediation.

In its provisions that guide court adjudication, PRC law has taken formalist Western principles about rights and altered their universalist claim and intent with practical stipulations that accord with Chinese realities. At bottom, the same mode of legal thinking—practical moralism—undergirds both contemporary and Qing law. The remainder of this chapter uses case records to delineate in broad strokes the main areas of civil provisions and adjudications. I begin below with tort law and tort cases, for they illustrate well both the importing of the formalist formulation of torts and the persistence of the older, practice-based approach to law.

Tort Law

In formalist Continental law—including the 1900 German Civil Code, which became the blueprint for the Guomindang Civil Code of 1929–1930—tort law begins with the abstract principle that if one party infringes on the rights of another, monetary compensation may be sought for such a "wrongful act." Crucial in this formulation is the idea of fault (in violating another's rights), which is entirely consistent with the more general notion that laws exist to protect individual rights. Thus, part 5 of the Guomindang code, "Wrongful

Acts," began with the stipulation: "A person who, intentionally or by his own fault, wrongfully injures the rights of another is bound to compensate him for any damage arising therefrom" (Article 184). The General Principles of the Civil Law of the PRC adopted in 1986 substantially follows that formulation: "Citizens and legal persons who through their fault (*youyu guocuo*) encroach upon state or collective property or the property or person of other people shall bear civil liability (*minshi zeren*)" (Article 106). On the surface and in theory, at least, PRC law seems consistent with modern Western formalist law in its treatment of torts.

But Article 106 of the General Principles continues: "Civil liability shall still be borne even in the absence of fault, if the law so stipulates." And Article 132 spells out the implication: "If none of the parties is at fault in causing damage, they may share civil liability according to the actual circumstances." A legal formalist might find a logical inconsistency here. How can the law stipulate first that the obligation to compensate another for damages rests on fault, and then go on to say that such obligation may obtain even if there is no fault? How can there be civil liability with no fault? Nothing of this kind appeared in the German Civil Code or the Guomindang Civil Code.

Case records show, first of all, that the courts have employed consistently throughout the post-1949 period the principle of civil liability in case of fault.[5] In 1977 in county A, the plaintiff, a woman about sixty years old, was injured and had to be hospitalized for treatment when the defendant, a teenage student, ran into her during a stone-throwing fight with two other students. Her medical fees and sickness pay were covered by her unit. She sued for the difference between her actual wages and the sickness pay, plus expenses incurred in resting at home for three months. The court took the adjudicatory posture that the defendant was indeed at fault and then "persuaded" the defendant's father to agree to pay the 41.70 yuan difference in wages, and 51 yuan for convalescing expenses. The resulting "mediation agreement" stipulated that the full amount was to be paid by the third month of 1978 (A, 1977-015). In another example, a 1995 case from county B, the plaintiff, while riding a bicycle, was injured by the defendant on a motorbike. The court, on the basis of the report of the traffic police who had investigated at the scene and taken testimony from eyewitnesses, found the defendant at fault and adjudicated (*panjue*) that he pay 3,826 yuan in compensation, plus 400 yuan in court fees (B, 1995-3).

The more interesting cases for our purposes are those in which the other party was not at fault. By the strict formalist principle of wrongful acts, there could be no obligation for compensation. But Chinese courts, at least in the

5. My sample of cases includes only four tort cases from before 1978. All involved clear-cut findings of fault (A, 1977-015; B, 1977-4, 6, 14).

Reform era, have in fact employed consistently in such situations the principle of "civil liability even in the absence of fault." In county A in 1989, for example, a seven-year-old boy running home from school ran into an elderly woman carrying a bottle of boiling hot water. The woman dropped the bottle, spilling the hot water on the boy's chest, back, limbs, and face. The total medical costs (including transportation costs) to treat the burns suffered by the boy came to 2,009.70 yuan. The township government paid 573.70 yuan of that total, and the father of the boy brought suit against the woman for the balance (A, 1989-9).

If torts are conceived of as wrongful acts, then the father should be unable to "win" any compensation, since there is no way to establish fault on the part of the woman. Lacking insurance, or (as here) granted inadequate payment by the township government, the injured could do little more than lament his bad luck. But Chinese courts in such situations typically treat the damages as a social problem caused by the joint actions of the principals involved, for which both parties thus bear some measure of responsibility.

In this case from county A, the judge, after a detailed investigation of the facts, took the adjudicatory posture that the defendant, though not at fault, should share in covering the damages, citing precisely Articles 106 and 132, discussed above, which specify civil liability even in the absence of fault. The court then set about working out a "mediated agreement" (*tiaojie xieyi*) acceptable to both sides, calling for the old woman to help bear 250 yuan of the medical expenses (A, 1989-9).

Numerous other cases illustrate such an approach to obligations for compensation in the absence of fault. In a "vehicular tort" case from county B in 1988, a woman riding a bike on a rainy day slipped and fell, and the vehicle traveling behind her—a small tractor, commonly used in the countryside to transport goods—ran into her. Her collarbone was broken as a result. She was taken to the hospital, where the bone was reset and she spent five days recuperating. The defendant, the tractor driver, willingly paid for those expenses.

But then complications arose because the bone had not been set properly. The woman had to go to another hospital for treatment, and she sued the tractor driver for the additional medical expenses.[6] The township government had tried to mediate, suggesting that the defendant bear 300 yuan of her total expenses, but she wanted more and came to court. Once again, the court took the position that though the defendant was not at fault, he had an obligation to help resolve the problem. It therefore helped to work out a mediated agreement for the defendant to pay 350 yuan (B, 1988-3).

6. Some readers may wonder why she did not sue the hospital instead, since it was responsible for a kind of "malpractice." In China at the time, however, filing a complaint against a state institution was clearly not an option; hence her suit against the other citizen. The extent to which the Administrative Litigation Law of 1990 has changed the situation is not yet clear.

Finally, in a case from B county in 1989 of what we might call a "bicycle tort," the plaintiff was walking home along a road, followed by the defendant, who was traveling, slowly, on his bicycle. The plaintiff turned suddenly, and the defendant ran into him. The unlucky plaintiff suffered a concussion from his fall, requiring a CT scan and incurring considerable medical expense. He filed suit for damages, including the costs of hospitalization and of missing work—a total of nearly 3,000 yuan. The court, after interviewing two witnesses (one in court and one at the witness's work unit) to make sure that it had the facts of the case straight, took the adjudicatory position that neither party was at fault but that both parties should nevertheless bear responsibility for what happened. A mediated agreement was then worked out (B, 1989-16).

The above cases show that depending on the nature of the case, courts rely in adjudicating both on the formalist principle of wrongful acts and on the notion of civil liability in no-fault situations found in the General Principles of the Civil Law. As I have already suggested, the General Principles could make such a stipulation and not speak to its evident logical inconsistency with the formalist rubric because of the practical moralism mode of Chinese legal thinking, not immediately evident in the legal provision. Given a basic attitude of giving priority to actual situations over abstract principles, it simply seemed commonsensical to acknowledge that no-fault accidents occur, despite the formalist formulation of wrongful acts. A civil problem still existed, one that could not be resolved by blaming an at-fault party. The practical solution, so obvious to the lawmakers as to require no further comment, was the principle of "civil liability even in the absence of fault."

Because formalist law has greater prestige than the commonsensical approach of the courts, the wrongful-acts principle is placed first in the General Principles. The relegation of the old practice-based approach and principle to a subordinate position should hardly be surprising, given that this stipulation was preceded by nearly a century of imitating and borrowing from modern Western Continental law, which carried (and still carries) with it all the force and prestige of superior power and more advanced economic development, as well as the added attractions of democracy and human rights. Nevertheless, consistent with their tendency to use practical realities as their point of departure in legal conceptualization, the authors of the General Principles took for granted that fault and no-fault situations both exist in life. The apparent contradiction between the two stipulations, in other words, is present only from the viewpoint of legal formalism, which demands logical consistency with its abstract legal proposition about fault-based "wrongful acts." From the Chinese epistemological outlook, based on fact situations, the combination appears not inconsistent but true to life, and hence in need of no further explanation.

Though the supplementary stipulation, like the method of thinking grounded in fact, is not allowed even by the Chinese lawmakers themselves to take precedence in codified law over the formalist legal principles that have been transplanted from Western Continental law, it provides evidence that the old mode of thinking has persisted down to the present. The law has effectively taken the imported principle of wrongful acts and transformed it from a formalist universal into a guide resembling the moral ideals of the Qing code. Rather than demanding that all fact situations be subsumed under its logic, it is open to modification in practice.

We need to add here that some Chinese civil law specialists have advanced an interpretation different from the analysis presented above. In their view, Chinese civil law has adopted, in addition to the principle of liability for wrongful acts, two other principles of modern Western law, one being "strict liability" (*yange zeren*) and the other, "equitable liability" (*gongping zeren*). According to them, the former has to do with obligation for compensation in situations without fault, and the other with judges' taking into account concrete circumstances (including no fault) to determine civil obligation. Therefore, they believe that what China has imported from the West includes the principle of civil liability without fault (Zhang Xinbao, 2006: 28–30; Ma Yuan, 1998: 414ff.).

However, if we examine closely the concepts, we will see that "strict liability" in fact employs the same original fault logic, only with a looser requirement for proof of fault than with other wrongful acts. Thus, with those who manufacture dangerous products, the victim seeking compensation need only prove that the product is faulty and need not prove fault on the part of the manufacturer. The purpose here is to lower the proof requirement for dangerous products in order to ensure that those manufacturers would take stricter precautions. The logic remains that of obligation on account of fault, by a stricter standard (Huang, 2006a: 153, n10; Zhang Xinbao, 2006: 28).

As for the principle of "equitable liability," some of its advocates (as, for example, Justus Wilhelm Hedemann) did intend to include under "equitable liability" the concept of liability in fact situations without fault (as well as of special considerations for the weak). But the principle was in the end rejected by German lawmakers for inclusion in the civil code (Tunc, 1986: 145ff.). The fact of the matter is that, under the influence of what Weber called "formal rationality," the guiding mode of thought of German civil law was to start from abstract principles and to apply those through legal logic to all fact situations, not the reverse. For this reason, German civil law did not accept the principle of obligation for compensation (in a fact situation) without fault.

The way in which some Chinese civil law scholars have interpreted these two concepts actually illustrates precisely the mode of thinking I am talking about. In the case of the seven-year-old boy recounted above, what the judge called upon was neither the principle of "strict liability," nor of "equitable liability," but rather the distinctive Chinese principle of civil liability without fault. Precisely because Chinese legal thinking habitually starts from concrete fact situations rather than from abstract principles (and considers such a mode the self-evidently correct one), it has (deliberately or not) reinterpreted (or mistaken) the strict liability principle as obligation (in fact situations) without fault, and done the same with the "equitable liability" principle rejected by German civil law.

We can give another example of this difference in modes of thinking. Twelve states in the United States have now adopted so-called no-fault car insurance. On the surface, this appears to be an adoption of the principle of liability (in fact situations) without fault, in addition to the original principle of fault-based obligation. But the logic of no-fault car insurance actually goes like this: the principle of fault-based obligation had led to expensive contestations to prove fault—for this reason, the decision was made to exclude completely considerations of fault in determining compensation. The insured would obtain compensatory payment for damages directly from the insurance company, without any consideration as to the fact situation. Its logic is not that, in light of fact situations that involve damages without fault, the civil liability without fault principle is therefore adopted, but rather that, because of expensive past contestations over fault, the decision was made to not consider fault at all. The logic of no-fault insurance is not to start with the fact situation (as to fault or no fault) to determine the obligation for compensation, but rather to not consider the fact situation at all (Huang 2006a: 153).

The principle of no-fault divorce that was adopted in the West during the 1960s and 1970s was based on the same logic. It is very different from Chinese law, which sees two kinds of fact situations in divorce disputes, those involving fault (such as a third-party or abuse) and those not, and the law is to act accordingly, but rather, because the fault principle that governed divorce disputes for so long led to so many expensive arguments over fault, legislators decided to adopt the general principle to not consider fault at all in any and all divorce disputes. The meaning of the English term "no-fault" is to "not consider fault," not that there are fact situations without fault. The logic of the legal system as a whole remains that of fault; the logic of the system has not been overturned or revised by the adoption of "no-fault divorce."

Property Rights and Obligations: Inheritance and Old-Age Support

PRC law, much like the Guomindang law before it, emphasizes the imported principle of property rights: "'Property ownership' means the owner's rights to lawfully possess, utilize, profit from and dispose of his property" (General Principles of the Civil Law, [1986] 1987: Article 71).[7] But at the same time, as we will see, the law has incorporated the older practice-based principle that took account of the realities of the peasant family farm, in which individual property claims or rights were constrained by familial claims and obligations. Similarly, the law blends the new imported principle of equal inheritance rights for daughters ("Law of Succession,"[8] [1985] 1987: Articles 9, 10, 13) with the older practice and principle of inheritance by sons only.

Property rights to rural land and houses in imperial China generally came with legal and customary constraints. No peasant patriarch, for example, could legally disinherit a son or elect to pass his land and house to others outside the family in preference to his sons. Land and house ownership was in fact seen largely as cross-generational and familial, not individual. The father's rights resembled more those of a custodian (albeit with wide discretionary powers) holding property in trust for his sons than those of an owner with absolute rights to dispose of the property as he saw fit. At the same time, the son's inheritance of the father's land and house came with obligations for his parents' old-age support. Those obligations did not cease when he formally became the head of his own household.

These were principles and practices born of the economics of the peasant family farm. Peasant households were not simply consumption units, as are most households in modern urban society; they were also production units, owning their source of livelihood (land) in common. Production and consumption were inextricably entwined, as A. V. Chayanov so cogently pointed out already in 1925 (Chayanov, [1966] 1986; see also Huang, 1985: 3–9; 1990: 5–11). Property rights, we might add, were therefore fitted to the life cycle of the family as both consumption and production unit, as the able producers provided for the consumption of the entire unit: parents would support their offspring during their nonproducing years, and children would in return support their parents in old age.

Those property principles and practices have continued into the post-1949 period. Collectivization, to be sure, put an end to private ownership in land: household divisions of land and market transactions in land ceased altogether.

7. In contemporary Western corporate practice, ownership has in fact come to be broken up into a "bundle of rights" shared by multiple parties, including not only stockholders and managers but also bondholders, boards of directors, and even labor unions, tax authorities, government regulators, labor unions, large suppliers and customers, and so on. For a more detailed discussion, see Grey (1980); see also Cui (1996) and Huang (2001: 109–10).

8. "Law of Succession" is the official English translation, though perhaps a better rendering is "Law of Inheritance," since under PRC law succession to the patriline is no longer the major issue it had been under the Qing (Bernhardt, 1999). But I use here the official English translation, as I have with almost all other citations from PRC law in this chapter, unless otherwise noted.

But it did not put an end to peasants' ownership of their houses. Though almost never bought and sold in the collective era, they were divided and passed on to heirs just as before the revolution. Nor did collectivization put an end to the household as the basic production-consumption unit. Workpoints for peasant cultivators were calculated individually, but they were paid to each household through its head. The old model—that the able producers of the household should support those not able—persisted. With the de-collectivization of farming in the 1980s, the old family-farm economy returned, and the household is once more the basic unit of both production and consumption. In the absence of any viable pension plans in the countryside, the old principles and practices remain the only feasible answer to the problem of old-age support.

Inheritance has therefore continued to be accompanied by obligations to support parents in their old age, just as before the revolution. The Qing code had put the matter negatively, specifying punishments: sons who failed to provide adequately for their parents were to be punished (Statute 338). The Republican Civil Code of 1929–1930, we have seen, put it positively, laying out the mutual obligations of lineal blood relations to support one another. Post-1949 inheritance law, though not formally promulgated until the 1985 Law of Succession, would explicitly link the right to inherit and the obligation to provide old-age support: "At the time of distributing the estate, successors who have made the predominant contributions in maintaining the decedent or have lived with the decedent may be given a larger share. At the time of distributing the estate, successors who had the ability and were in a position to maintain the decedent but failed to fulfill their duties shall be given no share or a smaller share of the estate" (Article 13).

In the countryside, this legal principle applies mainly to the family house, not the land, which remains collectively owned. The samples from county A and county B contain a total of fifteen cases over the inheritance of the family house; four of them involve issues of old-age support as well.

These examples suggest, first of all, that the courts were consistent in upholding the equal rights of inheritance of sons. In two cases, stepbrothers battled over their rights of inheritance.[9] In 1965, a younger man sued his elder stepbrother for his share of the house left by their natural father. His stepbrother had sold one room of the four-room house ten years earlier to pay for the house's repair (after a typhoon) and for the reconstruction of the remaining three rooms into a two-room house. The court, after repeated attempts to "mediate" (i.e., to persuade the litigants to willingly accept its position), ruled

9. There are no examples of blood brothers suing one another, probably because in their case, the principle of equal inheritance is universally accepted.

(*caiding*) that the two were entitled to equal shares of the inheritance, or one room each of the rebuilt house (A, 1965-02). In 1988, similarly, a plaintiff sued his two elder stepbrothers for his share of the old family house. The two, without consulting him, had torn down the center room of the old house to build a new home. The court took the position that by law, the old house belonged equally to the three brothers. But since the two elder brothers had already built their new home, they were to compensate the younger brother for his share. The "mediation agreement" worked out under the court's adjudicatory posture was for the two defendants to compensate the plaintiff 250 yuan for his share of the house's value (A, 1988-9).

When it comes to daughters, the courts have applied the new principle of gender equality in inheritance selectively—mainly in the towns and cities, and generally not in the countryside. Thus, in a 1989 case from the town of Huayangqiao, a sister sued her brother for part of their deceased father's house; he was occupying seven of its eight and one-half rooms. The court's judgment (*panjue*) was that brother and sister should have equal shares, in accordance with the letter of the code (A, 1988-11). In the villages, however, the old principle of inheritance by sons and not daughters generally prevailed. Since women by and large continued to marry out into their husband's village, dividing the father's house between sons who continued to live in the same village and daughters who had moved to another village would be enormously complex.[10] The obvious solution—selling the house and parceling out the cash proceeds—was not a realistic option in the Maoist era, given the absence of market transactions in real estate. In Huayangqiao village and Huayang(qiao) Township down through the 1980s, there was not a single instance of a married-out sister attempting to sue a brother for a share of the family's house (INT90-6). The standard social practice was for the daughters marrying out to give up any claim to it (INT91-6).

The post-1949 court has in fact been consistent during both the Maoist and Reform periods in linking inheritance rights with obligations for old-age support. The Supreme People's Court issued multiple directives to that effect beginning in 1950 (Zuigao renmin fayuan, 1994: 1279, 1286, 1292–93), and the lower courts acted accordingly. In a case from 1953, for example, a granddaughter-in-law brought suit against her stepmother-in-law for the house of the grandparents-in-law. While both were equally entitled to it as the sole surviving legal heirs, the plaintiff, unlike the defendant, had not borne any of the burdens of maintaining the elderly couple before they died. The court

10. Of course, families that had no sons frequently took in a son-in-law. The practice had been quite common in Huayangqiao village before 1949, and remained so. In this situation, the stay-in daughter customarily inherited her father's property just as a son would do.

explicitly took that fact into account and adjudicated that the plaintiff should receive just two and a half rooms of the ten-room house, and the defendant the rest (B, 1953-12).[11]

The obligation of children to support their elderly parents of course had application beyond the ownership of the family house. It also involved subsistence in other respects. Thus, in 1989, an elderly woman of eighty-one sued her stepson for old-age support. She had raised him from the time he was seven, and continued to maintain him from the time of his father's death in 1949 until his adulthood. From 1962 (when the woman was fifty-four) onward, her stepson had provided her with grain and fuel, thereby fulfilling his obligations. However, conflicts arose in 1979 between the plaintiff, her daughter, and the defendant over the division of the family house. The plaintiff ended up living with her daughter, and the defendant ceased thereafter to provide her any support. The court was unable to produce a mediated resolution. In rendering judgment (*panjue*), it cited two relevant paragraphs of the 1980 Marriage Law: "If children fail to perform their duty, parents who are unable to work or have difficulty in providing for themselves shall have the right to demand support payments from their children" (Article 15), and "The relevant provisions of this Law governing the relationship between parents and children shall apply to the rights and duties in the relationship between step-fathers or step-mothers and their step-children who receive care and education from them" (Article 21). The judgment required the defendant henceforth to provide his stepmother with twenty yuan per month in cash and 7.5 kilograms of rice, as well as to cover half of her medical expenses. He was also to pay the fifty yuan in court costs (A, 1989-020).

Thus the 1985 Law of Succession formally links inheritance rights to maintenance obligations, thereby incorporating principles and practices from the past to deal with social realities even after modern Western formalist legal principles have been adopted. Its provisions may be considered the codified justification for the long-standing legal custom of letting sons who stayed in the village, not the daughters who married out, inherit the family home. And, just as with the stipulation about civil liability in no-fault situations involving

---

11. In a 1976 case, a deceased man's sister-in-law, nephew's wife, grandnephew, and maternal grandnephew brought suit for the inheritance of his house. The man, who had died in 1975 unwed and childless, had worked as a doctor in the town health system until 1966. Thereafter, he had lived on a pension of 10 yuan a month (from the town clinic) until his death in 1975. The plaintiffs had provided some care when he was ailing, but they had otherwise offered no support in his old age. The court ruled (*caiding*) that because there had been no relationship of maintenance (*shanyang guanxi*), the plaintiffs, who were not legitimate heirs (limited to one's spouse, offspring, parents, and then brothers and sisters, grandparents, and maternal grandparents), had no legal basis for their claim of inheritance. The deceased was to be treated as a terminal household (*juehu*), whose property was to go to the state (A, 1976-01).

tort law, the lawmakers saw no need to speak to the apparent contradiction between the traditional approach and the new abstract principles about exclusive individual property rights and gender equality in inheritance. Once again, the principles that in Western Continental formalist law carried with them an imperative for universality and logical consistency were here incorporated into law under a mode of reasoning that takes for granted divergences between idealized principles and practical applications. Generalized principles can therefore be foregrounded in codified law, accompanied by a stipulation modifying them to fit the practical realities of the countryside.

Debt Obligations

Imperial and modern Chinese law, on the one hand, and modern Western law, on the other, showed no great dissimilarity in the requirement to repay legitimate debts; the difference was over the treatment of interest. On that score Chinese law, once again, has adapted steadily to the realities of a growing market economy, notwithstanding earlier Maoist principles that denied the legitimacy of interest.

In general, the Qing code had started from the logic of a subsistence economy. Its main concern was to control the usurious lending that accompanied borrowing to survive: the code thus stipulated a maximum interest rate of 3 percent per month, or 36 percent per year. It allowed some room for the idea that money capital was entitled to interest, but it set a ceiling—total interest might not exceed the original principal (Statute 149). That approach to interest, of course, was largely consistent with the reality of relatively stable prices in the Qing. (The code also went on to stipulate, as we have seen, that nonpayment of legitimate loans would be punished.)

The Republican code kept the stricture against usury (after stipulating the obligation to repay debts in the manner of the German Civil Code), setting a legal annual maximum of 20 percent interest. It also incorporated more fully the logic of a market economy, by making an interest rate of 5 percent the default rate on interest-bearing debts for which a contract did not fix a rate (Articles 205, 203; Huang, 2001: chap. 7).

And while the post-1949 state reaffirmed the principle that debts must be repaid, it did not address the issue of interest—consistent with its vision of a socialist economy of stable prices and no private capital. Thus, the 1986 General Principles stipulated simply that "legitimate loan relationships shall be protected by law" and that "debts shall be cleared. If a debtor is unable to repay his debt immediately, he may repay by installments with the consent of the creditor or a ruling by a people's court. If a debtor is capable of repaying his debt but refuses to do so, repayment shall be compelled by the decision of the people's court" (Articles 90, 108). With the coming of marketization in the Reform era, however, the PRC courts too have increasingly come to modify the earlier Maoist vision to treat interest as legitimate, in accord with the realities of the price changes and inflation accompanying a growing market economy.

The sample from the two counties contains fifteen debt cases. In all five from county A in 1953, the court took the position that the loan must be repaid. In four of them, the defendants agreed to repayments within a specified amount of time (A, 1953-21, 012, 018, 019).[12]

Disputes over debts became rather rare after the early 1950s, but the courts acted consistently when they did crop up. In two cases from county A in 1965, the court took the position that the debts must be repaid. In one, involving a debt of 1,150 yuan for an ox, the plaintiff agreed to a symbolic compromise, taking a loss of 50 yuan to placate a defendant who thought after the fact that the agreed-on sale price was too high (A, 1965-016). In the other, involving two state supply-and-sale agencies (*gongxiaoshe*), the full amount of the principal was paid (A, 1965-16). The issue of interest did not arise in those cases, as prices at the time were highly stable.

With the marketization of the 1980s, the number of lawsuits involving debt increased, approaching the frequency seen in the early 1950s. In Songjiang County by 1989 and 1990, they were accounting for more than 10 percent of all cases (Huang, 2005: 190). In the five cases from county A in 1988 and 1989, four involved simple payments of the principal, without interest (A, 1988-01; 1989-12, 03, 019). In a 1989 case, for example, the defendant had used for personal family expenses the 2,000 yuan given to him by the plaintiff

12 In the remaining case, two peasants, both classified as "poor peasant" in the Land Reform, had been involved in a credit society in 1947. Through that society, the plaintiff had lent the defendant 1.9 *shi* (ca. 160 catties) of unpolished, short-grain rice, under a contracted condition of prepayment in March 1953 of a total of 3.5 shi, to include principal and interest. The defendant paid the plaintiff back 2.0 shi, arguing that he was not liable for any more interest, since the credit society had since been disbanded. The court in its judgment first cited a regulation issued by the State Council on the handling of debt disputes in villages of farmed areas, to the effect that old credit arrangements should continue in force. However, in view of the fact that the society had been dissolved and that the defendant had already repaid 2.0 shi, and considering the concrete conditions of the case, the court ordered the defendant to pay the rest of the debt in two installments: 0.5 shi by 1 December 1953, and another 0.3 shi by 1 December 1954. "Thenceforth, the debt relationship between the two will be considered terminated." The defendant, in other words, was to pay another 0.8 shi, or one-half of the total interest of 1.6 shi claimed by the plaintiff (A, 1953-06).

The debt case from county B from 1953 shows the special circumstances and considerations surrounding the height of class revolution during the Land Reform. The plaintiff, who had borrowed 7.3 shi of corn from the defendant and then repaid just 1.8 shi, had been mistakenly classified a "landlord"; bearing the burden of being labeled a class enemy, he had actually begged the defendant to accept his repayment of the balance. But the defendant (classified a "middle peasant"), fearing that if he accepted payment he might be seen as a usurer, had actually refused to accept it. By 1953, however, things had settled down and the defendant sought repayment. But now the plaintiff, having been (correctly) reclassified as a middle peasant, took the position that the state's policy was that debts incurred during the Land Reform were to be forgiven. The court found for the plaintiff (B, 1953-9).

a year earlier (in September 1988) to purchase 20,000 bricks. The court took the position that the debt had to be paid, and managed to get the defendant to accede. "Through the mediation of the court," the case record states, the parties agreed that the defendant would make a single payment of 1,000 yuan before July 1989, and give back 150 yuan each month thereafter until the entire debt was paid. The defendant was also to bear the court costs of 40 yuan (A, 1989-12). There was no mention of interest, even though by February 1990—the date by which the plaintiff was to recover the full amount of his loan, according to the stipulated schedule—the purchasing power of 2,000 yuan would be substantially less than it was at the time of the original loan fifteen months earlier.

The fifth case, however, shows the beginnings of a change in attitude toward interest. In this case, the plaintiff had agreed to let the defendant tear down the central room of her house and use the building materials for his new home. Both had set the value of the materials at 150 yuan, but the defendant repaid only 50 yuan. The plaintiff brought suit for the balance, plus interest and "losses sustained in seeking repayment" (*cuikuan sunshi fei*). The court succeeded in getting the defendant to agree to pay the balance of 100 yuan immediately, plus another 50 yuan in interest and the 30 yuan in court costs (A, 1988-011).

According to the Songjiang County Court judges interviewed, their rule of thumb during the Maoist years was "If the principal is repaid, that is good enough." By the early 1990s, commercialization and inflation were leading to rethinking of the legality of interest charges. The Supreme People's Court issued regulations (*guiding*) in 1991 that set the legal maximum at four times the official bank rate (Zuigao renmin fayuan, 1994: 1194). In practice, the judges said, when an original loan agreement specified interest, they would consider acceptable a rate up to double the official bank rate (INT93-8).

By 1995, the cases from county B show, the inclusion of interest in debt obligations had become quite well established. In one case, the defendant, the deputy head of a town (*fu zhenzhang*), had contracted to buy a car from a car company for 33,000 yuan and had paid a 3,000 yuan deposit. But he then refused to pay any more, and the company brought suit. The defendant claimed that the company had been late in delivering the car to him, that the body of the car had some problems, that the starter mechanism had to be changed, and that he had to hire someone to help with the registration paperwork. Altogether, he claimed, he had to spend 6,000 to 7,000 yuan. The court took the adjudicatory posture that he had to pay the money owed, plus interest. In the end, he agreed (reportedly through the "mediation" of the court) to pay the balance of 30,000 yuan, plus another 5,000 yuan in interest in two payments within the next five months (B, 1995: 1). The law in action, once again, had taken practical realities into account in developing new guides to court adjudication. Formal provisions regarding interest seem likely to be added to the code in the future.

Divorce

We turn finally to divorce law, which deserves detailed attention because it has until recently been the largest of all categories of civil cases.[13] In addition, in this area even more than in other civil spheres of the law, official representations in the PRC would have us believe that the courts almost never adjudicated. Unlike other civil cases, all contested divorce lawsuits were procedurally required (rather than just encouraged) by both the 1950 and the 1980 Marriage Law to undergo mediation first before adjudication could be considered (Marriage Law, [1950] 1959: Article 17; Marriage Law, [1980] 1987: Article 25).

As in other areas of civil law, the imported principles and the practical stipulations and actions are at considerable variance in divorce law. As has been seen in chapter 4, PRC law on marriage and divorce had begun in the 1931 Jiangxi Soviet's Marriage Regulations of the Chinese Soviet Republic (Zhonghua suwei'ai gongheguo hunyin tiaoli), with the principles of gender equality (imported from the Soviet Union) and of divorce granted on the demand of either party. Those provisions had provoked a great deal of opposition in the larger society, especially from peasants, for whom marriage involved a huge, once-in-a-lifetime expenditure. The dimensions of the problem of rural resistance were demonstrated when efforts to implement the new marriage law targeted unacceptable old-style marriages: bigamy/polygamy, slave wives, *tongyangxi* (young girls brought into the home to be raised as prospective daughters-in-law), purchased wives, and parentally imposed marriages. By the party's own statistics, during the campaign of 1950–1953 as many as 70,000 to 80,000 people (mainly rural women) were killed or committed suicide annually.

The party responded not by discarding the promised principle of gender equality or the legitimacy of ex parte petitions but by seeking practical solutions through court actions. The 1950 Marriage Law had stipulated a single procedural requirement—"mediation" in all contested divorce cases—precisely in anticipation of rural resistance. That became the party's main coping mechanism. Ultimately, the Maoist courts took a strongly adjudicative posture against divorce, evinced by either outright adjudication or mediatory

13. "Economic" cases (mainly contract disputes) eventually became dominant. In 1989, there were 745,267 divorce cases and 634,941 contract cases (*Zhongguo falü nianjian*, 1990: 994). In 2003, the 1,264,037 "marriage, family, and inheritance" cases were far outnumbered by 2,266,476 contract disputes (*Zhongguo falü nianjian*, 2004: 1055).

adjudication against divorce, as they intervened actively and aggressively to try to "mediate" marital relationships. Thus was an imported radical general principle of gender equality (and divorce on demand) modified in actual application (see chapter 4; cf. Johnson, 1983; Diamant, 2000).[14]

Adjudications against Divorce

The following examples will illustrate just how restrictive and adjudicatory the legal system was toward divorce, after the relatively liberal period of the early 1950s. In 1977, a wife sued for divorce after her husband was sentenced to five years' imprisonment following his conviction for raping and impregnating his uncle's minor daughter. The husband, however, did not wish to divorce. The county A court took the position that in accordance with the state's policy of reforming criminals with relatively "minor" offenses, the woman should drop her suit. The record states that "after the court and the woman's unit worked on the wife to give up her request for the sake of her husband's reform and for the sake of their two children, she indicated that she trusted 'the organization' [*zuzhi*, i.e., the party], that she was willing to listen to the organization, but that if the man's behavior should fail to improve, she would ask again for divorce" (A, 1977-18). The court's stance was consistent with a basic tenet of post-1949 Chinese criminal law: in dealing with offenders, "education would be combined with punishment" (see, for example, Zhonghua renmin gongheguo zhi'an guanli chufa tiaoli, [1986] 1987: Article 4). It amounted to a judgment denying the request for divorce. In this instance, the woman was persuaded "voluntarily" to withdraw her lawsuit (*chesu*).

This approach continued even in the liberalized late 1980s. In 1989, a woman sued for divorce on the grounds that her husband was a good-for-nothing who liked to play and gamble, that he had committed adultery with a third party in 1982, and that he had been convicted of larceny in 1985 and sentenced to five years' imprisonment. The county A court further learned that while in prison the husband asked repeatedly for money and for this and that gift, at a time when the wife could barely support herself and their daughter. But the court noted that it had ascertained that the wife's main concern was the effect on her daughter's future of having a convicted criminal for a father. The judge therefore took the position that the wife should not seek a divorce. He advised her that "since the defendant will be released by February of next year, the court hoped that she would for the sake of the

14. In actual implementation of the "mediation" approach, of course, the influence of patriarchal attitudes was probably unavoidable. Johnson's argument (1983) could likely find support from an analysis of court actions.

daughter and for the reform of the defendant do all she could to reconcile." The plaintiff agreed, with the caveat that if the husband failed to reform after leaving prison, she would again ask for divorce. The case was thus reported as "mediated" (A, 1989-017).

According to the Songjiang County judges interviewed, another consistent adjudicatory posture, though never formally codified, was always to deny a request for divorce from the party deemed to be at fault if the aggrieved spouse objected (INT93-9). Such situations most commonly arose when an individual was involved in adulterous relations with a third party and wished to leave a spouse for his or her paramour. The sample provides two examples of such cases. In the first, a husband in 1988 sought a divorce, ostensibly because of incompatibility with his wife. He also charged that his wife, sister-in-law, and mother-in-law had ganged up on him and beaten him. On investigation, the court learned that the relations between the two had been good until the husband fell for a woman worker in his factory, and the new relationship was the true reason the husband wanted a divorce. Both the court and the work unit held that the married couple could reconcile if the man would just sever his relations with that third party. The husband, however, insisted on divorce. The court therefore adjudicated to deny permission for divorce (*panjue buzhun lihun*) (A, 1988-13).

In the second case, also from 1988, the woman sought a divorce because she had developed a relationship with another worker. The husband's violent reactions to her friendship with the third party aggravated matters. The court held that the husband was wrong to beat her and threaten her with a knife as he did, but that she was at fault for the improper relationship with a third party. On that basis, the court adjudicated to deny permission for divorce (A, 1988-14).

These cases demonstrate the courts' highly restrictive adjudicatory posture against divorce. The 1990s would see liberalization of divorce in general and most particularly in the treatment of cases involving third parties, as will be seen below.

Mediatory Adjudications against Divorce

As has been seen in chapter 4, in the face of rural resistance to its marriage law, the party's main response was the distinctive Maoist method and approach of "mediated reconciliations" (*tiaojie hehao*), invented to cope with seriously contested divorce cases. Judges would go down to the villages to actively investigate the foundation and history of a couple's relationship, interviewing their relatives, neighbors, and the village leadership. Unless they concluded that the relationship was utterly hopeless and beyond repair, they would deny the divorce petition as a matter of course and intervene aggressively to try to effect reconciliations. Their tools included moral and ideological persuasion as well as coercive measures, such as making clear the court's disinclination to grant divorce, sometimes flatly declaring that the court would rule outright against it. They would bring to bear pressure from relatives, the village leadership, and even the party organization. Sometimes they would go so far as to provide real material inducements against divorce—helping a couple build a house, arranging for improved employment for the husband or wife, and so on.

Such practices were at bottom adjudicatory (against divorce), often imposed against the will of the petitioner. They cannot be understood simply as "mediation" in the term's conventional English or traditional Chinese usage. They are much better understood as what I would call "mediatory adjudication."

Mediated reconciliation was in fact the courts' standard response to virtually all seriously contested divorce petitions. While national statistics do show a large number of mediated divorces and adjudicated divorces, in a large proportion of these both parties wished to divorce and the courts' real role was only to help work out the specifics of a settlement (see chapter 4; Huang, 2005: 167–69). The response to contested petitions was almost always denial accompanied by coercive mediated reconciliation and, if that failed, outright adjudication against divorce. In 1989, the courts claimed that about 80 percent (125,000) of the petitions were successfully resolved via mediated reconciliation, versus 34,000 adjudications against divorce. In 2000, the proportion was lower, though still considerable: 40 percent, or 89,000 mediated reconciliations to 108,000 adjudications against divorce (*Zhongguo falü nianjian*, 2001: 1257).

As those figures suggest, the 1990s would see considerable decline in the resort to Maoist mediated reconciliations (both absolutely and proportionally) and some relaxing of the strict adjudicatory postures taken by the courts in the past. Clearly, throughout the Maoist period the legal system was extremely reluctant to grant contested divorces.

Adjudication for Divorce

In some fact situations, narrow in scope, the post-1949 court did adjudicate for divorce over the objections of one party.[15] These cases serve to round out our picture of the adjudicatory sphere of the PRC's divorce law.

The 1953 cases stand out because they were brought during the campaign against old-style marriages following the passage of the 1950 Marriage Law. In

15. The sample contains eighteen outright adjudications for divorce from county A, and twenty-eight from county B.

county B, for example, a man who was a cadre in the labor union organization in Tangshan sued for divorce on the grounds that his wife was "backward and selfish" (*luohou zisi*). The wife, it turned out, had married into his family as a *tongyangxi* when she was just ten (and the two had married finally when he turned twenty-two). For the court, the latter fact was the crucial determining factor in its judgment for divorce, given the concerns of the time: "The feudal marriage system is most irrational and immoral. Such marital relations if continued would only add to the misery [of the parties]" (B, 1953-19).

In county A in 1953, similarly, the plaintiff's intent in bringing a complaint was to try to use the court for leverage against his adulterous wife. Two years earlier he had obtained the support of the ward (*qu*) government to punish his wife for her adulterous relationship with another man. In that instance, the ward government had "educated" her and required her to sever relations with her paramour. But relations between the couple had not improved, and she had recently left him again. This time he brought suit. The woman, however, countered that she had been forced to marry her husband (by his underworld sworn brother), that the age difference (sixteen years) between the two was too great, and that her husband was an unbearable male chauvinist who frequently beat her. The court, reflecting the climate of the time, ultimately took the side of the wife: after reprimanding her for her adulterous action, it nevertheless adjudicated for divorce, because of the campaign against the old society's forced and abusive marriages (A, 1953-01).[16]

Another major category of adjudication for divorce involved spouses of convicted criminals who had been sentenced for major offenses to long prison terms so that any hope for a viable marital relationship was unrealistic. One 1953 case involved a husband sentenced to twelve years for opium peddling; a second, a man who received a five-year sentence for collaborating with the Japanese (A, 1953-11, 20). Other cases involved two husbands sentenced to ten years for "counterrevolutionary" activities (A, 1965-012, 11); two repeat

16. In a related phenomenon, party leaders took advantage of the campaign to obtain divorces from their peasant wives, often in order to pursue new relationships with women comrades with whom they had fallen in love—an issue Ding Ling had raised as early as 1942, in her essay criticizing male chauvinism within the party on the occasion of International Women's Day (Ding, 1942). Thus, in county B, a party "commissioner" for the ward (*qu zhuanyuan*) petitioned the court for divorce on the grounds that his relationship with his wife had ruptured because of her "backward feudal thinking." The couple, it turned out, had four children and she was four months pregnant with the fifth. But the petition was nevertheless granted, as he conceded to her all of their property as well as custody over the children (B, 1953-1). In three other cases, leading local cadres successfully obtained divorce on similar grounds (B, 1953-5, 7, 8). In another case, a "revolutionary" woman cadre who was chair of the "women's committee" (*funü weiyuanhui*) managed to win divorce for similar reasons: she filed for divorce on the grounds that her husband's "thinking was backward," and that he "would not even allow her to attend meetings." The court granted the divorce on the grounds that because "the woman's thinking was progressive and the defendant's backward, the plaintiff was kept from participating in the revolutionary work" (B, 1953-20).

offenders, both jailed for larceny (A, 1977-2, 20); a husband convicted repeatedly for swindling (A, 1988-17); and a rapist sentenced to six years' imprisonment (A, 1989-10).

The courts also adjudicated for divorce when, in the court's judgment, both parties wished to divorce but one party was holding out to make unreasonable demands in the divorce settlement. In the eyes of the court, such opposition to divorce was not based on a genuine desire to reconcile. In a 1953 case, for example, a young peasant couple who had not known each other before marrying simply did not get along. Apparently, they did not sleep together. The disappointed parents-in-law accused the woman of having another lover and forbade her from visiting her natal home. They also gave her an ultimatum, threatening to "struggle" her (*douzheng*) if things did not improve within five days. At that, the woman ran back to her natal home and brought suit for divorce. The court ascertained that the husband likewise felt the marriage was unsalvageable but was insisting that his family's expenses for the betrothal gift and the wedding ceremony be repaid. After satisfying itself that there was truly no hope for a reconciliation, the court, "for the sake of the future of the couple," rendered a judgment for divorce over the objections of the husband (A, 1953-5; see also 16, a similar case). Another couple who had long lived separately both wanted to divorce, but the husband held out for repayment of one-half of his betrothal and marriage expenses (A, 1977-20). And when a husband and wife both wished to divorce but could not come to a financial agreement, the court adjudicated to set the terms for the divorce settlement (A, 1989-01).

In the final category of divorce adjudication, clearly very difficult to establish in the Maoist court, "the (emotional) relationship (*ganqing*) had truly ruptured."[17] In a 1953 case, for example, the couple's feelings had long ago soured. The man was apparently lazy as a peasant cultivator, and his wife earned most of the family's income by hiring out as a servant in Shanghai. She stopped sending money back a year before the lawsuit; by 1953, the couple had lived apart for four years and the woman was already raising two children with another man. The husband nevertheless objected to the divorce. The court ascertained that "the relationship had already ruptured to a point beyond repair" and adjudicated for divorce (A, 1953-04).

A later example involved two village teachers estranged during the Cultural Revolution. At the time of their marriage, the woman apparently had

17. The Chinese term *ganqing* is not easy to translate. The official English version of this law renders *ru ganqing que yi polie* as "if mutual affection no longer exists," but I prefer "if the (emotional) relationship between the couple has truly ruptured." As I noted in my earlier chapter on divorce law practices, judges customarily rate a couple's ganqing as very good, good, average, or poor. Because "(emotional) relationship," unlike "mutual affection," allows for such gradations, I believe it captures the meaning of the term more exactly (see chapter 4; Huang, 2005: 155n8).

concealed from the man her father's political background as a "counterrevolutionary." At the height of the Cultural Revolution, the husband wrote an open letter exposing his wife's family background and attacked her mother and brother for their "innate class character" (*jieji benzhi*). In 1977, when the woman brought suit for divorce, the couple had already been living separately for four years. The husband, moreover, had just been convicted as a hooligan (*liumang*). The couple's work units had made repeated efforts to get them to reconcile, but to no avail. The court determined that the feelings between the two were beyond repair because, the judge's report acknowledged, "The man's action had been one for which she could not forgive him." It therefore adjudicated for divorce over the husband's objections (A, 1977-13). As two Songjiang judges pointed out, there was general agreement among judges that for one spouse to attack another politically in the Cultural Revolution was an act so unpardonable as to make reconciliation impossible (INT93-9).

In both of the above cases, it should be noted, the couple had already been separated for a long period of time—four years. In general, the Maoist (and also the early reformist) court maintained a very strict position against granting contested divorces and insisted instead on trying to effect mediated reconciliations. That state of affairs, we have seen, has been dramatically depicted for English-language audiences in Ha Jin's prize-winning novel *Waiting* (1999).

Divorce Law in Transition

Substantial changes regarding divorce came only in the 1990s. The pattern of legal change is similar to that observed in other areas of civil law: new legal stipulations emerged first from changed circumstances, formulated in preliminary ways by Supreme People's Court directives and opinions to guide court adjudication and formally codified only after having been thoroughly tested in practice.

With the return of lawsuits over property and debt in numbers not seen since the early 1950s, plus the emergence of contract disputes, the courts have simply been overwhelmed. Partly in response, there came the call for giving up the Maoist requirements of systematic on-site investigations by the judges in favor of relying on evidence presented at the courts by the litigants (a method dubbed *tingshen diaocha*, or "investigate by adjudging at court") (chapter 4; Huang, 2005: 157, 170). Such a change would also put an end to aggressive Maoist intervention in the home communities to effect couples' mediated reconciliations. As two Songjiang County judges interviewed pointed out, this approach was simply less time-consuming and more efficient in dealing with mounting caseloads (INT93-9). The net effect was a decline in Maoist interventionist mediations, making divorce easier to obtain.

In addition, the Songjiang judges observed, there was also considerable rethinking about the practical consequences of the highly restrictive posture of the divorce courts in the Maoist period. According to them, typically half of all couples to whom permission to divorce was denied eventually ended up divorcing, despite the courts' attempts to effect reconciliation (INT93-9).[18] Vigorous court interventions often merely forced the petitioner to give in temporarily, only to return again and again—in the manner of Liu Kong, the protagonist seeking divorce in Ha Jin's novel.

These changes and changed perceptions, of course, reflected larger shifts. In the past two decades, party-state control has contracted at the same time that the role of the courts has expanded. And within the legal system itself, the (vertical) interventionist reach of the courts into the private lives of people has diminished even as the (horizontal) scope of activities covered by the courts has enlarged greatly.

The altered circumstances and rethinking were accompanied by new, more liberal formulations concerning divorce, most especially the "Fourteen Articles" issued by the Supreme People's Court in November 1989 to guide the lower courts in interpreting the law's broad instruction to use the emotional relationship (ganqing) of a couple as the criterion for determining whether to allow divorce (as codified in the 1980 Marriage Law).[19] As one informant put it, "The feelings between a couple are not something an outsider can easily ascertain; like an old shoe, you don't know how it feels unless you are wearing it." The new guidelines were intended in part to address that difficulty.

A major change was the court's posture toward an adulterous party seeking divorce. In a report to the National People's Congress in 1982 about the civil procedural law, Wu Xinyu, one of the nation's top jurists and deputy chair of the Law Committee of the National People's Congress, referred specifically to the past practice of denying divorce to an at-fault party. Such denials had, as he put it, been used as a kind of punishment for the perceived wrongdoing. He urged that the practice be discontinued and that henceforth the intended punishment be meted out in some other form (for example, in working out the property settlement). If the emotional relationship between the couple had truly ruptured, he recommended, judges should adjudicate for divorce

18. In 1988, the *Bulletin on China's Legal System* (*Zhongguo fazhi bao*) published an article from the Chongming County Court of Shanghai municipality showing that in the years 1985–1986, only 3 percent of couples denied divorce by the court later made genuine attempts at reconciliation (cited in Palmer, 1989: 169).

19. The full title of the guidelines is "Some Concrete Opinions of the Supreme People's Court Regarding How the People's Courts in Judging Divorce Cases Are to Determine Whether the Emotional Relationship of the Husband and Wife Has Truly Ruptured" ("Zuigao renmin fayuan guanyu renmin fayuan shenli lihun anjian ruhe rending fuqi ganqing que yi polie de ruogan juti yijian"; in Zuigao renmin fayuan, 1994: 1086–87).

in accordance with the new stipulation in the 1980 Marriage Law (INT93-9). The Fourteen Articles of 1989 were more explicit: "if the party at fault [i.e., committing adultery] brings the lawsuit and the other does not agree, after criticism, education, appropriate punishment, or denial of the request for divorce that party brings suit again for divorce," then it shall be granted (Article 8). Further, "if, after a judgment denying permission to divorce, the couple lives separately for a year and neither fulfills the obligations of a spouse" (Article 7), then divorce shall be granted. According to two Songjiang judges, these directives translated in practice into adjudicating against divorce on the first request, but permitting it on the second (INT93-9), a practice that would later in the new century become quite standardized. Such an application of the law, highly restrictive though it may still appear from the vantage point of today's United States, represented a substantial relaxation of the constraints on divorce and a concession to the reality that the state could have only limited influence on a couple's marital relationship.

Thus, the following example appears in the sample of divorce cases from county B in 1995. The wife sued for divorce after ten years of marriage on the grounds that she and her husband lacked a "common language" and that he was "narrow-hearted," groundlessly suspecting her of fooling around, and beat her when he was drunk. He did not deny her allegations but countered that she had improper relationships with other men, that he had twice bumped into her while she was with another man, and that she was the one at fault. To the Maoist court, this contested case would have seemed a likely candidate for aggressive court intervention—the judges going on-site to verify the accuracy of the husband's charges; if true, to pressure his wife to change her ways; and, of course, to deny her divorce petition because, among other reasons, she is the offending party. Nevertheless, the county B court granted the divorce (though the settlement it worked out favored the husband as the aggrieved party) (B, 1995-10).[20]

Other stipulations in the Supreme People's Court's Fourteen Articles of 1989 also helped to relax the restrictions against divorce. Articles 7 and 10 acknowledged "incompatibility" as acceptable grounds for divorce under certain conditions: for example, divorce would be allowed "if because of incompatibility in feelings, the couple has lived separately for three years, and there really is no hope for reconciliation" (Article 7). And Article 2 allowed for divorce in the case of hastily concluded marriages (*caoshuai jiehun*) in which "there was no mutual understanding before marriage, and no marital feelings have developed, such that it is difficult for the couple to live together." Some

---

20. The husband received custody of their child, their three-room home, and the big items owned by the couple—their television, refrigerator, chests and bureaus, and motorbike.

conditions that in the past were marginally acceptable gained formal recognition in the 1989 articles, which permitted divorce "if one party is lazy and does not like to work, has bad habits like gambling, does not fulfill the obligations of a spouse, does not reform after repeated education, and is difficult to live with" (Article 10); "if a spouse . . . breaks the law and severely damages spousal feelings" (Article 11); and for "other reasons leading to a rupture in feelings" (Article 14).

In another 1995 case from county B, a woman sued for divorce on the grounds that her husband mistreated her and her child (from a previous marriage). He tied her up, stuffed her mouth with cotton, and beat her. He countered that she had married him merely for his money (a 10,000-plus-yuan insurance payment he received after his father's death in an auto accident) and that she went off all the time—to see her previous husband, he suspected. And that's why he beat her. In the Maoist period, judges of such a case would have gone into the village to coerce the husband to change his ways and thereby effect a mediated reconciliation. In 1995, however, the court simply concluded that "the couple did not have adequate mutual understanding before marriage, had married hastily, and have not established a good emotional relationship after marriage." The petition was granted and, since both parties willingly went along, it was reported as a "mediated divorce" (B, 1995-5; for similar cases, see 6, 8, and 20).

Finally, we have an example of simple adultery in a relationship. The wife sued for divorce saying that their emotional relationship after marriage had been very good, but that her husband had fooled around and not done his duty as a husband. The husband refused to agree to a divorce, on the grounds that the couple had two children. The court learned that the husband was having an affair with a young woman in the village. Once again, while the Maoist court would have brought all the pressures of the relatives and the village to bear on the offending husband to change his ways and thereby reconcile with his wife, this county B court concluded that "the two sides were incompatible and fought over small matters of daily life, and their emotional relationship had in fact completely ruptured." It therefore adjudicated outright for divorce, over the objections of the defendant husband (B, 1995-19).

The Persistence of Maoist Practices

The above examples are by no means intended to suggest that divorce could be had pretty much for the asking. In China the 1990s were a time of transition, when judges of different generations and different outlooks worked together. That was certainly true of the Songjiang judges interviewed: the senior of the two, with just a grammar school education, had come through the army (in 1969, during the Cultural Revolution) and service as a cadre at the height of the Maoist period; the younger man, by contrast, was a recent graduate from the law department of a college of political science and law (Huadong zhengfa xueyuan), a product entirely of the Reform era (INT93-8). While someone like our younger Songjiang judge might be more inclined to simply follow the new Fourteen Articles, someone like the older Songjiang judge was more likely to adhere to old Maoist attitudes toward divorce, even if he was no longer in a position to employ Maoist methods of aggressive intervention to try to effect mediated reconciliations.

In 1995 in county B, a wife sued for divorce on the grounds that her husband had picked up a gambling habit, losing their money and putting them into debt. When admonished, he beat her. He responded that he gambled only when he was very sick, and that he had not done so for more than a year. His present condition still required her help, for he could not live alone. The court found that the couple's "emotional relationship had been relatively good." Moreover, "the couple has two children whom they should raise together." And, finally, "the husband is now sick and needs the help of the wife." The plaintiff's petition for divorce, the court concluded, was "not sufficiently justified." It therefore adjudicated outright against divorce (B, 1995-16).

In another case, the wife sued for divorce on the grounds that her husband made excessive sexual demands on her, over which they had frequent fights. He broke things when he was angry, and once even took a chopping knife to the dining table. The husband countered that their relationship had been good after they married but that recently she had been frequently visiting her natal home, and three times during their fights had actually beaten and injured him. The court investigated and found that the couple had lived together before they got married, that their emotional relationship had "always been very good," and that "tensions had arisen only recently over their sex life." The court ruled that the couple "should treasure their past emotional relationship, and bring up their children together." As in the previous example, the change from the Maoist period was that instead of seeking a mediated reconciliation, the court simply adjudicated against divorce (B, 1995: 17).[21]

Moreover, the 1990s moves toward liberalization would trigger something of a backlash by the turn of the century, with the result that the Standing

---

21. In another case, a wife sued for divorce after finding a letter of her husband's that detailed his "feelings of being with another woman." She said he often came home late. The husband asserted in response that she had taken up the practice of *taiji* sword under a male teacher and once did not come home until 2:00 A.M. The court concluded that the couple's emotional relationship was actually "relatively good" (*jiao hao*) and that the husband showed regret for his actions and a desire for change; he had been turning over all of his pay to his wife and had asked for her forgiveness and understanding. For these reasons, the court found, "the couple's relationship has not ruptured and the plaintiff wife's petition for divorce is therefore denied" (B, 1995-9; see also 14 for a similar case).

Committee of the National People's Congress adopted rather more stringent requirements for divorce in April 2001.[22] The provisions included making "separation for two years" one conservative standard for determining whether a couple's "relationship had truly ruptured." The liberalizing impact of a still more recent (1 October 2003) step, removing the requirement that the village or work unit certify a divorce, should not be overestimated, for the change applies only to divorces by mutual consent, not to those that are contested.

Of course, in the new century, as chapters 4 and 5 have shown in some detail, divorce law practice has undergone considerable change as a result of the conjuncture of a number of tendencies. One is the fading of the historical circumstances and considerations that had given rise to the party's strong adjudicatory posture against divorce; another is the greatly increased incidence of litigation, especially economic disputes, that has accompanied marketization; yet another is that formalistic changes in evidence procedures have led to unanticipated consequences, especially an inability to generate the evidence required for the court to adjudge what the law considers fault—such as issues of a third party, of spousal abuse, and domestic violence. The result has been a growing simplification and formalization of divorce court actions. Just as the two Songjiang judges had pointed out already in the 1990s, court judgments in contested divorces have tended more and more to disregard substantive issues, and have resorted to the simple formula of denying divorce upon the first petition, and allowing it on the second. This is also one side of the larger phenomenon of the rapid increase in the proportion of cases adjudicated.

The Process of Legal Change and Lawmaking in Contemporary China

As the evidence presented above shows, there has been both continuity and change in law between the Maoist and Reform periods. Insofar as the continuities seem to me less obvious than the changes, I have emphasized them more. They are especially evident in what might be called the "old" areas of civil law: namely, property and inheritance rights and obligations with respect to the peasant family house, debt obligations, marriage law, and, to a lesser extent, compensation for damages. Of course, during the tumultuous years of the Land Reform and the Cultural Revolution, political considerations sometimes entered into civil justice in all areas to an unusual degree. What is more novel in Reform-era legislation has been in the newer areas of the law,

22. "Guanyu xiugai 'Zhonghua renmin gongheguo hunyinfa' de jueding," Chinese text available on the web at www.people.com.cn (accessed August 2004).

designed to meet the changed socioeconomic conditions resulting from marketization, the rapid growth of private enterprises, the internationalization of the Chinese economy, and so on: these include new laws on contracts (1999), trademarks (1982), insurance (1995), individual income tax (1980, revised 1993 and 1999), enterprise bankruptcy (1986), and foreign trade (1994). They have little precedent in the Maoist era.

Extremely politicized periods aside, the survey above shows that practical realities have been consistently favored in lawmaking and legal change. Generally speaking, new statutes designed to guide court actions have come not at the beginning of change but only after a considerable period of testing in practice, usually via provisional and preliminary formulations issued in the form of directives and opinions of the Supreme People's Court. Only after their efficacy has been extensively tested would such provisions be formally codified into law.

Reliance on the quality of the (emotional) relationship of a couple, or ganqing, as the crucial criterion in determining whether to grant divorce was already widespread by the early 1950s, as our case sample shows (see also Huang, 2005). The standard was given provisional form in a Supreme People's Court opinion issued on 28 February 1950, in the very first of its rulings on divorce (Zuigao renmin fayuan, 1994: 1056; see also 1064), though it was not mentioned at all in the 1950 Marriage Law (Article 17). Its formal codification into law did not come until the 1980 Marriage Law (Article 25), after more than three decades of application. Changes in divorce legislation in the 1990s, similarly, first appeared in the trial practices set out in the Supreme People's Court's 1989 "Fourteen Articles," not in codified law. Throughout both periods, the ganqing formulation has remained the conceptual cornerstone of divorce law.

The treatment of interest on loans shows the same pattern. In the Maoist period, we have seen, it was simply taken for granted that borrowers were obligated to repay just the principal borrowed, not interest. Only with marketization in the Reform era have interest charges gradually come to be accepted as legitimate. The Supreme Court was the first to address the issue in a directive in 1991, instructing that each court should "act in accordance with actual conditions in its locale, but in no case is interest to run over four times that of the bank interest rate for a similar type loan" (Zuigao renmin fayuan, 1994: 1194).

Formal codification of legal principles concerning rights over the family house in the countryside similarly followed an extended period of trial practice. Our case records and ethnographic information for Huayangqiao village show that social practice consistently linked inheritance rights to obligations for supporting the parents in their old age. It was generally taken for granted that rural sons, not daughters, would inherit the family house. Yet, once again, it took more than three decades for the tie between inheritance rights and old-age maintenance obligations to be written into law. In the intervening years, although the Supreme People's Court consistently urged the linking of inheritance to maintenance in its directives, it gave no guidance on rural daughters in this regard, preferring to leave the matter to local society and to ad hoc court actions (Zuigao renmin fayuan, 1994: 1276–1301). Explicit codification, as we have seen, came only with the 1985 Law of Succession.

Finally, our tort cases show that the law adopted a practice-based, commonsense view that there should be some compensation in no-fault fact situations as well as those involving fault. For the latter, the law would apply the imported principle of "wrongful acts," which requires payment for the damages sustained. For the former, in contrast, the law and the courts have adopted the posture that damages to one party creates a social problem, for which the other party, though not at fault, still bears some share of "civil liability."

It should be clear from the above that the priority given to practical realities by no means implied an absence of guidelines to court adjudication in civil cases. Indeed, there was a sizable body of such legal guides, in the form of codified law, Supreme People's Court directives and opinions, and tacit agreement among the judges. It is also clear that contemporary as well as imperial Chinese civil justice had long resorted readily to adjudication according to law, official representations about the predominance of mediation notwithstanding.

The question is how to understand this factual record. Someone taking a strictly Weberian formalist position could argue that "adjudication" should be understood only as the legal application of universal principles about rights to all concrete fact situations, as has Shiga Shūzō. In that narrow sense of the word, the Qing courts did not adjudicate civil matters, and contemporary Chinese courts do so only in cases when they apply imported formalist principles. But such a stance would ignore a substantial body of legal provisions in both Qing and Maoist guiding court decisions, though derived from a logic very different from that of legal formalism. The Qing and the Maoist courts did not engage only in "didactic conciliation" in civil disputes. The widespread resort to adjudication of the Reform period had deep roots in the history of practice; it did not come in one leap but rather had long-standing antecedents in Qing and Maoist court practices.

The logic system of Chinese law supports a mode of legal reasoning that underlies the combination, in both Qing and contemporary civil justice, of official representations that emphasize mediation with actual court actions that regularly employ adjudication. It enables Chinese lawmakers to incorporate into statutory law both statements of moral ideals or rights and practical provisions that diverge from those without seeing any need to address the apparent contradiction. That mode of thinking, this chapter suggests, has persisted across all the sea changes undergone by China in recent centuries. Unlike the formalist mode so influential in Continental Western law, it was distinctive from the start for the insistence that legal codes be derived from and linked to concrete illustrations, not elevated to a level of universal principles under which all fact situations are supposed to be subsumed. It reflects a basic assumption that practical realities are too variable for abstract principles to encompass. Under PRC justice, that from-fact-to-concept mode of thinking was further extended by testing preliminary formulations in practice for extended periods before principles were codified in law.

Whereas Weberian Continental legal formalism demands logical consistency between universal principles and court actions, Chinese practical moralism readily tolerates divergence between them—and the addition of practical provisions that diverge from those principles requires no other justification than the observable reality itself. It also explains the coexistence of moralistic representations about mediation with the courts' actual adjudicatory practices. Contemporary Chinese justice, in fact, has in effect turned its imported formalist legal principles about rights, originally intended to be universal and applicable to all fact situations, into moral ideals intended to be modified in practice as the situation requires.

From the point of view of legal formalism, the mode of thinking typical of Chinese justice, past and present, can appear murky and inconsistent—instrumentalist, substantivist, irrational, or what Weber would call "empirical." Rights violations can be and indeed often are tolerated in the name of practical considerations—more readily than in systems that take a formalistic approach to legal rights. Yet the from-fact-to-concept-to-practice mode of Chinese legal reasoning, with its tendency to combine moralism with practicality, has some obvious merits. It provided the basis for a legal system of tremendous longevity in imperial China and conceptually grounded a mediatory justice that kept in check litigious and adversarial excesses. In recent times, that same practical moralism has enabled Chinese justice to continually change and adapt to a world undergoing tremendous and sometimes violent transformation. It has also enabled contemporary Chinese law to accommodate within a single evolving system both the legal formalism of modern Western law and the practical moralism of Chinese tradition. Strict legal formalism, by contrast, would demand out of logical consistency a simple choice of one or the other. Perhaps the challenge for both formalist and Chinese justice today is the continuing search for an appropriate balance between inviolable principles and practical imperatives.

Bibliographic Note

Linxia Liang's Book: *Delivering Justice in Qing China: Civil Trials in the Magistrate's Court*

Linxia Liang's new study (2007) confirms my argument that Qing magistrates acted mainly as adjudicators according to the law and not as mediators, but she goes much further than I would in claiming complete consistency between "law" and Qing magistrates' actions and nearly perfect effectiveness for the Qing legal system. The latter view represents something of a polar opposite to conventional wisdom; this note has been added to situate and clarify my thinking vis-à-vis that point of view.

Though Liang agrees with me that magistrates adjudicated rather than mediated, she strangely does not even mention Shiga Shūzō's "didactic conciliation" argument, still the dominant interpretation of Qing justice, especially in China and Japan, a view that I disputed at some length in my *Civil Justice in China: Representation and Practice in the Qing* (Huang, 1996). Instead, she concentrates most of her energies on a critique of my work, despite the fact that of all of the existing literature, the sources I used and my overall assessment of Qing law are probably closer to her own than any other.

Liang is so entirely focused on magistrates' adjudication by law that she does not address at all the question of whether and how they might have mediated at court; my book argued that they rarely did so, but still that is not a question that can be simply ignored. Liang tries to minimize even the role played by societal mediation (my "informal justice") in the civil justice system. She rejects my argument that Qing magistrates routinely gave priority to societal mediation, that they preferred to close rather than to pursue a pending case if the litigants should petition to close it on the grounds that the dispute had been settled through informal mediation or by themselves. This was not so, she argues, because such petitions were always subject to the magistrate's review and approval. My analysis, she says, "would undervalue the magistrate's power and overvalue the power of the informal mediator" (p. 88). For evidence in support, she presents a discussion of six case examples. But her own examples, on close examination, actually show that the magistrate rejected only one such petition (case 6), and then only initially; he thought better of his rejection once he saw that it was true that the litigants had resolved their differences (pp. 86–94). By contrast, my book had counted up 126 cases in which the litigants successfully petitioned to close the case on those grounds, out of a total of 628 from Baxian, Baodi, and Danshui-Xinzhu (Huang, 1996: 111, 118–21, 241).

Liang rejects also my suggestion that of the cases in which records do not show a final outcome (264 of 628 cases), possibly as many as one-half of them might have been the consequence mainly of litigants who had settled their differences outside of court but did not afterward come to court to petition to close the case (Huang, 1996: 111, 118–21). Liang disputes my suggestion by arguing that cases with no known outcomes were instead the consequence entirely of the two months' rule of Substatute 336-5 (pp. 94, 148), to the effect that if a plaintiff after filing a complaint does not show up at court for two months, the case is automatically closed. But she has no other evidence to support her argument, only inference, for she explicitly acknowledges in the discussion that she is leaving out of her consideration the 37 cases of unknown outcome in her 173-case sample from Baodi County (p. 148). Cases of unknown outcome, of course, are what I was talking about.

Further, Liang also rejects my argument about a "third realm" (in between formal magisterial adjudication and informal societal mediation, where preliminary expressions of magisterial opinion interacted with regalvanized community mediation), in which some of the cases show that the xiangbao sometimes acted on their own authority, and could abuse that authority, despite Qing legislation forbidding them to do so. My argument was that xiangbao acting on their own authority was a phenomenon observable to different degrees in different places in the nineteenth century: none in Baxian in the second half of the eighteenth century and the first half of the nineteenth century, but 6 of 118 cases in Baodi, mainly in the second half of the nineteenth century, and 31 of 202 in Danshui-Xinzhu in that same period (Huang, 1996: 113). Liang argues instead that the law was always followed: a magistrate did not let xiangbao handle things on their own; he required them to report, and everything was subject to his approval. But she has just one case example to support her argument (case 4, p. 88). One wonders: if the law really always operated as well and as consistently as she argues, why then was the 1765 substatute (No. 334-8) forbidding magistrates to allow xiangbao to handle cases on their own adopted in the first place (Huang, 1996: 113)? And, 200 years later in the second half of the nineteenth century, could that substatute really have been as completely effective as she believes?

On the larger conceptual level, Liang rejects my arguments about the "disjunction between representation and practice" of the law in the Qing, as for example in the ideal of no civil litigation over minor matters versus the reality of pervasive litigation, of the construction that litigation came only from evil litigation mongers or bad people versus the reality of widespread resort to the courts by common people, of governance by moral example and suasion versus the reality of court adjudication, of a formal court system existing alongside an informal societal mediation system, of moralistic statements versus practical actions by magistrates, and so on. She does this by taking a very broad interpretation of the law in the Qing. In Confucian thought, she argues, the ideal of "no litigation" (*wusong*) in fact came with the acknowledgment also of "antilitigation" (*yansong*) and "ending litigation" (*xisong*) (p. 11). Moreover, "law" includes not just *fa*, but also *qing* and *li*, as an integral part of the LAW. She interprets qing as meaning facts, and li, "true meaning of the law." For her, the three categories become in fact not only inseparable but also indistinguishable, together making up the single category of LAW as she interprets it (pp. 241–46). It is on that all-encompassing notion of LAW that Liang rejects my efforts to separate out legal code from actual application, representation from practice, and moral ideals from practical intent.

While it is certainly true that the Qing code embodied not just moral ideals but also practical stipulations, as I argued in my book (Huang, 1996: 14–15), it is not true as Liang argues that qing, li, and fa formed an indistinguishable whole. Qing, as I made clear, could mean not just "facts" (as in the terms *qingshi* and *shiqing*, and *zhenqing zhouli* and *chaqing lichu* [Huang, 1996: 101]), as Liang argues, but also in Confucian usage human compassion (close to *ren*, humaneness), and in popular usage, human feeling/relations (*renqing*). As for li, instead of Liang's "true meaning of the law," it more commonly meant "heavenly principle" as in Neo-Confucian usage (*tianli*) or "common sense right and wrong" (*daoli*), in popular usage (Huang, 1996: 12–13; 65ff. cf. 101). It does not help our understanding to think of a LAW that encompassed all this in a coherent and consistent whole. Nor does it help to insist that departures in practice from codified law are part of LAW itself. As I put it in the 1996 book, "This book argues that a view that takes into account both representation and practice and both official and unofficial aspects of the system points up the extent to which that system was characterized by built-in paradoxes. To identify the 'real' system only with the constructions of the state is as much off the mark as to identify it with the actions and consequences of the system. Rather, the system is really understandable only in terms of its paradoxical dimensions" (p. 15). Or, as I put it later and more colloquially in lectures to Chinese audiences in the past few years: in the Qing legal system "what was said was one thing, what was done was another thing; but together the two made up yet another thing" (Huang Zongzhi, 2008: 108–9).

Finally, Liang does present a provocative interpretation of the term *xishi*, or "minor matters." What it really means, she says, is "non crimes" (*wu zuiming*), as opposed to "crimes" (*zui*). In fact, the very term *susong*, she argues, should be understood as embodying the same distinction, with *su* referring to crimes, and *song* referring to disputes over "non crimes" (pp. 13–17). By this interpretation, the distinction between the "criminal" and the "civil" in the Qing is no longer a rather fuzzy one, as I believe it was, but rather every bit as clear-cut and exact as in modern Chinese law.

While this subject could use further clarification, it should be pointed out here that in making the argument, Liang does not consider the two more common meanings of *xishi*, which are the ones that I employed: first, of the sense of "minor matters" as opposed to "weighty cases" (*zhong'an*), both in terms of legal and of bureaucratic views and in terms of degrees of punishment; and second, less obvious, of the sense that minor matters should be settled by society itself and not by the courts. To make a more convincing argument for her interpretation, Liang needs to either refute or incorporate these two more common interpretations. As it is, Liang's argument seems to me an interesting way to extend, indeed "modernize," Qing legal concepts, but it is not convincing as history.

I should mention here also that Liang's book considers only my first volume, *Civil Justice in China: Representation and Practice in the Qing* (1996); it lists in the references but does not consider or mention at all the companion volume *Code, Custom and Legal Practice in China: the Qing and the Republic Compared* (2001), which follows the original inquiry into a number of selected areas of the law: dian (conditional sale of land), topsoil ownership, debt, old-age support, and women's agency. Nor does her book consider the series of major articles I have published since: "Divorce Law Practices and the Origins, Myths, and Realities of Judicial Mediation in China" (2005), "Civil Adjudication in China, Past and Present" (2006), "Court Mediation in China, Past and Present" (2006), and "Whither Chinese Law?" (2007).*

In a sentence, then, I believe Liang's book goes much too far in arguing for complete consistency and effectiveness of Qing LAW. Nevertheless, I believe Dr. Liang should be commended for being the first mainland Chinese scholar (though partly Western trained) to publish a substantial monograph based on systematic use of case records, and in going against conventional wisdom to document the fact of adjudication by law in the Qing. It should not be long before the question of whether magistrates were mainly adjudicators or "didactic conciliators," à la Shiga Shūzō, is settled for good. More important, further research based on archival case records should open up many more new perspectives and questions about the true nature of Qing justice and about just what role the Qing system has played and could play in a newly configured Chinese legal system today.

---

* Two errors in Liang's book seem to me serious enough to be worthy of mention in a footnote: on page 12, note 26, Liang writes, "I cite Articles and sub-statutes according to Xue Yunsheng's numbering in *Cunyi*." Xue, of course, never used such a "modern" numbering system; that was the work of editor Huang Tsing-chia [Jingjia]. In the bibliography on page 275, Terada Hiroaki's last name is given as Hiroaki (浩) rather than as Terada (寺田). Here I wish to note also that Liang is right to point out that in my one-paragraph discussion of a false accusation case involving one Zhou Fulai (Huang, 1996: 84), I failed to take into account the fact that he was a "superior relative" and therefore entitled to a reduction in punishment by two degrees (pp. 228–30), but that brief discussion was very peripheral indeed to the main concerns of the book and not at all relevant to the issues discussed above.

7

Court Mediation, Past and Present

MAOIST IDEOLOGY WOULD HAVE us believe that almost all Chinese court actions were mediatory. Such a claim obfuscates the realities of court practices and also greatly stretches the meaning of the language used. The root meaning of the word *tiaojie* ("mediation") in Chinese in pre-Maoist times was in fact much the same as the English—namely, the voluntary settling of differences through third-party facilitation or intervention—and it mainly referred to societal mediation. Under Maoist justice, however, court and administrative mediation became widespread while societal mediation shrank drastically under the expansion of party-state control. *Tiaojie*, which had originally emphasized voluntary agreement or at least compliance, came to incorporate the meaning of the term *tiaochu*, which earlier in some of the liberated areas had been carefully distinguished from *tiaojie* and applied mainly to administrative actions;[1] it included decisions imposed regardless of the will of the litigants. Maoist usage of *tiaojie* thus came to include adjudicatory and coercive actions even while they continued to be cast as demonstrating voluntary agreement or compliance.

This chapter uses the criterion of whether a resolution of a dispute is imposed against the will of one of the litigants to distinguish between genuine court mediations and adjudicatory actions that are represented as mediation. "Mediation" as used in this chapter will cover, first of all, the word's original core sense: voluntary settlement of differences through third-party

1. See chapter 6, notes 1 and 2.

facilitation. It will include also a range of actions that I term "adjudicative mediation"—that is, mediation with adjudicative features, so long as it is not imposed against the will of a litigant. But I will distinguish "mediation" from "adjudication,"[2] which results in a clear-cut finding of legal right and wrong, a "winner" and a "loser," as well as from a range of actions that I term "mediatory adjudication," which is adjudication with mediatory representations or features, imposed regardless of the will of the litigants. These different categories, of course, tend to shade into one another in practice; nevertheless, we must try to take into account the fundamental substantive difference between mediation and adjudication, a distinction that is made, in fact, by both Confucian and Maoist legal discourses.

The chapter is based, once again, mainly on the sample of 336 civil cases that I have collected from two counties, county A in the south and county B in the north.[3] In addition, I have used the 45 divorce cases from 1999 to 2004 collected from county R in South China. Such cases are not generally available to researchers and are discussed in considerable detail.

The purpose of the examination of the case records is, first of all, to delineate more exactly where mediation operated and where it did not. In addition, I will attempt to define what might be termed the "operative logic" of mediation, as opposed to its ideological constructions. My hope is to uncover the implicit logic guiding mediation in practice that is not apparent from an analysis of the official ideology alone.

Much has already been written on the subject of mediation. The early works by Jerome Cohen and Stanley Lubman pointed out some of complexities and ambiguities of the term "mediation" in contemporary Chinese law (Cohen, 1967; Lubman, 1967). The later work of Michael Palmer emphasized the high-handedness of contemporary Chinese mediation, while Donald Clarke stressed how its character differed according to the type of institution undertaking it (e.g., local judicial officials or government organs, the courts, "people's mediation committees," or a parent company) (Palmer, 1989; Clarke, 1991). In addition, K. C. Hsiao highlighted the use of compromise in traditional Chinese mediation, and Shiga Shūzō analyzed in depth the conceptual underpinnings of what he terms "didactic conciliation" by the Qing courts (Hsiao, 1979; Shiga, 1981). I aim to build on such past research as I emphasize a historical perspective and make still sharper distinctions between what was said and what was done, between official representations and actual practice.

2. See chapter 6.
3. The names of the counties are withheld to maintain confidentiality of recent court records. For a more complete description of the cases, see chapter 4.

This chapter will also seek to establish under what conditions Chinese court mediation has been effective and under what conditions not. The basic difference between adjudication, which is concerned with establishing legal right and wrong, and mediation, which is concerned rather with resolving disputes through compromise, has to a large extent determined when each has (or has not) worked well. And the operative logic contained in effective mediations tells us not only about the nature of Chinese court mediation but also about the distinctive nature of Chinese legal reasoning that has persisted from the Qing through the present, despite the great and obvious changes in Chinese society and law.

The Ideology of Mediation in the Qing

The point of departure of the formalist Continental legal tradition of modern Western law is universal principles about rights and their protection by law. As has been discussed in the previous chapter, in Max Weber's characterization, such formalist law requires that all court judgments be derived by means of "legal logic" from principles about rights.[4] In Weber's terms, Qing civil law is substantive or instrumentalist, more preoccupied with the ruler's concern to maintain social order than with a guarantee of individual rights (Weber, [1968] 1978: 844–48). Lacking the formalist requirement that court actions be derived logically from abstract principles of rights, it is susceptible to arbitrariness. These distinctions of Weber's between formalist and substantivist, rational and irrational, though idealized, overdrawn, and easily distorted into Eurocentric and modernist conclusions, nevertheless do point up some crucial differences between Chinese law and the formalist tradition of Continental modern Western law.

By contrast, Qing ideology regarding "civil" disputes among the people had as its foremost concern the resolution of disputes, not the protection of rights. To recapitulate, the ideal moral society is characterized by harmony and absence of conflict; no disputes, much less lawsuits, would exist. The moral Confucian gentleman was someone who would not stoop to disputes; he would rise above them by conciliation (*rang*) and forbearance (*ren*). The truly cultivated gentleman would not allow himself to be drawn into a dispute or lawsuit; such involvement was itself a sign of moral failure. It is a view, we might say, of disputes and lawsuits as inherently not matters of right or wrong but matters to be resolved through compromise.

4. Thus, in Max Weber's words, "every concrete legal decision [must] be the application of an abstract legal proposition to the concrete 'fact situation,'" and "it must be possible in every concrete case to derive the decision from abstract legal propositions by means of legal logic" (Weber, [1968] 1978: 657).

If a dispute nevertheless arose, society itself, in the form of the community or the kin group, not the court, should be the one to resolve it. The mechanism would be the facilitation or intermediation of a morally superior person, who would persuade and educate the disputants into voluntary compromises. Only failing such resolution, and only if the disputants were truculent enough to persist, would the courts become involved, though the courts would defer first to the intensified societal mediation that generally followed the filing of a lawsuit.

If such mediation failed, then and only then would the courts intervene. In that eventuality, the magistrates, consistent with the ideal of moral and benevolent governance, would engage in moral education and persuasion to gain the voluntary compliance of the litigants—an ideal evidenced in the standard practice of requiring litigants to file a pledge of "willingness to close the case" (*ganjie*) to show their voluntary acceptance of the court's decision (Huang, 1996: chap. 7; see also Huang, 2006b).

Such an ideology led to civil matters being conceptualized as "minor" or "trivial" (*xishi*) affairs that local governments would handle on their own authority without troubling the higher levels of the bureaucracy; under those constructions, litigation came to be seen as the activity of the morally inferior (*xiaoren*). If litigation proliferated, the individuals responsible were perceived as "litigation mongers" (*songgun*) and "litigation instigators" (*songshi*), or "yamen worms" (*yadu*), who goaded good people into litigating. And the litigants themselves, of course, were morally inferior (*xiaoren*) or crafty people (*diaomin*) (Huang, 1996: 152–52, 156–57, 166–67, 185–89).

On the other side of this highly moralistic construct was the magistrate, who was supposed to govern by benevolence (*ren*) and moral example. In his able hands, litigation mongers and instigators and yamen worms would be curbed or suppressed, as would the impulses of morally inferior and crafty litigants. The Confucian magistrate, a superior gentleman, would rule as the "father and mother official" (*fumuguan*) over the childlike "good people" (*liangmin*); there would be few disputes and little or no litigation, and society would be in harmony.

On the basis of these moralistic representations, Shiga Shūzō (1981) has argued that Qing courts engaged not in adjudication but only "didactic conciliation," whose conceptual foundation lay in the triadic principle governing Chinese law: *qing*, *li*, and *fa*, or compassion based on Confucian humaneness (*ren*, *renqing*), moral principles governing both nature and society (*tianli*), and the laws of the state (*guofa*). In Shiga's analysis, laws occupy in the triad a relatively small place, which he likened to that of an iceberg in the ocean; the main guides to court actions are instead Confucian compassion and society's moral principles. Didactic conciliation, not adjudicatory judgment, was the task of the courts (Shiga, 1981).

It should be pointed out in this connection that even in the original Confucian representations, societal and not court mediation was paradigmatic. When it came to court actions, Qing law and Qing magistrates in fact acknowledged readily that in practice the courts adjudicated (*duan* or *duan'an*, and *pan*, not *tiaojie*), *pace* Shiga. I have already discussed and documented this point at length and will not repeat the argument and evidence here (Huang, 1996: chap. 8; see also chapter 6, this volume). Indeed, mediation by the courts was largely new to Chinese justice in its modern period, not a legacy from the Qing.

Shiga's construction of Qing court actions aside, the Confucian representations outlined above are at once revealing and misleading about the real nature of Qing justice. They are revealing in that they clearly set forth the mediation ideology and also disclose important aspects of the logic that informed it. But they are misleading, we will see, because the ideal of societal mediation can obfuscate the practical reality of codified provisions and court adjudications over "civil" matters; they also tell us little about the unspoken logic of mediation as it actually operated.

The Actual Practice of Qing Courts

As has been seen in the previous chapter, by analyzing 628 Qing court cases—drawn from the counties of Baxian in the southwestern province of Sichuan, Baodi in the capital prefecture of Shuntian, and Danshui-Xinzhu in the province of Taiwan—my 1996 volume showed that the courts did not engage in the kind of "didactic conciliation" suggested by Shiga. In the great majority of the 221 cases that persisted into a formal court session (most of the others being settled through societal mediation spurred by the filing of a lawsuit),[5] the courts ruled according to the law. In the second volume (2001), I examined in detail the main areas of the specific laws involved, comparing Qing and Republican Guomindang laws. In the Qing, civil adjudication was guided by a host of laws in the Qing code about property (mainly land and houses), debt, inheritance or succession and old-age support, and marriage and divorce, all couched in the form of illustrative fact situations. These moral ideals (e.g., no household division while one's parents are alive) were placed in the foreground and presented a framework of punishment for offenses. They therefore are quite easy to mistake for provisions about criminal offenses. But the "civil" stipulations were in fact plentiful and specific, many of them in the form of substatutes added on over time that often originated—much like the precedents in common law—from actual case experiences reported by local

5. See chapter 6, note 4.

officials. Thus did property "rights," for example, come to be formulated in terms of punishments for fraudulent sales or taking the fruits of another's land. Likewise, debt obligations were formulated in terms of punishments graded in severity by the amount of the debt and the length of time it was unpaid; inheritance rights and obligations in terms of punishments for not allowing sons to inherit, violating parents' wishes, and failing to support the parents in their old age; and rights involved in marital contracts in terms of punishments for false representations to the other party, failing to comply with the time frame set by the marital agreement, and so on. Fact situations not covered by the law were to be adjudicated by analogy to those that were.[6]

The local courts adjudicated civil disputes accordingly, both because that was the law and because their sizable caseloads did not really allow the magistrates the time needed to persuade litigants to accept a conciliatory resolution voluntarily, certainly not in the manner expected of the later Maoist courts. Part of the difficulty was that litigants who insisted on a formal court session despite all the obstacles set up along the way were generally either the most truculent or the most aggrieved, and therefore also the least open to persuasion or compromise. For all these reasons, the magistrates adjudicated readily.

The adjudicatory practices of the courts could coexist with the ideology of societal mediation because of a distinctive mode of legal reasoning that gave priority to fact situations over abstract principles, practical application over moral ideals, as I have analyzed in detail in the previous chapter. While insisting on the necessity of foregrounding moral ideals, it also acknowledged the reality of divergences from such ideals in practice—hence the moral packaging of the code, which simultaneously contained divergent or even contradictory provisions intended to guide actual practice. It was an epistemological method that went from fact to concept, rather than the reverse; it coupled moralizing with practical actions, in what I termed "practical moralism" (Huang, 2006a; see also Huang, 1996: chap. 8). Practice and the practical adaptations of the law, however, were never allowed to supplant the original moral visions about what ought to be. Despite the reality of adjudicatory actions by the courts, the Qing held on tightly to the ideal of settling disputes among the people by societal mediation.[7]

Though societal mediation as it was practiced did not come close to resolving all disputes as the Confucian ideal required, it did conform with the official ideology in important respects. I dealt with this subject in my 1996 book and in greater detail in chapter 2 of this book. To summarize very briefly here:

6. Elsewhere I have documented the specific legal areas that saw the highest incidence of litigation (Huang, 2001) and provided a more detailed summary (Huang, 2006a).
7. The conceptual underpinnings of Qing adjudication are analyzed in chapter 6.

Our best available evidence shows that in most villages, there were one or more respected individuals to whom the community turned to mediate disputes as needed. These individuals were generally endogenous to the community and possessed no formal official connections. The moral norms they appealed to resembled those of the official ideology, albeit interpreted in unsophisticated and commonsensical ways. The methods they employed were chiefly those of persuasion, as they talked with one party and then the other before seeking common ground, generally through compromise. It was a system that worked best among disputants who were roughly equivalent in status and power. Under those conditions, and so long as the disputants possessed the necessary resources, they could opt out of the process as they wished by deciding to go to court (see chapter 2, this volume; Huang, 1996: chap. 3).

The system served some very practical needs. As entities in which people lived together year after year, generation after generation, villages did indeed find it necessary to do everything possible to seek amicable resolutions to disputes, in order to avoid the creation of lasting enmity if at all possible. The official ideology of mediation in fact both expressed and shaped the mechanisms and processes of village dispute resolution.

It was also in such relatively insular and cohesive communities that a certain number of respected individuals would come to be seen as "of advanced age and of moral uprightness" (*niangao youde*), or as particularly "trustworthy" (*you xinyong*). Someone who was especially effective as a mediator could even come to be known as "the well-doer of the village" (*yixiang shanshi*), perhaps even developing a trans-village reputation as a mediator able "to turn big problems into small ones, and small problems into non-problems" (*dashi hua xiao, xiaoshi hua liao*) (see chapter 2, this volume; Huang, 1996: 58–59).

My concern here, however, is mainly with the courts. As we have seen, they operated mainly by adjudicating cases, within a system that held up societal mediation as the ideal. The combination of adjudication and mediation rested on the tendency to give priority to practical realities while continuing to foreground moral ideals, displaying the distinctive practical moralism of the Qing legal system and indeed of Qing governance as a whole (see chapter 6, this volume; Huang, 2006a; see also Huang, 1996: chap. 8).

Mediation in the Republic

During the Republican period, China tried almost wholesale Westernization in its legal system. The Civil Code of 1929–1930 was modeled after the German Civil Code of 1900, one of the most formalist (in Weberian terms) of all Western models. It began with rights stated in the abstract, and constructed the entire code around such rights of the person, of property, of debt (rights and obligations), of marriage and divorce, and of inheritance (Civil Code of the Republic of China, 1930–1931; German Civil Code, 1907). The lawmakers themselves were mainly Western-trained (including in Japan), and Wang Chonghui, a major figure in the small group overseeing the drafting of the code, had published an authoritative translation of the German Civil Code. The courts were expected to adjudicate as to right and wrong for the protection of rights, in the manner of the formalist Western model (Huang, 2001: chap. 4).

The Guomindang government did try to implement a court mediation system as a way to lessen the burden on the courts.[8] It formally promulgated on 27 January 1930 a Civil Mediation Law (Minshi tiaojie fa), calling for all courts of first instance to establish a supplementary mediation office (*minshi tiaojiechu*) that would screen all cases. The express purpose was to "prevent disputes and lessen litigation" (*duxi zhengduan jianshao susong*) (*Fengxian xian fayuanzhi*, 1986: 187–88; see also *Zhonghua minguo fazhi ziliao huibian*, [1927–1937] 1960: 43, 44). Thus, in the years 1934, 1935, and 1936, just about the same number of cases reportedly underwent mediation as were concluded by the regular courts (*zhongjie*).[9] The numbers alone make clear that all cases received by the courts were routinely steered to the mediation office before they went on to the regular adjudicatory court.

The very frequency of the process suggests that the "mediation" was most likely rather perfunctory, as the mediation case records from Shunyi County, which had a mediation office in place well before the formal promulgation of the Mediation Law, illustrate quite well. To judge by those cases, the institutions and processes established for court mediation involved a minimal investment of time and effort. The mediation hearings tended to be rather simple and brief. The judge asked only simple questions of fact to see if the two parties themselves were willing to settle or compromise. When they were evidently willing, he would announce the settlement at the end of the brief session of questions, at which point the stenographic recording of the hearing would be signed by the two parties, and that would be the end of the process. When the parties seemed unwilling to settle, as happened the great majority of the time, the case would be referred on to the regular court for normal handling. The judge generally made little or no effort to work out a compromise between them.

In May 1931, for example, Liu Qixiang brought suit against Zhang Jizong. Two years earlier Zhang had purchased on credit, through a middleman,

8. The irony is that mediation as practiced by the later Maoist courts proved to be more time-consuming than adjudication.

9. In 1934, there were 113,757 cases that underwent mediation and 75,149 that were concluded by the regular courts; the numbers in 1935 were 82,174 and 105,286; in 1926, 84,317 and 83,121 (*Sifa tongji*, 1936: 16, 98).

thirty-four yuan worth of chickens and eggs from Liu to peddle. Liu had tried repeatedly to collect from Zhang, and he had a receipt to prove his sale. At the mediation hearing on 21 May, according to the stenographic record, the judge first asked Xu, representing Liu, to explain why Liu was not there. Satisfied that Xu had full authority to represent Liu, who was sick, he next asked for an explanation of why Liu had brought suit; Xu gave a brief three-sentence reply. The judge next turned to Zhang to ask why he had not paid. Zhang acknowledged that he owed the money but explained that he had no money and needed to wait until after the coming harvest to pay. The judge turned back to Xu, urging him to allow Zhang to wait, and Xu answered that he would agree to wait if Zhang would pledge before the judge to pay by the fifteenth day of the sixth month. On Zhang's agreement to pay by that date, the judge had the stenographic recording read out loud for approval by both parties, and pronounced the case successfully mediated. The entire text of the questions and answers took up only seventeen lines (Shunyi 3:483, 1931.5.31 [debt 19]).

Of the fifteen cases in my Shunyi collection that came before the county's mediation office or court in the years 1924–1931, just three were successfully mediated, corresponding roughly with the proportions reported nationally in 1936.[10] All had to do with a debt obligation that was documented and incontrovertible, as in the above example. In court, the defendants were placed in a position of having to acknowledge the obligation; the court was left simply to get the two parties to agree to a timetable for payment. All were settled in the same way (Shunyi 2:261, 1924.2.2 [debt 11]; 2:601, 1928.8.31 [debt 15]).

In the other twelve cases, mediation failed because the litigants themselves could not agree. In no case did the judge make a serious effort to help work out a compromise. For example, Wang Suoqing charged that Shan Yongxiang refused to pay rent for cultivating twenty-four *mu* of Wang's land. At the mediation session two weeks later on 19 May 1931, Wang stated that Shan's uncle Shan Fu had worked for his family as a hired laborer. Since Shan was related to his family by marriage (one of Wang's aunts had married into the Shan family), he was later allowed to cultivate the land (in Linhe village) rent free. Later, after Shan Fu died, the Wangs allowed his descendants to continue to cultivate the land, for a rent of five diao, but no lease was signed; Wang Suoqing had a land deed to prove that the land belonged to his family. He had to raise the rent because of the recent military levies, which actually exceeded the rent he received. All this came out in Wang's brief answers to eight short questions. Next, Shan Yongxiang told the presiding judge that the land actually belonged to his great-grandfather, who had bought it in 1844. Shan, too, had a deed to

10. Of the cases received in 1936 for mediation, 12,409, or 15 percent, were reported as successfully settled, compared to 68,016 not (*Sifa tongji*, 1936: 98).

prove his ownership. This information was elicited in two questions. The two parties, clearly, were some distance apart.

Whereas the later Maoist court might have taken upon itself the task of going down to the village to investigate the alleged facts and then try to push the two sides toward a mutually acceptable settlement, the Guomindang mediation office simply declared that mediation had failed and that the case was now to go to the regular court for adjudication. The entire transcript of the hearing filled just three thirteen-line sheets (Shunyi 3:478, 1931.5.6 [land 22]).

Mediation operated to greater effect in the Republican period in society itself, where it continued to work much as it had in the Qing. Generally speaking, the Guomindang government did little to alter what was already in place in the villages. There was a short-lived, halfhearted attempt to establish "mediation committees" (*tiaojie weiyuanhui*) or "committees to prevent litigation" (*xisong weiyuanhui*) in North China villages. But those modern-sounding institutions did not take hold there; by the late 1930s, at the time of the Japanese Mantetsu investigations of the villages, nothing remained of them but their memory among a few village leaders (KC, 3.30–31).

To judge by both the documentation from villages and the 128 civil cases preserved in the Shunyi County archive, as chapter 2 has shown in detail, community mediation still played a significant role in the justice system as a whole. Many of the cases in Shunyi ended much as they had in the Qing: withdrawn or closed after the filing of a lawsuit provided the impetus for successful societal mediation. The business of the courts was mainly to adjudicate; mediation was done extrajudicially, by community and kin groups. In that respect, little had changed from the Qing (Huang, 1996: chap. 3; 2001: table A.2 and passim).

Thus, court mediation seems to have figured rather modestly in the Republic, especially by comparison with the Maoist justice that followed. While community and kin group mediation continued to operate in society, the Guomindang by and large adopted the adjudicatory court system of its German model. The Shunyi case examples and the national judicial statistics indicate that the courts' experiment with mediation had only limited impact, which should perhaps not be surprising. Guomindang lawmakers in fact prided themselves on their formalist German model. Court mediation was tried somewhat perfunctorily.

The Ideology of Mediation in Post-1949 China

Maoist ideology put enormous emphasis on mediatory justice, in many ways even more than did the Qing. The language is different, to be sure. Rather than the Confucian qing, li, fa (although those categories are still often used by judges and judicial officials in their work), the terms used are those of "socialism" in its distinctive formulations by Mao. Disputes are conceptualized as, or at least called, "contradictions." And contradictions, in turn, are separated into the "antagonistic" (i.e., between the enemies and "the people") and "nonantagonistic" (i.e., "among the people"). While those in the former group are seen as requiring violent resolutions (and punishments), the latter are to be resolved peacefully, relying especially on the mediation of differences to result in amicable settlements, much as in Confucian ideology (Mao, [1937a] 1971, [1957] 1971; a representative academic statement of this same position is Han, 1982; see also Yang and Fang, 1987).

Of course, a very practical reality underlay this emphasis: in the Communist base areas (*bianqu*, "border regions"), severed from the urban centers where a Western-style court system had been instituted under Guomindang rule, the Communists needed to draw on rural practices and nonspecialists before 1949. The mediation tradition in local communities turned out to be an important source of inspiration for the entire Maoist justice system. Justice in the central Shaan-Gan-Ning border region, in fact, came to be conceptualized as a three-tiered system: "folk mediation" (*minjian tiaojie*) was at the bottom, and above it were "administrative mediation" (*xingzheng tiaojie*) by local government officials and organs and "judicial mediation" (*sifa tiaojie*) by the local courts. It was a system built on top of existing village traditions and practices.[11] The schema was formally stipulated in the 1943 Regulations for Mediating Civil and Criminal Matters of the Shaan-Gan-Ning Border Region (Han and Chang, 1981–1984: 3.630–33).

Maoist mediation was also couched within the ideology of the "mass line": that is, judges do not just sit at court but must go down to the village to investigate the truth with the help of "the masses" and then resolve or "mediate" a case. Judges must rely on the masses because their eyes were "the clearest" (*zuiliang*) and because the justice system, like governance as a whole, was to proceed according to the formula "from the masses, to the masses." This method was supposed to minimize "contradictions" between the leadership and the followers, the courts and the masses. By this ideology, judges would ascertain from the masses whether a marriage was worth reconciling and, if so, would call on them to help work things out. The judges would manage other disputes the same way, investigating to learn the truth from the masses and then working with them to resolve the dispute. The entire approach was summed up as the "Ma Xiwu way of adjudging cases" (*Ma Xiwu shenpan fangshi*) (see chapter 4, this volume; Mao, [1943] 1971; see also Huang, 2005: 173, 182–83).

---

11. The categories of "administrative mediation" and "judicial mediation" clearly anticipated the expansion of the meaning of tiaojie to include the more high-handed tiaochu.

Reinforcing this ideology of mediation was the nationalistic claim for the superiority of harmony-based Chinese justice over adversarial Western justice. On this account, mediation reflected the finest ideals of Chinese justice in the past and Chinese socialism in the present (Huang, 2005: 153–54). This theme has been sounded even in the post-Mao Reform period, and it has struck quite a chord in recent years with some Western analysts, who believe that much can be learned from Chinese mediation by those who seek to overcome problems of excessive litigation and adversarial confrontation by developing ways to resolve disputes through arbitration or mediation (as discussed below).[12]

Nowhere was the mediation ideology applied more persistently and vigorously than in contested divorces: the goal of court action was to minimize the incidence of divorce through aggressively implemented "mediated reconciliations" (*tiaojie hehao*), as I have discussed in detail in chapter 4 (Huang, 2005; see also below). The stated rationale was that marriages would not be taken as lightly in "socialist China" as in the capitalist West. Divorce would be and should be much harder to obtain, despite the justice system's emphasis on freedom of marriage and divorce and on gender equality. Over time, the judicial system has come to rely on the standard of *ganqing*, or the quality of the couple's (emotional) relationship, for making decisions as to whether to grant divorce.[13] If the ganqing foundation is good and has not "ruptured," the couple would be required to attempt a mediated reconciliation rather than divorce. In this way, divorce law in contemporary China would be true to the twin ideals of socialist harmony and of gender equality and freedom of divorce, while making very practical concessions to the reality of peasant opposition to the radically new marriage laws. Thus did the law come in practice to reject the great majority of contested divorce petitions and engage in high-handed methods to impose mediated reconciliations, regardless of the will of the petitioners.

As has been discussed in chapter 4, that aggressively interventionist ideology of Maoist mediation with respect to divorce shaped the contemporary Chinese civil justice system as a whole. The strongly adjudicatory posture of the courts, the use of party and community pressures, and even the use of material inducements became methods entirely acceptable for mediation in other spheres of civil justice, even if less commonly employed there. As a consequence, the very word "mediation," or *tiaojie*, took on a far more adjudicatory, aggressive, and interventionist meaning than the mediatory

12. This new emphasis on finding alternatives to confrontation is perhaps another important reason that past Western scholarly works on Chinese justice, cited at the beginning of this chapter, have focused on mediation. Among Chinese works, Fan (2000) is representative of this line of analysis.

13. Official translations render *ganqing* as "mutual affection," but that translation, as I have suggested, does not allow for the routine grading by the courts of *ganqing* as very good, good, average, or poor. "(Emotional) relationship" seems to me to more accurately capture the term's customary legal usages (Huang, 2005: 155n8).

ideal of voluntary settlement of differences through third-party facilitation. (Although, as chapter 5 has shown, the coercive "mediated reconciliations" of the Maoist period have largely fallen into disuse after the 1990s under new social-economic conditions and the new evidence procedures; other kinds of court mediations that grew up alongside, especially those involving no fault, have shown strong resilience. In 2006, of all civil lawsuits, 1.426 million were still resolved by mediation, compared to 1.744 by adjudication [*Zhongguo falü nianjian*, 2007: 1066].)

The contemporary mediation ideology also envisions extrajudicial mediation. As has been shown in chapter 2, at the village level, "mediation committees" (*tiaojie weiyuanhui*) are supposed to form "the first line of defense" (*diyidao fangxian*) of the entire justice system. By resolving disputes at early stages and amicably, mediation supposedly lessens the number of court cases and curbs more serious offenses. At the system's height, according to official constructions and tallies for 1989, for example, basic-level mediation of some 7.3 million disputes is credited with having "prevented" a total of more than 80,000 instances (*qi*) of possible fatal incidents (*fei zhengchang siwang*), affecting some 137,000 people, that the disputes might have provoked (*Zhongguo falü nianjian*, 1990: 62; cf. Shanghai shi lüshi xiehui, 1991: 264). Good local officials (village and township leaders) are those who stay below certain target numbers of disputes and lawsuits by resolving disputes early.[14]

Here I am focusing on the court system itself; community mediation has been dealt with in chapter 2. It is worth pointing out, however, that while the Maoist ideology of mediation bears close resemblance to the earlier Confucian ideology, its differences are also stark, in envisaging a much enlarged role for the new party-state, in directing societal mediation, in instituting court mediation, and in expanding the meaning of mediation to include a range of interventions, up to and including adjudicatory actions taken irrespective of the will of the litigants.

The Practice of Court Mediation in Post-1949 China

Court-administered "mediated reconciliations" in contested divorce cases, as I have shown, had their origin in a very practical concern: trying to minimize

14. In 1991, with the formal promulgation of the "Resolutions on Strengthening Public Order in Society by Unified Governance" ("Guanyu jiaqiang shehui zhi'an zonghe zhili de jueding," 1991), a kind of blueprint or master plan for public security, villages, towns, and townships actually "contracted" with their superior agencies for certain quotas of disputes and lawsuits (INT91-KB:2). Huayangqiao Township, for example, had a target figure of three disputes (to be handled at the township level) per thousand residents (INT91: 4).

conflicts with society over the new (1950) Marriage Law, especially peasant opposition, on a case-by-case basis (chapter 4, this volume; Huang, 2005). In effect, their default position came to be adjudication against divorce. As the court practices evolved over time, a host of more or less standardized measures were developed; these included the codified requirement that all contested divorces first go through mediation, obligating judges to make on-site visits to talk with the work units, relatives, and neighbors and friends to ascertain the quality of the couple's relationship and the roots of the problems ("contradictions"), and then to intervene actively to effect reconciliation through moral-political education, through political pressures (applied also by the local party leadership) and social pressures (applied also by relatives and neighbors), and even through positive material inducements.

Such actions and methods are better characterized as "mediatory adjudication," since the main thrust of the court action was adjudication against divorce, regardless of the will of the litigants—though serious efforts were made toward mediating a reconciliation. A great deal of what was called *tiaojie* by contemporary Chinese courts in fact fell into this category.

Yet voluntary mediation does occur in the contemporary Chinese justice system. Below, I first delineate that mediatory sphere, in order to bring out more clearly its operative logic, before returning again to the subject of involuntary mediations.

No-Fault Mutual-Consent Divorce Cases

In mutual-consent divorce cases, there is generally no question about whether to permit divorce or about which party is at fault. The court is concerned almost exclusively with working out a settlement that both sides can agree to. Those were precisely the cases in which what transpired most closely approximated mediation in the word's original core sense.[15]

The basic approach of the 1950 and 1980 marriage laws to property settlements in divorce was to leave the specifics to mutual agreement (*xieyi*). The 1950 Marriage Law excluded from the divorce settlement only "such property as belonged to her [the wife] prior to her marriage," which would revert to her

15. Not all cases categorized as "mediated divorce" involved mediated compromises. Sometimes, the parties involved managed to reach agreement on their own and came to court merely to formalize it and their divorce, leaving the court merely a pro forma role (see, for example, B, 1977-19, 20; B, 1988-11). But those cases too would be included in the count of mediated divorces, consistent with the judicial system's tendency to claim for "mediation" as high a proportion of cases as possible. At other times, the court's role could be mainly adjudicatory—for example, when one party withheld agreement to divorce in order to extract more favorable terms in the settlement, terms that the court saw as unreasonable. Such cases would likewise be categorized as "mediated," so long as the court managed to get both parties to accept the settlement, even if it were largely court-imposed (see, e.g., A, 1988-4).

(Article 23). The rest was to be settled by mutual agreement. The 1980 Marriage Law reaffirmed this principle, stipulating simply that "the husband and wife shall seek agreement regarding the disposition of their jointly possessed property" (Article 31). (By implication, their individual properties would remain separate.) Beyond that, the laws added a provision that would give a woman unable to support herself fully some measure of protection. As to the property settlement, "If they fail to reach an agreement, the people's court shall make a judgment, taking into consideration the actual circumstances of the property and the rights and interests of the wife and the child."[16] As for support and custody of the child (*fuyang*),[17] neither law took any position on which parent should be responsible, beyond noting that "the mother shall have the custody of a breast-fed infant after divorce" (i.e., an infant still being breast-fed—Article 20 of the 1950 law, and 29 of the 1980 law). The code thus set up a broad negotiatory framework that allowed for much latitude and flexibility in working out mediated compromises.

In many cases in the sample, the court's role was to help work out the specifics of a divorce settlement. The county A sample alone includes fifty-six mutual-consent divorces, in thirty-three of which the court took no adjudicatory posture as to fault. In those cases, once the courts had determined that both parties wanted to divorce, they took a fairly low-key, facilitative approach to fashioning the property settlements.

Consider first a case from county B, in 1988. The marriage was a failure from day one. The husband suing for divorce said in his complaint that his wife mistreated his parents and had wanted to separate the household from them after just thirty-eight days of marriage. She countered in her response that he beat her, but she did not object to the divorce. The judge and the secretary (*shujiyuan*) went down to the village and interviewed the plaintiff husband at the village government office, in the presence of the village leadership (the village head and an unidentified villager); he repeated much of what he had written in his divorce complaint. The judge then interviewed the wife, this time at the nearby local (Xinjun tun zhen) branch of the county court. She too basically reiterated her countercomplaint. Next the judge, as was standard in what I term "Maoist justice," interviewed the parents, the neighbor in the house east of the couple's home, and then the neighbor facing the couple's home, as he sought to ascertain the true nature of the couple's relationship. From those interviews, and presumably also from unrecorded

16. In the 1950 Marriage Law this sentence concludes "and the principle of benefiting the development of production," a clause deleted in the 1980 law.

17. Here I deliberately render *fuyang* as "child support and custody" (where the official translation has "child custody") to emphasize that the issue of support looms much larger in the Chinese countryside than in America.

discussions with the village cadres, the judge concluded that this divorce was an instance of mutual consent and not an adjudicative matter of fault or of right and wrong. The only issue was to work out a divorce settlement to which both parties would agree.

Using standard mediation techniques, the judge talked first with the husband and the wife separately. He learned that the wife wanted two articles left at the house when she had moved out: the bicycle she had been using and a luggage set that was hers. The husband resisted this demand but was open to some kind of a compromise. The judge then met with both of them at the same time, and initially they simply repeated their separate complaints about the other. After these were aired, the judge suggested a compromise solution: the husband would pay his wife 200 yuan in lieu of the bicycle and the luggage. This session ended with the husband agreeing to consider the solution. At the next session, the court obtained the couple's voluntary agreement along the lines of its suggestion. A mediation document (*tiaojie shu*) was drawn up, with the two agreeing to a (mutual consent) divorce (*xieyi lihun*) and to the terms of the settlement (200 yuan in compensation from the husband for the disputed bicycle and luggage set). The court fee of 30 yuan was to be borne by the plaintiff husband (B, 1988-20).

We have numerous other examples of such mediatory work by the courts. In 1977, a woman in county A sought divorce from her husband. She claimed that he was sexually too demanding and was too crude in his behavior. The husband did not object to the divorce. The court ascertained that the couple "lacked understanding before they married," that they had argued frequently after marrying because of personality differences, that tension had grown worse after he had been punished for mishandling archival materials in his charge, and that matters had degenerated to the point that the man sometimes mistreated the woman verbally and physically. The relationship between the two had in fact ruptured, the court concluded. At issue, then, were only the property settlement and the support and custody of their nine-year-old son. The court was able to bring the two parties to agreement fairly easily: the properties that each had brought to the marriage would go back to each. As for their joint properties, the sewing machine would go to the woman, and the large wardrobe to the man. The child's custody and support would go to the mother (A, 1977-012).

In 1989, to give one more example, a man in county A sued for divorce. The court ascertained that the marriage's foundation had been weak: the woman had married hastily because she wanted to move away from her stepmother, while the man had borne a grudge because he thought she had demanded too much money for the marriage agreement. After the marriage, the couple never got along well and frequently fought over small matters of daily life and over their child. They had in fact separated six years earlier, in 1983. Both wished to divorce. The court concluded that "the relationship between the two had in fact ruptured" and went along with the divorce. Once again, only the specifics of the divorce settlement were at issue. The court helped to work out the following agreement: (1) the child would live with his father; (2) the house the two had rented would be rented by the woman; and (3) the bed, the chest of drawers, the large wardrobe, the square table, the pair of bedside chests, and two wooden chairs would go to the woman, and the rest of their property to the man. A mediated agreement spelling out the specifics was drawn up accordingly (A, 1988-02).

Finally, an example of a case from the new century, under new evidence procedures (R county, 2002: no. 339). The wife seeks divorce, claiming that the husband abuses her. She wants custody of the five-year-old daughter; the three-year-old son to go to the husband. The husband claims that he is actually good to his wife. In the "trial" under new evidence procedures, the court reaches the finding that the couple's relationship had been so-so but that later, under financial pressures, they had fought constantly. For that reason, she had left a year earlier to seek work but was later persuaded to return home. However, a few months later, she went off to work again. In the course of the court process, the husband comes to see that his wife is determined to divorce, and in the end, goes along. With the help of the court, the agreement was reached for the husband to compensate the wife 2,000 yuan, to give her the washing machine and other big items that had been part of her dowry, and to give her custody of the daughter; he would have custody of the son. As for the court expense of 450 yuan, it was to be paid by her, the plaintiff. Thus did the two sides reach voluntary agreement. The court in this case example did not, like a Maoist court would, go down to the village and talk to the neighbors and kin, but rather mediated at court. However, its logic of operation was the same as before.

The role played by the courts in cases such as these in some ways resembles the no-fault approach that has come to dominate Western divorce cases since the transitional period of the 1960s and 1970s. Earlier in the West—mainly because of the legacy and influence of the Catholic Church, which steadfastly maintained the sanctity of marriage—divorce was possible only when fault could be proved. The result was an adversarial framework for divorce cases similar to that for other kinds of civil lawsuits about violations of rights. But recent Western divorce law has moved steadily away from assigning fault toward a greater emphasis on dispute resolution (Phillips, 1988), rendering fault largely irrelevant.[18] It is an approach with some similarity to the reasoning underlying Chinese mediation.

18. Even in divorces by mutual consent, relative fault may be assigned, as discussed later in this chapter.

There is a crucial difference, however. Weberian Continental legal formalism, as we have seen, demands that law start with universal principles, to be applied by "legal logic" to concrete fact situations. The recent no-fault approach to divorce, though a striking departure from the fault-based divorce of the past, retains the formalist mode of thinking. Thus, the no-fault approach begins with the no-fault premise, which is then applied to all divorces. The Chinese approach, by contrast, takes the fact situation as the starting point. The court first determines whether the divorce is by mutual consent; if so, then divorce will be granted. It also seeks to determine whether fault is involved; if not, then the working out of the divorce settlement will strictly be finding a compromise agreement that both sides will willingly accept.

The Chinese approach in fact inverts the formalist method. Instead of starting from a generalized principle that would be applied to all fact situations, it acknowledges that in real life both fault and no-fault situations obtain. The court begins by determining which kind of fact situation it is dealing with, and then acts accordingly.

No-Fault "Tort" Cases

Chinese court mediations have worked similarly to determine compensation in damages (*peichang*, "tort") cases that involve no fault. As has been seen in chapter 6, the 1986 General Principles of Civil Law, even though it adopted the Western conceptual framework of "wrongful acts" for tort cases (thereby requiring the establishment of fault—the violation of another's rights—before granting monetary compensation), went on to acknowledge the reality of no-fault "tort" situations and that, even in such situations, "civil liability shall still be borne" (Article 106, 132).

The key here is the recognition that compensation for damages may arise in some fact situations that do not involve fault. To the extent that the defendant accepts the principle of civil liability even in the absence of fault, such cases truly follow the mediatory ideology: to resolve disputes, courts focus not on establishing legal right and wrong, but rather on minimizing conflict and working out a compromise that both parties can accept.

For example, in the case already discussed in the preceding chapter, in county A in 1989, a seven-year-old boy rushing home from school ran into an old woman carrying a bottle of boiling hot water. She dropped the bottle, spilling the water on the boy's chest, back, limbs, and face. The medical treatment of his burns cost more than 2,000 yuan, of which the township government paid less than 600 yuan. The father of the boy brought suit against the woman for the balance.

The judge investigated the case and concluded that the woman was not at fault. Nevertheless, he held that she had civil liability, citing precisely Articles

106 and 132 of the General Principles of Civil Law. Under that legal rubric, the court then persuaded both parties to agree to a settlement: the woman was to pay 250 yuan to help cover (a part of) the boy's medical expenses. In the course of trying to gain their assent, the judge appealed especially to the (old) moral ideal that the two, living in the same small community, should be compassionate and not create lasting enmity (A, 1989-9).

In the "vehicular tort" case from county B (also in 1988), cited earlier, in which a woman riding a bike was run into by the small tractor behind her when she suddenly slipped and fell from the wet road and her collar bone was broken as a result, the driver willingly paid for the medical care she received. But then complications developed, because the bone had not been set properly, and the woman brought suit for the additional expenses. Once again, under the legal stipulation that the defendant bore civil liability despite not being at fault, the judge worked on both parties to persuade them to accept a 350-yuan settlement (B, 1988-3; see also B, 1989-16, a similar case).

These cases, it can readily be seen, are similar to mutual-consent divorces in that the court's concern was to devise a settlement that both parties could willingly accept, once it had determined that no fault was involved. In contrast, a "wrongful acts" rubric imposes an adversarial framework on cases, encouraging savvy lawyers to establish that the other party is at fault—as seen in divorce cases in the West before the transition to no-fault divorce.

They also may bring to mind recent developments in the United States regarding no-fault auto insurance. Under such insurance, drivers are covered by their own policies, regardless of who is at fault. It is intended to be more cost-effective than the old fault-based approach to auto torts, and to date has come to be adopted in twelve states in the United States (Auto Insurance In-Depth, 2004).

However, once again there is a crucial conceptual difference. No-fault auto insurance in the twelve U.S. states takes as its point of departure a principle that is generalized to apply to all fact situations, regardless of actual circumstances. The basic premise remains "no fault, no liability," and there is no role for mediation. In the Chinese approach, by contrast, the courts begin from the fact situation, and mediation comes into play after the courts have determined that the specific case involved no fault.

Both Parties Equally at Fault

Disputes in which both parties are seen as more or less equally at fault are also generally mediated according to the same reasoning and methods used in mutual-consent divorce and no-fault compensation cases. In county A in 1989, for example, two neighboring couples in an apartment building fought over water that collected in the hallway. First the plaintiff wife began fighting with the defendant husband, then their respective spouses joined the fray. All were injured to some degree, and all incurred medical expenses. The plaintiff husband's right little finger was broken at the last joint (208.95 yuan), and his wife's breastbone was bruised (126.57 yuan); the defendant husband's left index finger was fractured (186.60 yuan), and his wife's stomach was bruised (25.25 yuan). The township and village governments tried to mediate, but failed. The plaintiffs sought 500 yuan in damages and the defendants countersued, seeking 800 yuan.

The court investigated and concluded that in this situation, both parties were at fault. Because there was no one "wrongful act," the court was not concerned with adjudicating as to right and wrong. In the end, it succeeded in working out an agreement: the defendants were to pay the plaintiffs 120 yuan, to more or less even things out (the parties suffering the lighter injuries bore more of the medical fees), and the court costs of 100 yuan were to be equally split (A, 1989-16).

In a similar case in county B in 1988, two neighbors had a fight over the boundary of their residential plots (*zhaijidi*), the subject of two previous disputes. This time, the defendant had planted two trees on the disputed property. The plaintiff uprooted the trees when the defendant refused to remove them, and the two women then got in a physical fight that left the plaintiff with a concussion. The village leaders tried to mediate, arranged for the defendant to visit the plaintiff bearing a gift, and suggested that she pay 200 yuan in compensation to resolve the matter. But the plaintiff, left with headaches that persisted after her two-week hospital stay and complaining that she could not do housework or farm her five mu of "responsibility land," would not agree and brought suit.

The judge (and a secretary) came down to the village to investigate and talked with the village leaders and the witnesses to the fight. Apparently, the defendant had first grabbed the plaintiff's hair, and the plaintiff in turn had scratched the defendant's face with the stick in her hand before receiving the more serious injury. The judge concluded from his investigations that "both sides have responsibility" and "both should be criticized." He then turned to working out an agreement acceptable to both parties.

The judge met first with the defendant and summarized his findings: though both bore responsibility, it was the plaintiff who had an injury that caused her to be unable to farm or do housework, while the defendant's injury was very slight with no lasting consequences. The plaintiff's medical expenses alone came to about 300 yuan, he pointed out, and by law, the defendant had civil liability (even in the absence of fault). He spoke with all the authority not only of the court but also of the knowledge gleaned from his thorough investigation of the facts. After initial resistance, the defendant and her husband finally said that they would follow the court's opinion. The judge got them to agree to compensation amounting to "no more than 700 yuan." He then met with the plaintiff, represented by her husband, and urged a compromise. The plaintiff insisted on no less than 600 yuan. At that figure, agreement was reached (B, 1988-15; see also B, 1977-12, a similar case).

Again, the court followed logic similar to that used in mutual-consent divorce cases and no-fault tort cases. Once it had determined that both parties were at fault, not just one of the two, its task was then to fashion a mutually acceptable agreement regarding the shared "civil liability" for the damages, through a mediated compromise.

Both Parties Bearing Equally Legitimate Claims or Obligations

The operative logic in situations involving no fault or equal fault applies also to cases in which both parties have equally legitimate claims or equal obligations in the eyes of the law. Thus the court's main role, once again, is not to adjudicate as to legal right and wrong, but rather to resolve the dispute by working out a compromise solution acceptable to both parties.

For example, in county B in 1988, a widow sued her parents-in-law for her husband's death benefit and for her and her husband's property. The young couple and the parents had not undergone household division (*fenjia*), even though they had eaten separately since 1986. The main issue was how to distribute the husband's 5,000-yuan death benefit (he was killed while working in the village's hillside production facility), but there were other complications: the widow wanted her dowry and everything she and her husband had bought as a couple, while the parents-in-law wanted custody of their nine-year-old grandson and some of the couple's property. The court took a straightforward adjudicatory posture on those issues that did involve legal right and wrong: by law, the dowry she brought into the marriage was unequivocally hers, and a mother had precedence over grandparents for custody of her child. That left just the property of the couple and the insurance benefit, to which both parties (the widow and her child on the one hand, and the two parents on the other) had equal claim, with all four persons of the same family (of undivided household) being the "first in order" to inherit the property of the deceased, according to Article 10 of the 1985 Law of Succession.

The court, after verifying the facts by interviewing the relevant parties (including the insurance agent and the village government) and going to the couple's home to inventory their property, worked out a solution acceptable to both sides: the couple's belongings were divided up according to the wishes of both sides, with a 100-yuan adjustment in cash to be made in the sharing of the death benefit to even out the division. Both parties then agreed (B, 1988-17; for similar cases, see B, 1988-16; B, 1977-7).

We see here the court performing simultaneously its adjudicatory and mediatory roles. On issues involving clear-cut right and wrong in law (i.e., the widow's rightful claims to her dowry and custody of the child), the court took straightforward adjudicatory positions. But concerning the couple's shared property and the death benefit, to which both parties had equal claim, the court acted as a facilitative mediator to work out a resolution acceptable to both sides.

In another case in 1989, also from county B, a mother sued her three surviving sons for maintenance support, seeking fifty yuan a month from each of them. At the time, the widowed mother was living with her sixteen-year-old granddaughter fathered by her deceased third son (whose wife had remarried). From the start, it was clear that the three brothers still living were all obligated to contribute to her support, as everyone agreed. At issue were the specifics of how the burden was to be shared among the brothers, whose financial situations differed and who felt different degrees of obligation. The first son, relatively well off, wanted to provide just ten yuan a month—possibly a few yuan more, he said. The second son said he was willing to give whatever was agreed to by everyone. The fourth son, a worker on temporary status (*linshigong*) in the worst financial situation of all the brothers, earning just seventy yuan a month, said he wanted the mother to live with him (which would improve his financial situation). Otherwise, he said, he would be able to provide just eight yuan a month. There was also a daughter, quite well off, who volunteered to contribute thirty yuan a month, even though she had not shared in the inheritance from her deceased father as had the brothers (and therefore had no legal obligation to provide old-age support for her mother).

The court's first proposal, that each of the four (the three brothers and their sister) give twenty-five yuan a month, was resisted by the two elder brothers; it was also clearly unrealistic for the low-earning youngest brother. The mother, though the original plaintiff, was not involved in these disagreements. Discussions between the court and all the siblings ensued, until they finally came to an agreement: the first and second sons, and the daughter, were to give their mother twenty yuan a month; the fourth son, ten yuan a month. In addition, the brothers were each to provide half a ton of coal a year and to share equally in their mother's medical expenses, as needed. Everyone then signed the mediated agreement (B, 1989-10).

Here again, no one disputed the obligation and willingness of the brothers to provide old-age support for their mother. Only the specifics of the arrangement were in question. Under those circumstances, the role of the court was to facilitate the working out of terms acceptable to everyone. What could have become a rancorous dispute among the siblings was thus resolved through discussion and compromise.

Between Mediation and Adjudication

Despite its ideology of mediation and its from-fact-to-concept mode of thinking, contemporary Chinese justice in the Reform era has also drawn heavily on formalist Continental law, as did the Republic before it. The official adoption in the 1980s of laws modeled after Continental civil codes makes clear the intention of incorporating their features. The 1986 General Principles of Civil Law begins with rights, much as its formalist models do, and also attempts to stipulate provisions that follow logically from those abstract principles. The courts have adjudicated many cases accordingly, issuing verdicts of right or wrong and determining winner or loser, as do those in formalist legal systems, as I document in chapter 6 (cf. Huang, 2006a). In fact, the legal system comprises both adjudicatory and mediatory spheres.

We should recall that the new General Principles of Civil Law of 1986, the Marriage Law of 1980, and the Law of Succession of 1985 were not utterly new transplantations from Western models. Rather, in many respects they formalized principles that had been tested on a trial basis in the People's Republic for decades, mainly in the form of Supreme People's Court directives and opinions (see chapter 6; Huang, 2006a). Their scope has widened with formal codification, to be sure, but we can see an essential continuity (the extremely politicized Land Reform and Cultural Revolution years aside) in laws and court actions in older areas of civil law such as those discussed above: divorce, rights of ownership or inheritance of the family house and residential plot, debt obligations, obligations to maintain aged parents, obligations to compensate another for damages from "wrongful acts," and so on. These should be distinguished from the newer areas of the law born of the rapid growth of private enterprises and foreign trade in the Reform era, such as the laws on income tax (1980; revised, 1993 and 1999), trademarks (1982), foreign trade (1994), insurance (1995), and contracts (1999), for which there is little Maoist precedent.

Of course, I do not mean to deny that important changes occurred between the Maoist and Reform eras. In divorce law, for example, I have considered in detail (in chapters 4 and 6) the repercussions of the liberalization brought in 1989 by the so-called Fourteen Articles, which set forth how courts should determine whether the emotional relationship of the husband and wife has truly ruptured ("Zuigao renmin fayuan," 1990). Moreover, court mediation in general is unquestionably becoming a less and less prominent part of the total justice system, especially the Maoist period's "Ma Xiwu" mode of operation and the coercive "mediated reconciliations" in contested divorce cases, because of both mounting caseloads and changing ideas about the rule of law (see chapter 5). I have nevertheless elected to focus here mainly on some of the abiding characteristics of contemporary Chinese law, for they seem to me much less readily apparent than the changes. Persisting features include the mode of practical moralism in legal thinking, the combination of mediatory and adjudicatory justice under a single system, and basic characteristics of court adjudication and mediation. Between adjudication and mediation, of course, is a large intermediate zone in which the two overlap to varying degrees. But within that intermediate zone, two broad categories can be identified, as noted above: mediatory adjudications and adjudicative mediations.

Mediated reconciliations of contested divorces, as has been seen, were more often than not basically adjudications against divorce. I cited numerous case examples in chapter 4; here it suffices to recapitulate with just one example: in county B in 1977, a peasant woman sought divorce because her father-in-law had molested her, and her husband, thoroughly dominated by the father as he was, could not or would not stand up for her. The judges went down to the village and found that the woman and her family were determined to divorce. Nevertheless, the judges were bent on rejecting the woman's petition and working out a "mediated reconciliation."

They ascertained that the father-in-law had indeed made inappropriate advances toward the woman, and they tried their best to resolve the problem by lecturing and warning him. They worked out a solution with the village leadership to help the young couple build a new house and also threw in the additional material inducement of arranging a better position for the husband in the seed farm of the brigade. At the same time, they worked hard on the woman and her family, bringing pressure to bear from the village leadership in addition to making completely clear that the court did not look favorably on the proposed divorce. They also pushed the father-in-law into helping the young couple build their new home and promising to leave them be.

In the end, they managed to make all sides agree to the mediated reconciliation, after the team of three people from the court (the senior judge, junior judge, and a "people's assessor," *peishenyuan*) had made no fewer than four separate and joint trips to the husband's village and two to the wife's. The entire process was then concluded with a "family reconciliation meeting" at the young couple's newly built home (B, 1977-16; chapter 4, this volume; see also Huang, 2005: 156–66). This case may be considered a good example of the lengths to which Maoist courts went in their attempts to effect mediated reconciliations of couples.

In the later reflections in the 1990s about such mediated reconciliations, the Chinese legal community acknowledged that very often such aggressive "mediations" produced no lasting "reconciliation." By the reckoning of the Songjiang judges interviewed, perhaps half the time the "reconciled" couples would eventually end up divorcing (INT93-9). One widely read study of Chongming County's divorce cases in 1985–1986 even claimed that only 3 percent of all the couples "reconciled" by the court later made genuine attempts at reconciliation.[19] In a context in which one-party divorce petitions were almost routinely denied, most of those who nevertheless elected to come to court strongly desired a divorce. The denials of such petitions as a matter of course were necessarily often imposed against the will of the petitioner. The fact is that mediated reconciliations could not reshape the emotional relationships of couples in quite the manner that the party-state had hoped. Such court actions, in the end, can be called "mediatory" only by greatly distorting the word's normal sense.

But this is not to say that all cases with adjudicative features necessarily went against the will of the litigant. We have seen in the preceding section how the court exercised adjudicatory powers even in cases involving no fault or equal fault, insofar as it had the final authority to determine the nature of the fact situation. We have also seen a variety of cases in which the court mediated under an adjudicatory posture: these concerned civil liability even in the absence of fault, equal entitlement to the property of a deceased man on the part of the "first-order" heirs, the obligation to support an aged parent on the part of the sons, and so on. To the extent that those factual determinations and adjudicatory principles were accepted by the defendants, voluntary mediation took place. Some additional types of such adjudicative mediation are considered below.

In one case from county A, in 1965, the peasant couple had been married in 1960 and were separated in 1961 when the husband joined the army. She had an affair with a "third party." The husband filed a complaint to have that person disciplined under the regulations protecting enlisted men. The court had verified that the charge was true, and the man involved was consequently "locked up in punishment" (*guanya chuli*) for an unspecified period. The husband, represented by his father, went on to seek divorce from his wife, on the grounds that their relationship was irreparably damaged. She opposed the petition when she first met with the judge, but then, when the judge talked with her at greater length, she admitted that she did not really object to the divorce. Because the divorce at bottom was by mutual consent, it would unquestionably be granted. The only issues for the court were the property settlement and the custody of their young daughter.

The judge, consistent with usual procedures, met with the parties separately—first, the wife. She wanted to be given custody of the child and to continue to live with her husband's family until she found a new mate (*duixiang*). But her husband's father wanted her to move out; he also sought to keep custody of their child as well as the couple's property. The court then brought both

19. The article was published in the *Zhongguo fazhi bao* (Bulletin on China's Legal System) in 1988 (Palmer, 1989: 169).

parties together to work out a compromise resolution—arrived at with the understanding of everyone involved that the wife was the one at fault. The final terms were (1) the wife would be allowed to stay with the husband's family for one year, with use of the couple's furniture for that time only; and (2) during that time the wife would be given temporary custody of her daughter, and the husband's family would be required to provide child support, but the husband and his family would have custody thereafter. Both sides agreed to the terms and a "mediation agreement" was executed spelling them out (A, 1965-014; see also A, 1977-06, a similar case).

The final agreement plainly favored the husband. As my Songjiang informant judges made clear, the courts customarily viewed the adulterous party as the offending party, and the other as the victim. If suit for divorce was brought by the offending party, it would generally be denied. If the aggrieved party brought suit, as in this case, then that party would be favored in the court's efforts to help work out a settlement (INT93-9). Here, the husband had the advantage both in the property settlement and in child custody.

Even in such a situation, there was probably a substantial voluntary dimension. To be sure, the outcome was strongly influenced by the adjudicatory posture of the court. But the court's posture also represented the general mores of society. Thus the wife, too, most likely felt, at least to some degree, that she was the offending party and could not expect to be treated the same as the husband she had cuckolded. That was no doubt a factor at work in her willingness to accept the arrangement arrived at, or at least not insist on her position and force the court to adjudicate outright. Insofar as she truly shared the court's views on fault, her compromise may be seen as voluntary.

In the 1990s, the courts relaxed their posture against divorce to a considerable extent, specifically in cases in which the "offending party" brings suit for divorce. In large measure, two factors were responsible for the change. One was mounting caseloads: with marketization came the return of property and debt disputes, plus many new types of cases, especially concerning contracts. The courts of the 1990s could no longer afford to devote to Maoist "mediated reconciliations" the time and energy they required. The other was the increasing evidence that such forced reconciliations more often than not merely postponed the inevitable. In addition, the considerations of peasant opposition that had given rise to this approach to contested divorces no longer figured quite so prominently as they had earlier. The altered circumstances of the Reform era, of course, were accompanied by altered conceptions of law and the role it should play (see chapter 6).

Thus, in a case from county B in 1995, the wife brought suit for divorce after ten years of marriage, saying that she and her husband lacked a "common language" and that he was often jealous for no reason. He countered that she behaved improperly with other men—in fact, he had twice seen her with other men. She did not dispute the allegations. The court, consistent with the directives of the Supreme People's Court set forth in the Fourteen Articles, approved the divorce petition instead of attempting to force a mediated reconciliation. It did, however, favor the husband quite strongly in the settlement: he received custody of their child, their three-room home, and the "big items" owned by the couple—the television, refrigerator, chests and bureaus, and the motorbike (B, 1995-10). To the extent that the wife voluntarily accepted these unfavorable terms, the case may be seen as falling within the scope of adjudicative mediations.

Another type of case in which the court's judgment as to fault on the part of one party entered the picture involves the physical abuse—ranging from light to severe—of one spouse (generally the wife) by the other. The sample from county A contains four such cases. In 1988, for example, the woman sued for divorce on the grounds of mistreatment by her husband. She had become seriously ill after giving birth to their second child, but her husband continued to make unreasonable sexual demands on her. When she would not oblige, he beat her, the last time actually rupturing her liver and spleen. The husband admitted his fault, but pleaded that they should stay together for the sake of their two children. When his wife continued to insist on divorce, he relented. The court helped to work out the specifics of the settlement, clearly favoring the victimized wife. The couple had loaned out a total of 950 yuan to three parties. All was to go to the wife, plus another 300 yuan of the couple's savings. While the wife gave up her share of their furniture, the defendant husband was to provide her an additional 35 kilograms of (polished) rice, plus 150 kilograms of unhusked rice. Custody of the two children was to be divided, one to each parent (A, 1988-09).[20]

As has been seen in chapter 5, in the new century, along with the change in evidence procedures, the judges no longer go deep into the site of the dispute to interview and investigate, but rather undertake "investigation at trial" (*tingshen diaocha*). For this reason, on issues that are hard to prove at court (like spousal abuse or the "third party"), the courts have been moving toward a kind of "no-fault" logic in practice, no longer so emphatic about fault in such

20. In the third and final type of divorce settlements involving what the court perceived as "fault" in one party, one spouse had some involuntary disability. In such cases, the court typically took the position that the able spouse seeking divorce should take on some responsibility for the support of the disabled spouse. Our sample contains five examples of this type for county A. One occurred in 1953, when a man sued to dissolve his contract to marry the *tongyangxi* (young girl brought into the home to be raised as a prospective daughter-in-law) who had lived in his family since she was about twelve years old. She had required medical attention four years earlier and the doctors had concluded that she would not be able to bear children. The woman was willing to agree to the dissolution but asked for some financial consideration. Through the mediation of the court, the man agreed to provide a cotton suit for her, plus 60,000 yuan (in the currency of the time) (A, 1953-14).

issues. At the same time, however, the courts still uphold in principle the idea of fault. Thus, as has been seen in one case example in chapter 5 from county R, the court found on the basis of a report of a hospital examination (under the old system, the judge would have gone to the hospital to investigate), that the husband defendant was indeed unable to have children; although the husband denied the allegation, he was not able to offer any countervailing proof. For this reason, the court thought the wife plaintiff in the right in her request for divorce. This adjudicatory posture was reached on the basis of the new evidence procedures. On that basis, the judges spoke separately with each side and (in the old parlance) "worked on their thought" (*zuole sixiang gongzuo*), and got them to agree to compromise and reach agreement: the wife was to compensate the husband 5,000 yuan (he had asked originally for 8,000 yuan, when the wife was only willing to pay 3,000 yuan). This kind of case example may be seen as an instance in which the old mediation approach and the new evidence procedure successfully worked together (R, 2000-10).

The Nature of Contemporary Chinese Judicial Mediation

It is mainly in no-fault cases and in cases involving equal fault, or equal entitlement or obligation, that mediation in contemporary Chinese courts comes closest to the term's original core meaning of voluntary compromise. Once the court concludes from its fact-finding that fault cannot simply be assigned to one party, it becomes concerned only with working out a solution that both parties can accept. Such mediations have a greater chance of gaining the voluntary acceptance of the litigant. Even in those cases, however, we should not minimize the adjudicative role and power exercised by the court in first determining the facts of the situation.

Cases in which the court attempts to mediate specific terms of a settlement under an adjudicatory rubric (e.g., civil liability even in the absence of fault, obligation to support an aged parent, preferential treatment of the wronged spouse in a divorce settlement, and so on) may also be seen as mediatory to the extent that the defendant willingly shares or accepts the court's adjudicatory posture. We have seen how the courts have used methods and procedures similar to traditional societal mediation, first talking with the litigants separately to search for common ground and then helping to facilitate the working out of a compromise that both can accept.[21]

21. This is not to say that court mediations always work as they should. As caseloads increase, the courts can be expected to look for ways to save time—and mediation can be extremely time-consuming. Woo (2003: 101 n161) refers to the complaint of a litigant who felt the court rushed things too much.

As pointed out above, although Chinese no-fault mediation may call to mind the contemporary Western no-fault approach to divorce, as well as the more recent development of no-fault auto insurance in some states in the United States, it is fundamentally different. In both of the Western approaches, a "no-fault" principle is applied to all (divorce and auto tort) cases, regardless of the particular situation. In contrast, the Chinese approach takes as its point of departure the fact situation as determined by the court. Only after the court has concluded that the case involves no fault does the no-fault mediatory approach come into play. Arguably, each approach has advantages: one provides formalist consistency, while the other offers flexibility. In one, complex legal maneuvers to demonstrate fault have been rendered pointless, because a victimized or wronged litigant can gain no preference in the settlement; in the other, litigants still can benefit from such efforts, which may become more elaborate with increasing wealth and reliance on high-powered attorneys by the new elites of Chinese society.

Chinese court mediation might also be compared to U.S. out-of-court settlements in which the judges play a substantial role in bringing opposing counsel to agreement. Marc Galanter, who calls such negotiations "judicial mediation," points to a survey of trial judges: a high proportion (more than 75 percent) of the 2,545 respondents categorized their own role in out-of-court settlements as "intervention," while 22 percent saw themselves as not involved at all. The majority of judges surveyed viewed the intervention as "subtle," involving suggestions and making themselves available for conferences with the lawyers; 10 percent called their own involvement "aggressive," citing the use of pressure tactics (Galanter, 1985).

Yet such intervention is quite unlike Chinese judicial mediation, as its very name makes clear. U.S. out-of-court settlements are just that: they take place outside the courtroom, and outside the judge's formal capacity. In China, however, mediation is part of the formal role of the judge, thereby giving the judge greater authority and more power to intervene. In addition, the impetus for mediation is very different in the two systems. In the United States, litigants generally opt for out-of-court settlements after calculating how costly, in time and money, a trial would be. In China, at least in the kinds of disputes between individuals examined in this chapter (as opposed to contract disputes between corporate entities, which are a recent development), such cost considerations have yet to figure prominently. Cases are more likely to undergo court mediation on the court's initiative than the litigants', and the primary consideration is the judges' view of the nature of justice. Indeed, as we have seen, in China adjudication and not mediation is seen as the less costly and quicker approach—a major factor leading to the decline in Maoist-style "mediated reconciliations." Finally, Chinese judges readily pass judgment on whether the fact situation involves fault in their formal capacity, something that U.S. judges do only informally, outside the courtroom.

To the extent that "mediation" or "alternative dispute resolution" (ADR) in the United States (as well as most other Western countries) is understood as an extrajudicial rather than judicial action (*pace* Galanter above), undertaken largely by organizations in civil society rather than judges in court, it differs sharply from contemporary Chinese mediation, which is mainly court based rather than societal. That too makes the nature of the processes very different. When mediation is outside of and distinct from the courts, the proceedings are generally kept confidential, with the understanding that they cannot be used subsequently in court (in part to encourage the disputants to be more forthcoming). But when mediation is a court activity, the mediator and trial judge are one and the same person, and fact-finding during mediation is not separate from that during trial. Thus, in the Chinese system, a failed court mediation is almost always followed by arbitration or adjudication by the same judge, a feature that gives much more weight to the suggestions of the judge and puts greater pressure on the disputants. The same is not true of current extrajudicial mediation in the United States or Europe.[22]

In the United States and Europe today, what might be considered mediation proper seems actually quite limited in the extent of its use. Reliable data are hard to come by because the process is largely informal. For the United States, especially, it is almost impossible to get an accurate count (Subrin and Woo, 2006: chap. 10). My preliminary search shows that there are reasonably credible data for the Commonwealth of Virginia. To take it as an example, in 2002–2003, there were in this state a reported total of 9,457 mediation cases (Virginia Judicial System, 2004a). This is a rather paltry number if we consider the fact that the United States counts its total number of civil cases filed per year in the millions (e.g., 14.6 million in 1980, *State Court Caseload Statistics: Annual Report*, 1980: 14, 55; cf. Huang, 1996: 180), and its fifty states, in the hundreds of thousands. In Virginia in 2003, of the three main court systems, the Juvenile and Domestic Relations Court saw a total of 216,850 new "civil support" cases filed; the General District Court (overseeing relatively minor civil and criminal cases) saw a total of 949,202 new civil cases filed; and the higher-level circuit courts, a total of 115,383 new civil cases filed, making for a total of 1.28 million new civil cases (Virginia Judicial System, 2003: A-50, 64, 112, 116, 131). In other words, mediated cases amounted to just 0.7 percent

22. These characteristics of mediation are well illustrated by examples from the Netherlands, whose experiments with mediation in recent years are perhaps the best documented anywhere (de Roo and Jagtenberg, 2002). See also the Committee of Ministers of the Council of Europe's "European Principles on Family Mediation" (1998).

of all civil cases, a vast distance from the dimensions claimed for mediation in Chinese extrajudicial and judicial mediation.

The great majority of the mediated cases in Virginia, 73 percent, are "Custody, Visitation and Support" cases. To judge by fairly detailed data from one county, Richmond, perhaps 30 percent of all Custody, Visitation and Support cases underwent mediation. About half (498) of them were deemed appropriate by the court to refer the litigants to a mediation orientation session (while half were deemed inappropriate because one parent lived outside the state, was incarcerated, in drug rehabilitation, and so on). Of those about three-fifths (298) actually enter into mediation, making for just about 30 percent of all such cases filed. Of those, 83 percent reached agreement (Virginia Judicial System, 2004b).

Outside of "Custody, Visitation and Support cases," the other most frequent areas of mediated disputes were: "landlord-tenant" (10 percent), "business consumers" (7 percent), "contracts" (6 percent), and "employment," "neighborhood," and "divorce property," all just 1 percent.

To judge by the limited evidence above, then, mediation still plays a rather minor role in the American civil justice system, accounting for less than 1 percent of all civil cases, more than thirty years after the start of the ADR movement in 1976. It appears to be used principally in (child) custody-related cases. To be sure, of those that enter into mediation, the rate of success (i.e., with agreement reached without trial) seems quite high. Nevertheless, overall, the role played by mediation in the United States seems a far cry from that in China.

As for other Western countries, the Netherlands has possibly the most complete statistics, and we can use them to get a glimpse of the system's actual usage. There were in 2002 slightly more than 2,000 registered mediators in the Netherlands; but in the five-year period from 1996 to 2001, registered mediators handled a total of just 1,222 mediation cases, the majority of them divorce disputes (de Roo and Jagtenberg, 2002). Obviously, the number of people voluntarily opting to use mediation to resolve disputes was relatively small; the demand they generated fell well short of the supply of mediators and of the ADR ideal.

A comparison with China reveals striking differences. To be sure, Chinese figures on mediation are greatly exaggerated. In the Mao Zedong era, mediation was supposed to constitute the main approach of the entire civil legal system, and the courts tried their best to categorize all but the most strictly and narrowly adjudicatory cases as mediations in order to maximize the proportion of supposedly mediated cases, leading to the preposterous official claim that 80 percent of all cases were concluded by mediation. I have discussed this much-exaggerated claim in detail in chapters 4 and 7 (see also Huang, 2005, 2006b). In addition, chapter 4 showed how coercive Maoist "mediated reconciliations" began to contract in the 1990s, and chapter 5 demonstrated how it largely fell into disuse with the turn of the century. Even so, a substantial number of cases included some measure of genuine mediation (i.e., that did not completely disregard the wishes of the litigants). By my own preliminary research and analysis, their proportion is quite high among cases that do not involve fault, including divorce and tort cases, and also among cases in which the two parties both have entitlements or obligations, as in many legal actions over inheritance and old-age support. In disputes in which the fact situation does not really involve a matter of right and wrong, judges are more likely to be able to get both parties to compromise (with at least some degree of voluntariness) and thereby more nearly approximate the mediatory ideal in resolving disputes. The latest figures show that the total number of cases mediated amounts to about 41 percent of all civil cases (see chapter 7).

There are arguments for and against all the approaches to mediation discussed above. What seems indisputable, however, is that court or judicial mediation, or "the use of conciliation in arbitration," has recently been gaining considerable momentum in some parts of the world as a possibly viable alternative to court trials for settling disputes.[23] Even in the United States and Europe, there has been increased talk of "combining arbitration with conciliation" in an approach dubbed "Med-arb" (Schneider, 2003).

The Qing, the Republic, and Post-1949 China

Though contemporary Chinese mediation resembles traditional Chinese mediation in important ways, the institutional frames of the two are very different. The Qing courts almost never mediated; the contemporary courts, however, mediate a great deal—officially "80 percent" of the time in the Maoist period, but still about half the time in 2000, more than two decades into the Reform era, according to the official judicial statistics (*Zhongguo falü nianjian*, 1990: 993; 2001: 1257). Mediation in the Qing was almost entirely done by informal leaders of the communities; Maoist justice replaced most of those informal leaders with party-state cadres and instituted wide use of court mediation. In the Qing and the Republic, when societal mediation failed, the litigants could decide whether to go to court; today, failed court mediation—unless the plaintiff withdraws the case—is almost always followed by court arbitration or adjudication (by the same judge), those being parts of one and the same court process.

---

23. According to Tang Houzhi, countries beginning to use judicial mediation include Australia, Canada, Croatia, Hong Kong, Hungary, India, Japan, and South Korea (Tang, 1996). See also Chodosh (1999) and Schneider (2003).

But official representations from the People's Republic often conflate historical and contemporary mediation. Nationalistic reasons and historical exigencies lead to the assertion that mediation is simply "Chinese," the core of the great Chinese legal tradition that distinguishes it from and, by implication, makes it in some ways superior to that in the modern West. The state has, in other words, made of mediation an officially sponsored ideology, with all the exaggerated claims that such an ideology entails (chapter 4).

To be sure, the Qing-Republic and contemporary China are alike in that mediation has played a large role in the total justice system of both. But this similarity should not obscure the fact that court mediation in China is very much an invention of the modern period. Indeed, the contemporary Chinese example is above all characterized by in-court mediation, with all that such actions imply about the powers of the court and the blurrings of the lines between mediatory and adjudicatory justice.

Of course, there have been major changes from the Maoist to the Reform period. In the Maoist era, there was tremendous ideological pressure to make the great majority of court actions mediatory, in appearance even if not in actuality. The Reform era, in contrast, has seen explicit espousal of Western-model codes and an adjudicatory system. The space occupied by mediatory justice has shrunk considerably both in representation and in action. As has been shown in chapter 5, in the new century, the old Maoist forced reconciliations have largely fallen into disuse in the context of the new social-economic environment and the new evidence law. In many situations, adjudication has come to be seen as more efficient and appropriate than mediation. Where the balance between the two will be struck in the total justice system remains to be seen. Nevertheless, there can be no mistaking the continued reliance on and significance of court mediation in the contemporary Chinese civil justice system, both as a practice and an ideal. In 2006, the number of civil cases ending in mediation at court still totaled 82 percent of those adjudicated.

The Logic of Chinese Court Mediation

This review of the operative realities of the contemporary Chinese justice system shows that its point of departure, though only implicit, is the presumption that real-life disputes cover a wide range of fact situations, both involving clear-cut questions of right and wrong and not, both fault and no fault, with all mixes in between. This assessment of practical reality forms the basis of the legal system's inclusion of both imported, rights-protecting adjudicatory justice and traditional, compromise-working mediatory justice. The presumption is that either, or some mix of the two, is to be applied as the particular case might warrant, an outlook that underlies the paradoxical formulation in codified law about "civil liability even in the absence of fault." It is also what directs the courts to select an appropriate course of action, whether mediation or adjudication, after determining the nature of the fact situation.

This approach has created a mediation system that contrasts quite sharply with both traditional Chinese and current Western ADR approaches. The mediating Chinese court exercises great discretionary powers, as it determines the fact situation, decides whether to mediate, and decides whether to employ adjudicatory considerations in mediation. Moreover, the authority of its mediatory efforts is enhanced because it will arbitrate or adjudicate should mediation fail. That is a great deal more power and discretion than traditional Chinese or current Western ADR mediators (or even trial judges in out-of-court settlements) wield, and more than most Western jurists would likely find acceptable.

Yet there can be no denying that Chinese courts have been quite effective in resolving disputes with compromises that are at least to some degree voluntary. Success is more likely in cases in which fault or questions of right and wrong are truly not involved, or those in which the disputants accept as legitimate the adjudicatory position under which the court mediates. In contrast, court mediations have clearly been unsuccessful when the courts have acted with utter disregard of litigants' wishes, employing highly coercive methods to impose resolutions. Such cases reveal the courts' scope for abusing their great discretionary power. But those aside, it is perhaps not going too far to say that Chinese mediatory justice has been able to mitigate, at least to some extent, the kinds of adversarial excesses that advocates of alternative dispute resolution have criticized in Western legal systems.

At the same time, we must acknowledge that Chinese mediatory justice can turn clear-cut cases of legal right and wrong into unclear cases for compromise. Indeed, this is a common complaint of foreign observers and businesses operating in the Chinese environment, and even of some Chinese citizens themselves. The courts sometimes seek compromises rather than uphold rights and obligations. Since Chinese legal theory itself has not distinguished clearly between the circumstances under which mediation or arbitration is to operate and those under which it is not, or provided guidelines to judges for making these determinations, the blurring of clear-cut cases happens all the more easily. Adjudications on matters of right and wrong can be sacrificed for the sake of the mediatory ideology and approach.

But before we simply dismiss Chinese justice as unmodern, fuzzy, or overly authoritarian, we should consider formalist law through the eyes of Chinese justice (or of the advocates of ADR). With their insistence on beginning with abstract premises about rights, and of subsuming all legal decisions by deductive logic under such principles, formalist legal systems can drive almost all disputes into an adversarial framework of rights violations and of fault, even when neither party is at fault or when both parties would prefer a compromise resolution. Lawyer advocates and the general legal culture can impose an adversarial approach that insists on clear-cut right and wrong on every case. With such a legal culture, even cases undergoing alterative dispute resolution can be pushed into an adversarial framework requiring winners and losers. That has certainly been the case with construction disputes in California, for example.[24] The resort to and demand for mediation have in any case remained relatively low compared to that in China, perhaps because of its still relatively limited effectiveness. This is true even of the more empirical, pragmatic common-law legal cultures of the United States and Britain, which have led the Western world in the development of ADR.

The practice and logic of court mediation in contemporary China, we have seen, are largely predicated on an epistemological approach that gives priority to facts over universalized principles. The very logic of mediation—as the voluntary settlement of differences through compromise, not an effort to establish right and wrong—works best in cases not involving clear-cut right and wrong or fault, whose plaintiffs are much more likely to be satisfied with a compromise resolution. The case records suggest that relying on the courts to separate those fact situations appropriate for a mediatory approach (followed by arbitration if mediation fails) from those that are not has contributed significantly to the success of court mediation in China.

Practical objections to the Chinese judge-*cum*-mediator wielding excessive power aside, advocates of formalist reasoning of the type outlined by Max Weber are understandably resistant to the Chinese epistemological approach, which begins with fact situations rather than abstract principles about rights. Imperial Chinese lawmaking born of that mode of thinking has enjoyed remarkable longevity, however. And case records show that such a mode of legal reasoning has been fundamental to contemporary Chinese court mediation and its relative effectiveness. The courts are to choose adjudicatory or media-

24. Construction disputes in California are typically handled by arbitration under the ADR rubric; one might therefore expect mediatory approaches different from those found in the regular court system. In practice, however, the disputants typically do everything possible to arrive at the finish line as the "prevailing party"—defined as the side with more legitimate claims against the other, even if by just one dollar, after the arbitration court has reviewed all the claims and counterclaims. The "loser" is expected to bear the court and attorney fees, which can run to tens of thousands of dollars even if the amount at question is much less. This system encourages a win-lose adversarial mentality (heightened by the coaching of seasoned attorneys who make a living on such disputes), even when both sides might have been willing to seek a compromise. An "alternative" approach seeking to place greater emphasis on dispute resolution through compromise cannot make much headway within a legal culture that remains fundamentally adversarial (interview with attorney Rodney Moss of Moss, Levitt & Mandell, Los Angeles, specialists in construction disputes, 28 June 2004).

tory justice, or some mix of the two, depending on their determination of the facts of each case. This implicit logic of contemporary Chinese law and legal practice, not clearly spelled out even in Chinese lawmaking itself, may yet have something to offer to both Chinese and formalist law as they change and evolve in the years to come.

8
Whither Chinese Law?

Most people have looked to theory/ideology to answer the question "where should China go from here?" It is a question that, in the Chinese discursive context, is couched in the form of "what is 'modernity' (*xiandaixing*)?" Some have looked especially to liberalism, others to Marxism. This chapter stresses that the true meaning of modernity should be sought not in any one theory or ideology but in historical process. On the very general level, the West's modernity lies not just in one of the two great intellectual traditions of the Enlightenment—rationalism and empiricism—but in both, in their long-term coexistence and mutual influence. The "scientific method," too, historically relies neither simply on the deductive logic of rationalism nor on the inductive logic emphasized by empiricism, but rather on their simultaneous use. In still more general terms, in my view, the modernity of the political economies of most Western countries is found neither in a completely laissez-faire type of capitalist market economy, as envisaged in classical liberalism, nor in the welfare state that followed it, but in the mutual adaptation of the two. The British and American political economies display not just a pure capitalism under the "invisible hand" of Adam Smith's free market, but rather what resulted historically after the compromises capitalism made with popular movements from the lower classes—thereby giving rise to so-called social rights (of the underprivileged groups) as well as to individual political and economic rights. The capitalist nations of today contain both capitalist and welfarist systems, not just one or the other. The modern politics of most Western nations actually consists of the long-term tug-of-war between these two tendencies and between different interest groups, not in the simple dominance of one or the other.

We need to distinguish between what is termed "modernity" here and modern history (in other words, we cannot simply equate modernity with modern history). I myself would view modernity as a range of historical processes—not reducible to any one theory or ideology—in the pursuit of modern ideals, including scientific knowledge, industrial development, citizen rights, and so on.

In the legal sphere, the essence of modern Western law similarly is found not just in the rationalism-inclined tradition of Continental formalist law or in the empiricism-inclined tradition of Anglo-American common law but rather in the coexistence and mutual penetration of the two. For example, the so-called classical orthodoxy tradition of American legal thought, though arising out of the common law tradition, was actually the result of a high degree of formalization. Scholars normally trace this orthodoxy to Christopher Columbus Langdell, who took over as dean of Harvard Law School in 1870 and greatly influenced the shape of modern American law. Unlike the German formalist tradition of the eighteenth century, which took as its point of departure the premise of individual rights, to be elaborated by logic, it begins from case precedents; but from there, it seeks to systematically delineate general principles underlying contracts and torts, employing deductive logic to construct an integrated body of legal principles and laws that are meant to be entirely consistent logically. In its claims to universality, absoluteness, and science, it in fact shares much in common with German formalist law.[1] As numerous scholars have pointed out, in Langdell's eyes, jurisprudence should resemble Euclidean geometry: it ought to be based on a limited number of axioms and multiple theorems derived therefrom, which are then applied to all fact situations. Small wonder, therefore, that some have simply labeled the classical orthodoxy represented by Langdell "legal formalism."[2]

But we cannot equate modern American law with its classical orthodoxy. From the start, it was profoundly affected by the criticisms of and attacks from legal pragmatists—represented above all by Langdell's colleague at Harvard Oliver Wendell Holmes, often considered the founder of legal pragmatism. Holmes particularly emphasized the historicity of law, rejecting any claims to immutability and universality and arguing that law must change with the times. It must, moreover, be tested in practice and evaluated according to its social consequences (Grey, 1983–1984). Later, legal pragmatism would lead to the rise in the 1920s of the legal realism movement (its two key figures being

1. For the leading, and most influential, statement of legal formalism, see Weber ([1968] 1978: chap. 8).

2. See White ([1947] 1976); see also Grey (1983–1984). Wiecek (1998), however, objects to the use of the term "formalism" and advocates instead "legal classicism."

Roscoe Pound and Karl Llewellyn, despite their avowed differences); objecting to simple reliance on the rationalist deductive method, it advocated instead the use of empiricist induction and, like legal pragmatism before it, emphasized the need to consider the social consequences of law. It called especially for incorporating in method the new social sciences, principally sociology (Wiecek, 1998: 197ff. cf. Hull, 1997).

At the same time, pragmatism as a system of thought gained even wider influence (its prime advocates in philosophy being of course John Dewey, who spent nearly three years lecturing and teaching in China, and William James). Later still, after the 1970s and 1980s, came "neo-pragmatism," which emphasized once more the pragmatist epistemological method, in opposition to the absolutist tendencies of rationalism and deductivism (Grey, 1983–1984; Tamanaha, 1996). Another strain has been the quite influential critical legal studies movement; its proponents include the Brazilian-born Roberto Unger, who endeavors to find a third path outside of capitalist-liberal law and socialist-statist law.

The essence of modernity in American law, I would maintain, lies not in any single theoretical orientation but rather in the coexistence and mutual influence of these different bodies of thought and of multiple interest groups within a relatively open political system. Modern American law displays pragmatist and realist dimensions as well as strongly formalist characteristics. The makeup of the Supreme Court is a good concrete illustration of this pluralism: the nine justices have long included both adherents of classical orthodoxy and those from traditions opposed to it. In the half century before the 1930s, the former held the upper hand, but the balance tipped thereafter; most recently, it has shifted back (Wiecek, 1998: 3). During the presidency of (Franklin D.) Roosevelt, realists occupied the majority and the Court made a host of historic decisions in support of workers' rights ("civil rights"), such as the 1937 decisions that workers' rights to organize unions, to unemployment benefits, and to old-age benefits were constitutional. It also made a series of decisions in support of black people's rights, heralding the civil rights movement to come later ("Social Security Online," n.d.; McMahon, 2000). To be sure, modernism carries with it a strong tendency toward ideologizing a singular theoretical persuasion; nevertheless, any effort to reduce modernity in American law to just one theoretical orientation would be a violation of historical reality.

Postmodernism and Modernity

Recent postmodernists have criticized modernism mainly in terms of theoretical representations rather than historical practice. The criticisms have been largely epistemological, aimed particularly at the modernist ideology about knowledge—the notion that one can arrive at absolute, universalist, immutable, and suprahistorical truths through reason and science. Clifford Geertz can be taken as an example of such a critic. He analogizes knowledge to opposing sides in a court trial: each is but the advocate of its employer, and there is no such thing as objective truth. Geertz insists instead on the localized nature of all knowledge—that is, its particularity and relativity—to emphasize the subjectivity of all knowledge (Geertz, 1983).

Such postmodernist ideas have enjoyed wide influence in China, for reasons that are easy to understand. By questioning the ideology of Enlightenment modernism, they carry definite implications for decentering a West that had long been presumed to reign supreme in a modernist world. For many Chinese scholars faced with the wave of wholesale Westernization that dominated China in the 1980s, this feature of postmodernist thought seemed especially attractive. Within the Western context itself, postmodernism's chief contribution has been mainly to cast doubt on the positivism that had come to wield so much influence since the nineteenth century, most notably in the social sciences. It has also amounted to something of a reaction against Marxist materialism, instead placing subjectivity at the center of its concerns. Some Chinese legal scholars have appropriated these dimensions of postmodernism to raise objections to the simple Westernization-ism (or "transplantation-ism") of their colleagues; they call for a more China-based approach that would rely instead on "indigenous resources," and on what they call China's "customary law" (*xiguanfa*) or "laws among the people" (*minjian fa*), which they analogize to Anglo-American common law (Zhu Suli, 2000; Liang, 1996).

In all these postmodernist critiques of modernism, the focus has been more on theoretical representations than on historical practice. We can turn once again to the example of Geertz. For him, we have seen, all knowledge is like that of adversarial lawyers on opposing sides of a trial, each just a hired gun. Whether in court or in the world of knowledge, there is no such thing as objective truth. But the fact is that, *pace* Geertz, American courts in practice do not depend just on the arguments of the lawyers representing the two sides; rather, and more importantly, they rely on the judge and the jury's search for truth. The practice of the court system is predicated on the notion that given access to opposed opinions, a jury selected from among average citizens can, using the common sense derived from their daily lives, make sound judgments as to the real facts of a case and the right and wrong of the litigants and thus can decide guilt or innocence, winner or loser. (It also acknowledges that the human-made system cannot arrive at absolute truth, knowable only to God and merely approximated by the courtroom truths obtained within the parameters of legal procedures.) This in my view is the true essence of what might be seen as "modernity" in the American justice system. It rests not in any one ideology or argument, but in a system that allows for opposing arguments and the search for truth. If the American court system were really as Geertz characterizes it, there would be no justice to speak of, and the system would surely not be able to last for any length of time. Though it abounds in problems and is far from ideal (if nothing else because it has become the single most litigious system in human history), it is nothing like the nihilistic system that Geertz describes.

A similar point applies to the American political system. Its modern history is not captured by representations of the Republican "right" about a laissez-faire capitalist market economy or by those of the Democratic "left" about statist interventions for social justice; rather, it consists of protracted seesawing and repeated compromises between the two. We cannot equate the modernity of this political system simply with the representations and discourses of either party. That kind of understanding, once again, would do violence to history.

Geertz's postmodernist theoretical construct is itself heir to a modernist demand leveled at all theories—that they be abstracted and elevated above empirical reality, and that they be unified by (deductive) logic. It, like much other modern theorizing, has therefore tended toward exaggeration and overstatement, a tendency already evident in the original twin traditions of rationalism and empiricism. More closely approximating modernity as an actual historical process are instead those bodies of thought that have sought to amalgamate opposed traditions. One example is American pragmatism, which rejects the absoluteness or immutability of any knowledge, yet still emphasizes the need to approach facts with judicious care and to systematically organize empirical evidence and concepts derived from them; in this respect it offers a sharp contrast to the epistemological skepticism of postmodernism. Modernity in history, once again, results from the coexistence and interactions of multiple theories, not from any one theory or ideology. We might also think of it as follows: the history of a practice is not as simple or elegantly consistent as a theory, but it is also not as one-sided or exaggerated. It is full of paradoxes and compromises, and precisely on that account it is closer to the reality of historical process. This is what I myself understand by modernity: the key is to place modernity within a given historical context and to grasp it as historical process. The meaning of modernity, I would maintain, should lie not in the propositions of any single theory but rather in the process of varied historical practices in pursuit of modern ideals.

Modernity in Chinese Law?

Viewed in terms of theoretical representations and discourse, the past century of Chinese legal reform displays one flip-flop after another, and it would be difficult to identify any abiding characteristics. There was first the late Qing and Republican rejection of imperial Chinese law, and the Guomindang's wholesale transplanting of Western, most especially German formalist, law. Next came the Communist Party's complete rejection both of traditional law and of what it called "bourgeois law," and the modeling of China's legal system after that in the socialist Soviet Union. Then, after the Sino-Soviet split, came the reliance mainly on indigenous resources, especially the mediation tradition from the countryside and from the revolutionary base areas. Finally, in the Reform period, came the second wave of importation of Western laws, amounting to almost wholesale Westernization, which in turn gave rise to the cry for relying on "indigenous resources." This history shows that Chinese law in the past hundred years has followed a truly tortuous path, with multiple reversals and with every step a conflicted one.

Precisely because of this discursive tradition and context, arguments today over modernity in Chinese law lapse easily into ideological disputes, each side aligning itself with one or another theoretical or legal tradition, or else identifying with something loosely conceptualized as Chinese culture, custom, or abiding values. The recent debates in 2005–2006 over the draft property law show precisely this kind of ideologizing tendency (Xiaoning, 2006; Zhu Jingwen, 2006). We need to set aside such ideological debates that have little to do with reality.

The key is in the practice of the laws, whether transplanted from abroad or drawn from indigenous resources. From the Westernizers' standpoint, the big problem of the moment is that imported principles and laws are difficult to implement. As is well known, legal provisions that are imported from the West and predicated on rights are much too easily drawn into the whirlpool of the present Chinese bureaucratic system, with the result that what are intended as rights protections become mere exercises of power and influence (*guanxi*) or else the administrative "balancing" (*baiping*) of different interests. For that reason, some scholars believe that the most urgent task in lawmaking today is not to craft substantive laws but rather to establish detailed and thorough procedures to guide their operation. The indigenous-izers, on the other hand, advocate searching for China's legal modernity in its culture and customs, an approach they oppose to wholesale Westernization.

By comparison, the indigenous-izers are perhaps less specific and concrete, especially in their opinions of what actually constitutes the culture or customs that they would call upon. This chapter therefore leans more toward citing and examining specific aspects of past laws and lawmaking that might be taken up as constituent parts of a Chinese legal modernity. The argument is, first of all, that if we set aside abstract ideological arguments and look instead at the legal practice of the past hundred years, we can see that a modern Chinese law has already taken a rough shape, one that embodies both Western and Chinese characteristics and carries with it a fairly clear set of moral values as well as a particular mode of legal thinking. It comprises traditions inherited both from the Qing and from the Chinese Revolution (setting aside, of course, its totalistic, or "totalitarian," aspects) and, in addition to those, transplanted elements from the West (selected and adapted by the Guomindang government). This mixture may seem on the surface like a hodgepodge, but in fact it contains definable characteristics, as well as the principle of coexistence of pluralistic elements and traditions. Together, these multiple tendencies are enough to add up to a preliminary composite of a distinctive Chinese modernity in law and lawmaking.

In thus isolating the modern characteristics of China's recent and distant past, I do not intend to call for excluding importations from Western law, or to deny the multiple difficulties involved in making imported laws work, or to minimize the multiple failings of Maoist justice. The point I wish to emphasize is that the future of Chinese legal reform does not lie just in either Westernization or indigenous-ization: it ought to rest on a protracted process involving coexistence and mutual interaction of the two in the actual practice of pursuing modern ideals.[3] What follows, then, are some specific examples given previously, sorted, elaborated, and summarized for the purposes of this chapter.

Inheritance and Old-Age Support

Inheritance and old-age-support law illustrates well the adaptation of imported law to Chinese realities and also the use of a distinctive mode of thinking. In the beginning, the Guomindang's 1930 Civil Code of the Republic of China adopted the 1900 German Civil Code's legal principle of gender equality in rights to inheritance (*Civil Code of the Republic of China*, 1930: Article 1138; hereafter cited simply by article number). As far as the text of the code goes, rural daughters were henceforth to enjoy rights equal with their brothers' to inherit the family's land and house. In actual practice, however, the law did not follow its declared intent.

First of all, as Kathryn Bernhardt has shown in her book on women and property in China, the new provisions of the law applied only to postmortem inheritance, not property dispositions before death (Bernhardt, 1999: 152–60). We know that rural families of the time commonly divided the

3. Ji Weidong (2006) makes the very constructive suggestion that legal "proceduralism" can provide a theoretical basis for an institutional framework in which agreement and consensus can be worked out despite the reality of the coexistence of multiple theories and values.

household while the parents were still alive, and only brothers were included in those divisions. But they did not violate the letter of the law. The basic spirit of the new law, moreover, was that an individual had the right to do with his or her property as he or she saw fit. The new code's principle of gender equality in inheritance therefore had only limited effect in practice. As for the rural social practice, widespread at the time, of setting aside "old-age-support land" (*yanglaodi*), when households were divided, to sustain the parents in old age and to cover their funeral expenses (what was called in the countryside "maintenance while alive and burial when dead"—*shengyang sizang*), it too persisted (Huang, 2001: 140). Overall, in the Republican period, rural inheritance practices basically still followed old ways, as I have demonstrated in some detail in my book *Code, Custom and Legal Practice in China: The Qing and the Republic Compared* (Huang, 2001: chap. 8).

The reason behind this continuity is obvious: at the time, most village girls still married out into other villages, and caring for parents in their old age had long been a responsibility of the sons who remained in the village. Under those circumstances, for daughters to divide up the land with their brothers would have immediately threatened the means of that support, whether from the family farm or from old-age-support land. Indeed, given the persistence of the small peasant economy, land was still something familial and not individual, used to maintain the entire family: it was what parents used to support their children, and what they themselves relied on for support in their old age. Daughters, precisely because they generally married out, were simply not in a position to bear the responsibility for the parents' old-age support. And for that reason, the right to inherit the land had to go to the son(s) and not to the daughter(s).[4]

The Guomindang law of the time did not deal directly with this contradiction between social reality and the letter of the law; it did not try to create a new legal principle, different from what it had imported from the German Civil Code, to govern inheritance. All it did was both espouse the principle of gender equality in inheritance and, in practice, refrain from interfering with the social reality of gender differences in household divisions. Guomindang law, we might say, in the end dealt with rural customs simply by shutting an eye as to what was done. Though it imported in toto Western inheritance laws, in actual practice it applied the new laws only to the cities and allowed old customs to continue in the countryside.

In the People's Republic, the Law of Succession formally promulgated in 1985 was like the Guomindang law in stipulating gender equality (Law of

4. Of course, this generalization did not apply to families with married-in sons-in-law, who made up a significant proportion of rural marriages; for example, in the Huayangqiao villages where I undertook long-term research, such marrying-in was fairly common.

Succession, [1985] 1987: Articles 9, 10, 13; hereafter cited simply by article number); but unlike the Guomindang law, it also created a new legal provision intended to reconcile the principle of gender equality with social practice by explicitly linking inheritance rights to (old age) maintenance obligations: "At the time of distributing the estate, successors who have made the predominant contributions in maintaining the decedent or have lived with the decedent may be given a larger share. At the time of distributing the estate, successors who had the ability and were in a position to maintain the decedent but failed to fulfill their duties shall be given no share or a smaller share of the estate" (Article 13). Thus, sons take precedence over daughters in inheriting family property because they fulfill the obligation of maintaining the elderly parents, and not because they are male; if the daughters and not the sons should fulfill this kind of obligation, they would be equally entitled to precedence in inheritance. The law thus attends both to the principle of gender equality and to rural realities. In so doing, it resolves the long-standing contradiction between the letter of the law and operative reality.

To be sure, in the Mao period land was collectivized, leaving little family property to speak of. Yet the basic logic of traditional rural maintenance of the elderly remained: parents in their old age still had to rely on sons who remained in the village for their support. Even though the system of the so-called five guarantees was then in place, most of the rural elderly still relied on their sons for old-age support, albeit expressed in workpoints and not in produce from the family farm. In addition, the family house remained a crucial item of private property—the elderly generally had to live in the family house, not the home of a married-out daughter.

The provision in the Law of Succession discussed above was not something that was formulated overnight. Rather, the approach emerged out of protracted experience, including trial practice over the course of many years in the form of directives and opinions issued by the Supreme Court, long before its formal codification in law. This is a point I have documented at some length in chapter 6. By examining case records and Supreme Court directives, we can see the actual process by which this principle took shape from the 1950s down to its formal codification in 1985 (Zuigao renmin fayuan, 1994: 1279, 1286, 1292–93).

This comparison brings out an important difference between the Guomindang's and the Chinese Communist Party's (CCP) lawmaking: Guomindang law took as its point of departure the German Civil Code, which was considered the best and the latest at the time. Though it made some revisions and compromises in response to social reality, its guiding approach was transplantation. Even its compromises were undertaken not for the purpose of creating a distinctive Chinese modern law but to provide temporary concessions. This point can be seen in the Guomindang code's disinterest in engaging on the level of legal principle in making concessions to rural old-age-maintenance practices. In contrast, the CCP dealt with the same issue by creating a fresh legal principle that is different from that of Western law, thereby evincing greater independence. However, in the Reform era that came afterward, the main guiding spirit in lawmaking has almost reverted to that of the Guomindang period in simply equating modernity with the West, without attempting to systematically develop China's own distinctive modernity. Still, the example of inheritance-maintenance law stands as one illustration of such an approach.

The example of inheritance-maintenance law also illustrates a particular mode of legal thinking, though one that has not been explicitly articulated or sanctioned. In that mode of thinking, practice takes precedence over (formalist) deductive reasoning, and the formulation of legal provisions, including fundamental legal principles, must start from practical experience, not from premises deemed universally valid in the manner of formalist German law. The practice of property law, discussed below, similarly demonstrates this point.

Dian Rights

Regarding rights to property, the Guomindang Civil Code imported from the West the principle of individual property rights. To wit: "The owner of a thing has the right, within the limits of the law or ordinances, to use it, to receive its benefits, and to dispose of it freely, and to exclude others from interfering with it" (Article 765). Such a concept of unitary and exclusive property rights is a fundamental principle of capitalist economies. And Guomindang lawmakers, like the advocates of institutional economics in China today, believed that clear stipulation of property rights was a basic requirement for economic development (Huang, 2001: 54). However, in actual operation, the Guomindang made definite concessions to social practice. At the time, in rural land sales, definitive sales (*juemai*) were rather rare; most took instead the form of Chinese *dian*, or "conditional sales," generally giving up the use rights (in return for about 70 percent of the land's value) but reserving the right to redemption. The custom was at once a form of borrowing and a form of exchange of land, and was widely followed. Insofar as its basic intent was to let those who were forced to give up their land by hardship reserve the right to favorable terms of redemption for a long period of time, it may be considered an expression of something of the survival ethic of a peasant society. The custom was condoned by the state and included in the Qing code.

In the face of the reality of such social practices, the Guomindang lawmakers decided to reincorporate the custom and legal category of dian into its civil code. As the Central Political Council that guided the drafting of the new civil code put it, dian is a Chinese custom, one that is different from the Western (German Civil Code's) concepts of "mortgage" and "pledge."[5] Rather than losing his land on account of nonpayment, as would be the case if he failed to pay a mortgage or pledge, a dian maker would retain his right to redemption. Precisely for that reason, according to the lawmakers, dian rights make possible a more benevolent type of system. Since most dian makers were "the economically weak," giving them the right to redemption reflects "the strong point of our country's morality of looking after the weak"; this provision is more progressive than the "individual-based" Western laws, and gives fuller form to the West's own latest tendencies toward more "society-based" laws (Pan, 1982: 107; see also Huang, 2001: 88). Hu Hanmin, the top Guomindang lawmaker, referred explicitly to the concerns for social justice shown in recent Western lawmaking and maintained that such a "spirit" (*jingshen*) was close to the Chinese "way of the sage kings" (*shengwang zhi dao*), distinct from the "way of the hegemons" (*bawang zhi dao*) (Hu, 1978: 857; see also Huang, 2001: 63). For that reason, the Central Political Council resolved to retain this legal category from the Qing code, assigning a separate chapter in the new civil code to it. Thus China's dian rights were tacked on to a civil code that had been transplanted from Germany. It was, we might say, a compromise made in the face of the long-term persistence of the peasant economy in modern China.

Under the People's Republic, land exchanges were basically terminated after the collectivization of the 1950s, as were the customary practices of dian. In the Reform era, codified law has adopted once more the unitary property rights principle of the West: according to the General Principles of the Civil Law of 1986, like the Guomindang Civil Code before it, "'Property ownership' means the owner's rights to lawfully possess, utilize, profit from and dispose of his property" ("General Principles of Civil Law of the People's Republic of China," [1986] 1987: Article 71; hereafter cited simply by article number).

In practice, however, property rights have more or less followed the customs before the revolution. First of all, "use rights" are distinguished from ownership rights over "responsibility land" (*chengbao di*),[6] a separation that can be found in German civil law but is also traceable to pre-1949 Chinese "topsoil rights" (*tianmian quan*) and dian rights. Already reemerging in the countryside today are the old tenancy system (the practice of subletting [*zhuanbao*] responsibility land may be equated with the pre-1949 renting out of topsoil rights) and conditional sales of responsibility land (*dianmai*, which may be seen as equivalent to the pre-1949 conditional sales of topsoil rights). The

5. The concepts of mortgage and pledge, we might note, are logically derived from the premise of unitary, individual property rights.

6. Peasants have the use rights for a defined period, but the collective owns the land, while the state reserves the prerogative to requisition it.

2007 "Property Rights Law of the People's Republic of China" (implemented from 1 October 2007), though it did not adopt the Qing-Republican category of dian, did formally recognize the legality of multiple forms of transfers of "responsibility land" (*chengbaodi*) (Article 128). That way, it adopted for the countryside the more pluralistic and complex property rights principles from China's rural tradition, while also adopting for the cities the more unitary and exclusive property rights principles of the West. The key factor here is the long-term persistence of China's peasant economy into the present (Huang Zongzhi, 2006a).

Tort Law

The pattern of compromise with and concession to social reality can also be seen in tort law. Contemporary Chinese tort law comes mainly from Western Continental law, since the Qing code contained no provisions at all about torts or compensation. As has been seen in chapter 6, the point of departure of the new tort law is the principle of "wrongful acts." The Guomindang Civil Code had modeled itself on the German Civil Code, and the key is the principle of fault: only fault makes compensation necessary; in the absence of fault, compensation would not be required. The General Principles of the Civil Law promulgated in 1986 adopted this same principle.

However, in real life, as actual case records show us, damages do not always involve fault and are often the result of purely accidental fact situations in which no one is at fault or negligent. The case of the seven-year-old child running home from the village kindergarten who collided with an old lady and was burned by the bottle of boiling hot water she was carrying is a particularly good illustration. The district (*qu*) government had paid part of the medical expenses incurred; the boy's father brought suit against the woman for the balance.

According to the logic of wrongful acts, if there is no fault, there is no obligation to compensate. The boy and his family, in the absence of insurance and more government compensation, can therefore do nothing beyond blaming their bad luck. Chinese law, however, takes the very different approach of proceeding from the fact situation, and acknowledging the reality of disputes involving damages incurred without fault. And, faced with this reality, the law chooses to add to the wrongful acts provision that "Civil liability shall still be borne even in the absence of fault, if the law so stipulates" (Article 106). Thus, in the case of the boy running into the old lady (and in many other similar cases), the judge explained that even though the old lady was not at fault, she should bear some civil responsibility. He persuaded both sides to agree that the woman would shoulder a part of the medical fees, thereby successfully mediating the case (see chapter 6, this volume; see also Huang, 2006a: 150–51; 2006b: 292–93).

From the point of view of the Western principle of wrongful acts, this legal provision and practice are illogical. Since the law stipulates that compensation is based on fault, how can it then go on to say that even without fault there has to be compensation? Within the framework of formalist logic, this is an irreconcilable contradiction. But from the vantage point of China's long-standing mode of legal reasoning, there is no necessary either/or conflict here. The fact is that in real life we find both damages that involve fault and damages that do not. The law makes different provisions in response to different fact situations. Because the reality is deemed to be obvious, the law need not try to explain the apparent logical contradiction between the two provisions. As has been seen in chapter 6, some Chinese civil law scholars have given the modern Western civil law principle of "strict liability" just that reinterpretation. In the West, "strict liability" is about lowering the standard of proof for fault when it comes to dangerous products, not about civil liability even in fact situations without fault, as in the Chinese reinterpretation. This mode of thinking can be further illustrated with marriage and divorce law, discussed below.

Marriage and Divorce Law

As has been seen, the point of departure for contemporary Chinese marriage law is the 1931 Marriage Regulations of the Chinese Soviet Republic ("Zhonghua suwei'ai gongheguo hunyin tiaoli," 1931). It imitated the then very radical Code of Laws on Marriage and Divorce, the Family and Guardianship enacted in the Soviet Union in 1926, allowing for divorce on the ex parte petition of either spouse (Article 9, cited in Huang, 2005: 175). The Western world would not adopt such laws until so-called no-fault divorce took root during the 1960s and 1970s (Phillips, 1988). In 1930s China, such a provision was very radical indeed, perhaps even extreme, for the cities and most certainly for the countryside.

It is not surprising that the regulations encountered widespread resistance almost immediately. For peasants, marriage was a once-in-a-lifetime big expenditure; an easy divorce after a marital spat, as occurs sometimes in the Western world today, was simply unthinkable. From the perspective of the peasants, to allow divorce based just on the preferences of one party did not accord with the realities of life or the wishes of most people. As for the Chinese Communist Party, the support of the rural people was simply crucial at the time—following its defeat in the Great Revolution, the party's very survival was dependent on peasants who provided the bulk of the recruits for the Red Army. Thus, the CCP quickly backpedaled on the matter.

First came the provision in the 1934 Marriage Law of the Chinese Soviet Republic placed immediately after a statement of the general principle about freedom of divorce: "Wives of soldiers of the Red Army when claiming a divorce must obtain the consent of their husbands" (Article 10). During the Sino-Japanese War, the Jin-Cha-Ji (Shanxi-Chahar-Hebei) and Jin-Ji-Lu-Yu (Shanxi-Hebei-Shandong-Henan) "border regions" allowed the spouse of a soldier to seek a divorce only after the soldier's whereabouts had remained unknown for "more than four years." And the central Shaan-Gan-Ning (Shaanxi-Gansu-Ningxia) region required a wife wishing to bring a divorce petition to wait until "at least five years" of "no information from the husband" had passed. These border regions went so far as to discard the Jiangxi Soviet legal construction and adopt instead the approach of the Guomindang's civil law, which stipulates a set of conditions—such as bigamy, adultery, abuse, abandonment, impotence, incurable diseases, and so on—under which divorce would be permitted, thereby giving up entirely the Soviet-period provision that divorce would be allowed on the petition of just one party (see chapter 4, this volume; Huang, 2005: 175–77).

After 1949, the law dropped the mode of expression of the Guomindang code but continued to allow the border regions to grant to the (largely peasant) soldiers the right to refuse to divorce. Even in the marriage law campaign of the early 1950s, which attacked the five kinds of "feudal marriages"—namely, bigamy or polygamy, slave girls, *tongyangxi* (i.e., a child raised to be a future daughter-in-law), and marriage by purchase and by parental imposition—this right was still protected, even if the wife were a tongyangxi or had been purchased or married by the will of her parents. I have documented and discussed these points in detail in chapter 4 (see also Huang, 2005: 178ff.).

Outside of the provision about soldiers of the Red Army, the concessions made by the law on this question centered on a single legal provision: namely, the requirement that prior mediation be undertaken, as provided in the 1950 Marriage Law. (Marriage Law, [1950] 1959: Article 17). Thus, in any disputed divorce, government mediation and court mediation became preconditions to granting that divorce. After the tide of the marriage law campaign of the early 1950s, almost all contested divorce petitions had to undergo high-pressure "mediated reconciliation" attempts before they could have any chance of gaining approval. The thinking behind this requirement is obvious: in the face of widespread peasant opposition to easy divorces, the party elected to minimize tensions between itself and the peasants by trying to mediate all contested divorce petitions, one by one (see chapter 4, this volume; Huang, 2005).

This was the historical context in which the rather distinctive Chinese court mediation system developed. As I have already shown in detail elsewhere, the courts of imperial China rarely mediated. As the famous Qing judicial secretary Wang Huizu observed, mediation was something done by people in their communities, while what the courts did was to adjudicate unequivocally. Precisely for that reason, from the perspective of the Confucian ideal of harmony, court adjudication was not as desirable as popular mediation, because community mediation can avoid leaving lasting enmity (Wang, [1793] 1939: 16; see also Huang, 1996: 204). Clearly, mediation by the courts, distinct from that by relatives and friends, was something created by a modern revolutionary party under specific historical circumstances. We will consider the "modernity" of this system in more detail in the next section.

During the Maoist period, the courts, in mediating contested ex parte divorce requests, gradually formed an entire set of methods, procedures, and styles of work: the judges would go down into the village communities, investigate and research the problem by interviewing "the masses" (i.e., relatives and neighbors) and party leaders, try to understand the past background and present situation of the marriage, and analyze the origins of its "contradictions"; on that basis they would intervene aggressively using a host of methods, including political education, pressures exerted through the party organization, material incentives, and so on—seeking by all means possible to save the marriage and trying to reach a "mediated reconciliation" of the couple in the great majority of contested divorce cases (see chapter 4, this volume; Huang, 2005). With the turn of the century, and the social-economic changes and new legislative perspectives, this rather coercive system has largely fallen into disuse. But the many other varieties of court mediation that grew up alongside it have shown continued vitality, especially with disputes not involving fault (or equal degrees of fault or of obligation).

In terms of juridical principle, already in the 1940s and 1950s the approach emerged of using the quality of the (emotional) relationship (*ganqing*) of the couple as the standard for judgment in all divorce cases. The reasoning goes as follows: precisely because marriage is supposed to be based on a good relationship, the new law does not accept "feudal marriages" that disregard how members of a couple feel about and behave toward one another. In doing away with such old-style marriages, the new law asks that marriages be founded on a good relationship, and not be entered into "rashly" (*qingshuai*). For that reason, unless the couple's "relationship has truly ruptured" (*ganqing queyi polie*), every effort must be made for them to "reconcile," with the government and the courts taking on the task of such mediation. In that way, old-style feudal marriages would be eradicated without individuals' lapsing into "rash" "bourgeois" marriages and divorces (see chapter 4, this volume; Huang, 2005: 183–88).

This reasoning was not incorporated into codified law when it first took shape; it was tried out only in practice and in the conceptualization and language provided in preliminary directives and opinions issued by the Supreme People's Court. By examining 336 cases drawn from two counties, one northern and one southern, I have shown how already in the 1950s the courts were widely using this standard and language in divorce judgments. Even so, the 1950 Marriage Law made no mention of the concept of a "rupture in the relationship" (*ganqing polie*). Not until thirty years later, in the revised Marriage Law promulgated in 1980, was the concept formally incorporated into codified law: to the original expressions "only when mediation . . . has failed" "will divorce be granted" was added the clause "if the relationship has truly ruptured" (Marriage Law, [1980] 1987: Article 25).

This reasoning, formulated after a long period of legal practice, emerged out of a particular historical context. Taking the couple's (emotional) relationship as the basis of all marriages could be a means both to attack "feudal" marriages and to oppose the "bourgeois" "rash attitude" (*qingshuai taidu*) and "liking the new and tiring of the old" (*xixin yanjiu*) (a fairly widespread tendency among early party members—to leave old rural wives for new female comrades—that had been criticized by Ding Ling in her 1942 essay "Thoughts on the Occasion of 8 March"). At the same time, because the term "relationship" encompassed such wide scope and was not easily pinned down, the formulation allowed the courts a great deal of flexibility to act according to the needs or policy of the time in dealing with each contested divorce case, as they attempted to minimize possible conflict between the marriage law and the people. As Wu Xinyu, the vice chair of the Legal System Committee of the People's Congress, explained: the provision "at once maintains the principle of freedom of marriage and also gives the courts considerable latitude"; it was therefore "well suited to the real conditions of our country" (Hubei caijing xueyuan, 1983: 46). Of course, in actual operation, this system could easily tilt toward being overly "conservative" and excessively coercive, in effect denying divorce without regard for the wishes of the litigants. This was precisely the main criticism Wu made at the time (and also the criticism made by the later "Fourteen Points" that were implemented in the 1990s). In fact, the "(emotional) relationship" formulation allowed both for strict (and overly strict) application and for loose application.

This conceptual foundation of divorce law may be considered a kind of "logic of practice," displaying a kind of modernity born of practice in modern Chinese marriage law. It is the crystallization of decades of practice in marriage law; it comprises legal principles that embody both modern ideals and adaptations to historical realities; it includes dimensions that are "imported" as well as those drawn from old traditions and from modern (including revolutionary) traditions; it is a principle born of particular historical conditions. It also embodies a rather distinctive modern court mediation system that is the focus of the discussion below.

Institutional Innovation in Court Mediations

Since the 1970s, in reaction to the litigious excesses of the legal system, there has emerged in the American legal world a movement for "alternative dispute resolution" (ADR) to seek ways to resolve disputes outside of the existing court system. The movement draws its inspiration from legal realism and is thought to have been born at a 1976 conference commemorating Roscoe Pound, the founder of that earlier movement. It has since gained a sizable following and has become a substantial force for legal reform (Subrin and Woo, 2006: chap. 10). The United States and Britain took the lead in ADR, but it now has influence throughout much of Western Europe (although in actual practice its effect remains rather limited). Partly on account of its influence, many American (and British) scholars studying Chinese law have focused their attention on mediation in the Chinese legal tradition, with the view that it is the most distinctive aspect of the Chinese legal system (see, for example, Cohen, 1967; Lubman, 1967; Palmer, 1989; Clarke, 1991), and some believe it may have instructive implications for American legal reform.

In contrast to contemporary Chinese court mediation, this Western legal reform movement insists that mediation must be entirely voluntary and must occur outside of the court system. The Committee of Ministers of the Council of Europe has in fact drawn up a set of guidelines for mediation, stipulating that it must be independent of the court process, that mediators of a case must not serve later as judges of the same case if the mediation should fail, and that records of the mediation process may not be used in subsequent litigation (a prohibition intended to encourage greater openness in the mediation process), seeking thereby to ensure that mediation be completely voluntary and separated from court litigation (Committee of Ministers of the Council of Europe, 1998).

When compared to Chinese court mediation, that kind of approach has obvious advantages and disadvantages. On the one hand, it would not allow the kind of coercive disregard of litigants' wishes that has often occurred in Chinese court mediation, especially in its "mediated reconciliations" of divorce cases—a coercion so common that it became the subject of Ha Jin's novel *Waiting*, in which the protagonist waits through many attempts and for no less than eighteen years to get his divorce from his wife (Ha, 1999). On the other hand, precisely because the process is purely voluntary, either disputant can elect not to enter into it or at any time to withdraw from it and opt instead for court litigation—a possibility that greatly limits the extent of its use.

Some scholars have further included "arbitration" with mediation as a part of ADR (Subrin and Woo, 2006: chap. 10). In my view, however, even though arbitration may originally have been intended to serve as a mediatory alternative to litigation, in actual practice in the United States it easily becomes nothing more than a kind of abbreviated litigation—still relying, like litigation, on a judge and still resulting in a determination of winner and loser, right and wrong, just as in a court trial. That is certainly the case, for example, with construction disputes in the state of California, as discussed in chapter 7. In the end, arbitration frequently achieves only a reduction in costs by employing retired judges, simplified procedures, cheaper facilities, and the like. At its core it often remains litigation, and it might even be considered nothing more than discounted litigation. Its basic approach and guiding principles ultimately remain the either/or adversarial framework of the legal system as a whole.

The tendency to insist on a win/lose outcome is closely tied to the notion of rights in the Western formalist tradition. Other facts aside, the very term "rights" itself is a form of the same word in "right" and "wrong." The presumptive wish to establish right and wrong, and hence also winners and losers, seems to me so deeply ingrained in the concept of rights as to be inseparable from it. Regardless, the predominance of the adversarial approach in Western legal culture is beyond question.

In addition, some American advocates of ADR have also included out-of-court settlements as part of its process (Subrin and Woo, 2006: chap. 10). On the surface, this "system," if it can be called that, does indeed resemble Chinese mediation in some respects. It is a process in which judges play an important role. And, as is well known, a very high proportion of all court cases are concluded through out-of-court settlements, with perhaps only 2 percent actually coming to trial (Subrin and Woo, 2006: 220).

But this "system" in fact works very differently than Chinese court mediation. Its driving force is usually not third-party mediation, as in China, but rather the litigants themselves (mainly their attorneys), who opt out of a court trial after making probabilistic calculations of expense and time. Very little here is comparable to the Chinese process of making compromises through mediation in order to "patch up a quarrel and reconcile the parties involved" (*xishi ningren*). The role the judge plays is also very different: it occurs outside the court system, in what we might call the shadow of the law. In such a procedure, the judge's power is far less than that of his or her Chinese counterpart. The judge can only be a facilitator; the power of the final decision rests mainly with the litigants and their attorneys. In Chinese court mediation, by contrast, the power rests mainly with the judge: it is up to him or her to decide whether to mediate with adjudicatory powers to work out the terms of an agreement. And the main concern is what the judge considers legal and just, not the expenses that might be involved.

Indeed, in the Chinese system the cost considerations are the opposite of what they are in the United States: what takes more time and expense is mediation, not adjudication. The latter is quicker and more straightforward, and it therefore has been used more in the Reform era as caseloads mount and the need to minimize time and expense for each case consequently grows. From this point of view, the American out-of-court settlement should perhaps not be seen as mediation at all; it is mainly a way to terminate an ongoing adjudicatory process, not the conclusion of a mediation process. (The difference between the two systems is also evidenced in the fact that the American system has been completely misunderstood and misconstrued in China, as it has been inaccurately equated simply with "out-of-court" or "extrajudicial" "mediation," *tingwai tiaojie.*)

We can also think of the difference this way: the concern of Chinese court mediation is mainly with resolving disputes, not adjudging right and wrong. Its substance, procedures, and outcomes may all be seen as part of a mediation process. But the American out-of-court settlement has as its starting point litigation to establish right and wrong, which is terminated only when the litigants decide to opt out. Again, out-of-court settlements appear to be just one kind of outcome of a litigation process. They do not result from a mediatory ideal but rather are mainly a practical means of coping with the litigation system's excessive caseloads and expenses. The point of departure and basic concern of the legal system as a whole remain adjudication about right and wrong predicated on premises about rights, and not the desire for compromise and reconciliation as in Chinese mediation. In my view, out-of-court settlements, like arbitration, should not be equated with mediation.

Another critical factor is that the mediating judges in China wield considerable coercive power. If a disputant does not agree to the mediation, the same court and judge will go on to adjudicate, a procedure very different indeed from what is found in Western mediation. The Western mediators do not wield any coercive power; whether they continue to mediate is entirely up to the disputants, and hence the process is easily terminated. In the Chinese system, though each disputant has the right to refuse to accept the mediated resolution proposed by the court, he or she may not refuse the adjudicatory process that follows. Therefore, disputants are under much greater pressure to accept the court's mediatory efforts.

Under the procedures of Chinese court mediation, moreover, the judge has the power to make a separate determination of the facts—for example, to conclude that the dispute does not involve fault on the part of either party—and use that to persuade the parties to agree to the court's recommendations. In the Western legal system, the mediators do not have the power to make such factual determinations. Mediation must rely more completely on the wishes of the disputants, and coercive pressures are simply not allowed. But the Chinese courts may first decide that the situation does not involve fault and is merely a dispute among two parties equally in the right, or equally entitled or obligated, and then persuade both sides to make concessions to reach a mediated agreement. This ability too is a critical factor in the greater use and rate of success of the Chinese system (see chapters 4 and 7).

In any event, the partly coercive court mediation system of China has made its appearance today in the Western world in the form of "arbitration with conciliation" (or "med-arb"). It is clearly becoming an ADR model with some influence. As has been pointed out, in the 1990s a considerable number of countries—including Australia, Canada, Croatia, Hungary, India, Japan, and South Korea, as well as Hong Kong—had already begun experimenting with such a method of mediation (Tang, 1996). In recent years, med-arb has been used more often in the United States as well (Brewer and Mills, 1999), and the system may have quite a bit of room for further development in the world. It certainly will not entirely replace trials, but it may help to lower their numbers somewhat. Regardless, we can at least draw this conclusion: the court mediation system that emerged in the historical process of the Chinese Revolution is something that is both modern and distinctively Chinese; not merely the product of Chinese tradition, not purely of the modern period, it contains both traditional and modern, Chinese and Western characteristics.

Here we need to point out again that in China there has been a good deal of misunderstanding of the ADR of the West, imagining the "out of court settlement" and arbitration systems to be the same as the Chinese mediation system, when they are in fact very different—both from Chinese community mediation and from Chinese court mediation. One scholar, for example, even assumes the Western ADR system to be far more effective than the Chinese system, and calls for the Chinese system to follow the lead of the West (Peng Bo, 2007). In point of fact, the Chinese mediation system, including both the community mediation system that has continued to the present and the court (and administrative) mediation system created in the Maoist period, is a distinctive system and a relatively more effective one. It has gained widespread popular acceptance, far more so than in the West. When faced with a dispute, the first option people consider is mediation—that was the case in the past, and remains the case today. In the West, by contrast, the first option that people think of remains litigation. That is a fundamental difference in legal culture between China and the West.

The Practical Moralism Mode of Thinking in Modern Chinese Law

As has been indicated above, Chinese legal reform of the past hundred years has evinced a fairly consistent mode of thought, one that can be seen in Guomindang law and even more clearly in CCP law. It is also something of a continuation of the traditional Chinese mode of legal thinking. Its "modernity" is evidenced not only in its appropriateness for current Chinese life but also in its commonalities with some currents of recent American legal thought.

Guomindang judicial practice, we have seen, though guided by an overarching approach of wholesale Westernization, still evinced a realistic and practical orientation. The method of applying the adopted principle of gender equality in inheritance showed this tendency. The courts did not really try to impose the new principle on a very different rural social reality. The same was even truer of dian rights. The lawmakers explicitly acknowledged that rural customs were different from the categories used by modern Western law, and set up a separate chapter for dian in the civil code. And Chinese Communist legal practice, precisely because it rejected from the start the formalist tradition of Western law as "bourgeois," shows even more strongly the Chinese reality-based mode of legal thinking. We have seen how, in inheritance, CCP law formulated a distinctive new principle, based on rural realities, that linked inheritance rights to old-age-maintenance obligations, attending thereby both to the principle of gender equality and to the social reality of sons maintaining their parents. In tort law, similarly, the CCP's law code took into account that some disputes over damages involve no fault, creating for them a principle different from that of the imported principle of "wrongful acts."

The pattern is perhaps clearest in divorce law. CCP lawmaking did not insist on the original principle imported from the Soviet Union—of allowing divorce when one party insists on it—and instead sought to find a compromise between the ideal of gender equality and rural realities, attending to both the goal of overturning "feudal marriages" and the need to make concessions to peasant opposition. It did not act in the manner of formalist lawmaking, which starts from rational and universal premises to deduce legal provisions. Instead, it relied on years of experience to formulate the principle of using the quality of the relationship of a couple as the final standard in marriage and divorce, incorporating that principle into codified law only after it had been used in practice for several decades. The process by which divorce law took shape illustrates well the characteristics of Chinese legal reasoning and the pattern of modern Chinese lawmaking.

Here it should be pointed out that even though modern Western divorce law had originally taken as its point of departure the rights premise of formalist civil law—seeing marriage as a form of contract, and its dissolution as the consequence of the violation of the contractual rights of one party—in practice during the modern era it eventually abandoned this stance and adopted no-fault divorce in accord with lived realities. This process, which began in the 1960s, had taken hold in nearly all the Western world by the 1980s (Phillips, 1988). The no-fault divorce that is now so common has in fact discarded completely the original core conceptual construct—that divorce requires a judgment about fault—and adopted instead the view that husband-wife relationships are created by the couple jointly, and that their dissolution should involve no question of fault or of one violating the other's rights. The result of the adversarial approach to divorce had long been protracted and exceedingly expensive disputes, and therefore it was no longer appropriate for contemporary Western society.

In the disputes over divorce law in China today, some advocate the "return to civil law" (*huigui minfa*): that is, to stop using a separate law for marriage (and divorce) and place marriage law back within the general civil law (as the Guomindang Civil Code had done) (Ma, 2003). What lies behind this argument is the wish to set up a marriage law that would be "self-governing" and anchored on individual rights, in the same way as Western private law approaches civil life; its promoters hold that this is what truly modern law ought to be (Liu, 2002; for a criticism of this position, see Wu, n.d.). Obviously, such a view neglects actual historical change in the West: even in a legal system dominated by the formalist rights perspective and mode of thought, marriage law has undergone a fundamental qualitative change in response to social realities, finally discarding the principle of fault derived from the rights premises of the private law tradition and adopting in its stead the principle of no-fault divorce. That change makes understandable why divorce (and custody) disputes have constituted the largest single category and have had the most success of all disputes handled by mediation (de Roo and Jagtenberg, 2002).

To come back to Chinese divorce law, what it illustrates is an epistemological method that has definite continuity with imperial Chinese law. As we have seen, the Qing code clearly shows the mode of thinking that I have termed "practical moralism" (Huang, 1996: chap. 8). Whether the legal principles concerned property or debt, the Qing code always used concrete illustrations—real fact situations—to express them. The entire code was based on such an epistemological approach, in sharp contrast to the formalist mode of starting with abstract general principles from which legal provisions were derived by deductive logic. It reflected the belief that no abstract principle could encompass all the myriad fact situations of real life, that the meaning of all abstract principles needs to be articulated through factual contexts, with unforeseen fact situations handled by analogy with those already defined.

But Qing law was not the product simply of empiricism. It did not hold that all knowledge must come from experience. Rather, it held that law must be guided by moral values. On this point, it is no less "prospective" than is formalist law (i.e., it assumes that law should be an instrument for pursuing given ideals and not just purely "retrospective"). The difference is that it did not insist that legal provisions be unified by deductive logic or that the same abstract legal principles be applied by logic to any and all fact situations. It acknowledged instead that moral ideals and practical reality are not identical, that what ought to be is not quite the same as what is, and that therefore law should be allowed to operate in ways that are not necessarily consistent with moral ideals as it takes into account practicality and the infinite variability of fact situations.

In the modern and contemporary periods, particularly the Reform era, Chinese law has imported many Western legal perspectives and principles, most especially provisions about individual rights. However, it has tended to implement them in a rather different spirit than the original formalist intent of those laws. Rights constructions have generally been interpreted not as universally valid abstractions that stand above factual contexts but more like the traditional moral values that allow for practical adaptations and flexibility in implementation (a process that frequently leads to fuzzy application, resulting in court actions that run counter to people's rights). The discussions above of inheritance and old-age-support law, torts and compensation, and divorce laws provide examples of such interpretations. I have already examined in detail these aspects of the mode of thinking behind lawmaking and legal practice in chapters 6 and 7.

To that tradition, the contemporary Chinese legal system has added the concept of "practice" derived from its modern revolutionary heritage, requiring that legal provisions be tested and evaluated in practice. As we have already seen, contemporary Chinese lawmaking's basic method is to formulate and adopt legal provisions only after extensive and protracted trials. Old-age maintenance and inheritance legislation are two examples; the "rupture of the relationship" in divorce law and compensation for fault and without fault are two others.

In addition, there is the court mediation system. The procedures of the formalist courts of the West do not allow factual determinations to be made separately and independently of legal principles. Those are seen as the proper starting point in adjudication, and the facts of individual cases are to be subject to them. But the Chinese mode of starting from reality and from facts is quite different: facts are seen as carrying their own independent existence and truth. As we have seen, Qing law always began from illustrative fact situations, and its principles were always conveyed through real examples. A similar epistemological mode is evinced in the courts today. Tort law provides for two entirely different principles—one for compensation for damages in fact situations that involve the fault of one party, and one for damages in fact situations without fault. The two kinds of concrete factual contexts require the use of two different legal principles. In the court mediation system, this mode of thinking is evidenced in the judges' determination of the facts in and of themselves, or prior to the decision as to whether to employ mediation. As I suggested in chapter 7, mediation has enjoyed the greatest possibility for success when factual conditions involve no fault, or involve equivalent rights or obligations.

The above are all examples of what I term the reality- and practice-based mode of thinking manifest in contemporary Chinese law. Though born of specific historical circumstances, it is not unique. Modern American legal pragmatism, for example, comes quite close to this kind of thinking. It too was born of a particular historical context: namely, a reaction against the "classical orthodoxy" championed by Christopher Columbus Langdell (Tamanaha, 1996). In opposition to formalist epistemology and legal theory, legal pragmatism emphasizes the historicity and particularity of knowledge and law, and it rejects claims to universality and immutability. It holds that law should take reality as its point of departure and should change in accordance with changing circumstances. In addition, legal principles are to be tested and evaluated in terms of their social consequences, not detached from social reality. On these basic points, modern American legal pragmatism is quite close to the practical bent of Chinese law. And, as I have already suggested, the true essence of modernity in American law consists not in its formalist classical orthodoxy but rather in the protracted coexistence, seesawing balance, and mutual penetration of that tradition with legal pragmatism and legal realism.

The difference between American legal pragmatism and Chinese practical moralism lies in the latter's explicit moral views. As some critics have pointed out, legal pragmatism is principally an epistemological method and does not have a clearly defined agenda (Tamanaha, 1996). China's practical moralism, by contrast, is accompanied by a rich tradition of moral thought that centers on the Confucian ideals of "harmony" (*he*), of a society without litigation, of morally "superior men" (*junzi*) who rise above disputes, of magistrates who govern by moral example and suasion, and so on; popular mediation is therefore seen as a better way to resolve disputes than court adjudication, making peace among disputants superior to strict or severe enforcement of the law, and reconciliation superior to winning. In the contemporary period, the revolutionary party's adoption of popular mediation was followed by the institutional invention of court mediation, which used the ideal of reconciling "non-antagonistic contradictions among the people" to replace and continue the ideal of (what is called today) the "harmonious society" (*hexie shehui*).

Another Chinese legal ideal concerns looking after the weak, an integral part of "benevolent government" (*renzheng*) that is shown in the social custom and legal category of dian rights. The modern revolutionary party further set forth the moral value of "socialism," a society in which the laboring people come first. Of course, as has been pointed out by others, the marketization of the Reform era has given rise to the phenomenon of a leadership that is very "left" in words but very "right" in actions. Nevertheless, at least on the level of conceptualization and discourse, the ideal of social justice undeniably occupies a central place in modern Chinese moral values. This too is different from American legal pragmatism, though that approach is clearly more concerned with social justice than was classical orthodoxy. China's modern tradition of socialism can become a kind of resource for the establishment of social rights. Here, of course, we have left the realm of historical reality for that of ideals.

Looking Ahead

The imperial and modern traditions of Chinese law today face the challenge of wholesale importation of formalist laws. Given the reality of their coexistence in Chinese law, this chapter has emphasized the need to comprehend modernity in terms of the process of historical practice, not in terms of any one theory or ideology. I believe that the present and future of Chinese law lies neither in traditional law nor Western law, nor even in practical moralism or formalism: it rests, as it ought to, in the long-term coexistence of, tug-of-war between, and mutual penetration of these strains. The traditional approaches to civil law that stress dispute resolution and mediation obviously have modern value, and they can appropriately be drawn on and used in contemporary China (and perhaps elsewhere in the world as well). More than a half century of practical experience of court mediation has accumulated; the approach should certainly not be discarded, but instead should be maintained, and more clearly and explicitly delineated. It seems especially well suited for disputes that involve no fault. At the same time, there is no doubt that the mediation and practical moralism tradition carries with it a strong tendency to muddle up questions of right and wrong and to fail to clearly distinguish disputes that involve rights violations and those in which no fault can be assigned. In situations in which disputants are of unequal power, such tendencies easily lend themselves to abuses of power and influence—for which the importation of Western, rights-based law is a good corrective. Rights should indeed be clearly stipulated and protected in fact situations that involve fault. Conversely, the Chinese mediatory tradition can be a good corrective for the tendency of Western court systems even in no-fault fact situations to adjudge right and wrong, winner and loser. In addition, the socialist tradition of the Chinese Revolution, leaving aside its accompanying bureaucratic and propagandistic excesses, can become a resource for developing modern social rights legislation.

The key is perhaps to establish a system in which those who want to Westernize and those who want to maintain indigenous practices can coexist and influence one another, allowing different interest groups to compete openly, interact, and compromise. As was emphasized at the start of this chapter, the essence of modernity consists in historical practice, in the law's being able to reflect an ever more complex social reality and the ever-changing interests of different groups, and not in any immutable so-called tradition or West, or any single theory or ideology. Practice, to be sure, is not so consistent as formal logic; it is more complex and more full of paradoxes. Precisely for that reason, however, it is closer to Chinese reality and its practical needs, and more balanced in its ability to bring together tradition and modernity, China and the West. If the essence of modernity in American law is indeed the coexistence of its classical orthodoxy with legal pragmatism, then the essence of China's modernity lies perhaps in the coexistence of Western formalism with Chinese practical moralism. The direction of development of Chinese law rests on fostering such coexistence, not on choosing one element in an either/or binary. This chapter's attempt to uncover modernity in imperial and modern Chinese legal practice is a preliminary search for principles and methods to support just such a selective amalgamation and coordination of the two approaches.

9
Conclusion
Past and Present

THIS BOOK BEGAN BY ADDRESSING mainstream legal opinion in China because that, in my view, is what will ultimately determine the fate of Chinese legal history studies, not only inside but also outside China. There can be no lasting vitality to a field of study in which the subject of study itself views its history as irrelevant to the present. For a few dozen outside scholars to talk to one another about Chinese legal history will not make for a vibrant field. It seems fitting, therefore, to end this book by returning once more to the larger context of legal history study within China itself. The purpose here is to summarize the main findings and arguments of this book in that context.

Hegemonic modernist discourse has led most Chinese lawmakers and legal scholars to think that Chinese law ultimately can only follow the path of wholesale Westernization. It is a point of view that stemmed originally from the combined pressures of external aggression and domestic crisis, but today it has become an indigenous Orientalism that is accepted almost unconsciously. It considers Western law the only kind of law that is modern, and past Chinese law (including revolutionary law) as having no present-day relevance. The main purpose of this book has been to challenge such a point of view, and to demonstrate a different kind of understanding.

This book demonstrated that in the past century even though the Chinese legal system lacked independence at the level of legal theory and codified texts, it has demonstrated substantial agency at the level of legal practice. This fact can be seen, first of all, in the strong persistence of the tradition of community mediation in the past century. Even though traditional law was completely rejected again and again, the tradition of community mediation within that legal system has persisted with very wide application in practice, showing great resilience, adaptability, and creativity. To be sure, it has undergone changes, from the tradition of relying on respected individuals of the community to help work out compromise resolutions in their mediation, to the Maoist period's reliance on cadres who privileged state laws and policies and often used coercive pressures in their mediation, to the later Reform period's reliance on both the cadre and the societal mediation systems. In the Reform period, the cadre mediation system has, to be sure, contracted in scope since its heyday in the Mao period, but it has most recently reversed its decline, in part because of vigorous support from the state in legislation and funding. Today, about half of all disputes each year are still dealt with first by community cadre mediation. As for societal mediation, it is undergoing a limited revival, though to an unquantifiable extent since most of them go unrecorded.

Outside of semiformal mediation by community cadres, the intermediate sphere ("third realm") born of interactions between societal organization and the formal state apparatus has shown great tenacity also in other spheres of governance. The principle of minimalist governance and the method of semiformal administration—reliance on quasi-officials without salary, and intervention of the state apparatus only in the event of disputes—have continued throughout. This can be seen in village governance of the collective era, in "people-operated state-assisted" village education of the Cultural Revolution period, and even in today's village governance and the "appealing to higher authorities" *shangfang* system. The fact is, traditional (informal) societal mediation and semiformal minimalist governance have formed an inseparable part of the Chinese system of law and administration, accounting for one important aspect of its difference from the modern West. Even while importing Westerns laws and theories, the history of practice of Chinese law and administration has shown definite continuities with the past in these distinctive aspects. Today, basic changes in the nature of the state's power—on the one hand retreating from direct control of villages and on the other hand expanding its infrastructural (especially the legal system's) reach, though not yet fully—have come with the spread of illegal influences and a mounting crisis in governance. The old minimalist approach needs now to find new ways to fill its role. Outside of the semiformal cadre mediation system, one possible direction of development for the future is for the state, in addition to providing basic security and order, to join with society in cooperative endeavors to make up for the inadequacies of the present system of public services. The ideal would be to also rebuild community bonds and public morality through such interactive cooperation.

The Chinese Communist Party and its modern revolutionary tradition, out of special historical circumstances, further created a new court mediation system above the traditional system, and employed it widely to deal with civil disputes. Though the system was not applied to the extent claimed by official propaganda, its reach nevertheless far exceeded that evidenced in any modern Western nation. And although from the late 1990s on, the old coercive Maoist system of (intervening on site in husband-wife disputes to effect) "mediated resolutions" has largely fallen into disuse, and the scope of the system has contracted, court mediation has continued to play an important role in the legal system as a whole, especially in cases of disputes that do not involve fault (or involve equal degrees of fault, obligation, or rights). In terms of numbers, of all cases handled by the court system, still about one-half are resolved by mediation. There is in China a tendency toward a deep-seated indigenous Orientalist outlook, which holds that China's tradition of mediation must be placed under the rubric of the fashionable "alternative dispute resolution" rubric of the West to gain legitimacy in the present-day world. That kind of outlook exaggerates the importance of this new Western "movement," which is, after all, a side-current that has not been accepted into the mainstream of the adversarial legal system. It also underestimates the modern tradition of China's court mediation system, and overlooks the reality of the community mediation tradition of the past. Such an Orientalist understanding is in fact mistaken both about the reality of "mediation" in the West, and about the reality of China's original tradition and its modern institutional innovation. It also overlooks the unusual efficacy of the system when compared with other legal systems of the world.

Recent changes in evidence procedures for civil disputes, based on careless and rather mindless copying of Western rules of evidence (for litigants to bear the principal responsibility in providing evidence, or what is called in Chinese "litigant-ism," *dangshiren zhuyi*), have come from the same indigenous Orientalism. Legislators, adopting Western rights theory as their point of departure and mistakenly equating civil cases (where the state is something of a detached third party) with criminal cases (where the state is a principal), took the position that they must ensure the "rights" of the litigants to provide evidence. They therefore discarded completely the past judicial practice (including revolutionary practice) of having the judge bear the principal responsibility for evidence gathering (what is called in Chinese "[judge's] authority-ism," *zhiquan zhuyi*). The result has been an operative reality in divorce law that is incongruent with what is really needed by the existing laws. In the absence of an effective witness system, there has been no way to determine what the law considers fault, no way to make a sound judgment as to whether there has been marital infidelity, spousal abuse, or domestic violence. The courts therefore have had to simply disregard these questions of fault under the law. There have also arisen problems of purely formalistic applications of the new procedural rules, with utter disregard for substance, to result in a system that is neither here nor there. What is needed today is to recognize the place that both the old Qing and modern revolutionary traditions occupy in contemporary law, and acknowledge the distinctive modernity contained in some past practices. Mindless transplanting of Western institutions and undigested acceptance of Western modernism without considering its necessary preconditions have in fact already resulted in a host of negative unanticipated consequences. What is needed today is to combine more appropriately the "judge's authority" and "litigant's rights" systems in evidence law.

In addition to the above, many scholars have concluded on the basis of traditional Chinese official representations that Qing courts privileged mediation and harmony, and did not render clear-cut decisions. This is another manifestation of the mentality of severing the present from the past, and of turning the past into treasured items fit only for the museum. What the history of practice reveals is that adjudication was always an important component of the past Chinese legal system. Qing law in fact contained quite detailed and unequivocal provisions on land, debt, marriage, and inheritance and old-age maintenance. And Qing archival records demonstrate that when litigants did not accept the societal mediations and persisted to a formal court session, magistrates would generally render clear-cut judgments on the basis of the law (not barring, of course, appropriate consideration to human relations and moral principles within the boundaries of the law). Even in the Maoist system that represented virtually all court actions as mediations, a sizable proportion of cases were in fact adjudicated. Precisely for this reason, when China adopted the adjudicatory system of Western adversarial law in the Guomindang period and in the Reform period, it did so not out of the blue in a complete rupture from the past, but rather out of definite continuity with a part of past practice. Seen from the point of view of the history of practice, court adjudication is in fact an important point of commonality between Chinese and Western legal practice that has implications for the present. To insist that Chinese and the Western systems are entirely different is actually yet another manifestation of the indigenous Orientalism considered in this book: on the one hand, to equate what is modern entirely with the West, and to exclude Chinese law completely from it; and, on the other hand, to insist on the museum-treasures quality of Chinese law, and exclude Western law completely from it. In this way, Chinese and Western law are reified into two entirely opposed systems, a reflection of the fracture in indigenous Orientalism between its own intellectual and emotional commitments. In my view, the present and future (or "modernity" in current Chinese discourse) of Chinese law cannot be sought through this kind of either/or mutually exclusive binary, but rather must be sought from mutual accommodation and fusion that transcend such a juxtaposed opposition between Chinese and Western law.

Even at the level of lawmaking, we can find evidence of such transcendence, though under an ideology of wholesale Westernization, and perhaps only semiconsciously. This book has explored a number of examples from practice-oriented lawmaking. In the face of the realities of rural life, legislation of the past century has always upheld certain maintenance obligations not found in modern Western law and, in the end, creatively linked inheritance rights to maintenance obligations. While upholding the principle of gender equality in inheritance, it also attended to the rural reality that it is generally sons who maintain the parents in their old age. Thus did the law reconcile the long-standing disjunction between codified law and judicial practice. In tort law, in the face of real fact situations both of civil damages that involved fault and those that did not, legislators adopted the Western wrongful-acts fault principle and yet also, on the basis of China's own long-standing mode of legal thought, established the principle of civil responsibility even when there is no fault, thereby reconciling law with lived realities. In divorce law, after importing the new principle of freedom of marriage and then faced with the reality of rural opposition, legislators instituted the method of dealing with disputed divorce petitions on a case-by-case basis, and further established the distinctive standard of whether a couple's emotional relationship has truly ruptured to determine whether to grant divorce. These are all examples of clear-sighted choices and innovation, even under the ideology of a complete rejection of the past legal tradition. Such examples, it seems to me, can serve as models for present-day legislation.

At the same time, post-1949 Chinese legislation has long employed in practice the method of experimenting for years in practice before incorporating a provision into codified law. In marriage law, the principle of using the couple's emotional relationship as the standard in deciding whether to grant divorce was used for decades before its formal incorporation into law (the 1980 Marriage Law). Similarly, the linking of the right of inheritance with the obligation for old-age maintenance was not written into law until after many years of judicial practice (the 1985 Succession Law). The same goes for the provisions on how to deal both with compensation cases that involve fault and those that do not (the 1986 General Principles of Civil Law). In retrospect, the People's Republic's model for legislation has obviously been to test a provision first in the form of Supreme People's Court opinions or instructions and, only after years of actual practice, incorporate it into a law code. This kind of legislative history embodies precisely the from-reality-to-concept-to-practice mode of thought that this book has emphasized.

The above are just a few examples from this book's preliminary exploration into the practice of the People's Republic's civil law; further research should bring to light many more. This mode of choice could be made explicit and given affirmation today, so as not to remain in the mentality of following blindly the hegemonic discourse of Western modernism. The purpose of the history-of-practice approach advocated in this book is precisely to break away from such a mentality, to demonstrate the modernity embodied in the above examples from past law, and to lend support to an independent spirit in law-making. That way, China could define its own modernity in law.

At the same time, this book has argued that these innovative mergings of the Chinese and the Western, and the old and the new, have come from a long-standing and distinctive mode of thought that has continued to the present, a mode of thought that is at once traditional and modern. This book has termed it "practical moralism." It is a mode of thought that is different from Western formalism: it places special emphasis on the close interlinking of experience and concept, and does not fall easily into the trap of modernist ambitions toward universality and ideologizing; it privileges experience and practical effect, and historical context and change; it does not demand total logical consistency between norms and practice in the manner of legal formalism, and will allow inconsistencies between them even when combined into a single system; it is more tolerant and balanced, and does not carry the overbearing aggressiveness of Western modernism.

Chinese practical moralism, it should be made clear, shares certain commonalities with American legal pragmatism (and legal realism), a tradition that is as mainstream in the United States as its formalist "classical orthodoxy." It too emphasizes practice and actual effect, rejects the either/or binary opposition between experience and theory and, in basic spirit, also rejects the universality and scientificity claimed by legal formalism. Where it differs is in its reliance on China's humanistic moral ideals for its prospective norms, and not just practical effects. It starts with traditional Chinese (as well as revolutionary China's) humanistic ideals, not from a pragmatism wanting in moral principles, and of course also not from legal formalism's "natural rights."

This book has documented in detail that this is the basic mode of thought in Qing law. It has also obviously continued to this day, and can be seen both in the revolutionary tradition of the Maoist period, as for example in its divorce law practice, and in the legal practice of the Reform period, as for example in its compensation, old-age-maintenance and inheritance laws, even while under the ideology of wholesale Westernization. It is precisely such a mode of thinking that allows for pluralistic coexistence of Chinese and Western, and old and new, law, and does not insist on logical unity as would legal formalism. The "practical" and the "moral" were long combined in the imperial and modern traditions of Chinese law; it is a resource that can serve to guide lawmaking and judicial practice today.

In my opinion, it is a mode of thought that can stand up to modern Western formalism. For example, Chinese mediation with its ideal of compromise can, in accordance with its own practical-moralism way of thinking, start closely connected to the fact situation and adopt the following principle: in disputes where there is no fault (or where both parties are equally at fault or have equivalent claims or obligations), use mediation; and in disputes involving fault or violation of another's rights, then use Western-style adjudication to protect rights. Looking back on the several decades of experience accumulated by Chinese court mediation, it is apparent that mediation has enjoyed the greatest success in no-fault situations. This is a principle that can be made explicit and applied widely; it would help avoid the problems with an adversarial Western formalist system that, even in fact situations involving no fault, pushes the litigants toward a battle to win. At the same time, in fact situations involving violations of rights and fault, the adjudicating tradition that already existed in the Qing (and also in the Maoist period) can be given wider application with the help of the Western rights-protection perspective.

The practical moralism mode of thought is something that has yet to gain deliberate approval from legislators. Even though it has long been the actual guide in Chinese legal practice and legislative innovations, its use has always been only half deliberate, perhaps even unconscious. In my opinion, China today would do well to officially affirm this approach and use it to build China's own kind of modernity. And Chinese legal studies would do well to try to develop this mode of thinking, perhaps by borrowing from Western formalist logic to raise its level of precision and rigor.

Needless to say, this is not a plan for restoration of the past or complete rejection of the West, but is rather one for blending the Chinese and the Western, the past and the present. Modern Western law's emphasis on rights should be seen as a good corrective to the long disregard for people's rights under the centralized power of the monarchs, just as it had been in modern Western history. At the same time, formal logic's insistence on precision and coherence are also good correctives for some tendencies in Chinese thought to be inexact; it should be appropriately adopted, whether in legislation or research and development. However, the lopsided tendency of formalism and deductive logic (and of postmodernism as well) to disregard experience and practice is something to be avoided. The key consists perhaps in using formalist logic as method and not as answer, as a way to make research hypotheses more exact and focused, and not as the way to absolute truth. Most important, in my view, is to use it in close connection with the empirical and with practice.

In retrospect, the history of the winning of citizens' rights by the lower classes in Western nations was one fraught with struggles and piecemeal change, while formalist law has represented it as a one-step adoption of universal principles. It carries for this reason strong tendencies to substitute/equate the ideal for the actual, and easily covers up actual realities. On the other hand, formalist law also possesses a definite practical advantage, because once the ideal has been established by law, there comes the strong imperative for logical consistency—something that can become a weapon in the lower classes' fight for rights. That was in fact the case in the history of their struggle for citizens' rights. Chinese practical moralism, by contrast, readily accepts departures in practice from stated ideals, does not insist on the equation of actuality with theory, and is more prone to acknowledge reality. But it has the disadvantage of lacking the kind of demand for making things logically consistent that comes with formalism. China today could possibly draw on the strengths of one to make up for the weakness of the other: for example, by acknowledging the gross inequalities that have arisen among different social groups during the broad process of marketization, face up to the fact that its laws do not carry the same strong imperative toward ideals that formalism can bring, and that therefore the state should deliberately help the weaker classes build organizations that wield genuine negotiatory power, in order to advance the cause of citizens' rights. Only thus could it become the true inheritor of the original ideals of its modern revolutionary tradition.

The above are some of my preliminary thoughts after two decades of work on my three-volume study of the history of practice of Chinese civil justice. This third volume, which deals with contemporary civil law, because of the much wider scope of the topic than for the Qing or the Republic, and also because of its very rapid changes, can only be a work in progress. Answers to the question of whither Chinese law ("modernity") is not something that can be done by just one or two people; it needs the united efforts of one or more generations. The points raised above can only be a small and modest beginning. Even so, I am convinced that the future of Chinese law (and indeed of other spheres of thought and scholarship) lies not in blindly following Western modernism, but rather in deeply critical reflections upon it, as well as upon China's own traditions, and therefrom to search for ways to transcend the simple juxtaposed opposition between the two, and to seek ways for them to coexist, compete, accommodate, and merge with one another. That way, China might be able to overcome the long-standing indigenous Orientalism it has fallen into under the hegemonic influence of modernism, with its presumption of the either/or binary opposition between China and the West. Of all the fields of the humanities and social sciences, legal studies and legal history perhaps exemplify most clearly that kind of Orientalist trap. Breaking away from that trap and developing China's own modernity might well be the most urgent task facing the legal field (indeed perhaps the entire intellectual world) in China today. Practical moralism, assisted by non-absolutizing use of formalist logic and positivistic research, could conceivably become the basic mode of thought for modern China.

Finally, I wish to emphasize again that the history-of-practice approach advocated in this book is intended to be a means and not an end. My purpose is to correct for past emphases on thought and institutions to the neglect of practice and actual operation. But I certainly do not believe that truth consists only of practice. In the end, the true nature of law, whether Chinese or Western, consists neither in any theory or institutional design nor simply in its practice, but rather in their long-term mutual interaction. That was the case in the past; it is also the case today. In the end, what we need is focused study of the interactions among thought and behavior, institution and actual operation, and theory and practice, with a broad historical perspective and a keen sense of reality. That is the way, I believe, to surmount the current problem of a present severed from the past and define a genuinely viable Chinese modernity. Then and only then can the field of Chinese legal history study, inside as well as outside China, gain the true vitality and importance it deserves.

Glossary

Baijiaxing	百家姓
baiping	摆平
ban shuren shehui	半熟人社会
baoban hunyin	包办婚姻
baojia	保甲
bawang zhi dao	霸王之道
beiyou sishan yongcai	卑幼私擅用财
bianqu	边区
biaoxian	表现
binü	婢女
bu zhengpai	不正派
bucuo	不错
buhao	不好
bumenfa	部门法
caiding	裁定
caili	彩礼
caoshuai jiehun	草率结婚
chaqing lichu	查情理处
chengbaodi	承包地
chesu	撤诉
chonghun	重婚
cuikuan sunshi fei	催款损失费
cunfu	村副

cungui	村规
cuntan jingkuan	村摊警款
cuntan xuekuan	村摊学款
cun tiaojie	村调解
cunzhang	村长
dang bagu	党八股
dangshiren zhuyi	当事人主义
daoli	道理
daomai tianzhai	盗卖田宅
dashi hua xiao, xiaoshi hua liao	大事化小，小事化了
dian	典
dianpu	佃仆
diaocha	调查
diaochaling	调查令
diaocha yanjiu	调查研究
diaomin	刁民
disanzhe	第三者
diyidao fangxian	第一道防线
douzheng	斗争
duan	断
duan'an	断案
duanding	断定
dou'ou sha	斗殴杀
duixiang	对象
duizhi	对质
duxi zhengduan, jianshao susong	杜息争端，减少诉讼
eba	恶霸
ermu suo buji, silü suo budao	耳目所不及，思虑所不到
fa	法
faguan zhiquan zhuyi	法官职权主义
fali	法理
falüshi	法律史
falü shiwusuo	法律事务所
fang	房
fanghai hunyin	妨害婚姻
fangwen	访问
fangwen bilu	访问笔录
fangzi	房子
fei zhengcheng siwang	非正常死亡
fengjian luohou sixiang	封建落后思想
fenjia	分家

fenjiadan	分家单
fujuan	副 卷
fumuguan	父母官
fuyang	抚养
fu zhenzhang	副镇长
ganjie	甘结
ganqing	感情
ganqing buhuai	感 情 不 坏
ganqing genben buhe	感 情 根 本 不 合
ganqing henhao	感 情 很 好
ganqing polie	感 情 破 裂
ganqing que yi polie	感情确已破裂
gongping zeren	公平责任
guan wenshu	官文书
guanxi	关系
guanya chuli	关押处理
guiding	规定
guli ban'an	孤立办案
guofa	国法
guoshi sha	过失杀
gusha	故杀
haohao guo rizi	好好过日子
he	和
hehao	和好,合好
hehao hui	和好会
hejie	和解
heshilao	和事佬
hexie	和谐
hexie shehui	和谐社会
he xini	和稀泥
heyiting	合议庭
hôgen	法源
hu hun tiantu	户婚田土
huigai	悔改
huigaishu	悔改书
huigui minfa	回归民法
hukou	户口
hunhun	混混
hunyin maodun	婚姻矛盾
jian	间
jiancha weiyuanhui	监察委员会

jiandu laodong	监督劳动
jianfu	减负
Jiang Ping	江平
jiansong	健讼
jianyi chengxu	简易程序
jianzheng	简政
jiaohao	较好
jiaotiao zhuyi	教条主义
jiating hehao hui	家庭和好会
jie'an baogao	结案报告
jiedai bilu	接待笔录
jiedao	街道
jieji benzhi	阶级本质
jiguan tuanti	机关团体
jin hou dui ni you haochu	今后对你有好处
jing qinyou tiaochu/tiaojie/shuohe	经亲友调处/调解/说合
jingshen	精神
jingyan zhuyi	经验主义
jinshi	进士
jiquan zhuyi	极权主义
ju ganjie	具甘结
juehu	绝户
junzi	君子
lao zhangpanzi	老掌盘子
li	理
liangmin	良民
lijia	里甲
lingdao	领导
linshigong	临时工
litu bu lixiang	离土不离乡
litu lixiang	离土离乡
liumang	流氓
liusha	六杀
liyi	礼仪
lizhang	里长
luohou zisi	落后自私
Ma Xiwu *shenpan fangshi*	马锡五审判方式
maiduan	买断
maiduan	卖断
maimai hunyin	买卖婚姻
manyi	满意

maodun	矛盾
meiyou diaocha jiu meiyou fayan quan	没有调查就没有发言权
menzili	门子里
minban gongzhu	民办公助
mingling zhuyi	命令主义
minjian	民间
minjianfa	民间法
minjian tiaojie	民间调解
minshi tiaojiechu	民事调解处
minshi tiaojie shu	民事调解书
minshi zeren	民事责任
minzheng zhuli	民政助理
mo	摸
mousha	谋杀
mu	亩
muyou	幕友
nao lihun	闹离婚
niangao youde	年高有德
nongmin gong	农民工
pan	判
pan'an	判案
panjue	判决
panjue bu lihun	判决不离婚
panjue buzhun lihun	判决不准离婚
panjue lihun	判决离婚
peichang	赔偿
peili daoqian	赔礼道歉
qi	起
qing	情
qingli	情理
qingshi	情实
qingshuai	轻率
qingshuai taidu	轻率态度
qita feiyong	其他费用
qiyue weizhi er qiangqu	期约未至而强娶
qiyue yizhi er gu weiqi	期约已至而故违期
qu	区
qu zhuanyuan	区专员
quanneng zhuyi	全能主义
quzhang	区长
quanquan ta	劝劝她

quanxuesuo	劝学所
qunzhong	群众
qunzhong yanjing zuiliang	群众眼睛最亮
rang	让
ren	忍
renmin peishenyuan	人民陪审员
renqing	人情
ren	仁
renzheng	仁政
ruzhui	入赘
Sanzijing	三字经
shangfang	上访
shanshi tianyuan guaguo	擅食田园瓜果
shantou zhuyi	山头主义
shanyang	赡养
shanyangguanxi	赡养关系
shehui	社会
shehui tiaojie zhongxin	社会调解中心
shendong	绅董
shengshi ziding, yong bu jiafu	盛世滋丁，永不加赋
shengwang zhi dao	圣王之道
shengyang sizang	生养死葬
shengyuan	生员
shenpanyuan	审判员
shi	石
shiqing	实情
shishi qiushi de sixiang	实事求是的思想
shoulifei	受理费
shoushi	首事
shujiyuan	书记员
shuohe	说合
shuoheren	说合人
shuren shehui	熟人社会
sifa tiaojie	司法调解
sishu	私塾
si wenshu	私文书
sixiang	思想
sixiangshi	思想史
songgun	讼棍
songshi	讼师
susong	诉讼

taiji	太极
tanhua	谈话
tanhua bilu	谈话笔录
tankuan	摊款
tianli	天理
tianmian quan	田面权
tiaochu	调处
tiaojie	调解
tiaojie bilu	调解笔录
tiaojie bu lihun	调解不离婚
tiaojie hehao	调解和好
tiaojie lihun	调解离婚
tiaojie shu	调解书
tiaojie weiyuanhui	调解委员会
tiaojie weizhu	调解为主
tiaojie xieyi	调解协议
tiaoting	调停
tigao	提高
tingshen diaocha	庭审调查
tingwai tiaojie	庭外调解
tizhi	体制
tizhi jingying	体制精英
tizhiwai	体制外
tongchi	同吃
tonglao	同劳
tongyangxi	童养媳
tongzhu	同住
tousu	投诉
tuanjie	团结
Wang Hanbin	王汉斌
wei baohu funü yu zinü liyi	为保护妇女与子女利益
weijin quli	违禁取利
Weizhai riji	《胃斋日记》
Wenshu	文书
Wu Changzhen	巫昌祯
wulai	无赖
wusong	吴讼
Wu Xinyu	武新宇
wusha	误杀
wu zuiming	无罪名
xiagang	下岗

xia zhihui	瞎指挥
xian	县
xianchang	现场
xiandaixing	现代性
xiang	乡
xiangbao	乡保
xiangdi	乡地
xiangyue dibao	乡约地保
xiaoren	小人
Xiao Xun	肖峋
xieyi	协议
xieyi lihun	协议离婚
xiguanfa	习惯法
xingfang	刑房
xingge buhe	性格不合
xingzheng tiaojie	行政调解
xisha	戏杀
xishi	细事
xishi ningren	息事宁人
xisong	息讼
xisong weiyuanhui	息讼委员会
xixin yanjiu	喜新厌旧
xunwen	询问
yadu	衙蠹
yange zeren	严格责任
yansong	厌讼
yanglaodi	养老地
yaoqiu zhengfu gei wo duankai	要求政府给我断开
yiban	一般
yikao qunzhong	依靠群众
ying gutou	硬骨头
yinsi	隐私
yitian liangzhu	一田两主
yitian sanzhu	一田三主
yiwugong	义务工
yixiang shanshi	一乡善士
you canji zhe, wangzuo wu ji	有残疾者，妄作无疾
you xinyong	有信用
youyu guocuo	由于过错
yuebao	约保
zaixu taren	再许他人

zhaijidi	宅基地
zhaoshangju	招商局
zhaotie	找贴
zhen	镇
zhenqing zhouli	斟情酌理
zhengdi	征地
zhengfu	政府
zhengji	政绩
zhengjuan	正卷
zhi'an baowei zhuren	治安保卫主任
zhidushi	制度史
zhiquan zhuyi	职权主义
zhong'an	重案
zhongbaoren	中保人
zhongjianren	中间人
zhongjie	终结
zhongren	中人
zhongshuoren	中说人
zhongzhi	中止
zhongzichang	种子场
zhua geming, cu shengchan	抓革命，促生产
zhuanbao	转包
zhuguan zhuyi	主观主义
zhujian polie	逐渐破裂
zhutixing	主体性
zibao gongyi	自报公议
zili	自理
zili gengsheng	自力更生
zimin	子民
ziwo piping	自我批评
zu	组
zui	罪
zuiliang	最亮
zuole sixiang gongzuo	做了思想工作
zuotang ban'an	坐堂办案
zuoting ban'an	坐庭办案
zuzhi	组 织

References

Interviews

I conducted interviews in Songjiang County, the Huayang Township, and the Huayangqiao villages (renamed Ganlu cun from the 1990s) between 17 and 26 September 1990, 13 and 17 September 1991, and 6 and 10 September 1993, from 9 A.M. to noon and 2 P.M. to 5 P.M.; six interviews with Jiang Ping, one of the main architects of the 1986 General Principles of Civil Law (Minfa tongze), and the main architect of the Law of Administrative Procedure (Xingzheng susongfa), between 30 January and 8 February 1995; one interview each with Xiao Xun, former deputy chair of the Civil Law Section of the Committee for Legal Work (Falü gongzuo weiyuanhui) of the Standing Committee of the National People's Congress about the drafting of the General Principles of Civil Law, on 15 March 1999, and Wu Changzhen, one of the drafters of the amendments (passed 28 April 2001) to the 1980 Marriage Law, on 16 March 1999. References to the interviews begin "INT," followed by the year of the interview and its number (in consecutive order for each year), preceded by a hyphen (e.g., INT93-2). The interviews in 1995 and 1999 are further identified by the initials of the interviewee (e.g., JP for Jiang Ping: INT95-JP-1). There are two citations from interviews conducted by Kathryn Bernhardt with judges and judicial personnel in Songjiang in 1993. Those are cited as INT93, followed by B and the number of the interview (e.g., INT93-B-3).

Case Records

The North China county B case files are cited by the abbreviation B, year, and my own case number, from 1 to 20 for each of the years 1953, 1965, 1977, 1988, and 1989, for the first batch of case records I obtained, and 01 to 020 for each year for the second batch I obtained (e.g., B, 1953-20; B, 1965-015). The B court itself numbers its case records by year and in numerical order by date of the case's closing. For reasons of confidentiality, I have avoided using the court's own identification numbers and the names of the litigants.

The Jiangnan county A cases are cited by the abbreviation A, year, and my own case number, from 1 to 20 for each of the years 1953, 1965, 1977, 1988, and 1989, and 1 to 40 for 1995.

The South China county R divorce cases from 1999 to 2004 are cited by the year and registration number (*dengjihao*). They were filmed at regular intervals of 20 according to their archived numbers (*guidanghao*, to be distinguished from the *dengjihao*).

The Qing Code and the Civil Code of the Republic of China

The Qing Code is cited from Xue Yunsheng (1970) by (editor Huang Tsing-chia's) Statute or Substatute number: Statute 89; Substatute 89-1.

The Civil Code of the Republic of China is cited by Article number, in English from *The Civil Code of the Republic of China* (1930–1931), and in Chinese from *Liufa quanshu* (1932).

Unless otherwise noted, most citations of codes of the People's Republic of China are from the official English translations, for the benefit of English-speaking readers. Sources for the Chinese originals of the codes are given in entries beginning "Zhonghua renmin gongheguo."

References

Administrative Office of the U.S. Courts (1981) *Annual Report of the Director of the Administrative Office of the United States Courts*. Washington, DC: U.S. Government Printing Office.

Auto Insurance In-Depth (2004) "No-Fault Insurance Explained: Understanding No Fault Auto Insurance Laws." At www.autoinsuranceindepth.com/no-fault-insurance.html.

Baodi xian dang'an 宝坻县档案 [Baodi County Archives]. In Diyi lishi dang'an guan (First historical archives) 第一历史档案馆, under Shuntianfu 顺天府. Beijing. [Cited by juan number, year, lunar month, and day (where applicable): Baodi xian dang'an, 87, 1814, 12. 4].

Bernhardt, Kathryn (1999) *Women and Property in China, 960–1949.* Stanford, CA: Stanford University Press.

Bodde, Derk, and Clarence Morris (1967) *Law in Imperial China, Exemplified by 190 Ch'ing Dynasty Cases.* Cambridge, MA: Harvard University Press.

Bol, Peter (1993) "Government, Society, and State: On the Political Visions of Sima Kuang and Wang An-shi." In Robert P. Hymes and Conrad Schirokauer (eds.), *Ordering the World: Approaches to State and Society in Sung Dynasty China*, pp. 129–93. Berkeley: University of California Press.

Bourdieu, Pierre (1977) *Outline of a Theory of Practice.* Trans. Richard Nice. Cambridge: Cambridge University Press.

Brewer, Thomas J., and Lawrence R. Mills (1999) "Combining Mediation and Arbitration." *Dispute Resolution Journal* 3 (November). At www.findarticles.com.

Chang Chung-Li (1955) *The Chinese Gentry: Studies on Their Role in Nineteenth-Century Chinese Society.* Seattle: University of Washington Press.

——— (1962) *The Income of the Chinese Gentry.* Seattle: University of Washington Press.

Chayanov, A. V. ([1966] 1986) *The Theory of Peasant Economy.* Ed. Daniel Thorner, Basile Kerblay, R. E. F. Smith. Madison: University of Wisconsin Press.

Chen Baifeng 陈柏峰 (2008) Xiangcun hunhun yu nongcunshehui huisehua—liang Hu pingyuan, 1980–2008 《乡村混混与农村社会灰色化—两湖平原，1980–2008》 [Rural hunhun and the graying of rural society—the Hunan-Hubei plain, 1980–2008]. PhD dissertation in sociology, Central China University of Science and Technology 华中科技大学.

Chodosh, Hiram E. (1999) "Judicial Mediation and Legal Culture." Electronic journal article 2520, distributed by the Office of International Information Programs, U.S. Department of State. At canberra.usembassy.gov/hyper/WF991201/epf312.htm.

Chūgoku nōson kankō chōsa 《中国农村惯行调查》 (1952–1958) [Investigations of customary practices in rural China]. Ed. Niida Noboru 仁井田陞, 6 vols. Tokyo: Iwanami. Cited in text as KC.

Ch'ü, T'ung-Tsu (1961) *Law and Society in Traditional China.* Paris: Mouton.

——— (1962) *Local Government in China under the Ch'ing.* Cambridge, MA: Harvard University Press.

Civil Code of the Republic of China (1930–1931). Shanghai: Kelly & Walsh.

Clarke, Donald (1991) "Dispute Resolution in China." *J. of Chinese Law* 5, 2 (Fall): 245–96.

Cohen, Jerome A. (1967) "Chinese Mediation on the Eve of Modernization." *J. of Asian and African Studies* 2, 1 (April): 54–76.

Committee of Ministers of the Council of Europe (1998) "European Principles on Family Mediation." At www.mediate.com/articles/EuroFam.cfm (accessed 29 July 2005).

Cong Hanxiang 从翰香 (ed.) (1995) *Jindai Ji-Lu-Yu xiangcun* 《近代冀鲁豫乡村》 [Rural Hebei-Shandong-Henan in modern times]. Beijing: Zhongguo shehui kexue chubanshe.

Cui, Zhiyuan (1996) "Particular, Universal and Infinite: Transcending Western Centrism and Cultural Relativism in the Third World." In Leo Marx and Bruce Mazlish (eds.), *Progress: Fact or Illusion*, pp. 141–52. Ann Arbor: University of Michigan Press.

De Roo, Annie, and Rob Jagtenberg (2002) "Mediation in the Netherlands: Past—Present—Future." *Electronic Journal of Comparative Law* 6, 4 (December). At www.ejcl.org/64/art64-8.html (accessed 29 July 2005).

Diamant, Neil J. (2000) *Revolutionizing the Family: Politics, Love, and Divorce in Urban and Rural China, 1949–1968*. Berkeley: University of California Press.

Ding Ling (1942) "Sanbajie yougan" 《三八节有感》 [Thoughts on the occasion of 8 March]. *Jiefang ribao* 《解放日报》, 9 March.

Dong Leiming 董磊明 (2006) "Cun jiang bu cun—Hubei Shangwu cun diaocha" 《村将不村——湖北尚武村调查》 [Villages will no longer be villages—an investigation of Shangwu village in Hubei]. Parts 1 to 3. *Zhongguo xiangcun yanjiu* 《中国乡村研究》, no. 5 (2007): 174–202. Fujian: Fujian jiaoyu chubanshe. At www.snzg.net.

——— (2008) *Xiangcun jubian zhong de jiufen tiaojie jizhi yanjiu—Henan Songcun shijian de jiedu* 《乡村社会巨变中的纠纷调解机制研究—河南宋村实践的解读》 [The dispute-mediation mechanism in the midst of gigantic changes—a reading of the practices in Henan province's Song village]. PhD dissertation, public administration, Nanjing Normal University 南京师大公共管理学.

Fan Yu 范愉 (2000) *Fei susong jiufen jiejue jizhi yanjiu* 《非诉讼纠纷解决机制研究》 [A study of the mechanisms of dispute resolution without litigation]. Beijing: Zhongguo renmindaxue chubanshe.

——— (2007) *Jiufen jiejue de lilun yu shijian* 纠纷解决的理论与实践 [The theory and practice of dispute resolution]. Beijing: Qinghua daxue chubanshe.

Fei Xiaotong 费孝通 (1983) "Jiating jiegou biandong zhong de laonian shanyang wenti"《家庭结构变动中的老年赡养问题》[The problem of old-age support in the midst of change in family structure]. *Beijing daxue xuebao*《北京大学学报》, 3: 6–15.

Fengxian xian fayuan zhi《奉贤县法院志》(1986) [Gazetteer of the Fengxian county court]. N.p.

Freedman, Maurice (1966) *Chinese Lineage and Society: Fukien and Kwangtung*. London: University of London, The Athlone Press.

Galanter, Marc (1985) "'A Settlement Judge, Not a Trial Judge': Judicial Mediation in the United States." *J. of Law and Society* 12, 1 (Spring): 1–18.

Ganlu cun tiaojie weiyuan hui tiaojie jilu bu 《甘露村调解委员会调解记录簿》 [Record book of Mediations, Ganlu Village] 1989–1992.

Geertz, Clifford (1983) "Local Knowledge: Fact and Law in Comparative Perspective." In Clifford Geertz, *Local Knowledge: Further Essays in Interpretive Anthropology*, pp. 167–234. New York: Basic Books.

"General Principles of the Civil Law of the People's Republic of China" ([1986] 1987) In *The Laws of the People's Republic of China, 1983–1986*. Compiled by the Legislative Affairs Commission of the Standing Committee of the National People's Congress of the People's Republic of China. Beijing: Foreign Languages Press.

German Civil Code (1907) Trans. and annotated, with a historical introduction and appendixes, by Chung Hui Wang. London: Stevens & Sons.

Grey, Thomas C. (1980) "The Disintegration of Property." *Nomos* 22: 69–85.

Grey, Thomas G. (1983–1984) "Langdell's Orthodoxy." *University of Pittsburgh Law Review* 45: 1–53.

Guanche hunyinfa yundong de zhongyao wenjian 《贯彻婚姻法运动的重要文件》 (1953) [Important documents on the campaign to implement the Marriage Law] Beijing: Renmin chubanshe.

"Guanyu jiaqiang shehui zhi'an zonghe zhili de jueding" 《关于加强社会治安综合治理的决定》 (1991) [Resolutions on strengthening public order in society by unified governance] Quanguo renmin daibiao dahui changwu weiyuanhui, 全国人民代表大会常务委员会 [Standing Committee, National People's Congress], 2 March. At www.dglaw.gov.cn (accessed 6 May 2005).

Guo Xinghua 郭星华 and Wang Ping 王平 (2004) "Zhongguo nongcun de jiufen yu jiejue tujing" 《中国农村的纠纷与解决途径》 [Disputes and their ways of resolution in Rural China], *Jiangsu shehui kexue* 《江苏社会科学》, no. 2. At www.usc.cuhk.edu.hk.

Ha Jin (1999) *Waiting*. New York: Pantheon.

Han Xiutao 韩秀桃 (2004) *Ming-Qing Huizhou de minjian jiufen ji qi jiejue* 《明清徽州的民间纠纷及其解决》 [Disputes among the people and their resolution in Huizhou in the Ming-Qing period]. Hefei: Anhui daxue chubanshe.

Han Yanlong 韩延龙 (1982) *Woguo renmin tiaojie zhidu de lishi fazhan* 《我国人民调解制度的历史发展》 [The historical development of our nation's system of people's mediation]. Beijing: Zhongguo shehui kexue chubanshe.

Han Yanlong and Chang Zhaoru 韩延龙、常兆儒 (eds.) (1981–1984) *Zhongguo xin minzhu zhuyi shiqi genjudi fazhi wenxian xuanbian* 《中国新民主主义时期根据地法制文献选编》 [Selected source materials on the legal system of the base areas during China's new democracy period]. 4 vols. Beijing: Zhongguo shehui kexue chubanshe.

He Xuefeng 贺雪峰 (2000) "Lun ban shuren shehui" 《论半熟人社会》 [On the society of the semi-well-acquainted]. *Zhengzhixue yanjiu* 《政治学研究》, no. 3.

Hsiao Kung-Ch'üan (1960) *Rural China: Imperial Control in the Nineteenth Century*. Seattle: University of Washington Press.

——— (1979) *Compromise in Imperial China*. Seattle: School of International Studies, University of Washington.

——— [Xiao Gongquan] 萧公权 (1982) *Zhongguo zhengzhi sixiang shi* 中国政治思想史 [A history of Chinese political thought]. Taipei: Lianjing.

Hu Hanmin 胡汉民 (1978) *Hu Hanmin xiansheng wenji* 《胡汉民先生文集》 [Collected works of Mr. Hu Hanmin]. Taipei: Zhongguo Guomindang Zhongyang weiyuanhui Dangshi weiyuan hui 中国国民党中央委员会党史委员会.

Huang Songyou 黄松有 (2000) "Jianjin yu guodu: minshi shenpan fangshi gaige de leng sikao" 《渐进与过渡: 民事审判方式改革的冷思考》 [Gradual change and transitioning: Cool reflections on the mode of civil adjudication]. *Xiandai faxue* 《现代法学》, no. 4.

Huang, Philip C. C. (1985) *The Peasant Economy and Social Change in North China*. Stanford: Stanford University Press.

——— (1990) *The Peasant Family and Rural Development in the Yangzi Delta, 1350–1988*. Stanford, CA: Stanford University Press.

——— (1993a) "'Public Sphere'/ 'Civil Society' in China? The Third Realm between State and Society." *Modern China* 19, 2 (April): 216–40.

——— (1993b) "Between Informal Mediation and Formal Adjudication: The Third Realm of Qing Justice." *Modern China*, 19, 3 (April): 251–98.

——— (1996) *Civil Justice in China: Representation and Practice in the Qing.* Stanford: Stanford University Press.

———(1998) "Theory and the Study of Modern Chinese History: Four Traps and a Question," *Modern China*, 24, 2 (April): 183–208.

——— (2001) *Code, Custom and Legal Practice in China: The Qing and the Republic Compared.* Stanford: Stanford University Press.

——— (2005) "Divorce Law Practices and the Origins, Myths, and Realities of Judicial 'Mediation' in China." *Modern China* 31, 2 (April): 151–203.

——— (2006a) "Civil Adjudication in China, Past and Present." *Modern China*, 32, 2 (April): 135–80.

——— (2006b) "Court Mediation in China, Past and Present." *Modern China*, 32, 3 (July): 275–314.

——— (2007) "Whither Chinese Law?" *Modern China*, 33, 2 (April): 163–94.

——— (2008) "Centralized Minimalism: Semiformal Governance by Quasi Officials and Dispute Resolution in China." *Modern China*, 34, 1 (January): 9–35.

Huang Zongzhi 黄宗智 [Philip C. C. Huang] (2005a) "Renshi Zhongguo—zouxiang cong shijian chufa de shehui kexue" 《认识中国—走向从实践出发的社会科学》 [Studying China: toward social sciences that start from practice]. *Zhongguo shehui kexue* 《中国社会科学》, no. 1: 85–95.

——— (2005b) "Beilun shehui yu xiandai chuantong" 《悖论社会与现代传统》 [Paradoxical society and modern traditions]. *Dushu* 《读书》, no. 2: 3–14.

——— (2006a) "Zhiduhua le de 'bangong bangeng' guomixing nongye" 《制度化了的'半工半耕'过密型农业》 [The institutionalized "half worker, half peasant" involuted agricultural system]. *Dushu* 《读书》, no. 2: 30–37; no. 3: 72–80 (corrected version in Huang Zongzhi, 2007b: 457–70).

——— (2006b) "Zhongguo falü de xiandaixing?" 《中国法律的现代性》 [Modernity in Chinese law?]. *Qinghua faxue*, no. 10: 67–88.

——— (2007b) *Jingyan yu lilun: Zhongguo shehui, jingji yu falü de shijian lishi yanjiu* 《经验与理论：中国社会、经济与法律的实践历史研究》 [Experience and theory: Studying the history-of-practice of Chinese society, economy and law]. Beijing: Zhongguo Renmin daxue chubanshe.

——— (2008) "Zhongguo falü de shijian lishi yanjiu" 《中国法律的实践历史研究》 [A history-of-practice approach to the study of Chinese law], *Kaifang shidai* (开放时代), no. 4: 105–24.

Huang Zongzhi 黄宗智 [Philip C. C. Huang] and Peng Yusheng 彭玉生(2007) "San da lishixing bianqian de jiaohui yu Zhongguo xiao guimo nongye de qianjing" 《三大历史性变迁的交汇与中国小规模农业 的前景》 [The conjuncture of three great historic changes and the outlook for China's small-scale farming]. *Zhongguo shehui kexue* 《中国社会科学》 [*Social Sciences in China*], no. 4: 74–88.

Huayangqiao xiang tiaojie jilu bu 《华阳桥乡调解记录簿》 (1990) [Record book of mediation of Huayangqiao township].

Hubei caijing xueyuan (ed.) 湖北财经学院编 [Hubei College of Finance and Economics] (1983) Zhonghua renmin gonghe guo hunyin fa ziliao xuanbian 《中华人民共和国婚姻法资料选编》 [Source materials on the marriage law of the People's Republic of China]. N.p.

Hull, N. E. H. (1997) *Roscoe Pound and Karl Llewellyn, Searching for an American Jurisprudence*. Chicago: University of Chicago Press.

Ji Weidong 季卫东 (2006) "Falü chengxu de xingshixing yu shizhixing: yi dui chengxu lilun de pipan he pipan lilun de chengxuhua wei xiansuo" 《法律程序的形式性与实质性: 以对程序理论的批判和批判理论的程序化为线索》 [The formality and substance of legal procedure: Using criticisms of proceduralist theory and formalization of critical theory as leads]. *Beijing daxue xuebao* (zhexue shehui kexue ban) 《北京大学学报》哲学社会科学版, no. 1.

Jiang Shigong 强世功 (forthcoming [2010]) "Written and Unwritten Constitutions: A New Approach to the Study of Constitutional Government in China," *Modern China* 36, no. 1 (January).

"Jiaoyubu ni jiang nongcun jiaoshi si bai yi gongzi lieru yusuan" 《教育部拟将农村教师四百亿工资列入预算》 (2005) [The Ministry of Education intends to incorporate within its budget the 40 billion yuan salaries of rural teachers] 19 Dec. www.edu.cn.

Jin Hua 金晔 (2005) "Lun minshi susong dangshiren quzheng quanli zhi chengxu baozhang" 《论民事诉讼当事人取证权利之程序保障》 [On procedural guarantees of the evidence rights of litigants in civil litigation], MA thesis, Fudan University. At www.wanfangdata.com.

Johnson, Kay Ann (1983) *Women, the Family and Peasant Revolution in China*. Chicago: University of Chicago Press.

Jones, William C. (1987) "Some Questions Regarding the Significance of the General Provisions of Civil Law of the People's Republic of China." *Harvard International Law J.* 28, 2 (Spring): 309–31.

KC. See *Chūgoku nōson kankō chōsa*, 1952–1958.

Kuhn, Philip A. (1990) *Soulstealers: The Chinese Sorcery Scare of 1768*. Cambridge, MA: Harvard University Press.

"Law of Succession of the People's Republic of China" ([1985] 1987) In *The Laws of the People's Republic of China, 1983–1986*. Compiled by the Legislative Affairs Commission of the Standing Committee of the National People's Congress of the People's Republic of China. Beijing: Foreign Languages Press.

Levenson, Joseph R. (1953) *Liang Ch'i-ch'ao and the Mind of Modern China*. Cambridge, MA: Harvard University Press.

Li Fangchun 李放春 (2005) "Beifang tugai zhong de 'fanshen' yu 'shengchan': Zhongguo geming xiandaixing de yi ge huayu-lishi maodun sukao" 《北方土改 中的"翻身"与"生产": 中国革命现代性的一个话语-历史矛盾溯考》 ["Fanshen" and "shengchan" in North China's land reform: A study of the origins of a discursive-historical contradiction in China's revolutionary modernity]. *Zhongguo xiangcun yanjiu* 《中国乡村研究》, no. 3: 231–92.

Li Huaiyin (2000) *State and Village in Late Qing and Republican North China: Local Administration and Land Taxation in Huailu County, Hebei Province, 1875–1936*. PhD dissertation, University of California, Los Angeles.

——— (2005) *Village Governance in North China, 1875–1936.* Stanford, CA: Stanford University Press.

Li Liang 李梁 and Xu Tonghui 许桐珲 (2005) "'Mianfei' yiwu jiaoyu bainian bashe" 《免费义务教育百年跋涉》 [The hundred-year journey of free universal education]. Nanfang zhoumo《南方周末》, 24 November. At http://hsyong.edublogs.org.

Liang Linxia (2007) *Delivering Justice in Qing China: Civil Trials in the Magistrate's Court.* Oxford: Oxford University Press.

Liang Zhiping 梁治平 (1996) *Qingdai xiguanfa: shehui yu guojia* 《清代习惯法：社会与国家》 [Customary law in the Qing: Society and the state]. Beijing: Zhongguo zhengfa daxue chubanshe.

Liufa quanshu 《六法全书》 (1932) [Compendium of the six laws]. Shanghai: Shanghai faxue bianyi she.

Liu Kaixiang 刘凯湘 (2002) "Jieding hunyin jiating guanxi de shizhi shi xiugai he lijie hunyinfa de qianti" 《界定婚姻家庭关系的实质是修改和理解〈婚姻法〉的前提》 [Fixing the boundaries of the actual substance of marital familial relations is the precondition for revising and understanding the marriage law]. At www.civillaw.com.cn.

Lubman, Stanley (1967) "Mao and Mediation: Politics and Dispute Resolution in Communist China." *California Law Rev.* 55: 1284–1359.

——— (1999) *Bird in a Cage: Legal Reform in China after Mao.* Stanford, CA: Stanford University Press.

Lu Xueyi 陆学艺 (2004) *Dangdai Zhongguo shehui liudong* 《当代中国社会流动》 [Social mobility in contemporary China]. Beijing: Shehui kexue wenxian chubanshe.

Ma Yuan 马原 (1998) *Zhongguo minfa jiaocheng* 《中国民法教程》 [Textbook of China's civil law]. Beijing: Zhongguo Zhengfa daxue chubanshe.

Mann, Michael (1984) "The Autonomous Power of the State: Its Origins, Mechanisms and Results." *Archives européennes de sociologie,* 25: 185–213.

——— (1986) *The Sources of Social Power.* Vol. 1 *A History of Power from the Beginning to A.D. 1760.* Cambridge: Cambridge University Press.

Mao Zedong (1927 [1971]) "Report on an Investigation of the Peasant Movement in Hunan." In Mao, 1971: 23–39.

——— ([1937a] 1971) "On Contradiction." In Mao, 1971: 85–133.

——— ([1937b] 1971) "On Practice." In Mao, 1971: 65-84.

——— ([1941a] 1971) "Preface to Rural Surveys." In Mao, 1971: 194–97.

——— ([1941b] 1971) "Reform Our Study." In Mao, 1971: 198–208.

——— ([1942] 1971) "Oppose Stereotyped Party Writing." In Mao, 1971: 230–49.

——— ([1943] 1971) "Some Questions Concerning Methods of Leadership." In Mao, 1971: 287–94.

——— ([1957] 1971) "On the Correct Handling of Contradictions among the People." In Mao, 1971: 432–79.

——— (1971) *Selected Readings from the Works of Mao Tse-tung.* Beijing: Foreign Languages Press.

Mao Tsetung 毛泽东 (1967, 1977) *Mao Zedong xuanji* 《毛泽东选集》 [Selected Works of Mao Tse-tung] Vols. 1–4, 5. Beijing: Renmin chubanshe.

Ma Junju 马俊驹 (2003) "Dui woguo minfadian zhiding zhong ji ge jiaodian wenti de cuqian kanfa" 《对我国民法典制定中几个焦点问题的粗浅看法》 [Undeveloped views on a few key problems in the finalizing of our nation's civil code]. Part 6. At www.civillaw.com.cn.

Ma Xiaohong 马小红 (2004) *Li yu fa: fa de lishi lianjie* 《礼与法：法的历史连接》 [Rites and law: The historical connections of law]. Beijing: Beijing daxue chubanshe.

Marriage Law of the People's Republic of China ([1950] 1959) Beijing: Foreign Languages Press.

"Marriage Law of the People's Republic of China" ([1980] 1987) In *The Laws of the People's Republic of China, 1979–1982.* Compiled by the Legislative Affairs Commission of the Standing Committee of the National People's Congress of the People's Republic of China. Beijing: Foreign Languages Press.

McMahon, Kevin J. (2000) "Constitutional Vision and Supreme Court Decisions: Reconsidering Roosevelt on Race." *Studies in American Political Development* 14 (Spring): 20–50.

Meijer, Marinus J. (1971) *Marriage Law and Policy in the Chinese People's Republic.* Hong Kong: Hong Kong Univ. Press.

Michelson, Ethan (2003) "How Much Does Law Matter in Beijing?" At www.usc.cuhk.edu.hk. Chinese text in Mai Yisheng （美）麦宜生 (2003) "Jiufen yu falü xuqiu—yi Beijing de diaocha weili" 《纠纷与法律需求—以北京的调查为例》 [Disputes and the need for law—an example from an investigation in Beijing], *Jiangsu shehui kexue* 《江苏社会科学》 2003年, no. 1.

Morohashi Tetsuji 诸桥辙次 (1955–1960) *Dai Kan-Wa jiten* 《大汉和辞典》 [Comprehensive Chinese-Japanese dictionary]. 13 vols. Tokyo: Taishūkan shoten.

Nakajima Gakushō 中岛乐章 (2002) *Mindai gōson no funsō to chitsujo—Kishū bunsho wo shiryō to shite* 《明代乡村の纷争と秩序—徽州文书を史料として》 [Conflict and order in Ming villages—using the Huizhou documents as source materials]. Tokyo: Kyūko shoin 汲古书院.

Neighbors, Jennifer Michelle (2004) *Criminal Intent and Homicide Law in Qing and Republican China.* PhD dissertation, Univ. of California, Los Angeles.

Palmer, Michael (1987) "The Revival of Mediation in the People's Republic of China: (1) Extra-Judicial Mediation." *Yearbook on Socialist Legal Systems* 1987: 219–77.

——— (1989) "The Revival of Mediation in the People's Republic of China: (2) Judicial Mediation." *Yearbook on Socialist Legal Systems* 1989: 145–71.

——— (1996) "The Re-Emergence of Family Law in Post-Mao China: Marriage, Divorce, and Reproduction." In Stanley Lubman (ed.), *China's Legal Reforms*, pp. 110–34. Oxford: Oxford University Press.

Pan Weihe 潘维和 (1982) *Zhongguo lici minlü cao'an jiaoshi* 《中国历次民律草案校释》 [Collation and annotation of the successive drafts of the civil code in China]. Taipei: Hanlin chubanshe.

Pei Minxin (1997) "Citizens v. Mandarins: Administrative Litigation in China, *China Quarterly* 152: 832–62.

Peng Bo 彭勃 (2007) "Tidai xing jiufen jiejue bentuhua wenti chutan" 《替代性纠纷解决本土化问题初探》 [A preliminary study of the problem of the indigenousizing of Alternative Dispute Resolution]. *Zhengzhi yu falü* 《政治与法律》, no. 4: 71–75.

Pepper, Suzanne (1996) *Radicalism and Education Reform in Twentieth-Century China.* Cambridge: Cambridge University Press.

Phillips, Roderick (1988) *Putting Asunder: A History of Divorce in Western Society.* Cambridge: Cambridge University Press.

Rankin, Mary Backus (1986) *Elite Activism and Political Transformation in China: Zhejiang Province, 1865–1911.* Stanford, CA: Stanford University Press.

——— (1993) "Some Observations on a Chinese Public Sphere." *Modern China* 19, 2 (April): 158–82.

Reed, Bradley W. (2000) *Talons and Teeth: County Clerks and Runners in the Qing Dynasty.* Stanford, CA: Stanford University Press.

"Renmin tiaojie weiyuanhui zanxing zuzhi tongze" 《人民调解委员会暂行组织通则》 (1954) [Ad hoc principles for the organization of people's mediation committees] Implemented from 22 March 1954. In *Renmin tiaojie zai Zhongguo* 1986. See also www.falvfagui.com.

"Renmin tiaojie weiyuanhui zuzhi tiaoli" 《人民调解委员会组织条例》 (1989) [Regulations for the organization of people's mediation committees]. Implemented from 17 June 1989. At www.yfzs.gov.cn.

"Renmin tiaojie gongzuo ruogan guiding" 《人民调解工作若干规定》 (2002) [Some regulations for people's mediation work], Sifabu 司法部 [Ministry of Justice]. Implemented from 11 November 2002. At www.people.com.cn.

Renmin tiaojie zai Zhongguo 《人民调解在中国》 (1986) [Mediation in China] Tianjin: Huazhong shifan daxue chubanshe.

Rowe, William T. (1984) *Hankow: Commerce and Society in a Chinese City, 1796–1889.* Stanford, CA: Stanford University Press.

——— (1989) *Hankow: Conflict and Community in a Chinese City, 1796–1895.* Stanford, CA: Stanford University Press.

——— (1993) "The Problem of "Civil Society" in Late Imperial China." *Modern China* 19, 2 (April): 139–57.

Said, Edward (1978) *Orientalism.* New York: Pantheon.

Schneider, Michael E. (2003) "Combining Arbitration with Conciliation." *Oil, Gas, and Energy Law Intelligence* 1, 2. At www.gasandoil.com/ogel/samples/freearticles/article_55.htm.

Scott, James (1998) *Seeing Like a State.* New Haven, CT: Yale University Press.

Shanghai shi lüshi xiehui 上海市律师协会 [Lawyers' Association of Shanghai City] (ed.) (1991) *Lüshi yewu ziliao* 《律师业务资料》 [Professional materials for lawyers]. Shanghai: Lawyers' Association of Shanghai City.

Shiga, Shūzō (1974–1975) "Criminal Procedure in the Ch'ing Dynasty, with Emphasis on Its Administrative Character and Some Allusion to Its Historical Antecedents." *Memoirs of the Research Department of the Toyo Bunko* (2 parts), 32: 1–45, 33: 115–38.

——— 滋贺秀三 (1981) "Shindai soshō seido ni okeru minjiteki hōgen no gaikatsuteki kentō" 《清代诉讼制度 における民事的法源の概括的检讨》 [A general analysis of the origins of civil law in the litigation system of the Qing]. *Tōyōshi kenkyū* 《东洋史研究》 40, 1: 74–102.

Shunyi xian dang'an 顺义县档案 [Shunyi county archives]. In *Shunyi xian dang'an guan* 顺义县档案馆. [Cited by the archive's category number, juan number, and date by year, month, and day (e.g., 1931.5.6). The bracketed numbers refer to my own files, which are organized by category with an assigned case number.]

Sifa tongji 《司法统计》 [Judicial statistics] (1936) Vol. 2, *Minshi*, 民事 [Civil]. Di er lishi dang'an guan 第二历史档案馆 [Number Two Historical Archives], Nanjing. Category 7: juan 7078.

"Social Security Online" (n.d.) At www.ssa.gov/history/a9r30html.

Song Binwen, Xiong Yuhong, and Zhang Qiang（宋斌文、熊宇红、张强）(2003) "Dangqian nongmin yiliao baozhang de xianzhuang fenxi"《当前农民医疗保障的现状分析》 [An analysis of the current state of health protections for rural people]. *Dangdai Zhongguo yanjiu*《当代中国研究》83, 4. At www.chinayj.net.

Soviet Law on Marriage ([1926] 1932). Moscow: Cooperative Publishing Society of Foreign Workers in the USSR.

State Court Caseload Statistics: Annual Report (1980) (National Center Publication No. R-092).

Subrin, Stephen N., and Margaret K. Woo (2006) *Litigating in America: Civil Procedure in Context.* New York: Aspen Publishers.

Sverdlov, G. M. (1956) *Marriage and the Family in the U.S.S.R.* Moscow: Foreign Languages Publishing House.

Tamanaha, Brian Z. (1996) "Pragmatism in U.S. Legal Theory: Its Application to Normative Jurisprudence, Sociological Studies, and the Fact-Value Distinction." *American Journal of Jurisprudence* 41: 315–56.

Tang Houzhi (1996) "The Use of Conciliation in Arbitration." Conference on Mediation, WIPO Arbitration and Mediation Center, 29 March, Geneva, Switzerland. At http://arbiter.wipo.int/events/conferences/1996/tang.html.

Tian Chengyou 田成有 (1996) "Li fa: zhuanxingqi de tiaozhan" 《立法：转型期的挑战》 [Lawmaking: the challenge of the period of transition]. *Dongfang*, no. 4. At www.lawsky.org.

Tsou Tang [Zou Dang] 邹谠 (1994) *Ershi shiji Zhongguo zhengzhi: cong hongguan lishi yu weiguan xingdong jiaodu kan* 《二十世纪中国政治：从宏观历史与微观行动角度看》 [Twentieth-century Chinese politics: From a macrohistorical and microbehavioral perspective]. Hong Kong: Niujin daxue chubanshe.

Tunc, Andre (ed.) (1986) *International Encyclopedia of Comparative Law.* Vol. 11, *Torts.* Dordrecht, Germany: Martinus Nijhoff Publishers.

VanderVen, Elizabeth (2003) *Educational Reform and Village Society in Early Twentieth-Century Northeast China: Haicheng, County, 1905–1931.* PhD dissertation, University of California, Los Angeles.

——— (2005) "Village-State Cooperation: Modern Community Schools and Their Funding, Haicheng County, Fengtian, 1905–1931." *Modern China* 31, 2 (April): 204–35.

Virginia Judicial System (2003) www.courts.state.va.us/reports/2003/SECTIONa.pdf: pp. A-50, 64, 112, 116, 131.

Virginia Judicial System (2004a) "Mediation Information System Reports." At www.courts.state.va.us/courtadmin/aoc/djs/programs/drs/mediation/resources/resolutions/2004/march2004.pdf.

Virginia Judicial System (2004b) "Study of Recidivism in Domestic Relations Cases." At www.courts.state.va.us/courtadmin/aoc/djs/programs/drs/mediation/resources/resolutions/2004/march2004.pdf.

Wang Huizu 汪辉祖 ([1793] 1939) "Xuezhi yishuo" 《学治臆说》 [Subjective views on learning governance]. In *Congshu jicheng* 《丛书集成》 Shanghai: Shangwu yinshuguan.

Wang Yaxin 王亚新 and Liang Zhiping 梁治平 (eds.) (1998) *Ming Qing shiqi de minshi Shenpan yu minjian qiyue* 明清时期的民事审判与民间契约 [Civil Adjudication and popular contracts in the Ming and Qing]. Beijing: Falüchubanshe.

Wang, Yeh-Chien (1973) *Land Taxation in Imperial China, 1750–1911.* Cambridge, MA: Harvard University Press.

Weber, Max ([1968] 1978) *Economy and Society: An Outline of Interpretive Sociology.* Ed. Guenther Roth and Claus Wittich, trans. Ephraim Fischoff et al. 2 vols. Berkeley: University of California Press.

White, Morton ([1947] 1976) *Social Thought in America: The Revolt Against Formalism.* London: Oxford University Press.

Wiecek, William M. (1998) *The Lost World of Classical Legal Thought: Law and Ideology in America, 1886–1937.* New York: Oxford University Press.

Wolf, Margery (1972) *Women and the Family in Rural Taiwan.* Stanford, CA: Stanford University Press.

Woo, Margaret (2003) "Shaping Citizenship: Chinese Family Law and Women." *Yale J. of Law and Feminism* 15: 75–110.

Wu Chongqing 吴重庆 (2002) "Wu zhuti shuren shehui" 《无主体熟人社会》 [A society of the well acquainted absent its principals], *Kaifang shidai* 《开放时代》 [*Open Times*], no. 1.

Wu Ruozhi 巫若枝 (2007) *Dangdai Zhongguo jiashi fazhi shijian yanjiu—yi Huanan R xian weili* 《当代中国家事法制实践研究—以华南R县为例》 [On the practice of the family law system in contemporary China—South China's R county as an example]. PhD dissertation, Chinese People's University.

——— (n.d.) "Lun woguo hunyinfa zai falü tixi zhong diwei yanjiu zhi wuqu—yu hunyinfa zizhi lun shangque" 《论我国婚姻法在法律体系中地位研究之误区—与婚姻法私法自治论商榷》 [On blind spots in studies about the place of marriage law in our legal system: A critique of the self-governing theory of marriage law]. Unpublished manuscript.

Xiao Yang 肖扬 (2006) "Chongfen fahui sifa tiaojie zai goujian shehuizhuyi hexie shehui de jiji zuoyong" 充分发挥司法调解在构建社会主义和谐社会主义和谐社会的积极作用 [Fully develop the positive role of judicial mediation in constructing a harmonious socialist society]. *Renmin fayuan bao* 《人民法院报》, 30 September.

Xiaoning [pseud.] 晓宁(2006) "Wuquanfa cao'an zhengyi zhong de wenti yu zhuyi" 《物权法草案争议中的问题与主义》 [Problems and isms in the debates over the draft property law]. 2 March. At www.chinacourt.org.

Xiong Yihan 熊易寒 (2006) "Renmin tiaojie de shehuihua yu zai zuzhi: dui Shanghai shi Yang Boshou gongzuoshi de ge'an fenxi" 《人民调解的社会化与再组织：对上 海市杨伯寿工作室的个案分析》 [The socialization and reorganization of people's mediation: The case of the Yang Boshan work office of Shanghai city]. *Shehui* 《社会》, no. 6. At www.usc.cuhk.edu.hk.

Xiong Yuanbao 熊远报 (2003) *Shindai Kishū chi-iki shakaishi kenkyū—kyōkai, shūdan, netto wa-ku to shakai chitsujo* 《清代徽州地域社会史研究—境界、集 团、ネットワークと社会秩序》 [A study of the social history of the Huizhou area—boundaries, groupings, networks and social order]. Tokyo: Kyūko shoin 汲古书院.

Xu Xin 徐昕 (2006) "Faguan wei shenme bu xiangxin zhengren? Zhengren zai zhuanxing zhongguo sifa guocheng zhong de zuoyong" 《法官为什么不相信证人？—证人在转型 中国司法过程中的作用》 [Why do judges not believe the witnesses? The function of witnesses in the judicial process of a transitioning China]. *Zhong wai faxue* 《中外法学》, no. 3: 337–50. At www.csu.cuhk.edu.hk.

Xue Yunsheng 薛允升 ([1905] 1970) *Duli cunyi* 《读例存疑》 [Doubts remaining after perusing the substatutes]. Reprint. Huang Tsing-chia 黄静嘉 (ed). 5 vols. Taipei: Chinese Materials and Research Aids Service Center. Cited by editor Huang's statute and substatute numbers (e.g., Statute 89; Substatute 89-1).

Yang Tuan 杨团 (2006) "Yiliao weisheng fuwu tixi gaige de di san tiao daolu" 《医疗卫生服务体系改革的第三条道路》 [The third way for reforming the system of medical and health services]. *Xuexi yu shijian* 《学习与实践》, no. 5. At www.sociology.cass.cn.

Yang Yonghua 杨永华 and Fang Keqin 方克勤 (1987) *Shaan-Gan-Ning bianqu fazhishi gao* 《陕甘宁边区法制史稿》 [Draft history of the legal system of the Shaan(xi)-Gan(su)-Ning(xia) border area]. N.p.: Falü chubanshe.

Yang Zhongxu 杨中旭 (2007) "Zuigao fayuan shouchang hexie susong" 《最高法院首倡和谐诉讼》 (The Supreme Court is the first to advocate harmonious litigation). At www.chinanewsweek.com.cn.

Ye Jianping 叶剑平, Jiang Yan 蒋妍, Roy Prosterman 罗伊・普罗斯特曼, Zhu Kekliang 朱可亮, Feng Lei 丰雷 and Li Ping 李平 (2006) "2005 nian Zhongguo nongcun tudi shiyongquan diaocha yanjiu—17 sheng diaocha jieguo ji zhengce jianyi" 《2005年中国农村土地使用权调查研究—17省调查结果及政策建议》 [2005 research on use rights of land in rural China—the findings and policy recommendations of an investigation of 17 provinces). *Guanli shijie* 《管理世界》, no. 7. At www.usc.cuhk.edu.hk.

Zhang Wenxian 张文显 (2001) "Gaige kaifang shiqi de Zhongguo faxue" 《改革开放时期的中国法学》 [Chinese legal studies in the Reform period], *Fashang yanjiu* 法商研究, no. 1: 30–42.

Zhang Xinbao 张新宝 (2006) *Qinquan zeren fa* 《侵权责任法》 [Laws on obligations of wrongful acts]. Beijing: Zhongguo renmin daxue chubanshe.

Zhao Xiaoli 赵晓力 (1998) "Zhongguo jindai nongcun tudi jiaoyi zhong de qiyue, xiguan, yu guojiafa" 《中国近代农村土地交易中的契约、习惯与国家法》 [Contracts, customs and state law in rural land transactions in modern China]. *Beida falü pinglun* 《北大法律评论》 1, 2: 427–504.

Zhao Xudong 赵旭东 (2003) Quanli yu gongzheng: xiangtu shehui de jiufen jiejue yu quanwei duoyuan 《权力与公正：乡土社会的纠纷解决与权威多元》 [Power and Justice: Dispute resolution and pluralistic power in rural society]. Tianjin: Tianjin guji chubanshe.

Zhongguo falü nianjian 1990 《中国法律年鉴》 (1990) [Statistical yearbook of Chinese law, 1990]. Chengdu: Zhongguo falü nianjian chubanshe.
Zhongguo falü nianjian 2001 (2001) Chengdu: Zhongguo falü nianjian chubanshe.
Zhongguo falü nianjian, 2004 (2004) Chengdu: Zhongguo falü nianjian chubanshe.
Zhongguo falü nianjian, 2007 (2007) Beijing: Zhongguo falü nianjian chubanshe.
Zhongguo tongji nianjian 中国统计年鉴》(1985) [Statistical yearbook of China]. Beijing: Zhongguo tongji chubanshe.
Zhongguo tongji nianjian (1986).
Zhongguo tongji nianjian (1990).
Zhongguo tongji nianjian (1991).
Zhongguo tongji nianjian (2004).
Zhongguo tongji nianjian (2005).
Zhongguo tongji nianjian (2006).
Zhongguo tongji nianjian (2007).
Zhonghua minguo fazhi ziliao huibian ([1927–1937] 1960) 《中华民国法制资料汇编1927–1937 年》 [Collection of source materials on the legal system of the Republic of China, 1927–1937]. Taipei: Sifa xingzhengbu 司法行政部.
Zhonghua minguo minfa (1929–1930) [Civil law of the Republic of China]. In *Liufa quanshu*, 1932. Shanghai: Shanghai faxue bianyishe.
Zhonghua renmin gongheguo fagui huibian—1985 《中华人民共和国法规汇编—1985》 (1986) [Comprehensive collection of the law and regulations of the People's Republic of China—1985] Beijing: Falüchubanshe.
Zhonghua renmin gongheguo fagui huibian—1986《中华人民共和国法规汇编—1986》 (1987) [Comprehensive collection of the laws and regulations of the People's Republic of China—1986]. Beijing: Falüchubanshe.
Zhonghua renmin gongheguo falü huibian—1979–1984 《中华人民共和国法律汇编—1979 - 1984》 (1985) [Comprehensive collection of the laws of the People's Republic of China—1979–1984] Beijing: Falüchubanshe.
Zhonghua renmin gongheguo falü shiyi daquan 《中华人民共和国法律释义大全》 (1992) [Comprehensive explanations of the laws of the People's Republic of China]. Beijing: Zhongguo zhengfa daxue chubanshe.
"Zhonghua renmin gongheguo hunyin fa" 《中华人民共和国婚姻法》 ([1950] 1983) [Marriage law of the People's Republic of China]. In *Hubei caijing xueyuan*, 1983.
"Zhonghua renmin gongheguo hunyin fa" ([1980] 1985) In *Zhonghua renmin gongheguo falü huibian—1979–1984* (1985).
"Zhonghua renmin gongheguo hunyin fa" (2001) 中华人民共和国婚姻法》（2001年修正）(revised 2001). At www.Law-lib.com.
"Zhonghua renmin gongheguo jichengfa"《中华人民共和国继承法》([1985] 1986) [Law of succession of the People's Republic of China]. In *Zhonghua renmin gongheguo fagui huibian—1985* (1986).
"Zhonghua renmin gongheguo minfa tongze" 《中华人民共和国民法通则》 ([1986] 1987) [General principles of the civil law of the People's Republic of China] In *Zhonghua renmin gongheguo fagui huibian—1986* (1987).
"Zhonghua renmin gongheguo minshi susong fa" 《中华人民共和国民事诉讼法》 (1991) [Civil Procedure Law of the People's Republic of China], passed 9 April

1991. At www.cnfalv.com.

"Zhonghua renmin gongheguo wuquanfa"《中华人民共和国物权法》(2007) [Law on property rights of the People's Republic of China], implemented from 1 October 2007. At www.gov.cn/flfg/2007-03/19content_554452.htm.

"Zhonghua renmin gongheguo zhi'an guanli chufa tiaoli" 《中华人民共和国治安管理处罚条例》 ([1986] 1987) [Regulations of the People's Republic of China governing punishments in the administration of public security]. In *Zhonghua renmin gongheguo fagui huibian—1986* [Comprehensive collection of the laws and regulations of the People's Republic of China—1986]. Beijing: Falü chubanshe.

Zhonghua renmin gongheguo zuigao renmin fayuan 中华人民共和国最高人民法院 [Supreme People's Court of the People's Republic of China] (1994) *Sifa jieshi quanji* 《中华人民共和国司法解释全集》 [Comprehensive collection of judicial explanations of the People's Republic of China]. Beijing: Renmin fayuan chubanshe. Cited as Zuigao renmin fayuan, 1994.

"Zhonghua suwei'ai gongheguo hunyin tiaoli" 《中华苏维埃共和国婚姻条例》 ([1931] 1983) [Regulations on marriage of the Soviet Republic of China]. In Hubei caijing xueyuan, 1983: 1–4.

Zhou Feizhou 周飞舟 (2006) "Shuifei gaige dui guojia yu nongmin guanxi zhi Yingxiang" 《税费改革对国家与农民关系之影响》 [The impact of tax-fee reform on state-peasant relations]. *Shehuixue yanjiu* 《社会学研究》, no. 3. At www.sachina.edu.cn.

Zhu Jingwen 朱景文 (2006) "Wuquanfa zhengyi yuan yu shehui shenceng maodun" 《物权法争议源于社会深层矛盾》 [Debates over the property law stem from deep-seated social contradictions]. 28 February. At www.chinacourt.org.

Zhu Suli [Su Li 朱苏力 [苏力] (1996) *Fazhi ji qi bentu ziyuan* 《法治及其本土资源》 [Rule by law and its indigenous resources]. Beijing: Zhongguo zhengfa daxue chubanshe.

——— (2000) *Songfa xia xiang—Zhongguo jiceng sifa zhidu yanjiu* 《送法下乡—中国基层司法制度研究》 [Sending law down to the countryside—a study of the judicial system of China]. Beijing: Zhongguo zhengfa daxue chubanshe.

"Zuigao renmin fayuan" (1994). See Zhonghua renmin gongheguo zuigao renmin fayuan, 1994.

"Zuigao renmin fayuan guanyu renmin fayuan shenli lihun anjian ruhe rending fuqi ganqing que yi polie de ruogan juti yijian"《最高人民法院关于人民法院审理离婚案件如何认定夫妻感情确已破裂的若干具体意见》([1990] 1994) [Some concrete opinions of the Supreme People's Court regarding how the people's courts in judging divorce cases are to determine whether the emotional relationship of the husband and wife has truly ruptured] In Zuigao renmin fayuan, 1994: 1086–87.

"Zuigao renmin fayuan guanyu minshi susong zhengju de ruogan guiding" 《最高人民法院关于民事诉讼证据的若干规定》 (2002) [The Supreme People's Court, some regulations concerning evidence in civil litigations], implemented from 1 April 2002. At www.china.org.cn.

"Zuigao renmin fayuan guanyu shenli sheji renmin tiaojie xieyi de minshi anjian de ruogan guiding"《最高人民法院关于审理涉及人民调解协议的民事案件的若干规定》 (2002) [Supreme People's Court, Some regulations for the people's courts in adjudicating civil cases involving people's mediation agreements], implemented from 1 November 2002. At www.jincao.com.

Index

Note: Page numbers followed by "*t*" refer to tables.

About the Author

Philip C. C. Huang was a professor of history at the University of California, Los Angeles, from 1966 to 2004, and (founding) director of its Center for Chinese Studies, from 1986 to 1995. He has been (founding) editor of *Modern China: An International Journal of History and Social Science* since 1975 and of *Zhongguo xiangcun yanjiu* (*Rural China: An International Journal of History and Social Science*) since 2001. His major publications include *The Peasant Economy and Social Change in North China* (1985) (awarded the Fairbank Prize of the American Historical Association), *The Peasant Family and Rural Development in the Yangzi Delta, 1350–1988* (1990) (awarded the Levenson Prize of the Association for Asian Studies), *Civil Justice in China: Representation and Practice in the Qing* (1996), and *Code, Custom, and Legal Practice in China: The Qing and the Republic Compared* (2001). He is currently Chiangjiang Chair Professor at the People's University of China.